A Century of Spirit

A Century of Spirit

Barbara L. Pederson

Los Angeles, California

1990

Unocal Corporation

Executive editor: Karen A. Sikkema

Managing editor: Michael W. Thacher

Additional writers: Marshall Lumsden, A. Donald Anderson

Designers: Ray Engle and Associates/Ray Engle, Debra Hampton, Jerry Jensik

Photo coordination: Michael T. Hogelund, Starlene Frontino

Historical photo research: Mildred Chong-Dillon

Copy editor: Joyce Madison

Indexer: Carol B. Pearson

Interviewers: Arthur H. Bentley, W. Barry Lane, Clark McCann, John L. Rafuse, Carol Scott, Timothy J. Smight

Technical reviewers: E. P. "Barney" Barnett; W. Clyde Barton, Jr.; Edmund W. Bluth; Ray A. Burke; Dennis P. Codon; A. J. Eliskalns; Edwin E. Johnson; John E. Kilkenny; Dr. Harold M. Lian; William C. Lieffers; Richard C. Lindwall; William S. McConnor; John R. Murphey, Jr.; Dr. Carel Otte; Carleton B. "Bud" Scott; Sam A. Snyder; Vane E. Suter; Jasmina A. Theodore; Timothy R. Thomas

Proofreaders: Joyce Madison, Doug White

Staff assistants: Valerian Anderson, Kathleen O'Malley, Sandra Patino, Heidi Sigmund, Mary Stipe

Photocopying: Unocal Office Services

Typographer: Typographic Service Co.

Printer: George Rice & Sons

Updating the history of Unocal has been a sizable task that could not have been completed without the participation of scores of employees and retirees of this company. On behalf of the editors, I thank you all. Everyone the editors and I contacted, or who contacted us, has been most generous with their time and recollections, or with their photographs or written records. They have enriched our corporate history.

We owe particular thanks to the writers of prior versions of the history: Earl M. Welty and Frank J. Taylor, who completed *The Black Bonanza* in 1950. An expanded and redesigned edition was published as *The 76 Bonanza* in 1966. Paul R. Waddell and Robert F. Niven updated that book in 1977 with the addition of several chapters and retitled it *The Sign of the 76.*

Mr. Niven, who joined Union Oil in 1932 and served as corporate secretary for 25 years from 1947 until his retirement in 1972, conducted more than 40 lengthy interviews for *The Sign of the 76.* In 1988 and 1989, members of the Corporate Communications Department conducted another 60 wide-ranging interviews for the current book. These have proved an invaluable resource.

Deep thanks are extended to Marshall Lumsden, who greatly assisted in the preparation of the early chapters and the story of the 1985 hostile takeover attempt.

We acknowledge a debt to the editors and writers of the *Union Oil Bulletin, The Minute Man, On Tour,* and *Seventy Six,* company publications that have faithfully documented history-in-the-making since 1921.

We are also grateful to Signe Wattenford and Lawrence Marshburn of the Rose Memorial Library at Biola University, who provided access to their document and photo archives; to Jim Bishop for historical materials related to Lyman Stewart's good works for both his church and his community; and to Harry W. Kairys, keeper of The Pure Oil Company archives in Schaumburg, Illinois.

A Century of Spirit is a complete rewrite and updating of the company's history. Since publication of *The Black Bonanza* in 1950, scholars have uncovered more detailed information about the early days of California oil and the founding of Union Oil Company. A review of their work and certain company records prompted some corrections of earlier versions of events.

In the truest sense, this book represents a team effort. I am grateful to those friends and colleagues whose invaluable assistance helped me complete this project.

Barbara L. Pederson
Los Angeles, California
September 1, 1990

UNOCAL'S FIRST 100 YEARS: A TIMELINE

Union Oil Company of California, doing business as Unocal since 1985, was founded October 17, 1890, in Santa Paula, California. The first years were difficult. The company struggled for survival during alternating times of boom and bust in the fledgling petroleum industry. Union Oil itself was torn by the differing priorities of its three cofounders, who disagreed often on the best way to meet ever-changing and fast-growing opportunities.

By 1900, only one of the three — Lyman Stewart — remained. For the next three decades, Lyman and his son Will led Union Oil to a position of prominence in the western United States. Both men recognized the importance of building an integrated company and worked to create an effective refining and marketing organization backed by a solid resource base. Later executives such as Reese H. Taylor, A.C. Rubel, Fred L. Hartley, and Richard J. Stegemeier continued to build on this legacy.

Thanks to the vision and leadership of these men, the creativity and dedication of thousands of employees, and the strong support of its many shareholders, Unocal has developed into a high-technology earth resources company with operations around the world. The timeline on the following pages provides a brief overview of the company's history. And it suggests that the next century holds equal promise for technological innovation and productive growth.

1890 ❖ Union Oil Company of California is incorporated in Santa Paula with Thomas Bard as president, Lyman Stewart as vice president, and Wallace Hardison as treasurer.

1891 ❖ Union establishes the first petroleum research laboratory in the western U.S. at its Santa Paula refinery.

1896 ❖ Union Oil opens a new refinery on San Francisco Bay; the Santa Paula plant is destroyed by fire.

1900 ❖ William W. Orcutt, a young Union geologist, organizes the first petroleum geology department in the West.

1901 ❖ Union moves its headquarters to Los Angeles.

1903 ❖ Union launches the *Whittier*, a steel-hulled, steam-powered oil tanker that serves as the prototype for tankers built over the next 60 years.

1905 ❖ Field operations manager Frank Hill and his associates complete the first successful well-cementing job at Union's Hill No. 4 near Lompoc.

1910 ❖ Union's Lakeview No. 1 comes in near Maricopa, California, as the world's greatest gusher. Eighteen months and 9 million barrels of crude oil later, the well is finally brought under control.

1913 ❖ Union opens its first gas station at the corner of Sixth and Mateo streets in downtown Los Angeles. The petroleum industry now refines more gasoline than kerosene from its crude oil.

1917 ❖ Union's new Wilmington (Los Angeles) refinery begins operation, gearing up for American participation in World War I. A new research facility is added in 1922.

1923 ❖ Founder and chairman Lyman Stewart dies in Los Angeles at the age of 83. His son Will, president since 1914, continues to direct Union's vigorous expansion.

1924 ❖ Union Oil Company is listed on the New York Stock Exchange for the first time.

1925 ❖ Union introduces its first credit card, one of many marketing innovations. Company advertisements emphasize quality products and research.

1926 ❖ A fierce electrical storm ignites major fires at Union's San Luis Obispo and Brea tank farms. The loss spurs creation of a far-reaching fire-prevention training program.

Union Ethyl, an antiknock gasoline advertised as "the new super fuel," is introduced.

1930 ❖ Will Stewart dies at the age of 62. Press St. Clair is appointed president to guide the company through the Great Depression.

1932 ❖ The new Union 76 gasoline, its name invoking the patriotic "Spirit of 76," is a great success with motorists.

1934 ❖ Union introduces Triton, the first premium motor oil refined from heavy western crudes. In rigorous test runs, auto engines show little wear—and the new oil is enthusiastically received.

In Kern County, a Union drilling crew sets a record for the world's deepest well at a depth of more than two miles.

1938 ❖ Under new president Reese Taylor, a 38-year-old former steel company executive, Union begins to rebuild after the Great Depression.

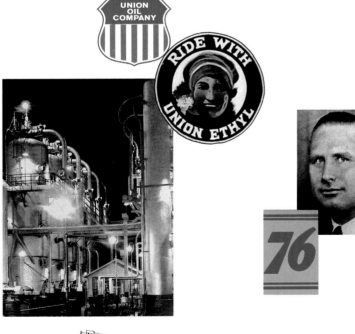

1939 ✶ Union establishes a Gulf Division, which makes its first discovery at East White Lake in Louisiana. The division's subsequent discoveries help fill the huge demand for oil during World War II.

1941–45 ✶ Union Oil supports the war effort, boosting crude production to the highest levels in the company's history. Major refinery expansion increases the output of aviation gasoline sevenfold by the end of the war.

Two Union tankers are lost — the *Montebello* to a Japanese submarine off the California coast near Avila with all hands rescued, and the *Gurney E. Newlin* to a German U-boat in the Atlantic with the loss of 38 of the crew of 41.

1951 ✶ A new research center opens in Brea as the company prepares to meet the demands of a booming industrial post-war economy.

1952 ✶ Union establishes Brea Chemicals, Inc., to manufacture and market oil by-products. Brea later merges with another Union subsidiary to form the Collier Carbon and Chemical Company.

1954 ✶ A major discovery at the East Lake Palourde field in Louisiana begins a new series of large strikes for Union Oil in the Gulf region.

1955 ✶ Union's new Santa Maria refinery, designed to handle heavy California crudes, comes on stream.

1956 ✶ Union drills the first well in the Gulf's Vermilion Block 26, six miles offshore Louisiana. It blows out, earning the nickname "Wild Tiger" — but signals the discovery of one of the Gulf's most prolific gas fields.

1958 ✶ Union employees move into the company's seventh headquarters since 1890 — the modern, 12-story Union Oil Center dominating the downtown Los Angeles skyline.

1959 ✶ Union discovers the first natural gas field in Alaska. It provides gas for Anchorage, 80 miles away — and, a decade later, feedstock for the nitrogen fertilizer plants Union builds on Kenai Peninsula.

1961 ✶ Union finds oil in Queensland, the first commercial oil discovery in Australia.

Union expands its fertilizer business with the purchase of Pacific Guano of California, later renamed the PureGro Company. The company's parent was founded in 1890 just five months before Union.

1962 ✶ Cy Rubel, president under Reese Taylor from 1956–1960, comes out of retirement to reassume the post when Taylor dies.

1964 ✶ Fred L. Hartley becomes president and chief executive officer.

At the Los Angeles refinery, the company starts up the first Unicracker, utilizing Union's revolutionary technology to produce nearly five barrels of high-grade fuels from four barrels of feedstock.

1965 ✶ A merger with The Pure Oil Company — the largest merger in the oil industry until that time — makes Union the ninth largest oil company in the United States.

1966 ✶ Union discovers oil in Alaska's Cook Inlet, becoming the state's biggest oil producer until the North Slope is developed.

1967 ✶ Union Geothermal Division is formed to operate holdings at The Geysers in Northern California. Union becomes the world's largest producer of geothermal power.

INTRODUCTION

In 1990, Unocal achieved a milestone few companies can claim. We completed a century as an independent business enterprise. Of the top 100 American companies in existence in the early 1900s, only 22 continue independently today.

That the company survived its first ten years is a tribute to the perseverance of Lyman Stewart. By 1900, he was the only one of the three cofounders still with Union Oil Company. At times, even he seemed ready to give up—trying to sell out when the future looked bleakest. Fortunately, he found no buyers.

In 1890, Union was a small part of an industry still defining itself. Stewart and his partners had to virtually create markets for petroleum, whose potential had barely been tapped. Refining methods were rudimentary; gasoline (merely a by-product at the time) was considered useless, even dangerous.

Soon enough, however, America's growing economy and rapidly developing technology found myriad uses for petroleum. The rise of the motorcar after the turn of the century made crude oil one of the world's most important natural resources. Scientists, engineers, and marketers have since developed hundreds of useful products from the hydrocarbon molecule.

In 1914, Will Stewart replaced his father as Union's president, with Lyman serving as chairman until his death in 1923. The elder Stewart lived to see horses replaced by horsepower—and Union rise to prominence in the industry.

In 1930, Will Stewart died. As the Great Depression began, Press St. Clair stepped forward to see the company through that very difficult period. One bright spot was the introduction of the famous Union 76 marketing symbol, first used on a new gasoline in 1932.

In the late 1930s, Union, with new president Reese Taylor, began to rebuild, supplying vital fuels for the Second World War. During the postwar boom, the company expanded aggressively. Cy Rubel, president under chairman Taylor and then successor to leadership after Taylor's death in 1962, helped establish Union as an explorer and producer in the high-potential lands and offshore areas along the Gulf of Mexico and in southern Alaska.

In 1964, Fred L. Hartley became president and CEO and, through a merger with Pure Oil, helped Union establish an international reputation as a producer, refiner, and marketer. The company made huge oil and gas discoveries in Southeast Asia and pioneered the development of geothermal energy.

Today, we are a lean and flexible organization, building on our legacy of success. We respond quickly to business opportunities. We realize, however, that the role of the modern earth resources company is not solely to discover and produce needed resources, but also to safeguard the land, air, and sea as we conduct our operations.

I am proud to be part of Unocal's remarkable history. In the final analysis, this company has been built on the creativity and effort of its employees, past and present. *A Century of Spirit* stands as both a tribute to our accomplishments and a commitment to carry on with the strength and spirit that have been our hallmarks from the very beginning.

Richard J. Stegemeier
Chairman, President and
Chief Executive Officer

1969 ❖ Union-operated Platform A blows out in the Santa Barbara Channel, spilling thousands of barrels of crude oil. The company launches a massive cleanup effort; the coastal environment recovers quickly.

1970 ❖ Union discovers oil in Indonesia, offshore East Kalimantan. The Attaka field, developed under a landmark production-sharing agreement, turns out to be one of the world's giant oil fields.

The company dedicates the new 140,000-barrel-per-day Chicago refinery, with innovative pollution control systems and advanced technology.

1971 ❖ Union scientists announce the development of "popcorn" sulfur, made from hydrogen sulfide gas, normally a waste by-product of refining. The product makes soils better able to absorb moisture and nutrients.

1972 ❖ The Tiwi geothermal field is discovered in the Philippines. Steam from Union geothermal operations will eventually generate 30 percent of the electricity for the island of Luzon, which includes the capital city of Manila.

1973 ❖ Union codevelops the Beavon Sulfur Removal process to recover 99.9 percent of the sulfur from refinery emissions and reduce air pollution.

1977 ❖ Union acquires Molycorp, Inc., a major producer of molybdenum and niobium, as well as lanthanides — used in numerous high-technology applications.

1978 ❖ Union signs the first gas sales contract with Thailand, opening up a new industry in that country. Production from the giant Erawan gas field and others eventually provides more than 50 percent of Thailand's electrical power.

1979 ❖ Union's research department becomes the Science & Technology Division.

1982 ❖ Union, following its success with Platform Heather in the U.K. sector of the North Sea, begins production from the Helm and Helder fields, recovering the first oil from offshore the Netherlands.

1983 ❖ Unocal Corporation, formed in Delaware, becomes Union's parent company.

1985 ❖ After a heated battle, Unocal defeats a hostile takeover attempt led by Mesa Petroleum.

Richard J. Stegemeier becomes new Unocal president and chief operating officer.

1988 ❖ Stegemeier, elected chief executive officer, accelerates major restructuring prompted by increased debt from the failed takeover attempt and the crude oil price collapse of 1986.

1989 ❖ At California's Salton Sea, Unocal becomes a commercial supplier of electric power with the opening of a 49,900-kilowatt generating plant, driven by steam from the company's geothermal wells.

1990 ❖ Unocal celebrates its one hundredth year in business.

Los Angeles Times

Unocal Defeats Takeover Bid

Pickens May Lose Money on Attempt

"What I was to find
in the West I knew not—
except that it was opportunity,
and that was all I asked."

Lyman Stewart

Part 1

Lyman Stewart:

WILDCATTER WITH A DREAM

Lyman Stewart—born July 22, 1840 —was only 19 years old when Edwin L. Drake punched a hole 69½ feet into the earth near Titusville, Pennsylvania, completing the world's first commercial oil well. Drake's discovery of petroleum so far underground set off an oil boom—and a new industry— within a few miles of Stewart's home. History does not record whether Stewart and Drake ever met (chances are they did; Titusville's population was only 400), but the well that Drake completed on August 27, 1859, changed the course of Stewart's life.

Over the next 64 years, Stewart's vision, audacity, and grit would rank him among the giants of the oil industry. Those qualities would also lead him into precarious ventures and narrow escapes. He lost and regained several fortunes before he died, but his resilience was astonishing. In the end, his legacy was both huge and far-reaching.

Petroleum—or "rock oil," as it was then known—had been part of the landscape in the Venango Valley long before "Colonel" Drake arrived. It was a constant presence along the banks of Oil Creek and collected in sumps that dotted the area. Drake's well was scarcely a gusher—the oil bubbled up only to within a few feet of the surface and then had to be pumped out—but the news hit the countryside like thunder.

Crude oil had ready markets as a source of kerosene, which would soon replace whale oil and coal oil as an illuminant in homes, offices, and factories. Crude oil was also used for lubricants and even patent medicine— but its major impact would come as it challenged coal to fuel the ongoing Industrial Revolution.

And, at $20 a barrel, crude oil promised enormous profits. Thousands of adventurers streamed into Titusville and the Venango Valley.

In 1851, at the age of 11, Lyman Stewart had quit school in Cherrytree, where he was born, to work in his father's tannery. As he learned the trade, he came to detest it. The hides reeked and, after handling them all day, so did Lyman. He saved up a small stake, intending to become a farmer. But oil proved to be a much more enticing possibility. Within a few months of Drake's discovery, Lyman succumbed to oil fever.

On December 5, 1859, his name was listed as a one-eighth partner in a drilling lease on the farm of John Benninghoff. His $125 stake was lost when the partnership failed to come up with enough funds to finance a well. Disappointed but undaunted, Stewart returned to the tannery. No doubt, he looked with new interest at the ubiquitous black ooze he saw as he rode horseback collecting hides from local farmers. In time, he developed a "nose" for oil—an ability to spot properties where petroleum might be found.

By 1861, Stewart had saved enough to take his second plunge as an oilman. This time the investors did everything right—got their lease, saved enough money to drill, and even struck oil—only to see their dreams of wealth vanish as oil prices collapsed in a production glut.

On April 12, 1861, Confederate troops fired on Fort Sumter beginning four years of bloody civil conflict. Stewart enlisted in the Sixteenth Pennsylvania Cavalry in 1862, serving the next three years as a private assigned chiefly to tend the unit's

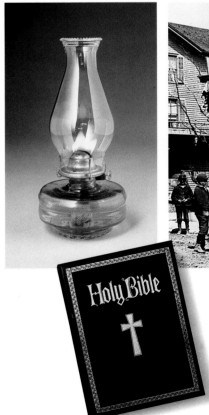

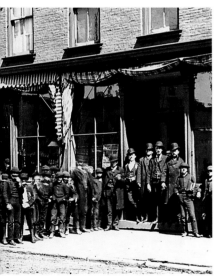

Top: Young Lyman Stewart prospered in oil, settling his family in a house in Shamburg shortly after the birth of his son Will in 1868. Center: Drillers in Pioneer Run created a forest of derricks. Bottom: The Titusville Oil Exchange, circa 1880, brought buyers and sellers together.

horses. While war raged, so did the oil boom in Titusville. Stewart returned to find the village had grown into a bustling town of 6,000 people.

Feeling the need to supplement his public education, Stewart went to Poughkeepsie, New York, for a short course in bookkeeping and finance at Eastman's Business College. In 1866, he settled in Titusville, where his family had moved, and opened a modest oil leasing office in nearby Pioneer Run. He soon attracted a steady clientele of investors impressed with his knowledge and integrity. Lyman and his older brother Milton accumulated a considerable number of producing properties.

"The Stewarts were known as gentlemen," recalled one of their contemporaries. "They dressed immaculately. They were courteous and soft-spoken. A profane word never came from their lips. Lyman could go out to the roughest and toughest field and mix with the most foul-mouthed scum and riffraff and command the respect of everyone. He was never a hypocrite." Milton stayed out of the oil fields, preferring the financial end of the business.

The Stewart brothers, with interests in more than 100 wells, amassed what for the time were impressive fortunes. In 1867, Lyman married Sarah Adelaide Burroughs, originally from New York. Their first son, William Lyman Stewart — later a major figure in Union Oil — was born April 7 the following year. Two more children, May and Alfred, followed.

Unfortunately, Lyman Stewart became involved in an ill-advised venture as backer of a new company that manufactured mowing machines for farmers. The investment proved a bottomless pit. "It took every cent I had made, including my home," Stewart later recalled. "By 1872, I was flat broke."

For the next five years, Lyman Stewart worked for wages, trying to put aside enough money for another oil play. In 1877, still far short of his goal, he was approached by Wallace L. Hardison, the brother of two men he had befriended during his more successful years. "You know oil and I don't," Hardison said. "I have money and you don't. We'll be partners. I'll put up the money and you put up the experience."

The deal was sealed by a handshake, and the alliance became an almost immediate success. Their first important play — in the Bradford field not far from the New York state line — generated a modest fortune for both men just before oil prices crashed again in the face of another glut. But the industry, not quite 20 years old, began to fall under the control of John D. Rockefeller and other big operators. Small players like Hardison and Stewart found it increasingly difficult to prosper in the eastern fields.

"Things in Pennsylvania were pretty much under the influence of one company, which controlled all the pipelines, and also had contracts with the railroads. We were getting pretty tired of working under those conditions," Stewart explained.

The West beckoned. "There were reports that extensive oil lands could be had for practically nothing in California," he said. "The idea of the new, open country, with the opportunity for unhampered effort, appealed to me very strongly."

Stewart and Hardison sold off their Bradford properties, realizing about $70,000 each. Hardison intended to settle on a cattle ranch he had bought in Kansas. Stewart shipped two drilling rigs to California in September 1882 and, on a spring day in 1883, boarded a train headed for an uncertain but tantalizing destiny.

"What I was to find in the West I knew not," he said. "With me I carried a small Bible Mrs. Stewart had given me years before. That Bible was to be my guide and protector, my inspiration during the hectic and discouraging times ahead."

Rocky Beginnings

Lyman Stewart and his son Will, circa 1880. Lyman Stewart was 42 when he arrived in Los Angeles (opposite) in early 1883 for a new start.

Los Angeles in 1883 was a raw, fast-growing community of 15,000, full of spirit and fired by visions of boundless opportunity. Lyman Stewart and his 15-year-old son Will were met at the River Station depot of the Southern Pacific Railroad by Isaac E. Blake, a one-time driller in Titusville whose accounts of oil discoveries and promises of plentiful land on which to drill had lured the Stewarts to California. Blake took them to Newhall, a dusty clapboard town on the rail line about 30 miles northwest of Los Angeles.

From there they traveled by horse three miles west, across rolling hills that 80 years later would be bulldozed into sites for tract housing, a golf course, and a college of fine arts — today's city of Santa Clarita. They rode through scrub land, where automobiles and semitrucks now pound along U.S. Interstate 5, and on into Pico Canyon.

There was much to make Lyman Stewart feel at home here. Like the Venango Valley, Pico Canyon was dotted with oil seeps, and leases were cheap. The area had already yielded discoveries that were enriching some of Stewart's Titusville friends with production of several hundred barrels a day, all from shallow wells. Stewart sent off an enthusiastic telegram to Wallace Hardison, who was still in Pennsylvania winding up his business affairs. Apparently, Stewart's friend and former partner was easily lured away from his intention to become a rancher. "Hardison replied in his usual crisp manner," Stewart said, "merely stating the date he could come out and commence operations."

Hardison and John Irwin, a cousin of Stewart's who had a good reputation as a driller and oil finder, arrived in California in mid-May 1883 and toured the properties Stewart had picked out. Hardison agreed with Stewart's appraisal, and they immediately formed a partnership, Hardison, Stewart & Company (HS&C), with Hardison as president and Stewart as treasurer. They opened a tiny office in Newhall, a single room upstairs in a crackerbox building on the main street, and Stewart began to arrange for leases on which to drill. In such arrangements, the drilling company would take the risks, then share in the profits with the company that owned the land. The landowners could control production to keep from flooding the small markets opening up in the West for crude oil. Stewart and Hardison believed they were drilling on proved lands, but such was not necessarily the case.

By November, when Stewart returned to Pennsylvania to bring his family to California, a series of dry holes had him flirting with financial ruin once again. Even though California crude was more sulfurous than the Pennsylvania variety,

it proved difficult for him to "nose" out. And the California formations were more challenging—resulting in crooked holes, cave-ins, and lost tools.

In December 1883, Pacific Coast Oil (PCO) was having trouble with a well and, through the influence of Blake, asked Hardison and Stewart to complete it for them. It came up dry, but the skill of the HS&C operation impressed a local landowner, Thomas R. Bard, who later played a prominent role in the formation of Union Oil. Early in 1884, HS&C participated in drilling on the Ojai Rancho on lands owned by Bard. They found heavy oil at a shallow depth, but the well was a poor producer.

"We owed a total of $183,000 with no cash on hand to meet the current bills which were pouring in," Stewart said later. "We had used up our personal resources and had borrowed wherever we could."

The situation was desperate and Lyman was discouraged. On April 23, 1884, in one of his weekly letters, Milton Stewart wrote with obvious concern to his younger brother: "You view the future from a despondent standpoint to which you have brought yourself by this long and constant strain…You must bear in mind that you are of a very sanguine temperament and that this is only the natural reaction following hopes deferred…Your nature is hopeful and it would soon resume its normal condition if you would but give it half a chance…By all means get away from business."

Whether or not Lyman took Milton's advice to take a vacation, he was soon back in the fray. He appealed to PCO for a chance to drill on proven land and was finally granted a prime site known as the Star lease in Pico Canyon. (The land was owned by California Star Oil, which was controlled by PCO.) Drilling was difficult. Stewart came close to shutting down the operation, but in late November the well, Star No. 1, came in at 1,620 feet—unusually deep for the time—with production settling down to about 30 barrels a day. It was the turning point after more than a year of disappointment and near ruin.

"We were elated. We had finally struck oil," Stewart recalled. "But that was about all. Our resources were gone. We didn't have enough funds left to develop the oil we had found in Star No. 1." Hardison and Stewart were forced to sell the well back to California Star for enough capital to continue drilling.

Nevertheless, the struggling little company was on its way to becoming a player to be reckoned with on the California oil scene. Hardison and Stewart were learning valuable lessons. In the petroleum environment of the mid-1880s, making money required staying somewhat independent of the large oil

Wallace Hardison (above) followed Lyman Stewart west, and they soon founded a new oil enterprise. Top left: Many HS&C drillers hailed from the Pennsylvania fields, including Stewart's cousin John Irwin (middle row, with the beard) and, on his left, Hardison's nephew Lewis. Top right: Hardison and Stewart opened their first office in rooms above a store in Newhall (photo circa 1920). Opposite: Later, they shared quarters with the Mission Transfer Company in Santa Paula.

combines. Rockefeller's giant Standard Oil of Ohio had virtually taken over the eastern oil fields, and the same pattern was taking shape in California. For a small operation like HS&C, independence meant having control not only of its own properties, but also of its own refining, marketing, and transportation operation.

Stewart turned his sights northwest from Pico Canyon to a similar area along the Santa Clara River near Santa Paula. Backed with capital from Milton Stewart in Pennsylvania and Hardison's eastern connections, the partners acquired some acreage. They then "leveraged the leverage" by borrowing against the property to finance their drilling ventures.

Looking for ways to cut drilling costs, Stewart hit upon a new application for oil that ultimately revolutionized the petroleum industry. At the time, drillers used coal to fire the boilers that provided steam for the drilling-rig engine. Why not burn oil just as it comes from the well, Stewart reasoned. He set his drilling crews and shop mechanics to work on the problem. Soon, they came up with a cheap, practical nozzle that could successfully feed a continuous flame to heat the drilling-rig boilers. Before long, most oil-field engines were equipped with oil burners. In later years, Stewart went on to promote oil as the best fuel for a wide range of industrial uses, helping to pioneer vast new markets for petroleum.

By 1885, Stewart had settled his family in Los Angeles. In the summer of 1884, Milton had freely offered his advice on this matter, as he did on most everything. "You speak of moving to Los Angeles," Milton wrote. "Do you think it prudent to locate there? As I understand it, the drainage is not good and that in consequence fevers are quite prevalent. You can't find a healthier locality, according to all accounts, than Santa Barbara, and you had better consider well before making the change."

In 1886, the partners moved their company office to Santa Paula, and Hardison settled his family there. The town was a little rough under the growing influx of oil-field workers. It had three saloons. The 200 residents were mostly single men, some of them badmen—rustlers and thieves. Hardison plunged into community activities, helping to organize the Santa Paula Universalist Church and becoming active in local business and politics. The influence of men like Hardison and Stewart soon brought respectability to Santa Paula, and it became a thriving center of commerce.

Over the next few years, Stewart and Hardison's individual horizons broadened. Stewart became involved in several ventures in Los Angeles, including real estate and an oil play on Rancho La Brea. Hardison began buying up property in the Santa Paula area and helped develop the arid countryside into rich orchards of citrus and walnuts. Hardison's interests in new ventures eventually led him away from the oil patch.

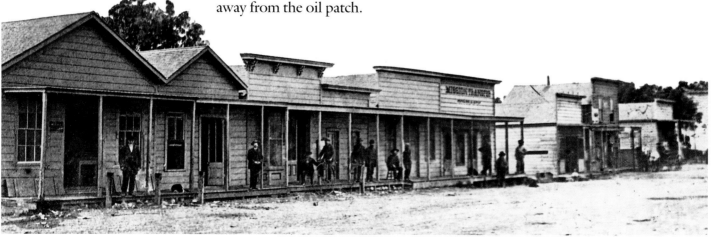

Top left: Edwin Drake, field superintendent for the Seneca Oil Company,
was given the title "colonel" by his
employer to boost the company's image.
Top right: The first oil wells were
drilled with rudimentary spring-pole
rigs. *Left:* "Colonel" Drake (in top hat)
hired "Uncle Billy" Smith to drill the first
successful oil well — originally dubbed
"Drake's folly" — near Titusville.
Above: Stewart had an interest in
the Lady Stewart well — probably
named for his mother — near
Shamburg, Pennsylvania.

CALIFORNIA'S BLACK GOLD

In 1855, four years before Drake made oil-drilling history in Pennsylvania, a California entrepreneur produced axle grease, lamp oil, and medicinal products from a small crude oil still in San Fernando, a few miles northwest of Los Angeles. Don Andres Pico, whose brother Pio was California's last Mexican governor, extracted his crude from oil seeps in the Newhall area. Other oil pioneers produced crude from seeps near Carpinteria and Ventura, and "mined" oil by tunneling into hillsides. In 1865, California's first successful oil well was drilled in the north, at Ferndale in Humboldt County. The jumbled western formations proved tougher to drill than the Pennsylvania oil fields, and the crude was heavier and mixed with more impurities, particularly sulfur. At first, these "sour" crudes produced acceptable grease and lubricating oil, although the kerosene could not compete with cleaner-burning eastern varieties. As the automobile age dawned, however, the need for high-grade lubricating oils and gasoline grew rapidly. "Sweet" eastern crudes prevailed in the marketplace, until refining innovations developed by Union and others during the 1920s and 1930s helped eliminate the eastern advantage.

By 1888, Santa Paula was well established as California's first oil center.

At the same time, Stewart and Hardison became more closely associated with Thomas Bard. Also from Pennsylvania, Bard came to California shortly after the end of the Civil War to look after property owned by his uncle. Early on, he had developed some interest in oil, but he had established himself mainly as a local businessman and property owner of considerable substance. He made his home near Hueneme, on the coast south of Ventura.

Both Stewart and Bard were Presbyterians and shared high moral principles. Stewart was devoted to the personal observance of his religion. After settling in Los Angeles, he served for three years as president of the Young Men's Christian Association. In 1887, even though his oil company was in dire need of cash, Stewart found time to raise $14,400 for the YMCA. "I have had a hard week raising money," he wrote. "I could not endure it, or rather would not, were it not...for 'Him who giveth us all things to enjoy.'"

His interest shifted to the poorer men and boys on Los Angeles's skid row, and he helped to organize the Pacific Gospel Union Mission, later known as the Union Rescue Mission. In 1888, he was a founding member of the Immanuel Presbyterian Church.

Bard, while not a consistent churchgoer, was a generous donor to religious causes, including Stewart's Pacific Gospel Union, and an active participant in the higher councils of his church. He supported the YMCA on the local, state, and national levels. As Presbyterians, Bard and Stewart both became founding trustees of Occidental College in Los Angeles.

At first, Bard and Stewart seemed highly compatible. They complemented each other in business. Bard had property, influence in banking circles and politics, and a solid reputation as a business leader in the Ventura area. Stewart had imagination, nerve, and unmatched skill and experience as an oilman. But there were deep differences between the men that would ultimately lead to the rupture of their business relationship. Bard was a cautious and conservative businessman. Stewart was more of an entrepreneur—a wildcatter with the vision to see beyond the temporary setbacks that so bedevil the petroleum seeker.

The California oil business could be discouraging in those years. The crude brought in by the shallow wells, which averaged less than 1,000 feet in depth, was heavy and viscous, good mostly for making roofing paper or burning as fuel oil. The most valuable petroleum product at the time was kerosene, but the

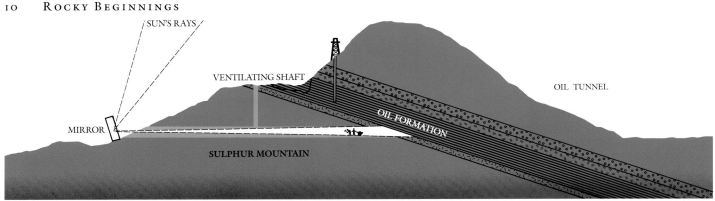

SUN'S RAYS

VENTILATING SHAFT

OIL TUNNEL

OIL FORMATION

MIRROR

SULPHUR MOUNTAIN

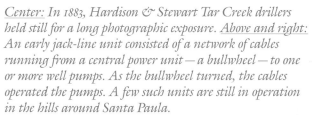

Center: In 1883, Hardison & Stewart Tar Creek drillers held still for a long photographic exposure. <u>Above and right:</u> An early jack-line unit consisted of a network of cables running from a central power unit — a bullwheel — to one or more well pumps. As the bullwheel turned, the cables operated the pumps. A few such units are still in operation in the hills around Santa Paula.

TUNNELING FOR OIL

Hardison and Stewart were determined men. Where they couldn't drill for oil, they dug for it. Such was the case on the steep southern flank of Sulphur Mountain about ten miles northwest of Santa Paula. The mountain oozed oil, but the terrain would not easily accommodate drilling rigs. In the late 1880s, H&S crews adapted a method pioneered by Josiah Stanford 20 years earlier. Stanford had applied his mining expertise to the problem and dug some 30 tunnels to produce oil. H&S crews (Union crews after October 1890) excavated another 26 tunnels. Each tunnel floor was angled slightly upward to allow the oil to flow down a central gutter toward the mouth. Sun rays reflected up the shaft from a mirror at the tunnel's mouth provided light, as well as a directional beam to guide the diggers. The "Boarding House" tunnel in Adams Canyon was the longest, penetrating 1,940 feet and exceeding the depth of most wells drilled at that time. Serious tunnel accidents were rare. In some, ventilation was provided by an ingenious device called a "water blast," which forced a stream of aerated water deep into the shaft where the air separated out of the water to help dissipate explosive gases. The Boarding House tunnel produced only water, causing the demise of a spring near the summit of Sulphur Mountain. But other tunnels produced up to 40 barrels of oil a day. Of the almost 60 tunnels dug a century or more ago, 28 still dribble oil today.

California variety tended to be mixed with a bothersome component, gasoline, that caused it to explode unexpectedly. The market for crude as fuel oil was uncertain at best. Coal was industry's primary fuel, and the public was wary of anything that packed the explosive punch of oil.

Nevertheless, HS&C persevered, driven by Stewart's zeal and vision, and aided by continuing infusions of capital from the East—mainly from Milton Stewart, who frequently admonished his brother to be more restrained in his approach to business. "At present we must plod along slowly and feel our way carefully," wrote Milton, "until we get established on a paying basis."

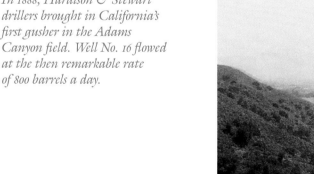

In September 1886, Thomas Bard, Lyman Stewart, and Wallace Hardison formed the Sespe Oil Company. Bard, who had studied law as a young man in Pennsylvania, drew up the incorporation papers and was named president, although Hardison and Stewart held majority control of the new company. By this time, HS&C was operating under a rather restrictive long-term agreement with Mission Transfer Company, which was controlled by PCO. Hardison and Stewart were forced to sell oil produced on PCO lands to Mission Transfer for a relatively low price. PCO, one of the largest oil companies on the West Coast, held the oil claims on a large area around Ventura and Santa Paula. In one of its first actions, Sespe made a bid for half of Mission Transfer and, somewhat surprisingly, PCO agreed to sell.

In December, Hardison and Stewart decided to incorporate, forming the Hardison & Stewart Oil Company (H&S), which absorbed their partnership. Lyman Stewart became the first president of this new corporation. Within a year, Sespe, with help from H&S, purchased the other half of Mission Transfer from PCO, giving Hardison and Stewart a transportation network of pipelines with ready access to the growing Los Angeles fuel oil market.

Thus, Stewart, Hardison, and Bard were linked in the oil business through a series of tightly interlocking, complex corporate relationships. H&S, Sespe and its subsidiary Mission Transfer, along with the Torrey Canyon Oil Company (incorporated in 1889 and controlled by Bard), formed the nucleus of what would become Union Oil Company of California.

In 1888, Hardison & Stewart drillers brought in California's first gusher in the Adams Canyon field. Well No. 16 flowed at the then remarkable rate of 800 barrels a day.

These incorporations, with their assessments, placed a heavy financial burden on Lyman Stewart, and he would struggle for many years to get free of it. However, events began to justify his faith in the business. Some of the Sespe wells turned out to be good producers. And in January 1888, in the Ex-Mission area stretching northeast from Ventura, H&S's Adams Canyon Well No. 16 came in with a roar, California's first bona fide gusher. Oil burst out of the casing pipe from a depth of 750 feet, spewing 100 feet into the air and flowing at the unheard of rate of 800 barrels a day. The oil streamed down into the Santa Clara River. Nine months later, Adams Canyon No. 16 was still producing 500 barrels a day, more than doubling previous production from all H&S wells.

H&S's income from crude oil in 1888 totaled close to half a million dollars, but it was still not enough to finance the ambitious drilling program Stewart and Hardison were pressing. The result was more borrowing and more leverage, and the diminished cash flow cut deeply into the partners' living standards. Creditors' complaints continued to arrive at the desk of the young company's general manager, Thomas Bard.

Meanwhile, Stewart worked to increase sales of fuel oil. But the high cost of transporting the oil by rail, particularly to the growing industrial market in the San Francisco area, was a problem. Southern Pacific Railroad had Hardison, Stewart, and every other producer at its mercy when it came to freight rates. The railroad refused to negotiate rate increases.

Stewart disliked being at anyone's mercy, so he hit upon a solution. While recovering from an illness, Lyman summoned Hardison and Bard to his bedside. He suggested they build a new kind of ship — an oil tanker with the capacity to carry two weeks' worth of production. It could make the run to San Francisco for half the cost of rail freight.

Hardison and Bard agreed, and by early 1889 the steam-powered *W.L. Hardison* was launched and ready for trial runs. Even before the vessel was completed, it earned its owners a handsome return on their investment. Southern Pacific cut its freight rates from $1 to 30¢ a barrel.

The *Hardison*'s boilers were fired by oil burners, an idea that Stewart, Hardison, and their competitors had quickly translated from oil-field use to much broader application. California oilmen knew about the uses of fuel oil in Russia, particularly as fuel for marine and rail transportation. Russia, like California, was short on coal but virtually swimming in petroleum as drillers in the great Baku field on the western shore of the Caspian Sea made more and bigger

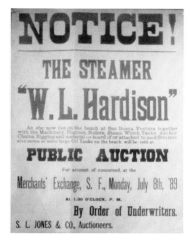

Above and right: Before it was destroyed by fire, Hardison & Stewart's first tanker induced Southern Pacific to lower its rail freight rates for oil. Opposite: The first Benz attained a speed of 9 miles per hour on its first public run in 1886, proving the viability of the gasoline-powered internal combustion engine. Opposite, below: In 1887, when H&S's Santa Paula refinery was built, gasoline was just a bothersome by-product.

discoveries. The Russian oil industry made tremendous strides in developing refining techniques and expanding uses for petroleum in the 1870s and 1880s, and many of California's industrialists welcomed the convenience and efficiency of fuel oil.

Stewart and Hardison, as aggressive in sniffing out new markets as they were in sniffing out new oil, made steamships one of their early sales targets—not always with good results. Stewart convinced the owner of the lumber carrier *Pasadena* to convert it to oil, but the boiler fires could not be sustained on the first trial. The fuel was contaminated with water, and the ship had to be towed back to port. The tug *Waterwitch* was abandoned after its oil furnace exploded.

These setbacks were chalked up to experience, but a more serious accident involving a passenger boat threatened the demise of the infant fuel oil industry. An oil-burning ferryboat, the *Julia*—operated by Southern Pacific, which bought its fuel from PCO—blew up in San Francisco Bay in February 1888. Twenty-eight people were killed. The disaster led to a federal ban on the use of oil as a marine fuel on the Pacific Coast and a San Francisco ordinance placing restrictions on industrial use of fuel oil.

In order to equip the *W.L. Hardison* with oil burners, Thomas Bard wielded his considerable political influence. He enlisted the support of a local congressman to push through a federal measure permitting the use of oil for experimental purposes on vessels that did not carry passengers. The *Hardison* made only six trips to the Bay Area before it burned to the waterline at its dock in Ventura—but the oil burners were not to blame for the fire. The story goes that a crewman lowered a lantern into a tank to check the oil level, turning the ship into a floating inferno.

Despite accidents, Stewart remained convinced that oil could be as safe as it was efficient and continued to push for expanded markets. Manufacturers who had tried fuel oil were reluctant, some even outraged, at the prospect of giving it up. The demand for fuel oil proved so compelling that legal restraints on its use were only temporary.

Like their ill-fated tanker, Stewart and Hardison's fortunes foundered as the decade of the 1880s drew to a close. Oil production from some of their wells had fallen sharply, and new exploration efforts had not panned out. Their peak California production of 444 barrels a day in 1888 slumped to only 175 barrels a day in 1889. The following year, Hardison suffered a personal tragedy when his brother Harvey was killed in an explosion in one of H&S's oil tunnels at Sulphur

Mountain. (Tunneling horizontally into the steep cliffs to reach the oil formations was easier—given the level of technology then—than vertical drilling.) Meanwhile, bankers soured on the value of H&S stock as collateral against outstanding loans, while creditors continued to nag.

Lyman Stewart wrote to Hardison: "I saw Mr. Bixby today and he wants some money from me on account of what I owe him, in time to use it in payment of his taxes. Can you help me out to the extent of $750?...I am not very well. My head has given out again."

An attempt to expand the H&S product line by building a refinery at Santa Paula in 1887 also proved disappointing. Stewart wanted to meet head-on the increasing invasion of eastern oil into the West Coast market. But the refining technology had simply not yet been invented that could turn California's thick, odorous crude into clean-burning refined products. Eastern producers, refining higher quality crude oil, could export their products—particularly kerosene— to the West Coast and beat local producers in both price and quality.

The H&S refinery was rudimentary, with a capacity of 14,000 barrels a year. Its output of naphtha and kerosene was limited and of poor quality. But late in 1889, Milton Stewart identified an eastern group with a new refining process that supposedly could double the value of H&S's thick Santa Paula crude oil as feedstock. If so, the process could revolutionize the oil business on the West Coast. H&S's directors agreed to sell the syndicate 49 percent of the company—which, of course, included the intertwined ownerships of the Sespe and Torrey Canyon oil companies—for a little under $900,000.

Spooked by price or sobered by reality when it came time to put their new process to the test, the syndicate backed out of the deal. But the exercise proved an instructive one for Hardison, Stewart, and Bard, who had never before reckoned the value of their tangled petroleum empire. Having already packaged their assets, the three partners decided to create a new company to consolidate them. It was capitalized at $5 million with majority ownership in the hands of Hardison and Stewart. Bard was named president, Stewart vice president, and Hardison treasurer. The incorporation papers were certified in Ventura on October 17, 1890. The name of the new company: Union Oil Company of California.

Hardly had their signatures dried on the incorporation papers than Thomas Bard and Lyman Stewart became embroiled in a long-running struggle for control of the infant company. Bard was convinced that Stewart was an inept

In 1890, Santa Paula's elegant two-story office building became the headquarters of the newly founded Union Oil Company of California. The building's construction began in 1889. Oak logs were imported from the East around Cape Horn, then dragged the last 16 miles from Ventura by teams of horses. Rock was quarried locally, and bricks hand-molded in the town's brickyard. Architectural details included imported European tiles, hand-carved woodwork, and ornate bronze fixtures.

business manager, and Stewart saw Bard as an overcautious obstructionist to his plans for a growing oil enterprise. Hardison, meanwhile, became less and less of a presence at Union's Santa Paula offices. An impulsive man of large appetites, he was turning his attention to real estate, fighting off creditors with one hand while signing up for new debt with the other. Hardison also became more active in Republican Party politics.

The problems that afflicted Union Oil over the next decade rose in part from the differing priorities of its top executives. Bard and Stewart tried to work together to determine the new company's direction. But Bard's annoyance mounted as Stewart kept borrowing to expand the company, seemingly oblivious to the pressures this put on Bard and the company's credit standing. Stewart, having been squeezed out of more than one profitable drilling deal because he didn't control the land, felt that acquiring potential oil property was the key to long-term success.

Although Bard was certainly not against vertical expansion, Stewart apparently better understood the importance of strong "downstream" operations — refining, transportation, and marketing — in creating a successful petroleum company. Only by controlling the oil from wellhead to customer, Stewart believed, could Union hope to survive against industry giants. And while Bard remained ever cautious about moving away from the business of producing and marketing fuel oil, Stewart had a much clearer vision of the possibilities of new, higher value products and new markets.

One of the major business conflicts between the two men was Stewart's insistence on paying dividends, even in uncertain economic times. Bard and Stewart fought over the issue constantly, voting dividends in at one board meeting and out at the next. In general, Stewart prevailed, setting a policy for the company that continued even through the Depression of the 1930s.

Stewart's insistence on paying dividends can perhaps be explained by his personal circumstances. He needed the income from dividends to service his debts. At the same time, his debts were secured by company stock, the face value of which was shored up at least partly by the paying of dividends. To the conservative Bard, however, it was almost immoral for a company so dependent on borrowed money to pay out dividends, a practice that became commonplace in later times.

Years after Bard had resigned from the company, Stewart was asked if it would be fair to say that Bard felt he was too venturesome, and that he felt Bard was too conservative. "Yes, I guess that was about the situation," Stewart said.

In 1890, Union Oil Company's 26 producing wells yielded 84,421 barrels of crude oil (231 barrels a day), equaling one-fourth of California's petroleum production that year. Ownership of Union Oil Company was held by the three original companies — Hardison & Stewart Oil Company, Sespe Oil Company (which owned Mission Transfer), and Torrey Canyon Oil Company. Lyman Stewart, Wallace Hardison, and their families and friends controlled 53 percent of the shares (which included the majority interests in H&S and Sespe), while Thomas Bard and his allies controlled 40 percent (including a majority of Torrey Canyon).

The struggle continued, with Stewart plugging for expansion and Bard for what he felt was a more prudent approach. Stewart never lost sight of the need for new reserves, and he took advantage of Bard's frequent absences by going on land-buying binges or committing the company to major expenditures for pipelines and refinery equipment.

Stewart was convinced there were untapped reservoirs of petroleum deep below California's broken hills and valleys. In 1884, W. E. Youle, another Titusville driller, had gone down to 1,600 feet for oil in the Puente Hills east of Los Angeles. Stewart and Hardison had followed that example in the Star No. 1 well in November 1884, and later in Adams Canyon, drilling down to almost 3,000 feet with some success.

Again and again, Stewart went to Union's board with the same argument: Let me buy promising oil lands while they're available and cheap. In late 1890, when the board put a lid of $5 an acre on the price he could pay, Stewart found ways around it. By purchase and lease, the acreage kept accumulating. By the end of 1892, Stewart was picking up oil lands so fast that Union's directors appropriated funds for a temporary assistant in the office of the Ventura County recorder — to make sure the land records were kept current.

Meanwhile, the battle for petroleum product markets, particularly kerosene, warmed up. San Francisco, by far the largest city on the West Coast, had been staked out by the Standard Oil Company for early conquest. "They are preparing for a war west of the Rockies, and soon there will be firing all along the line," wrote an embattled Union Oil sales manager at the time. "They are building the largest oil refinery in the world in Chicago and will cut the life out of our prices within a year."

Lyman Stewart concluded that the one way to compete was to upgrade the art of petroleum refining on the West Coast, where technology lagged behind the East. By developing new and more valuable products from its Ventura crude, Union might double the value of its oil. Stewart was on the right track, but early attempts to follow through proved discouraging at best.

Milton Stewart learned of a researcher in New York with a tempting idea. Dr. Frederick Salathe, a Swiss chemist, had been experimenting with crude oil to develop cheaper dyes for the textile industry. The Union board agreed to hire Salathe at the then fabulous salary of $10,000 a year. (Bard's salary was only $5,000, although he never collected the full amount, and Stewart's was $2,000.) In early 1892, Union put Salathe in charge of its refining operations.

It was an unfortunate decision. Salathe promptly quarreled with the refinery superintendent, F. H. Dunham, who was fired (and later rehired). Salathe then took over the duties of managing the refinery, for which he had neither talent nor interest. He turned out a steady stream of new products — illuminating oils, kerosenes, and lubricants in a rainbow of colors (a big selling point in those days) — but could not produce them in large quantities.

Early oil-field workers, such as these Hardison & Stewart drillers of 1884, often lived up to the name of roughnecks with bawdy talk and behavior. Lyman Stewart grew more and more concerned about their spiritual welfare, providing traveling preachers, forbidding work on the Sabbath, and building a chapel in the Torrey Canyon field. Later, he made sure Bibles were available to office workers.

The Torrey Canyon field provided more than a third of Union Oil Company's production during the company's first four years.

Refinery operations deteriorated, customers went elsewhere, and Union Oil's sales plummeted.

"Our chemist is somewhat visionary," Stewart wrote to an associate, "and we have been a good deal disappointed in the result of his work."

Bard complained: "The great failure of this lubricating oil business is our inability to supply our customers a second time with the oil we have sold them on trial."

Stewart, Bard, and the rest of the board tolerated Salathe's eccentricities during the two years of his contract, then eased him out in late 1893. Bard estimated the Salathe experiment had cost the struggling company $56,000.

This was not the only misstep in Union's effort to build a sophisticated refining capacity. In 1891, Hardison got the company involved in a process to produce ink from petroleum, which also proved a steady cash drain. The ill-conceived project resulted in losses totaling $55,000 before it was essentially scuttled, also in late 1893.

Meanwhile, the state legislature — no doubt under the goading of the Rockefeller interests — threatened to impose tighter requirements on kerosene sold in California, requirements Union and other western refiners could not meet. Hardison and Bard quickly put their political connections to work and got the legislation killed.

Undaunted by these setbacks and legislative threats, Stewart kept pushing Union's board of directors to underwrite expansion. In 1892, the company increased its crude production to 180,000 barrels — more than half of the total crude produced in California. Most of Union's new production came from Torrey Canyon, east of Santa Paula, on lands originally controlled by Bard. Production on old H&S properties, meanwhile, had fallen sharply.

Hardison's sale of his interests in Union Oil changed the management dynamics of the young company in 1892. His shaky financial position had resulted in rising pressure from several banks and other lenders to whom he owed money. Bard, fearful that Hardison's creditors might start coming after Union Oil, pressed Hardison to get his finances on a sounder footing. Finally, with three other investors, he offered to buy Hardison out. Hardison reluctantly agreed but served on Union's board for another two years.

With Hardison sidelined, Stewart could no longer count on his old friend and partner to back his dreams for Union Oil against Bard's fiscal conservatism. To make matters worse, Bard had increased his stake in the company, and with it his voting power, in the event of a showdown with Stewart. Bard's personal holdings amounted to 25 percent of Union's outstanding shares, the largest individual stake held by anyone. Through allies, he controlled a good deal more. But when the dust settled, Stewart was still in charge.

While Bard and his friends bought out Hardison, Lyman and Milton quietly acquired the holdings of another investor, giving the Stewarts a majority interest. The stage was set for a new period of struggle between Lyman Stewart and Thomas Bard. The backdrop was one of dramatic change in the oil patch and approaching crisis in the country's economy.

Edward L. Doheny, a hard-rock miner, had been lured to California from New Mexico by the scent of oil. He staked out a claim on a city lot just west of downtown Los Angeles, near today's intersection of Second Street and Glendale Boulevard. Unschooled in the ways of oil drilling, Doheny hunted for petroleum the only way he knew how, by digging. He sank a 4-by-6-foot shaft that encountered thick, black crude oil at 46 feet. He managed to produce four barrels a day, which financed his acquisition of a small rig that he used to drill several successful wells in the vicinity.

Thus, in late 1892, was born the Los Angeles field, which quickly became the biggest producer in the state and threw the West Coast oil market into temporary chaos. Hundreds of cheap, shallow wells were drilled, rapidly glutting the market for all petroleum products. Residents of the area rebelled at the smelly, unsightly rigs mushrooming around them. The city council declared derricks a civic nuisance and prohibited drilling for oil within the city limits. Drillers

In the 1880s, Santa Paula became the West's Titusville as numerous discoveries were made in the surrounding hills and valleys. Below: In late 1892, Edward Doheny struck oil near downtown Los Angeles, and oil fever soon had the city forested with derricks. The resulting oil glut threatened the viability of Union Oil Company.

circumvented the ban by saying they were looking for water. If they found oil "by accident," so be it.

As crude prices crashed, Union Oil was forced to retrench sharply. Drilling was curtailed and several wells producing heavier crudes were shut in. Dividends were temporarily suspended, and Stewart and Bard fought over building a pipeline from Santa Paula to Los Angeles. Bard prevailed, arguing that Stewart's proposal to build the line was based on an unrealistic estimate of costs. Nevertheless, Union used the threat of a pipeline to win better shipping rates from the railroad.

Stewart continued his aggressive marketing efforts, with the company opening a sales office in Los Angeles. But it was a difficult time. The New York stock market crashed in April 1893, triggering bank closures, business failures, and unemployment across the country. Many of Union's potential fuel oil clients shut down, even as crude oil production continued to rise.

Union's executives made another weary round of creditors, seeking more cash to continue operating. Bard wrote to Stewart: "I do not intend to make any provision for loans to pay dividends, and am so strongly opposed to borrowing any more money that I will insist on retiring from the management if that cannot be avoided."

This was the first of several threats to resign that Bard made but did not carry out over the next few years. They were effective because Stewart, although chafing under Bard's restraining hand, feared the consequences to the company's standing in the financial community if Bard withdrew. Stewart had reason to be grateful for Bard's solid reputation and referred to him as "one of the most substantial and conservative Christian businessmen of this coast."

The notes of Union's directors' meeting held December 7, 1893, stated: "The President referred to the unsatisfactory condition of the Company's business; to the losses that had been incurred by the various new enterprises that had been begun by the Company in the last two years; to the prospect of competition with oil to be brought from Peru, and recommended that the Company make reduction in price of fuel oil, pushing our sales in Southern California and competing promptly in San Francisco with Peru oil by offering to contract to deliver oil as low as $1.25 per barrel at Santa Paula; also, to confine our work at the refinery to the manufacture of only such products as are readily salable and to stop all further experimental work and investigations, and to cut off every part of the business that was not profitable or in a promising condition, and to confine our business largely, if not entirely, to the one object of increasing the sales of fuel oil."

(The threat of oil imports from Peru never amounted to much. California production was constantly increasing, and government tariffs protected domestic oil. It is interesting to note that Wallace Hardison, who attended his final board meeting as a Union director in the fall of 1894, was involved in the deal to import oil from Peru.)

In 1894, Union retained Stephen F. Peckham, a University of California chemist, to see what he could salvage from the refinery wreckage left by Salathe. Much of the equipment had been misused and was beyond repair. Peckham managed to get some operations up and running and even improve product quality. But his tenure was brief. Peckham returned to university life in less than a year, and the refinery was shut down.

As to the development of a clean illuminating oil and other new products, Peckham's report to Union's directors was not encouraging: "The trouble with California oil is, no one knows anything about it; we do not know what we are working on, and the results of our labors thus far have been thrusts in the dark."

Peckham estimated that it would take two years for a proper analysis—time

he would not have. At this critical juncture, Union was focused on sales, not on long-term research.

Production from the shallow wells in the Los Angeles field began to peter out by 1894, and the oil finders—who had streamed to Los Angeles as avid for wealth as the gold prospectors of 1849—turned their attention northward to the San Joaquin Valley and the Santa Maria area. Ironically, in departing the Los Angeles basin, they were leaving behind one of the largest oil regions in the country. In later years, deep drilling would produce more than 10 billion barrels of petroleum liquids, and the basin remains a solid producer to this day.

In 1894, as the country's economy began to improve, Union's innovations in marketing helped revive the company's sales. For example, a deal Stewart had made with the state-run Whittier Reform School two years earlier was bringing in other new business. To sell the Whittier school on switching its heating system over to oil-burning furnaces, Stewart had agreed to wait a year for payment. The state legislature had approved the plan and, when the furnaces worked beautifully, Union Oil had the edge on the competition to supply other state-run institutions.

Also in 1894, Stewart won over the Los Angeles Iron and Steel Company by promising to install oil burners at Union's expense, then take payment in company stock rather than cash. Many other sales followed, prompting the *Los Angeles Times* to note that "Union Oil has long been known as 'Old Reliable.' Union makes it a special business to introduce oil for any new work wherein oil has not been used before, and puts forth every effort to make a success of same."

Stewart applied the same basic marketing idea to the railroads, which were interested in the efficiencies of fuel oil even though they were prime beneficiaries of the coal trade, hauling thousands of tons a year at advantageous rates. Stewart and Bard were well aware of Russian successes in using oil to power steam engines, and both worked hard to sell the railroads on fuel oil.

Santa Fe's Southern California Railway finally agreed to let Union experiment with one of its engines, and company mechanics installed an oil burner. The initial results were less than satisfactory. The wheezing engine managed a couple of runs on level track but clearly lacked the power to pull a string of cars. But by late 1894, the mechanics had modified the burner's design so that it provided enough heat to steam the engine, with a full load of cars, up the tough Cajon grade above San Bernardino.

OIL PATCH GUNSLINGER
Legal contracts and leases were often loosely drawn in the California oil fields in the late nineteenth century. Such was the case for Sespe Oil Company formed by Thomas Bard, Wallace Hardison, and Lyman Stewart in 1886. The incorporation papers and subsequent lease agreements, carelessly drafted, led to endless litigation. Among the disputants at Sespe Canyon was one Joe Dye, a former Indian fighter and peace officer who had explored there in 1876 and claimed to hold rights to his old properties. In disputes about his claims, he gunned down a local stalwart named Herman Haines and threatened others. Alarmed, Hardison wrote to Bard: "Dye is now out on bail and is a bad man. Within six months he has threatened to shoot three different men. Owing to my connection with the oil business at the Sespe, I do not want my name mentioned just now as a party urging vigorous prosecution, but I am in favor of putting such fellows where they can't shoot any other person. Dye passed through here tonight full of whiskey." Dye remained at large for five years, during which time his enmity spread to include Bard, who began keeping a brace of pistols at hand. But Dye met poetic justice. On May 14, 1891, he was gunned down on a Los Angeles street by a former associate named Mason Bradfield. A sympathetic jury gave Bradfield only five years.

Top left: Union Oil's mechanics perfected an oil burner for a locomotive in late 1894, part of Bard and Stewart's diligent—though ultimately unprofitable—efforts to sell the railroads on burning fuel oil instead of coal.

Unfortunately, the company never profited from this innovation. Once Union's technology proved that it could be done, the railroad devised its own burners and went elsewhere for fuel oil. Eventually, many railroad companies began their own petroleum operations, supplying their trains and competing with oil companies for customers.

Bard and Stewart continued to have their differences. Stewart put Bard through an embarrassing interlude in early 1894 when Bard tried to relieve himself of growing management pressures by naming a new general manager. The man Bard had in mind was Stewart's brother Milton, who was an experienced oil producer and marketer in Pennsylvania and a constant adviser to Union. During a trip to Los Angeles, Milton met with Bard and agreed to take the job. Bard wrote immediately to Lyman, telling him of his plan, "of course, presuming that this would be agreeable to you."

Curiously, Lyman Stewart said the arrangement was not agreeable to him. Perhaps he did not relish the prospect of his somewhat meddlesome brother looking over his business shoulder and counseling caution on a daily basis. At any rate, Bard let Milton think he had merely changed his mind, hoping Lyman would explain things later. Lyman never did, however, and Milton apparently never suspected that his brother had objected to his being hired. Instead, Milton nursed a smoldering resentment toward Bard for years to come.

Still anxious to find a general manager for the company, Bard offered his resignation in May to try to get action from the board. But the board refused his offer, with Stewart joining in the unanimous vote. Bard would have to try a different approach.

What appeared to be the final breach between Bard and Stewart occurred just before Stewart's extended trip east over the summer of 1894. During a heated argument, Bard vowed to do everything in his power to defeat the ambitions of the Stewart family. Then, in July, with both Stewart and Hardison absent, Bard persuaded the board to accept his resignation as president and appoint David T. Perkins—his long-time associate and fellow Union board member—in his place.

It was in this angry atmosphere that I. H. Warring, corporate secretary and a Bard ally, yanked Will Stewart out of his new job in the refinery—where the young man hoped to learn downstream operations—and confined him to the barrel factory. When Lyman Stewart returned to California, he was furious to learn of the action against his son, not to mention Perkins' appointment. Lyman immediately reassigned Will to work as a driller's helper in a field crew—and prepared for a showdown with Bard at Union Oil's annual meeting in October.

Stewart intended to oust Perkins and get himself elected president, as well as general manager. By the time of the meeting he had the necessary votes, and the deed was done. Now Stewart was boss of the company Bard had run for four contentious years. Bard told Stewart afterward, "Well, you have us where you want us now."

Indeed, Stewart had won. But Bard was still a major stockholder, and Stewart valued his presence on the board. Stewart was convinced that Bard and his banking connections were vital to Union Oil's future. He may also have realized that the company needed Bard's influence to counterbalance his own boldness and vision with a dose of economic reality. So, instead of sweeping the Bard forces from the company, or at least cutting their voting strength on the board, Stewart offered to let Bard name five of the nine directors. Bard accepted, and Union Oil faced another six years of turmoil.

2

Finding New Markets

Thomas Bard was a key figure during Union Oil Company's first ten years. Opposite: In 1897, E.C. Erie took a spin in an automobile of his own construction — the first built in Los Angeles. Erie's passenger was former mayor W.H. Workman.

In 1895, the efforts of pioneer oil marketers like Lyman Stewart began to pay off. While kerosene was still the major high-value component refined from a barrel of crude oil, fuel oil — Union's major product — was rapidly displacing coal in industrial applications. Naphtha and benzene were becoming popular fuels for stoves. Municipal gas companies used benzene to enrich gas made from coal. New lubricants were produced for engines and equipment, along with new grades of distillate for cooking and heating. Asphalt — Union produced seven different grades — found markets as an excellent paving and roofing material.

Automobiles, still a rich man's diversion, would soon usher in a new era of transportation, creating a huge demand for yet another product of crude oil, gasoline. In 1890, when a motorist putted up to the Santa Paula refinery in his horseless carriage, he was told there was no gasoline in stock — but to check back in several days.

The first gasoline-powered automobiles had been unveiled in Germany in 1886 by Karl Benz and Gottlieb Daimler. In 1893, J. Frank Duryea of Massachusetts built America's first gasoline-engine car using the designs of his brother Charles. A small but important event in the advance of automotive technology occurred in 1895. In an auto endurance test on a 55-mile course outside Chicago, some of the cars actually held together long enough to cross the finish line. The winner was a Duryea, which averaged — including time out for repairs — 7½ miles per hour.

The demand for crude oil products was growing, and production out of the Los Angeles field — which had glutted the markets in 1893 and 1894 — was lessening. Union had cut back production during the glut. As the company geared up again in 1895, it desperately needed a new refinery. The Santa Paula refinery — worn out and obsolete — was shut down that year. Better technology had been developed to turn out the widening range of new petroleum products.

Union's directors appointed a board committee to locate a site for a new California refinery somewhere on the coast. The committee's first choice, Ventura, was overruled by Stewart, who favored "the great city of the future," Los Angeles. But city fathers there opposed the plan because of fire risk. So the committee proposed a site on San Francisco Bay, near the Carquinez Strait, called El Rancho Chino. It had five fathoms of water close in and was located on the Southern Pacific main rail line from the south. Union bought the property for $15,000.

Construction of the new petroleum facility, capable of processing 1,200 barrels of crude a day, began almost immediately. The new refinery, named for the nearby town of Oleum, went on stream in February 1896. Coincidentally, the Santa Paula refinery was destroyed by fire four months later.

The new Oleum facility was soon acquired by Mission Transfer Company, which leased it back to Union for $60,000 a year. The arrangement gave Mission Transfer a source of income so that it could pay dividends to its shareholders, primarily Lyman Stewart, who was strapped for cash as usual.

Oleum was supplied with Southern California crude from the outset by Pacific Coast Oil's new ship, the *George Loomis,* probably the first true tanker built on the West Coast. The hull of the *Loomis* served as one great oil tank, unlike the earlier *W.L. Hardison,* which had been equipped with steel tanks.

With its crude production centered in the south and its refinery in the north, Union needed to expand its transportation capabilities to remain competitive and out of the clutches of the railroads. The board approved several pipeline projects.

Over the next decade, the Oleum refinery became a key to Union's growth as a marketer in California. A state-of-the-art facility, it gave the company a wider range of products to sell, and it was ideally located near the state's largest population center. Union Oil was becoming a major industrial force in California.

The fast-growing company began to attract the attention of investors and corporate suitors, including Standard Oil of New Jersey. As early as 1891, Union had approached Standard Oil proposing to restructure the company and offering to sell them half of it in order to raise funds. Standard, however, wanted all or nothing.

In 1896 Stewart, worn down by years of indebtedness, approached Standard three separate times. Standard showed some interest and Stewart, after consulting with Thomas Bard, set a price. In New York, Standard's executives apparently could not reach a decision, so nothing came of it. Bard and Milton Stewart became suspicious that Standard had feigned interest only to get an opportunity to spy on Union's properties.

The exercise was repeated in 1898 with the same outcome. Just when Rockefeller's negotiators appeared to reach agreement with Lyman Stewart and Bard, the deal was suddenly called off on orders from the East. Stewart, who had envisioned a cash windfall, was crestfallen. Bard probably felt relieved, because

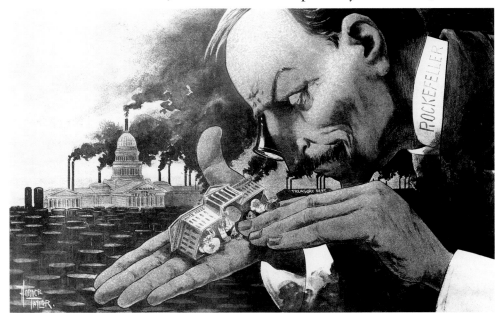

"The Trust Giant's Point of View: What a Funny Little Government!" Horace Taylor's cartoon, published in 1899, echoed many others of the period that focused on the acquisitive John D. Rockefeller and Standard Oil Company.

Union's second refinery, much larger and more sophisticated than the one in Santa Paula, was built near Oleum on the northeast shore of San Francisco Bay. It started up in 1896 with four crude oil stills (at right), each with a 150-barrel capacity.

he had been concerned about what would happen to his minority interest if Union Oil fell into outside hands.

In 1897, an English woman, Serena Lightfoot, appeared in Los Angeles looking for opportunities for European investors. She persuaded Union management that she could find buyers, and Stewart was eager to explore the possibilities. After her first efforts failed, Bard became skeptical. Nevertheless, he packed his money belt with Union stock and traveled to London in May, where she promised to produce a buyer. Her deal fell through, but Bard took the opportunity to visit the Clippens Oil Company in Edinburgh. He obtained samples of the shale rock from which Clippens extracted oil. This was probably Union's first contact with the shale oil process, which would play a significant role in the company's story in the late twentieth century.

Stewart, in addition to his tireless efforts to build the company, worried about improving the character of his drill crews. Arriving unannounced at the Torrey Canyon field in 1898, he caught the drillers stretched out in the shade, while a sweating boy pumped a bellows for the furnace. The hard-working youngster was obviously tired.

Stewart walked over to the lad, glanced at the sleeping men, then said sympathetically, "Well, son, this is pretty heavy work for a fellow your size, isn't it?"

"Mister, she is a ____ and you can tell the whole ____ world I said so," the boy replied, adding a few more sizzling expletives to describe the sleeping crew.

Horrified, Stewart backed out of earshot. At the next meeting of Union's directors, he received authorization to build a chapel in Torrey Canyon and to employ the Reverend Mr. Johnson of Piru to conduct services.

As the century drew to a close, hostilities between Bard and Stewart continued to escalate. Though no longer an officer of the company, Bard wielded considerable influence as a board member and major shareholder. Stewart, very

much in control of company operations, still bristled over what he regarded as
Bard's resistance to his plans for making Union Oil bigger and better. For his
part, Bard felt that the debt-ridden Stewart, with 51 percent of the company,
jeopardized Bard's investment. All of Stewart's shares were pledged against
loans, and if Stewart died or were to be foreclosed, control could pass to
an outsider.

Once again, Bard prepared for battle. The field would be the tangled corporate structure upon which Stewart, Hardison, and Bard had built Union Oil —
a structure that encouraged manipulation and power plays. Bard fired the first
shots at the 1898 shareholders' meeting of the Sespe Oil Company, whose directors were empowered to name several members of the Union board. Using an
obscure legal loophole, Bard took control of the Sespe board and so gained the
authority to name the swing vote on Union's board for the next 12 months.
Apparently, he had taken full control of Union; Stewart seemed to be finished.

Stunned, Stewart told associate R.W. Fenn, "It's all up. I'm a ruined man."

Fenn reminded Stewart that another vote was coming up by the directors
of the Torrey Canyon Oil Company, which also controlled some Union board
seats. Unless Bard won the Torrey Canyon vote, he would not control the Union
board. Bard had assumed that with three votes, including Fenn's, he had the
Torrey Canyon vote locked up. Bard was mistaken.

"He has only two directors of the Torrey Canyon Oil Company," Fenn told
Stewart. "You have two, and I am the fifth — and I will cast my vote for you."

Bard thus lost the Torrey Canyon vote, and with it control of Union Oil
Company. Furious at Fenn's desertion, Bard charged — with some reason — that
Stewart had pressured Fenn by reminding him of interest-free loans Stewart had
made him.

Before long, Bard threatened to sue Union Oil over its unfair and possibly
illegal corporate structure, squeezing a promise from Stewart to dissolve the
holding entities — Sespe, Torrey Canyon, and H&S oil companies — and make
Union Oil a straight stock company. While this would not immediately dislodge
Stewart, it would make his hold on Union more tenuous. Bard knew that Stewart
and his allies held a bare majority of company stock, and if any of it were ever
sold, Bard could buy it up and regain control.

For several weeks, Stewart dragged his feet, failing to dissolve the holding companies, so Bard once more employed the threat of resignation to get action. Fearful that Bard's departure from the board would expose the company's internal conflicts and diminish the value of the stock as collateral, Stewart finally made good on his promise. Bard, as usual, drew up the papers.

On April 13, 1899, Union Oil shed its contorted structure of corporate governance and became a free-standing, publicly held company. Bard received 12,168 new shares worth about $45 each, representing 25 percent of the shareholders' equity. Stewart and his allies controlled 26,941 shares, or approximately 54 percent of the company.

One final battle remained. Stewart realized that under the new corporate structure he was in a vulnerable position. So early in 1899, he consolidated the shares he controlled under the shield of a new holding company whose directors would have total control of the Union Oil board. The new entity, called the United Petroleum Associates, would make the possibility of an unfriendly takeover much more remote.

Bard countered by amassing his shares in another new holding company, United Stockholding Associates. But, for the last time, Bard came up short. His bloc controlled only 16,000 shares, while Stewart could vote nearly 27,000. The game was over; Stewart had won.

Stewart's victory was a critical turning point in the history of Union Oil. The company had already fully integrated its production, refining, and marketing activities, but now Stewart could aggressively pursue his vision of the future, expanding in all phases of the industry. Had Bard won, it seems likely he would have followed a more conservative policy, and no doubt Union Oil would have been a far different company today.

Once the fight was settled, the bitterness drained away. Bard continued as a board member and minor player in Union's destinies for another 18 months but decided to retire from the oil business when he accepted an appointment to fill out a term as a United States senator. He offered Stewart an option on his United Stockholding Associates shares, but the two men couldn't come to terms. On November 18, 1900, Bard optioned his stock to a group of Los Angeles businessmen for $43.25 a share, thus ending his formal association with the company he had helped found.

Bard remained a friend of Union Oil and even lent the company substantial sums from time to time, until his death in 1915. He also contributed to Stewart's Bible Institute of Los Angeles, founded in 1908. Stewart supported Bard's bitterly fought — and unsuccessful — bid to retain his Senate seat in 1904. Bard wrote Stewart that year:

"I greatly appreciate your own friendly interest in my campaign. It is particularly gratifying to me personally that the men with whom I have been associated in business, who know my shortcomings and defects of temperament, are able nevertheless to believe that I have the qualifications fitting me for such great responsibilities."

In a letter to a San Francisco banker, Bard explained the sale of his Union interests: "For some time the Stewarts have been desirous of expanding the business beyond the scope of our original scheme, and for such purpose to borrow or otherwise raise large sums of money. This we might consent to if the management were entrusted to more competent and conservative men....The Stewarts are honest and, in the best sense, trustworthy. But they are not competent to carry on the great business of the company....I learn, however, that they have indicated to our option holders that they are disposed to let new men share in the management. They have come to the realization that the new blood is needed to give the body corporate new health and vigor."

Will Stewart, who joined Union in 1894, became general manager late in 1898. <u>Left:</u> Late in 1900, Union's directors voted to move corporate headquarters to Los Angeles. In February 1901, new offices were opened in the Tajo Building (at left), a five-story structure on the corner of First and Broadway. Parking was not a problem in the community of slightly more than 100,000.

Indeed, changes had already occurred in Union's management. In December 1898, 30-year-old Will Stewart, with Bard's approval, had become general manager of the company at a salary of $300 per month. After some initial misunderstandings, Will had forged a close relationship with Bard. Later, Bard proposed that Will's salary be raised to $375 a month because he was "working very hard and spending his whole strength in the interests of the corporation." The board agreed and made Will a vice president as well.

A gregarious and earthy young man, Will Stewart had received a first-rate education in the petroleum business from his father. He had worked in the fields, tool shops, and the refinery during school breaks. In 1890, he dropped out of the University of California in Berkeley, where he was a football star, to work full time in the oil fields for a year. He then tried his hand at farming, planting an orange grove on a tract of land in Upland east of Los Angeles before returning to Union Oil in 1894.

Drillers liked Will Stewart for his willingness to plunge into the grimy, sweaty labor around the rigs. He did not refrain, as his father had, from drink and tobacco, and his language could be as colorful as any rowdy's in the oil field. His tolerance for the foibles of his crews was demonstrated in an exchange he once had with his father.

Lyman Stewart had urged Will to dismiss one of his drilling foremen, saying, "No man who starts work sober but ends up half drunk should be retained on Union's payroll."

Will, reluctant to lose a good foreman, assured his father the report must be wrong. "I know the man," he said, "and I can tell you he never showed up sober and ended up drunk."

Pleased with the reassurance, Lyman relented, and the foreman was kept on.

Recalling the incident later, Will said he had been strictly accurate, though not altogether candid. "The man's never showed up sober," he explained. "He's always half drunk when he starts to work."

Yet the bond between the two Stewarts was close. As a boy, Will had often served as his father's secretary, taking down his dictated letters and memos during the frequent spells of illness that afflicted the elder Stewart in those tense years of struggle to get the company on a solid footing.

Together, the Stewarts began to reinvigorate Union Oil. The company enjoyed a period of rapid expansion, with several new oil discoveries and a firm market for its products. A 7,500-barrel full-rigged schooner, the *Santa Paula*, was built to help move the new crude production to the Oleum refinery. In 1901, the oil-burning tug *Rescue* displayed what may have been the company's first advertisement—a banner reading, "We burn Union Oil for fuel."

In late 1900, Union Oil's directors voted to move the corporate headquarters from Santa Paula to Los Angeles. Stewart's "city of the future" had become the financial and business center of Southern California, and Union's operations spread south through Los Angeles County and beyond.

Below: After a century, the Union Tool mark can still be found on operating equipment in oil fields around Santa Paula. Bottom: In 1896, Union Tool Company craftsmen posed with a steam engine built in their Santa Paula shop. Alfred C. Stewart (seated on oil can) was Lyman's younger son. Then 21, he later became a well-known inventor, making many contributions — notably the Stewart carburetor — to automotive science.

In 1901, Union Oil Tool Company set up shops in Los Angeles to service not only Union's crews but those of competitors. Even before they founded Union Oil Company, Lyman Stewart and Wallace Hardison had understood the importance of servicing operations in the oil fields with quality drill bits, cable, and other tools of the trade. Unable to find reliable suppliers, they had created their own hardware subsidiary, the Santa Paula Hardware Company, which was assimilated into the new Union Oil Company in 1890. Bard had felt that it was an unnecessary, money-losing proposition and talked the board into selling it.

Stewart simply went ahead and started another tool company. His ace in the hole was Edward Doble, whom he had recruited on a trip east in the 1890s. With a gift for tool design, Doble quickly established a shop that could "make anything." Under Doble's leadership, Union Tool Company became one of the outstanding supply companies in the industry. (In 1920, it was sold to the National Supply Company.)

A vital part of the Stewarts' strategy for Union Oil as they entered the

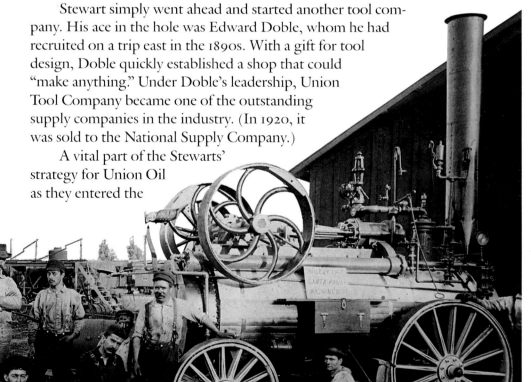

new century was the infusion of new talent into the management team, men who would help build a bigger, more sophisticated Union Oil. In some cases, their direct influence was felt into the mid-twentieth century. When John Baker, Jr., took over operations of the Oleum refinery in 1899, for example, the facility had been losing money heavily, and Union's directors were considering either selling or leasing it. With Will Stewart's backing, Baker convinced the board not only to keep the refinery, but to double its size and later to triple it. Then Baker set out to widen Union's marketing operation; before long, his salesmen were handling all the product the refinery could manufacture.

William W. Orcutt had grown up around Santa Paula, working at odd jobs at the Union refinery before entering Stanford to study engineering and geology. Hired by Union in 1899, he was soon running the geology program. He started the first petroleum geology department in the West in 1900, made the first geological maps of many of California's most important oil fields, developed a staff of topflight oil finders, and built a reputation as the dean of West Coast petroleum geologists.

Although the world was becoming mechanized in the early 1900s, the vehicle had not yet been invented that could get Orcutt and his crews into the craggy California mountains they wanted to explore. A typical expedition in those days consisted of a wagon drawn by a pair of saddle-broken horses (in case the going got too tough for wheels), equipped with a grub box, blankets, tools, maps and compass, a bale of hay, a sack of grain, water, and something stronger to ward off the chill. Also useful were a few sides of bacon, a favorite of the Basque shepherds of the area, who knew the locations of oil seeps or unusual outcroppings of rock that might indicate the presence of oil.

Frank F. Hill also joined the company in 1899. Union's directors had approved the hiring of "a young man of good education and some geological knowledge and experience as a mountaineer, but also inexperienced as an oilman who would work for a very small salary and his expenses." Hill had been knocking around Union's fields as a teamster since he was a teenager. Once on staff he demonstrated a flair for invention and improvisation, always coming up with ideas to make equipment run faster or more efficiently. His innovations would make a lasting impact on drilling practices.

It was certainly the right time for a problem solver in the oil patch. By the

DEAN OF OIL GEOLOGY
William W. Orcutt was involved in Union's geology and exploration operations for somè 40 years. One of the industry's most gifted explorationists, he is credited with organizing the first oil company geology department in 1900. His early maps of California oil fields confirmed his brilliance and made it possible for Union to select the best sites to drill. Born in Minnesota in 1869, Orcutt grew up in Santa Paula, California, where he sometimes worked at odd jobs at the Hardison & Stewart refinery. One of his friends — later a close business associate — was Lyman Stewart's son Will. Orcutt was one of Stanford University's first four-year graduates, a member of the pioneer class of 1895. He worked as a civil and hydraulic engineer until 1899, when Union Oil's directors hired him "to look after the company's interests in Fresno and San Benito counties." His horizons quickly expanded. He hacked through tangled tropical jungles, slept on frozen ground, forded rivers, and climbed mountains in the search for oil. In 1908, Orcutt became Union's chief geologist, land department manager, and a company director. He was named a vice president in 1922, and added development and production to his portfolio in 1933. When Orcutt lost his left arm in an automobile accident in 1934, he adjusted so quickly that a friend referred to him as "one of the old iron men" of the early days of oil. He retired in 1939 and died in 1942.

turn of the century, drillers were pushing against the limits of their technology.
Although the rotary drill was coming into fashion, particularly in Texas, most
drilling in the West was still done with a cable rig, in which the drill bit was fixed
at the end of a drop rope or cable and battered into the earth repeatedly. As the
hole deepened, the cable had to be lengthened. Manila rope stretched too much
to allow drilling deeper than 2,000 feet. Steel cable was an improvement, but
beyond depths of 5,000 feet the weight of the cable put too much strain on the
underpowered steam engines of the day. Hill turned his fertile imagination to
the problem, developing a series of innovations that made drilling faster, easier,
and more efficient.

The scope of Union Oil's operations widened dramatically in the early years
of the twentieth century. Derricks sprang up all over the upper San Joaquin
Valley in Central California. On the heels of the Coalinga boom came discovery
of the McKittrick field, then the Midway-Sunset field. Across the valley, east of
Bakersfield, the Kern River field burst into production in 1900. Discoveries in
the Santa Maria and Lompoc valleys of Santa Barbara County followed.

The *Los Angeles Express* reported, "The state has gone oil mad. A feeling of
speculative unrest is abroad. Los Angeles operators just in from Kern County say
that a large number of people in that county appear to be actually oil crazed."

With each new oil strike, and sometimes ahead of them, Lyman Stewart was
there picking up land by purchase or lease. By 1902, Union held options on
50,000 acres in the Santa Maria and Lompoc areas that geologists decided had
all the features of an American Baku—Russia's great oil field. The company also
acquired valuable holdings in the Kern River and Coalinga areas in the San
Joaquin Valley. A new refinery went up in Bakersfield to handle production from
the San Joaquin region.

That year Stewart reported "the company's new acquisitions of oil lands,
with the extensions to its plants...have cost approximately $2,031,000, but they

Top left: When Texas's famed Spindletop gusher erupted in January 1901, markets were glutted and prices plunged. Lower left: A train on the island of Maui carries sugar cane to the grinding mills. After Spindletop, Will Stewart sent his master salesman John Baker to Hawaii to line up more fuel oil markets. Baker convinced sugar producers of the benefits of fuel oil over coal to power their mills. Opposite: The Fullerton *was built to serve Union's Hawaiian customers.*

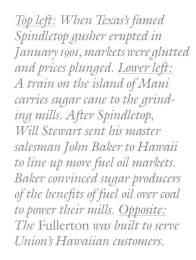

have doubtless doubled the value of its capital stock, and possibly quadrupled it."

Not surprisingly, the acquisitions continued to put a heavy strain on Union's lines of credit. In 1900, Stewart pioneered a new frontier in money-raising by borrowing almost $25,000 from the Protestant Episcopal Church of Los Angeles. He also touched Thomas Bard for money (at one point Union's debt to its former president rose to more than $120,000). These loans helped tide the company over until the sale of a new stock issue provided additional capital for expansion.

Along with the burst of drilling and land acquisition, the company expanded its marketing horizons. Oil prices, however, took another skid in 1901, after the famed Spindletop well in East Texas erupted on January 10. The well gushed 84,000 barrels a day, setting off panic in the nation's oil trading centers. Overnight, Spindletop nearly doubled total U.S. oil production.

As a result, Will Stewart turned his attention 2,500 miles west, toward the Hawaiian Islands, where he saw a promising market for fuel oil. He assigned John Baker to go after three large sugar plantation owners who were using Australian coal to fuel their cane-grinding mills on the island of Maui. Baker convinced them of oil's added convenience and efficiency and soon had lined up more Hawaiian customers than the company could handle with its existing facilities. By the end of 1901, the company had storage capacity totaling 227,000 barrels on three islands of the Hawaiian chain. Baker also struck a deal with

B. F. Dillingham's Oahu Railway and Land Company to serve as sales agent for Union fuel oil throughout the Islands. The deal gave Union its first tidewater terminal in Honolulu.

To service this profitable new market, Union built a 16,000-barrel barkentine (sail-powered) oil carrier, the *Fullerton*. Then, in 1902, the company ordered its first steel-hulled, steam-powered tanker, the *Whittier,* which represented a revolutionary step in oil carrier construction. The vessel's engines were set far aft to reduce fire danger, and the cargo tanks were an integral part of the hull. Galley and quarters for engineers and crew were also situated aft, with deck officers quartered amidships near the bridge. The ship established a new maritime prototype and, until the early sixties, tankers followed its basic design. The *Whittier,* built in San Francisco and delivered in 1903, cost $198,000.

In a dramatic demonstration of marine technology, the *Whittier* was ordered shortly after its commissioning to steam to Hawaii, where a critical oil shortage had developed. The vessel not only carried 11,000 barrels of oil in its own tanks for the 2,500-mile voyage, but towed two other vessels: the *Fullerton,* with a cargo of 16,000 barrels, and the *Santa Paula,* which had been unmasted, converted into a barge, and loaded with 8,200 barrels of oil. It was the largest single cargo of petroleum ever delivered by sea up to that time.

Oil companies were constantly jostling for position in the rapidly growing and highly competitive marketplace for petroleum products. In 1901, Standard

The tanker Whittier, *commissioned in 1903, was Union's first steel-hulled tanker—a prototype for tankers to come.*

Oil, Union, and Associated Oil Company each tried to increase its market share by consolidating forces with small producers. No permanent arrangements resulted. In Union's case, Will Stewart threw his support behind an idea to shift fuel oil operations over to a company being formed by several independents who wanted more control of the California fuel oil market. Lyman backed his son, but the majority of Union's directors were leery of any involvement with syndicates or other companies.

Led by two of the directors who had bought out Bard's shares in 1900, Union's board decided in 1901, "This company...is destined of itself to form the nucleus of a great organization and ought to be free to act independently of any other concern."

As Union expanded in the century's first decade, it continued to need infusions of capital. In 1903, Lyman Stewart approached Standard, as he had several times before. This time he offered to swap Union's downstream operations—refining, transportation, and marketing—for a guaranteed market for Union crude and enough capital to develop Union Oil properties: in other words, to take Union back to being simply a producing company. While this seemed to contradict Stewart's strategy of building an integrated oil company, his key concern, as it had always been, was to assure a market for Union's crude. However, once again, Standard headquarters turned Stewart down. Milton Stewart, for one, was relieved because he still felt that Standard could not be trusted.

Shortly after Stewart's negotiations with Standard Oil had broken down, Edward Doheny was invited to join Union's board of directors. Since launching the 1893 oil rush with his discovery of the Los Angeles field, Doheny had gained widespread recognition for his success as an oil finder and investor. As a board member, he was permitted to buy 1,000 shares of Union Oil treasury stock with a year's option for another 1,500 shares. Although the treasury stock (a special class not available for public sale) gave him no particular leverage on the board, it enriched him considerably.

Doheny's tenure on the board was brief. In 1904 he resigned, preferring to concentrate his energies on oil ventures he could control. He went to Mexico and helped discover the big fields around Tampico.

Asked if he had ever tried to influence Doheny while he was on the board, Stewart admitted to one try, saying, "Mr. Doheny offered a resolution increasing the salary of the president of Union Oil to $1,000 a month. I refused the offer

A NON-OIL BONANZA
In 1901, Union geologist
Bill Orcutt was drawn to the
La Brea tar pits just west of
Los Angeles. Tar seeps often
indicated oil deeper down,
but when Lyman Stewart and
partner Dan McFarland had
drilled at the La Brea site in
1888, all they found was dust.
Orcutt found evidence of a
scientific treasure house—
"a mosaic of white bones,
uniform in shape, lying in an
exact pattern…a beautiful
contrast with the black surface
of the hard asphaltum." Orcutt
kept his discovery quiet to save
the tar pits from "relic hunters."
Eventually, he contacted John
C. Merriam at the University
of California in Berkeley, who
confirmed the find in 1906.
Scientists from around the world
were soon digging through
the muck. Property owner
G. Allen Hancock assigned
sections of his land to a dozen
universities and museums.
"The remarkable thing," Orcutt
noted, "was that every bone of
most of these skeletons was
recovered." His "mosaic" was
identified as the bony armor
plating of a giant ground sloth.
In Orcutt's honor, a species of
extinct coyote was named
Canis orcutti. The tar pits have
yielded thousands of paleonto-
logical wonders, including one
human mystery—the 9,000-
year-old La Brea woman. Unlike
animals that were trapped by
tar, she was probably the
victim of sacrifice or murder.

*Edward Doheny visited the
Los Angeles oil field in 1904,
twelve years after he discovered it
by digging a pit near what later
became the intersection of Second
Street and Glendale Boulevard.*

and asked for a salary of $3,000 a year." But the board voted with Doheny and gave Stewart his first real salary increase since the formation of the company.

Lyman Stewart's devotion to his faith and church continued to guide his management of Union Oil. Periodically, he asked the board to approve small sums for constructing chapels near oil fields or to compensate clergymen who held prayer meetings on company premises. When he decreed that only emergency work be carried out on Sundays, at least one foreman complained that most of the big wells seemed to come in on Saturday nights, making it impractical to take Sundays off.

Stewart's appetite for prospective oil properties remained prodigious. In 1903, he added 4,800 more acres in the Santa Maria fields and 3,400 acres of the La Habra Rancho, near Whittier, on a site known as the Sansinena tract. (After 50 years as a "sleeper," the Sansinena field would become one of Union's richest producers.)

Meanwhile, drillers brought in new wells around Coalinga in the San Joaquin Valley and made a remarkable discovery in the Lompoc area on the central coast. Stewart had rounded up drilling options at grazing-land prices on 72,000 acres in and around the Purisima Hills near Lompoc. But the options allowed barely enough time to sink exploratory wells.

Sweating out a tight deadline at Hill No. 1, the drill crew worked around the clock for several weeks. Finally, they struck oil late on a Saturday night, just three days before Union's option on the property was due to run out. Frank Hill, drilling superintendent on the project, recalled years later how word of this discovery of the Lompoc field reached Lyman Stewart.

Wishing to keep the strike secret from other operators in the area, Hill caught a train to Los Angeles around midnight Saturday. He was met at the station by Frank Garbutt, a company director, who drove him in his brand-new gasoline buggy to Stewart's home at Sixth and Lucas streets. They pulled up just as Stewart was coming out the front door, Bible under his arm, on his way to church. They knew very well "Uncle Lyman" didn't do business on the Sabbath, so they simply stood on the sidewalk and waited for Stewart to provide an opening.

OIL PATCH WIZARD
Frank F. Hill joined Union Oil
in 1899, and his innovative
approach to drilling had a lasting impact on the industry. He
is credited with the first successful oil-well cementing job, done
at Hill No. 4 near Lompoc,
California, in 1905. "After being
licked from bringing in a field
in 1900 due to water...I resolved
to really try to do something
about it," Hill recalled some 50
years later. "I soon concluded
that cement should do it, but
getting it down the hole and up
back of the casing was a problem."
Hill sketched a valve and tripping
device for a local blacksmith,
but when he returned the next
day no work had been done.
The blacksmith, who knew a
thing or two about pumping
sand out of water wells, told
Hill not to waste his time and
money. "When I told him I
wasn't trying to take something
out of the well but, on the contrary, was trying to put some
special material in, the blacksmith finished the tool." Hill
and his coworkers — Bill Wigle,
Roscoe Stephens, and Billy Scott
— perfected the system. During
40 years with Union, Hill supervised operations at virtually
every company field, overseeing
the fabulous Old Maud and
Lakeview gushers. He introduced high-speed rotary drilling to the West Coast and
improved much of the associated technology. He contributed significantly to the
standardization of oil field
equipment and helped develop
deep-drilling procedures.

As the story goes, Stewart, after some awkward foot-shuffling, finally asked, "What have you got?"

"We've got an oil well," said Hill.

"What does it look like?"

"Pretty heavy," said Hill, taking a bottle out of his pocket and handing it to his boss. "Here's a sample."

Stewart stuck his finger in and rubbed the oil back and forth between his finger and thumb. After some hesitation, he said, "We'll take up the options tomorrow. This is Sunday. Had you forgotten?" He then resumed his stroll to church as if nothing had happened.

In 1905, at Hill No. 4, Frank Hill and his associates made oil-drilling history. They came up with a practical way to use cement to seal off water-bearing sands from the well casing (steel pipe used to line the well bore). Water flowing into the wells from higher strata slowed down production, and drillers had tried wood shavings, chopped rope, burlap, and other materials to close up the space between the steel casing and the walls of the hole. Cementing had been tried before, unsuccessfully — but Hill and his men found a way to make it work. They pumped cement directly into the well and, when it hit bottom, a packer diverted it back up the outside of the casing.

Cementing enabled drillers to go deeper into the big oil reservoirs and doubled the amount of oil that could be recovered. The method devised by Hill soon became common practice, yet the company never took the time to patent the idea. Others did, obliging Union to pay royalties for its own innovation.

The year before, Frank Hill had also been in charge when Union's drilling crews made a dramatic discovery in the Santa Maria field (in an area renamed the Orcutt Hill field in the 1930s). The well was Hartnell No. 1, which got the name "Old Maud" almost from the day it was spudded — June 22, 1904 — for reasons long since forgotten. Old Maud was destined to become one of the historic wells in California oil development — the result of a lucky mistake. As the crew approached the site where they intended to spud the well, a heavy piece of equipment fell off the transport wagon. Rather than wrestle the gear to the pre-scribed spot for the well, the crew simply moved the derrick.

"On December 2, when no one was expecting much of a well, Old Maud starts rumbling," related one of the hands working there. "Then, with a roar, a column of oil and gas shoots up to a height of one hundred fifty feet. We can't control it, what with twelve thousand barrels of oil pouring out in a day. We

Opposite, far left: In 1897, the Torrey Canyon field provided 56,000 barrels of crude oil, almost half of Union's production for the year. <u>Right</u>: In June 1904, Bill Orcutt jotted down a layout of Mrs. Hartnell's property in his field book. Could she have been the Maud for whom the gusher was named? <u>Below</u>: Old Maud was a spectacular gusher in 1904, spewing a million barrels in her first 100 days.

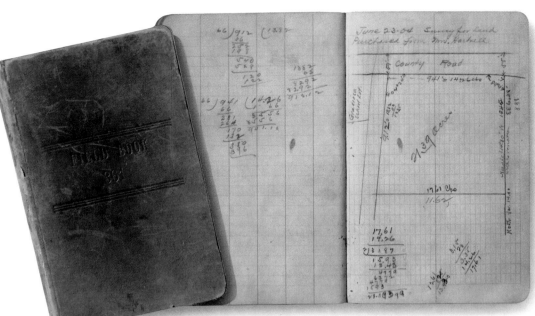

don't even have tanks or pipelines big enough to handle the flow. Pools of crude collect for miles below."

Old Maud poured out a million barrels of crude in its first hundred days, the champion producer in California to that time. Nobody could believe it.

"After we had guessed Old Maud's tremendous yield I phoned Frank Garbutt, our treasurer," recalled Frank Hill. "He asked what I figured the well would make. I told him ten thousand barrels a day. He yelled, 'Spell it out! It sounded like you said ten thousand barrels.' So I spelled it out for him. Garbutt next called Will Stewart and told him we had a ten thousand-barrel producer. Will also asked that the figure be spelled out and commented, 'That's a good story, anyway!' Will phoned his father, who asked, 'Did you say ten thousand barrels?' So for the third time that night, we spelled it out over the phone. Lyman Stewart said, 'Thank you. I have been expecting something big from up there. Good night.'"

Fourteen years later, Old Maud was still producing a respectable 250 barrels a day when a section of casing collapsed. Rather than spend a lot of money fishing out the broken material, the crew decided to drill another well nearby. They expected to hit the same formation, but Hartnell No. 7 proved something of a fizzle, never producing more than 75 barrels a day. In 1943, under wartime pressure to raise production, Union reworked Old Maud, cleaning out the well bore and installing a new pump. When it came back on stream, the well produced a steady 175 barrels a day.

In 1906, Union completed a 6-inch pipeline from the oil fields in Santa Barbara and San Luis Obispo counties to Port Harford, where the company built a tank farm with storage for 250,000 barrels. These facilities, combined with the terminal in San Pedro, gave Union two shipping ports and positioned the company to serve a broader world market. John Baker, Jr., by 1906 the manager of sales, manufacturing, and marine operations for Union Oil, set out to do just that.

In one of his boldest moves, Baker won a commitment from President Theodore Roosevelt giving Union the rights to build and operate a trans-Panama pipeline. Eastern interests fought the agreement, but T.R. stood by his word. The line, completed in 1906, supplied fuel for the builders of the Panama Canal (constructed between 1904 and 1914) and, briefly, moved some California crude to the Atlantic side of the Isthmus. Ultimately, this oil found no market in the eastern United States, and the pipeline was abandoned.

Left: Ship traffic in San Pedro harbor was growing as the century drew to a close, and Union built oil storage facilities there. By 1903, the company operated three oil carriers, which plied routes along the West Coast and to Hawaii. Below: Olds Curved-Dash Runabout, 1902. When a fire destroyed his factory in 1901, Clarence Olds subcontracted for parts and subassemblies, helping create the industries that made Detroit "Motor City." He used mass-production techniques to assemble the runabouts, which he then sold at affordable prices. The automobile was no longer just a costly luxury.

In one year, Baker traveled 50,000 miles (in the era before air travel), marketing Union crude and products in Central and South America, Europe, and in the eastern United States. He was so successful that the company had to acquire a tanker fleet, along with six first-class steamships, to haul asphalt to New York, which had gone on a street-paving binge to accommodate the invasion of horseless carriages.

Baker also pioneered in the art of business entertaining. Compared with the austere expense accounts of teetotaler Lyman Stewart, Baker's reports were a constant source of amazement in the accounting department. Finally, Stewart asked the board to clamp down, and a tough new rule was passed, eliminating "wine and cigars and extravagant hostelry expenditures" from the list of approved items. The more pragmatic Will Stewart, who had been absent when the vote was taken, balked at the harsh restriction—whatever might be said about Baker's expenses, they certainly got results—and persuaded the board (including his father) to approve an amended list restoring most of the items.

Union Oil's operating growth during this period was matched by growth in its outstanding stock. Lyman Stewart issued additional stock periodically in order to finance expansion—at the same time, of course, diluting his family's hold on the company. When a group of outside investors began to acquire large blocks of Union securities in 1905, Lyman decided to take precautions.

His strategy was similar to the one he had employed in 1899: the formation of a holding company that would name a majority of Union Oil board members. He and his allies would control the holding company and, even though they didn't control the

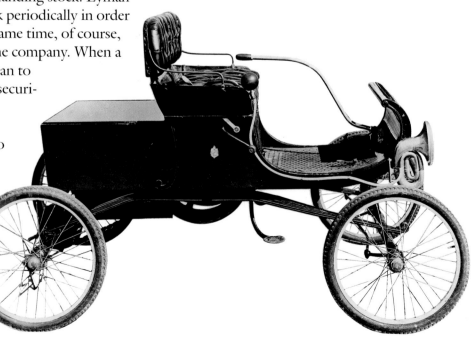

majority of Union Oil stock, they would continue to control the board.

The device worked beautifully. The company remained a Stewart family enterprise for another 11 years, despite the fact that their share of outstanding stock continued to dwindle. (In 1916, the courts — with new statutory tools like the Sherman and Clayton antitrust acts — found Lyman Stewart's machinations imaginative but illegal, and dissolved the holding companies.)

Disasters marked a difficult 1906 for Union Oil. The San Francisco earthquake caused major damage to storage facilities and destroyed records at the Oleum refinery. Badly needed expansion work was delayed. The Bakersfield refinery had to take up the slack and operated at full capacity most of the year. In Portsmouth, Oregon, a Union storage facility blew up, killing the workman who accidentally set off the blast. About the same time, the Union tanker *Santa Rita* ran into a heavy storm at sea and suffered serious damage, along with the loss of its entire cargo of oil.

Yet Lyman Stewart could report at year's end that the company had shown "substantial progress...notwithstanding disappointment in the amount of net earnings resulting from a depressed market, inadequate transportation facilities, deplorable labor conditions, and so forth following the earthquake and fire."

By early 1907, most of the prior year's difficulties had been resolved. Union management looked for new frontiers to explore.

"Our company in the short space of twelve months has risen from local to national prominence," wrote John Baker in a memo to Lyman Stewart early that year. While customers beat on Union's door, Baker worried about one problem: Would the company be able to supply all the new orders he was taking?

Stewart reassured him: "If there is any question, even the slightest, about the quantity of oil to meet these contracts, we'll put more tools in the field. If necessary, we'll run thirty, forty, fifty strings of tools in our territory. You get the contracts, we'll get the oil."

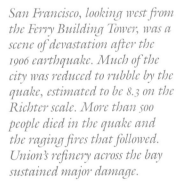

San Francisco, looking west from the Ferry Building Tower, was a scene of devastation after the 1906 earthquake. Much of the city was reduced to rubble by the quake, estimated to be 8.3 on the Richter scale. More than 500 people died in the quake and the raging fires that followed. Union's refinery across the bay sustained major damage.

3

Survival of
the Fittest

In 1910, Lyman Stewart had to deal with the aftereffects of Lakeview No. 1, the world's biggest gusher (opposite), which spewed 125,000 barrels of oil skyward in its first 24 hours.

In the 50 years after Drake drilled his well in Titusville in 1859, the world's thirst for oil grew from a few thousand barrels to more than 180 million a year. It doubled in the decade from 1910 to 1920, and doubled again before 1930 — a spectacular rate of growth.

Massive production from Spindletop and other fields in the early years of the century pushed down crude prices, thus helping to assure the economic supremacy of gasoline-powered automobiles over electric and steam models. In Detroit, Clarence Olds introduced mass production of automobiles in 1901. When Henry Ford perfected the technique with his moving assembly line in 1913, a set of wheels became widely affordable.

Another gasoline-powered industry — aviation — began with the Wright Brothers' brief but portentous flight in 1903. By the time World War I broke out in 1914, France had 1,500 military airplanes to Germany's 1,000. The renowned French Marshal Ferdinand Foch, who at one critical juncture commandeered Parisian taxis to ferry troops to the front lines, declared that "a drop of gasoline was as valuable as a drop of blood."

In 1910, the petroleum industry produced more gasoline than kerosene from its crude oil for the first time. Union bought its first motorized truck, although it was still making most of its deliveries by horse-drawn wagons. For a time, the company's marketing department boasted one of the largest stables in the state. The last 65 "hay-burners" were not sold until 1922.

By 1910, Union had accumulated more than 225,000 acres of oil properties, thanks to Lyman Stewart's voracious appetite for land. Oil exploration and production in California were the "greatest in history," noted Bill Orcutt. The state's production hit 74 million barrels, more than a third of the nation's total, with predictable consequences: The bottom fell out of the market again.

Union's annual production averaged 4.5 million barrels from 1909 through 1913. Part of that figure represented the output of the world's greatest gusher — Union's Lakeview No. 1. It was also one of the last gushers, since drilling technology soon found ways to contain even the most powerful oil streams, preserving the crude for efficient production.

Lakeview No. 1, located between Taft and Maricopa along the western edge of the lower San Joaquin Valley, came close to being someone else's discovery. A group of seven investors operating on a shoestring had spudded the well in early 1909, hoping for a quick strike. Before long they ran into problems, finally losing their tool string down the hole. With no money to fish out

the tools and resume drilling, the partners approached Union to take over the project. Union's crews had their hands full with other wells nearby, but the company reluctantly agreed to become a 51-percent partner, putting Lakeview No. 1 on the back burner.

Over the next few weeks, the Union crews managed to fish out Lakeview's drill stem and, sporadically, resumed punching hole until they had reached 2,200 feet. The foreman in charge was a luckless driller named Charles L. Woods, who had earned the moniker "Dry Hole Charlie." In the next few days, he would give the lie to his nickname.

Early on the morning of March 15, 1910, a Union crew drilled at Lakeview No. 1 while waiting for some technical problems to be cleared up at a more promising well nearby. When the drillers pulled up the bailer, they were surprised to find it dripping with oil. They dropped it down again several times, each time finding oil at a higher level. Clearly, they had hit something big. By dawn, the hole gurgled out a steady stream of water, shale, and sand.

When Dry Hole Charlie arrived at eight o'clock that morning, a column of gas and oil roared hundreds of feet out of the hole, drenching the area. Over the next several hours, the gusher continued to build, until it had blasted out a crater so deep and wide that the derrick and drill equipment completely disappeared.

"My God!" yelled Charlie. "We've cut an artery down there!" And so it seemed, as the well continued to spew oil out of control for months.

Witnesses estimated Lakeview No. 1 produced 125,000 barrels in its first 24 hours—half again as big as the famed Spindletop gusher and more oil than Union's entire production in its first full year of operations. Workers threw up earthen dams to hold the gusher's flow, but the barriers were soon overwhelmed by

DRY HOLE CHARLIE

Charles Lewis Woods stood out even in an industry that abounded in characters. Good-humored and resourceful, he was an outstanding driller who learned his trade well, working 12-hour shifts as part of a two-man team. Woods took over as foreman on Union's Lakeview No. 1 well near Bakersfield in 1909. But in 29 years of hard work, he had drilled a lot of straight holes in all the wrong places, earning himself the nicknames "Dry Hole Charlie" and "Dusty" Woods. Lakeview changed his luck; it came in as the biggest gusher of all time in early 1910. Woods hired everybody from "college boys to convicts" to build the dikes, pile up mountains of sand bags, and dam up the mouths of canyons with 20-foot-high walls in an effort to contain the gushing oil. Woods continued drilling long after Lakeview — punching more than 250 holes all over the state. As Union's division superintendent of operations, he established an exceptional safety record. During two periods of more than 14 months each, he ran his drilling and production crews of approximately 200 men with no lost-time accidents. When Woods died at the age of 62 in 1933, hundreds of veteran oil men gathered at the University Masonic Hall in Los Angeles to pay their final respects to "Dusty."

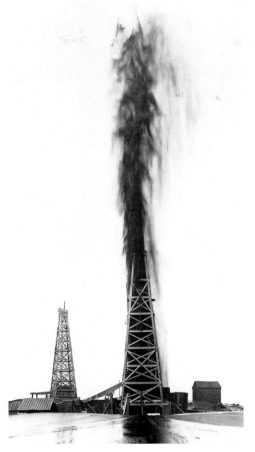

AND STILL SHE SPOUTS

Efforts to Harness Lakeview Well Prove Fruitless and She Still Continues to Gush

The Lakeview gusher continues to gush as hard and fierce as ever. Today it rounds out its thirty-third day of continuous spouting and gives every promise of keeping it up indefinitely.

All kinds of attempts hav...

More than a month after Lakeview blew, the Maricopa Oil News *reported it was still gushing — as it did for another 17 months. Union crews and volunteers worked around the clock to dam up the oil. The site, 30 miles southwest of Bakersfield, received California historical landmark status in 1952.*

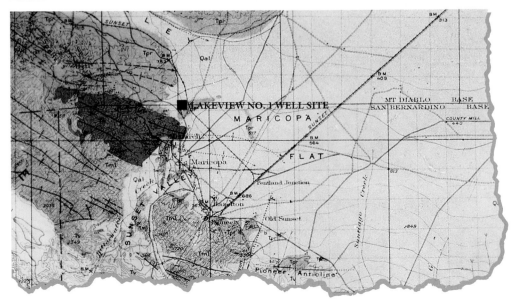

the torrent of oil. Finally, the crews moved downstream and built a massive containing wall to create a 16-acre reservoir, which they called the Cornfield. Just as they finished, a strong earthquake shook the area, fracturing the earlier dams and unloosing a flood into the Cornfield.

It would be 18 months and 9 million barrels of oil before Lakeview No. 1 could be brought under control. On September 9, 1911, almost as abruptly as it started, the well stopped gushing. The hole caved in, and the well settled down to an unremarkable production rate of 35 barrels a day. Of its total output, only 5 million barrels could be saved; the rest was lost to seepage and evaporation. Clearly a costly lesson in the waste of uncontrolled production, Lakeview No. 1 helped speed the technology of well containment.

In Los Angeles, Lyman Stewart dealt with Lakeview's consequences. The gusher had splattered vehicles, homes, and farm crops in a 15-mile radius, provoking angry lawsuits. Even as the complaints mounted, Union and other California independents confronted a serious problem on another front.

In 1909, the state's independent producers were still in the grip of the railroads, particularly Southern Pacific, when it came to moving their oil. And Standard, still the major buyer of production in the state, strongly influenced prices. So a group of independent producers in the San Joaquin Valley—organized as the Independent Oil Producers Agency—approached Union Oil with a plan to create a consortium in which Union would become sales agent for the entire group. Their leader was Leonard P. "Press" St. Clair, who was destined to become a Union director and eventually the company's president. A ten-year agreement was signed, giving the producers new leverage with Standard Oil on setting prices. This move doubled the amount of oil Union had to sell, establishing the company as a player in world markets.

To break Southern Pacific's hold on transportation, the consortium decided to build a pipeline from the San Joaquin Valley to the sea, where the oil could be shipped out on tankers. In a project that was the trans-Alaska pipeline of its day, the newly formed Producers Transportation Company laid an 8-inch line and built 15 pump stations in only eight months. The line carried oil 240 miles over the coastal mountains to Port Harford (later renamed Port San Luis) in San Luis Obispo County. Completed in 1910, the pipeline was designed to transport 20,000 barrels a day but was soon moving more than 30,000 barrels. At $4.5 million, the project exceeded its budget by $1 million— but signaled the end of expensive rail transport of petroleum in California. Union owned half the pipeline at the time of construction and eventually acquired the remaining 50 percent.

The Producers' Pipeline was a joint project of Union Oil and the Independent Oil Producers Agency, which represented about 150 small San Joaquin Valley oil producers. The project was massive—an 8-inch line laid 240 miles in record time to rush the independents' oil to market. Left: Boilers were hauled across arid flatlands to pumping stations along the route. Opposite: Hardy construction crews dug trenches and hefted pipe across desert and mountains.

This was an era of explosive growth for Union. By 1910, the company had more than 20 subsidiaries. One — the Outer Harbor Dock and Wharf Company — played a major role in the construction of Los Angeles's deep-water port. Other subsidiaries were involved in businesses ranging from toolmaking to pipe-line operations. Union Oil Company, in fact, had reached a kind of corporate "critical mass." Its continued success attracted investors and lenders, creating ideal conditions for further growth. Over the next decade, the company became a full-fledged corporate giant.

As Union grew, so did its management structure. In 1910, for example, Chester W. Brown was hired as head of a new production department to oversee the growing number of fields. At the time, Union operated more than 300 wells spotted over wide areas of California. Just returned from 17 years of wildcatting and mining in Peru, Brown had helped his uncle, Wallace Hardison, and Lyman Stewart develop many of the fields around Santa Paula in the early days. Highly respected, he was lauded as a leading oil pioneer when he retired in 1931.

Lyman Stewart summed up his company's position at the end of 1910 in typical fashion. "You will doubtless share my opinion," he wrote to shareholders, "that we have abundant cause for being grateful to the Supreme Ruler of all things for the remarkable growth of our business, the profitable development of our properties, and the important service we have been enabled thereby to render the public."

His words gave no hint of the financial tumult that would overtake the company in the next few years. The seeds of the problems had been planted by

Milton Stewart (above) was instrumental in providing financial backing for Union Oil in its early days. He also supported many of his brother Lyman's charitable projects, including the Bible Institute (left), which opened in downtown Los Angeles in 1915 (the building was razed in 1988 to make room for a high-rise), and the Hunan Bible Institute (below) in Changsa, China, which operated during the 1920s.

Stewart's borrowing policies, which had kept Union in a precarious position for years, along with his selection in 1909 of Robert Watchorn as the company's treasurer. Stewart extolled Watchorn to the board as a true Christian gentleman.

"He is a very popular man," Stewart said. "Every time he appears at a Presbyterian convention, he is greeted with a Chautauqua salute [in which the audience stood and waved handkerchiefs]." Watchorn became one of the most controversial figures in the company's history as he gained greater and greater influence over Lyman Stewart.

Early in 1910, Stewart was approaching his seventieth birthday. Never very robust, he became convinced that his days were numbered. Death seemed to be hanging in the air. Stewart's friend and one-time partner, Wallace Hardison, had recently died in an auto accident. Lyman's wife, Ada, was on her deathbed, and his brother, Milton, was seriously ill. Milton was the company's largest single shareholder, and the prospect of the Stewarts losing control of the company seemed imminent.

Lyman wanted to put his affairs in order. He turned for support and counsel to Watchorn, and the treasurer began to exert more influence on the affairs of Union Oil than the directors had ever intended.

After persuading the stockholders to increase Union's debt limit to $20 million, Stewart sent Watchorn to New York to borrow $1 million for the company and another sum for Stewart's personal use on behalf of the Bible Institute of Los Angeles, of which he was president and founder. (The Institute's

STEWART'S BIBLE INSTITUTE
Lyman Stewart grew up in a
deeply religious home. He was
active in the Presbyterian church—
a faithful tither and a member of
the evangelism program. But as
his oil investments grew, Stewart
put aside tithing, intending to
make up for it later. "My judgment was taken away," he said,
and he lost his fortune. When
he rebuilt it, he never again
neglected the duty he felt to
support God's work. He became
well known for his philanthropy
in Los Angeles after settling
there in 1885. In 1898, at the end
of the Spanish-American War,
Stewart was distressed when told
that the last two Bibles in the
Philippines had been destroyed.
He founded the Los Angeles Bible
Institute (later the Bible House)
to publish Spanish-language
versions of the Scriptures and
disburse them in more than
20 countries. As time passed,
Stewart became increasingly concerned with apostasy—the turning away from God. In 1908, he
founded a second Bible Institute,
this one a nondenominational
school that taught Christian
fundamentals. Many students
became ministers and mission-
aries. Stewart raised funds for
the Institute's building, completed in 1915 at Sixth and Hope
streets in downtown Los Angeles.
The Institute evolved into Biola
University and broke ground for
a new campus in La Mirada, east of
Los Angeles, in 1958. Biola offers
programs in psychology, theology,
and intercultural studies.

*Union's second Santa Paula
refinery was built in 1912 and
closed during the Depression.*

evangelical project at that time was distributing Bibles in China: "A Bible for
Every Chinaman" was the slogan.) Watchorn didn't mind such mixing of business with church activities, a practice that got both men in trouble.

As part of Stewart's plan to raise money for himself, he authorized Watchorn
to sell options on most of Stewart's Union holdings. The options carried the
rather steep exercise price of $150 per share, which may have lulled Stewart into
thinking they would not be exercised in his lifetime. Apparently, he overlooked
the effect the option sale might have on investor confidence in his company.
Later, Stewart would claim that Watchorn had misled him, setting off a violent
disagreement between the two men. Stewart had intended, he said, to keep a
large block of the optioned shares in his own name.

Nevertheless, the deed was done. Watchorn returned from New York with
a check for nearly $500,000 as down payment on the options from Eugene
de Sabla, president of Esperanza, Consolidated (which later became General
Petroleum Company). Another $500,000 was due in installments over the next 15
months. De Sabla's ownership of the options gave him, or anyone he sold them
to, the right to buy controlling interest in Union Oil at any time, provided he
was willing to pay $150 per share for the underlying securities. The arrangement,
which came to be known around the company as the "million-dollar mystery,"
cast a fiscal shadow over Union Oil as the options drifted from hand to hand in
the investment community over the next few years.

In a burst of expansion from 1910 to 1912, Union Oil committed itself
to a major role in the growth of Los Angeles's harbor, built new refineries in
Santa Paula and Fullerton, and was (as usual) acquiring oil land at a rapid rate.
The company's capital was stretched thin, and a day of reckoning was near.

In 1913, two $1 million notes fell due, one in May and one in August. The
New York company that held the notes told Union through its Los Angeles
representative, John H. Garrigues, that if the notes weren't paid at maturity
Union would be forced into receivership. Such a step would certainly have
caused a panic among Union Oil's old creditors and also would have destroyed
prospects of ever finding new ones. Bankruptcy became a real threat.

Watchorn made another trip to New York, where he lined up a $5 million
bond issue from Hallgarten & Company. When the deal fell through, the financial community began to smell blood. Stewart's "mystery options," his ferocious

appetite for borrowed money, and his ill-considered appointment of Robert
Watchorn were adding up to financial disaster.

Stewart was forced to take a desperate gamble. When Garrigues had delivered the threat of receivership, he had offered Stewart an alternative: Hire him as
treasurer for $25,000 a year, give him a free hand in Union's financial affairs, and
he would bail the company out of its dire straits. Stewart, his back to the wall,
asked the Union board to approve the deal "as insurance — as cheap insurance as
we could get." The board agreed.

Garrigues wasted no time in asserting his authority. He fired Watchorn,
along with the company's auditor, its comptroller, the managers of the marine
and manufacturing departments, and several others. And he ordered dividends
suspended, insisting that Lyman Stewart write a note to shareholders detailing
Union's financial plight.

Meanwhile, Will Stewart had been working with a syndicate of Los
Angeles financiers to secure another emergency loan. He wanted $2
million, which the syndicate at first appeared disposed to let Union
have. But Garrigues tried to browbeat the financiers into more favorable terms,
and they promptly reduced their commitment to $1 million, attaching a shock-
ing condition: Lyman Stewart must resign as president.

"We felt the public laid the blame — for the appointment of Robert Watchorn
…and the consequent sale of the de Sabla options — to Lyman Stewart," explained
John E. Jardine, an official with the banking firm that headed the syndicate. "We
felt that putting new men on the board…who were successful in business in this
city, would have a beneficial effect."

Opposite: Lyman, Ada, and their grandchildren in 1908, two years before her death. Bill, the tallest of the children, and Art, front row center, followed their father, Will, into the oil business. Right: Mule teams pulled graders during the final stages of construction of Union's refinery in Wilmington, near Los Angeles, in 1919. Below: Union Oil employees and their families gathered for a St. Patrick's Day picnic in 1917 on the Stearns fee property in Orange County. First drilled in 1898, Stearns, along with other fee properties in the Brea field, proved impressive. By 1990, the field still produced 2,100 barrels of oil per day and was expected to outlive the company's other Los Angeles basin fields.

With nowhere else to turn, Union — and Lyman Stewart — capitulated. On April 22, 1914, Stewart tendered his resignation. At age 73, after 24 years as the company's chief architect, he had lost control of Union Oil. The board immediately elected his son Will, 45, to replace him as president.

A few months later, the banking firm that headed the syndicate agreed to underwrite the entire $5 million borrowing on which Hallgarten had defaulted the year before. This gave Union the financial breathing room it needed to put its house in order and gird for the demands that would be placed on it in the upcoming wartime years.

With the ink barely dry on the $5 million financing deal, Garrigues began to throw his weight around with California's independent producers, suppliers of much of Union's crude and its long-time allies in the battles against the railroads and eastern producers. Summoning the independents' leader, Thomas A. O'Donnell, president of the California Petroleum Company, Garrigues spelled out tough new terms on a take-it-or-leave-it basis. When O'Donnell objected, Garrigues angrily threatened to smash the independent organization.

"You talk as if you were the whole Union Oil Company," O'Donnell said.

"I am the whole Union Oil Company," replied Garrigues.

Getting nowhere, the principals broke off the discussion. A peace meeting was arranged with the executive committee of the Independent Oil Producers Agency. One of the independent operators, S. A. Guiberson, Jr., reported what happened: "Garrigues told us the oilmen of California were a bunch of boobs and that…he was the Moses who had come out to California to lead us out of

Edward Doheny headed a group that tried to buy Union Oil in 1915. Left: Union's distribution terminal at Sixth and Mateo in Los Angeles provided a site for the company's first gas stand (far left), opened in 1913 (photo circa 1930).

our troubles. 'Nothing can prevent me from accomplishing my purpose,' he said, 'not even Standard Oil. You can get on my bandwagon…or you can get in the road and be run over.' "

After listening to this diatribe, Guiberson replied, "Mr. Garrigues, you are either a fool or you have been taking dope. You won't have to wait two or three days for my answer. So far as I am concerned, you can go plumb straight to Hell."

At this, the "peace" meeting broke up. On their way out, Guiberson and Garrigues met in a hallway. Garrigues stuck out his hand. "I like you, Guiberson. I like a man who says what he thinks." Garrigues' arrogance would plague Union Oil for another two and a half years.

For a company recently pulled back from the brink of disaster, Union remained remarkably attractive as a takeover prospect during this decade. Lyman Stewart's "mystery options" continued to cloud the company's financial future as they passed from hand to hand, finally ending up with British financiers who proposed in 1914 to form a new international company around the nucleus of Union Oil. The payoff for Union shareholders would be $15 million in cash.

The Union board agreed to the British deal, but soon after the contract was signed and the first payment of $2.5 million was made, war broke out in Europe. The deal was called off. The British financiers kept $2.5 million in Union treasury stock, which remained another question mark for several years.

Shortly after the British backed off, Edward Doheny hatched a scheme to take over Union. He and a group of associates offered to buy 51 percent of the company's stock for $85 a share, then fold it into the Pan-American Oil and Transportation Company, which they hoped would rival Standard Oil and Royal Dutch Shell in the increasingly centralized crude market.

Union's directors turned down the Doheny deal. They felt they had received a better proposal — albeit a more complicated one — that would consolidate California's independent producers, the British interests, and Union into a $100 million international oil company. The Stewarts and most of the other Union directors favored the plan; Garrigues was adamantly opposed.

Apparently willing to go to extraordinary lengths to promote his own position, Garrigues came up with a bizarre twist. Claiming knowledge from occult sources, he told the Reverend W. E. Blackstone, a former missionary to China who held the power of attorney to Milton Stewart's shares, that relinquishing the stock would be an evil act. The Reverend Mr. Blackstone replied that he would pray for divine guidance and voted the stock in favor of the consolidation.

For the plan to work, the Stewart family holdings had to be amassed into a single voting block. But with the uncertain status of Lyman Stewart's "mystery options" and some peculiar arrangements Milton Stewart had made with his shares, this proved difficult. Then other parts of the deal — particularly at the British end — came unraveled.

Before long, the ever abrasive Garrigues put the company through another internal spasm. He persuaded one of the directors, Giles Kellogg, to offer a resolution doubling Garrigues' salary to $50,000 a year. Will Stewart and the other directors refused, and Garrigues offered to resign immediately. While the directors must have savored the idea of getting rid of the contentious treasurer, they feared the consequences in the financial community. They turned down his resignation. But when he tried to dictate to them again a few months later, they'd finally had enough. They fired Garrigues. In January 1916, Will Stewart added the treasurer's responsibilities to his portfolio as president.

Garrigues' departure quickly broke the pall of austerity he had imposed on the company for two long years. At Lyman Stewart's urging, a special dividend was declared and another 50,000 shares of $100 treasury stock were created to raise new capital for expansion. The directors turned down offers from the British backers and Doheny to buy larger shares of the company. And the company bought a 200-acre site (more than doubled by later purchases) for a new refinery in Wilmington, near Los Angeles's harbor.

Will Stewart began to be a stronger president. With company earnings running about 28 percent on shareholders' equity — an after-tax return half that size today would be considered respectable — he moved to establish one of the first employee profit-sharing plans in the industry, as well as broad medical and life insurance plans.

Meanwhile, the persistent Garrigues plotted a new strategy to take control of the company. Motivated by revenge, or perhaps piqued by Union's rapid return to freer spending, Garrigues organized the Union Oil Company Stockholders' Protective Association. He filed suit in its name to dissolve the holding

Auto races — such as the San Diego Expo Race in 1915 — were popular events. Union and other marketers used them to show off their products.

companies through which the Stewarts controlled Union.

The litigation caused a sensation in the local press, as both sides hurled charges and countercharges. The *Los Angeles Examiner* called the case "perhaps the largest lawsuit in the history of the state courts of Southern California. This litigation involves the total $50 million capitalization of the Union Oil Company and the interests of about 4,500 stockholders."

During the long trial, Lyman Stewart tried to organize a voting trust that would take the place of the holding companies. But when he could get only 163,000 of the necessary 170,000 shares to approve the plan, he dropped the action. Then, in hopes of staving off a negative decision, the Stewart family voluntarily dissolved one of the holding companies. It did no good.

On October 2, 1916, state court judge Louis M. Myers handed down his decision: The holding companies were illegal and must be dissolved. From then on, Union Oil Company would be run by directors selected by all the shareholders. The Stewart family, still owners of the largest single block of Union Oil stock, no longer held ironclad control of the company.

"I never sought to control the company for any personal reason," Lyman Stewart told an interviewer after the decision. "The one idea of having control of the company was to assure stability of management. The Stewarts hold 57,000 shares of stock in the company. In making them valuable, they have made the shares of every other stockholder valuable."

The successful lawsuit cleared the way for a truly democratic vote of the shareholders, and Garrigues felt he could wrest control from the Stewarts at the shareholders' meeting in early 1917. The proxy battle over the next few months resulted in two postponements of the meeting, which was finally held on Washington's Birthday at the Oleum refinery. (Because of a tax dispute with the city of Los Angeles, Union's corporate business was conducted in Oleum from 1908 through 1920.) The shareholders voted overwhelmingly to support the Stewarts, giving the family control over nine of the eleven seats on the Union board. Garrigues was finished.

As Will Stewart assumed greater responsibility for running the company, he began to find himself increasingly at odds with his father. The battles with Garrigues behind him, the elder Stewart had regained his old spirit. His health also bloomed, perhaps rejuvenated by marriage to his private secretary, Lulu M. Crowell, who shared her husband's evangelical interests.

Lyman felt that his son, much like Thomas Bard, was too conservative in his management style as company president. The younger Stewart responded that he wouldn't be so conservative if his father weren't out to buy all the oil land in

Opposite, far right: In 1916, Union crews stopped drilling at 3,500 feet and just missed discovering the rich Signal Hill oil field near Long Beach, California. Below: In 1910, Union mechanics mounted an oil tank on a truck, spelling the end for horse-drawn delivery wagons.

SERVICE — FROM THE START
In 1913, the same year Henry
Ford's assembly line clanked
into motion, Union opened its
first gas stand — little more
than a shed — at Sixth and
Mateo streets in downtown
Los Angeles. Station operators
dispensed gasoline with a hand
pump; one turn of the handle
transferred a gallon from a drum
to the tank of a car. Customers
could also buy kerosene, lubricants, and fuel oil — if they
brought their own containers.
It was just the start. By 1923,
Union's chain grew to 304
stations, extending from
Canada to Mexico and to the
Hawaiian Islands. There was
keen competition for the best
station locations, described by
Union's marketers as on "a
well-traveled thoroughfare,
preferably on a corner." By
marketing through service
stations instead of grocery or
hardware stores, oil companies
were able to establish brand
identity, assure uniform product
quality, and capture customer
loyalty. Station design improved.
In 1923, Union introduced
"Super Service Stations,"
where the motorist could get
his battery charged, tires
repaired, engine lubricated,
and car washed and polished.
Union set one rule above all for
its station operators: "Profit is
the legitimate reward for service, but service is the *sine qua
non.*" The first Union station
(above, circa 1932) reported
brisk sales for the 21 years of its
existence. When it was replaced
with a larger modern station in
1934, sales jumped 300 percent.

California. When Lyman proposed to acquire the Pinal Dome Oil Company for
$3.6 million, Will objected strenuously. Eventually, Lyman prevailed, but most
decisions went Will Stewart's way.

The company was growing in all directions, not the least in exploration.
Wells were spudded in a score of new fields. One was a hole at the western base
of Signal Hill, located in Long Beach south of Los Angeles. The well was abandoned at 3,449 feet and the drilling rights surrendered. Had the crew drilled a
few hundred feet deeper, they would have nicked one of the richest reservoirs in
Southern California — but that discovery remained for later explorationists.

As the 1920s approached, the automobile had become a major force in
Southern California. Union scrambled to meet the burgeoning demand
for gasoline and lubricants. The company had opened its first service
station in 1913 in Los Angeles, at the corner of Sixth and Mateo streets. Its
purchase of Pinal Dome in 1917 brought 20 well-established service stations into
the company's growing network. New stations were going up as fast as builders
could finish them.

Appalled by the poor appearance of many of the hurriedly built outlets,
Union's marketing department launched a competition among western archi-
tects to come up with more functional and attractive designs. Meanwhile,
the company rushed to complete the first units of its Wilmington refinery to
boost its production of gasoline and keep its stations supplied. Bulk marketing
operations were already established in several key cities on the West Coast and in
Hawaii, the Orient, Latin America, and Alaska.

Shortly after the fateful shareholders meeting in February 1917, Will Stewart
pushed through proposals to increase Union Oil's capitalization to $100 million
and to disincorporate the last remaining holding company, distributing its assets
to Union Oil shareholders. Later that year, the company also completed its takeover of the San Joaquin-to-the-ocean pipeline and acquired the terminal facilities
at Port Harford.

On April 6, 1917, the United States entered the war against Germany.
American industry was quickly drafted into the war effort. Three Union Oil
tankers were commandeered that August, one by the United States and two
(under United Kingdom registry) by the British. Two other tankers were lost at

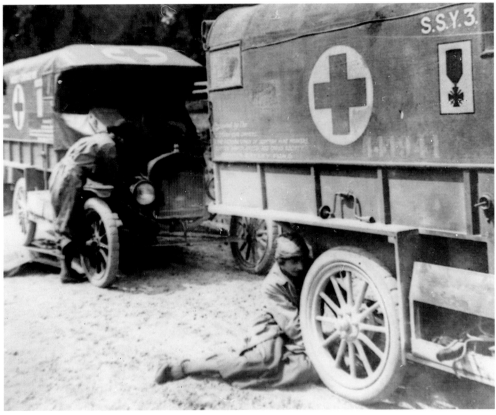

Above: When German torpedoes
sank the British liner Lusitania
on May 7, 1915, nearly 1,200 people
— including 128 Americans —
drowned. The incident inflamed
American opinion against
Kaiser Wilhelm, caricatured
by W.A. Rogers. *Left:* In 1914,
Parisian taxis were commandeered to rush troops to the front
line near the Marne River,
where the French stopped the
advancing German army.

sea during the war, one to German torpedoes, another in an Atlantic storm.

Demand for fuel for the Allied war machine pressed companies like Union to further expand their exploration programs and squeeze every drop of product from the crude they found. Union crews began drilling in Wyoming, Texas, and Mexico. The new Wilmington refinery was pushed to handle 10,000 barrels of crude a day. The Bakersfield refinery, destroyed by fire late in 1917, was rushed back into operation by mid-1918.

Union Oil Company's growth during the war years was astonishing. Once more, eastern investors took an interest. In July 1919, a syndicate of bankers offered to buy $20 million worth of Union's treasury stock. Needing money for expansion, the company's directors accepted the deal.

The syndicate included several heavy hitters from the New York financial community, including Percy Rockefeller (a nephew of John D.) and Charles Sabin, head of Guaranty Trust Company. Were they out to take over Union Oil Company? The investors denied such aspirations, and Will Stewart relayed their assurances to shareholders.

However, after picking up the shares owned by the British group that had made an earlier run at Union, the easterners took the ominous step of incorporating in Delaware under the name of Union Oil Company of Delaware. Soon, the new entity acquired other loose blocks, including Union stock held by the late Wallace Hardison's Columbia Oil Producing Company of California.

Wall Street was swept up in a buying frenzy, with the price of Union stock zooming to $200 a share.

By December 1920, Union of Delaware owned 126,000 shares, about a fourth of Union of California's outstanding stock. Alarmed, the directors sent Will Stewart and three other directors to New York. They met with Percy Rockefeller and were able to convince him that the price of a takeover was too high: If the syndicate intended to gain absolute control — that is, increase its holdings to 51 percent of the stock — it could end up paying more than the company was worth. The syndicate abandoned its buying spree, and the takeover threat lay dormant — but not for long.

Meanwhile, Southern California was building up to a crisis — a gasoline shortage. During the five years from 1915 to 1920, the auto population in California more than tripled, from 150,000 to half a million. The result, early in 1920, was a shortage of product that forced some gasoline stations to close down and others to impose rationing on customers. Not for another 53 years, with the dislocations following the Arab oil embargo of 1973, would the region experience peacetime shortages.

As a temporary expedient, Union brought in 2 million gallons of gasoline by railroad tank car from Texas. Other companies followed suit. The first load of the precious fuel was greeted with joy by the almost immobilized community. Wrote the *Los Angeles Express:* "Its entry into the city was heralded by Mayor Snyder, who rose early and journeyed to the outskirts of the city to hop aboard the locomotive and ride it into the station, where cheers reminiscent of a political rally welcomed the precious fluid."

The shortage was eventually corrected by diverting shipments from overseas and increasing refinery capacity in the western states. But nothing could have prepared the petroleum industry and Union Oil Company for the dramatic growth in motor fuel demand that California would experience in the decade to come.

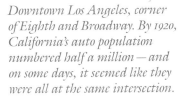

Downtown Los Angeles, corner of Eighth and Broadway. By 1920, California's auto population numbered half a million — and on some days, it seemed like they were all at the same intersection.

1

2

4

3

UNION OIL ALOFT

In January 1928, Union appointed Charles F. Lienesch chief pilot and manager of the new aviation department. Lienesch had taught himself to fly before getting formal training from the U.S. Army in 1917. Union bought a Travelair 2000, an open-cockpit biplane, and soon added three more planes to carry exploration teams to remote locales. But in the late twenties, there was a lot more to flying than just getting there faster. Enthusiasm for aviation hit a peak after Charles Lindbergh's 1927 solo trip across the Atlantic, and Union was caught up in it — particularly to promote its gasoline. The company sponsored many air racers and would-be record setters, a daring breed of men and women who sometimes courted death along with glamour. Marvel Crosson, who set the women's altitude record on Union gasoline in 1929, was killed later that year in the first cross-country Women's Air Derby (the "Powder Puff" derby). Amelia Earhart, Bobbie Trout, and the flamboyant Florence "Pancho" Barnes set records on Union aviation fuel, as did many less well-known flyers: Gordon Mounce, for example, set an "outside loop" record of 22 in June 1930, which was soon broken. Lienesch mingled "glamorous" flight duties — he was in charge of the Women's Air Derby in 1930 — with company field trips. But his last flight for Union ended in tragedy. On November 21, 1931, he was overcome by carbon monoxide fumes leaking from his exhaust system and crash-landed near Gifford, Texas. His passengers, two Union geologists on an aerial survey, were killed. Lienesch worked for Union until 1938 and later served with the Civil Aeronautics Board. He died in 1982, at the age of 88.

1. Union fueled the Southern Cross on its historic trans-Pacific flight in 1928. 2. Air races helped promote Union products. 3 & 4. Marvel Crosson set a women's altitude record at 24,000 feet in May 1929. 5. A new company Travelair in 1928. 6. Pancho Barnes, fastest woman pilot in 1930. 7. Charles Lienesch. 8. Amelia Earhart, preparing for a 1932 trans-continental flight. 9. Ruth Elder, a fifth-place finisher in the first Women's Derby. 10. The 20-seat Patrician was called a "leviathan" when introduced in 1929; its manu-facturer, Keystone, was already at work on a 36-passenger model.

4 A World on Wheels

*In 1929, Will Stewart cele-
brated 35 years with Union,
15 as president. Opposite: Los
Angeles — looking south on
Broadway, circa 1925 — had
become a bustling city of almost
a million people, nothing like
the frontier community Will
and his father found when they
moved west in 1883.*

The 1920s roared in many ways, but no roar was more audible than that of the millions of new automobiles produced during that busy decade. This transportation explosion pushed Union Oil Company to new heights of prosperity, lifting it among the industrial giants of the West.

The production of motorcars between World War I and the end of the Coolidge presidency in 1929 was breathtaking. In 1917, the nation boasted fewer than 3 million automobiles. Twelve years later, there were 23 million automobiles, all dependent on products derived from petroleum. They were fueled with gasoline and lubricated with oil and grease, and they rode on thousands of miles of roads either paved with asphalt or saturated with tar. Truly, it was a glorious time to be in the oil business.

The industry had built up enormous momentum supplying the Allies during the Great War, but the demands of war were soon dwarfed by the needs of an exploding civilian economy. Where would all the oil come from? A noted petroleum engineer predicted that America would run out within the decade, but events proved him wrong. The search for new oil intensified, and the industry experienced temporary gluts during the 1920s. Between 1918 and 1929, U.S. crude production nearly tripled, from a little over 350 million barrels a year to more than 1 billion.

Like other petroleum companies, Union Oil widened its exploration activities and employed ever more sophisticated techniques. Bill Orcutt had introduced aerial photography to Union's exploration effort shortly after the war, crisscrossing the Southern California landscape with flimsy biplanes to take pictures that might reveal the possible presence of oil and gas.

Another new tool was seismic sounding of the earth's strata with explosives. By shooting off small charges of dynamite in shallow holes, then measuring the "echoes" that bounced back from the formations below, oil finders began to identify rock layers where petroleum might be found. The science of petroleum geology in the 1920s — though light years ahead of Lyman Stewart's "nose" for oil — was still primitive. But each year brought improvements.

The 1920s also saw Union's first purchase of oil shale lands. Billions of barrels of petroleum were locked in the rugged cliffs of west-central Colorado. The vastness of these rich deposits sparked an oil shale boom.

Union geologist Roderick D. Burnham and chemist Albert S. Crossfield were assigned to check out the possibilities. Guided by mountaineer Pete Lindauer, the men collected rock samples at several locations near Parachute Creek,

Colorado. Tests indicated potential yields of as many as 39 barrels of high-grade oil per ton of shale. Extracting the oil, however, required pulverizing the rock and then cooking it in high-pressure retorts at temperatures of several hundred degrees Fahrenheit. The costs at that time were clearly prohibitive, but if the country really were running out of oil, shale would be a valuable resource in the future. Over the next few years, Union acquired the rights to thousands of acres of shale lands, banking on long-term technological and economic developments to make this play viable.

As the 1920s began, Lyman Stewart was over 80 and in his seventh decade as an oilman. He had enjoyed the longest tenure at a single company of any executive in the industry. Union Oil Company rode the postwar boom, well positioned with oil properties Stewart had fought to acquire. Union produced more oil — peaking in 1923 at 18.7 million barrels (51,000 per day) — than any other producer based in the West. The company seemed impervious to any attack from outside, but one last battle remained for the elder Stewart.

In May 1921, a takeover threat surfaced that would occupy the attention of Union's executives for the better part of the following year. It would also seize the front pages of California's newspapers, setting off a wave of public indignation throughout the state. By successfully casting the struggle in nationalistic terms — industrious American capitalists versus a cabal of foreigners — Union Oil enlisted popular opinion behind its struggle to remain independent.

The takeover threat began when Percy Rockefeller, who had promised a few months earlier not to acquire more stock in Union Oil of California, sold his holdings in Union Oil of Delaware. The buyer was Royal Dutch Shell, which directed its worldwide operations from headquarters in The Hague, Holland, and was backed largely by British capital. Union of Delaware held about a fourth of Union Oil of California's stock.

What did this giant foreign oil company have in mind? Obviously a takeover was afoot, and it roused patriotic ire. A U.S. Senate resolution called for an investigation into what looked like a brazen attempt by foreigners to take over an American oil company. The Navy Department voiced its concern about national security if U.S. petroleum supplies fell into foreign hands. The *San Francisco Chronicle* put the question squarely: "Where will Union Oil of California stand if this deal [the takeover] goes through?"

While press and politicians voiced apprehension, Royal Dutch Shell,

Above: Union directors Henry M. Robinson (top) and Isaac Milbank were chief among the Stewarts' allies when they fought off Royal Dutch Shell.
Top left: Union's modest discovery well in the Santa Fe Springs field in 1919 was followed by a 4,000-barrel-per-day producer in 1921, triggering a scramble for oil rights. Soon, derricks of competing producers covered the area. The field proved to be a "super giant," producing well over 500 million barrels in its first 32 years.

In July 1924, these Union drillers were one of three five-man crews that completed the deepest rotary-drilled well to date. In just under a year, the drillers reached the then remarkable depth of 7,319 feet. The well, in Union's Dominguez field in Southern California, was a duster.

through its Wall Street representatives, went after more Union Oil of California stock. The arithmetic appeared simple: To gain control of the California company, Royal Dutch Shell would need to acquire another 125,000 shares from among the 314,000 shares it did not control. These shares were in the hands of some 3,800 stockholders, about 80 percent of them in California. Clearly, the Golden State was going to be the battleground, though the stakes were global.

Lyman and Will Stewart's impressive array of allies included Union Oil directors Isaac Milbank, who was the former general manager of Borden Milk Company, and Henry M. Robinson, head of the powerful First National Bank of Los Angeles. The defense centered around a newly formed stock pool called Union Oil Associates, which would fight Royal Dutch Shell for the independently held shares.

Meanwhile, the media warmed to the struggle. The *San Francisco Examiner* invoked military metaphors to sum up the situation: "Under the Union Jack, with here and there a Holland ensign, are marshalled the forces of the Royal Dutch Shell combination...formidable by reason of their heavy artillery, manned by a regiment of Rothschilds and equipped by a plentiful supply of ammunition from the British treasury. Across the field...stretch the squadrons of Union Oil under command of W.L. Stewart and his venerable father, Lyman Stewart. An American flag of the very largest size waves proudly over this array."

Thanks to the Stewart family holdings and other friendly owners of large blocks, Union Oil Associates quickly lined up a solid 200,000 shares. But another 50,000 shares would be needed to assure victory in the coming proxy vote. First set for November 17, 1921, the vote was postponed, then postponed again. Finally the date was fixed: March 20, 1922.

The bidding for Union Oil of California stock pushed its price up sharply — it rose $22 in a single day on the Los Angeles and San Francisco exchanges. A massive public relations campaign was launched, featuring stockholder mailings, newspaper advertisements, mass meetings, and door-to-door solicitations. The Union campaign stressed national security and the need to assure control of domestic oil supplies. Royal Dutch Shell, through its Wall Street surrogates, argued the economic case: The price was right. Shareholders, even those with a single share, were wooed and cajoled. An Ohio man with only four shares received visits from both camps in a single afternoon.

As the proxy fight gained momentum, the prize suddenly became more valuable. In November, a Union crew drilling in virgin territory east of Los Angeles near Santa Fe Springs brought in a 4,000-barrel-a-day producer of high-gravity crude. The company owned 1,000 acres in the area, meaning it had a solid piece of what was to become a major Southern California field. Meanwhile, six producing wells were drilled in Wyoming and another in Texas. The company's production for 1921 set a new record: 9.8 million barrels. Union's tanker fleet had a capacity of over a million barrels; a new lube oil plant was on stream at Oleum; and a Canadian subsidiary, Union Oil Company of Canada, Limited, was operating a refinery near Vancouver to supply British Columbia.

Throughout California, support for the homegrown Union Oil Associates increased. Newspapers and civic groups urged shareholders to "get aboard the Union Oil Associates bandwagon." The Los Angeles Chamber of Commerce warned against "the real danger of foreign domination of this company, which has been heretofore 'of and for' Californians."

The *Los Angeles Express* joined the fray, urging "all Americans to do their duty." The paper said: "The manner and very daring of the plan conceived by foreign interests to acquire control of Union Oil of California have never been equaled in the annals of the financial world for plain audacity....Every stockholder owes it to his pocketbook, to California and to his nation to keep the American flag flying over California's oil fields."

On the morning before the meeting, full-page ads for Union Oil Associates ran in newspapers up and down the state, urging shareholders to "save the company from foreign control" that could make Union Oil of California "a pawn...

Above: The propane-solvent plant at the Oleum refinery produced Triton motor oil. Below left: In 1930, Union drillers in Santa Fe Springs raced against neighboring companies to tap deep oil zones some 8,000 feet down. Opposite: The Ole & Um cartoon series emphasized safe operations at Union's Oleum refinery in the 1920s. Opposite, right: Union's Los Angeles refinery, circa 1927.

OLE & UM
—by ANDY JARVIS

They take in the bright lights.

Moral: You don't have to go to Hollywood to get "Klieg-eyes."

shoved back and forth across the international chessboard in a worldwide war of the nations for control of the oil supply."

These appeals had a strong impact on a population that had recently gone through a world war. The vote wasn't even close. When the proxies were counted the next morning, Union Oil Associates controlled 275,000 shares — 25,000 more than were needed.

Union Oil Associates immediately incorporated into a new holding company — capitalized at $20 million — that held tightly to its 57.5 percent share of Union Oil of California stock for the next decade. Despite the court ruling that had broken up the earlier holding companies in 1916, the new structure was accepted by the courts as the only means to preserve the company from foreign control. Two years later, Royal Dutch Shell disposed of its last holdings in Union Oil of California. (In 1932, as the Depression deepened and the company retrenched, Union Oil Associates was merged into Union Oil of California.)

While the company battled Royal Dutch Shell, it skirmished with the city of Los Angeles. The city wanted to take over one of Lyman Stewart's pet projects — Union Oil's Outer Harbor Dock and Wharf Company in San Pedro — to expand Los Angeles Harbor.

The harbor was becoming a major Pacific port. Los Angeles's city fathers had envisioned just such a development years earlier. In 1907, they acted on their optimism, forming a harbor commission before the city even owned oceanfront property. In 1909, they annexed two coastal communities — San Pedro and Wilmington — via a narrow corridor of gerrymandered county land. Beginning in 1910, private investors — primarily Union and other oil companies — played the major role in building harbor facilities. The rapid growth in the harbor's commerce was largely due to petroleum exports from California's vigorous oil industry.

Harbor traffic increased when the Panama Canal opened in 1914, cutting 8,000 miles off the ocean route from the East around Cape Horn. During World War I, Los Angeles Harbor became home to U.S. Army and Navy installations, including a submarine flotilla. After the war, ship traffic in the harbor more than tripled in a few years — from 900 in 1919 to 2,900 in 1922 — and the ships were carrying more cargo, with average tonnage rising from 400 to 2,200.

As the harbor prospered, Union had invested heavily to dredge channels and build wharves and piers to accommodate its growing tanker fleet. When the city of Los Angeles filed suit to eject Union from its property, the reaction of the usually restrained Lyman Stewart was understandable. He was outraged. The company filed a countersuit that called the city's action "an unwarranted attempt to confiscate our property — property as justly and lawfully acquired as any property can be."

Stunned by Stewart's vehemence, the city agreed to a compromise in the spring of 1922: Union would hold its acreage under a 30-year lease, and then allow the city to buy it. (On April 4, 1952, the agreement culminated in the transfer of Union's wharves, piers, channels, and bulkheads to the city. The company retained the buildings and other installations, which it sold to another party in 1955.)

By the summer of 1922, Will Stewart could once again concentrate on the company's fundamental businesses. Buoyed by the run-up in Union's stock price, he obtained financing for expansion of downstream operations, including the establishment of a new research department at the Los Angeles refinery — one of Lyman Stewart's early dreams.

Over the next year, Union Oil expanded with an impressive array of new capital projects. The company boasted storage capacity of more than 30 million barrels of crude oil and products, including a major new bulk distributing station on the Honolulu waterfront. Union Oil trunk and gathering pipelines stretched more than 900 miles, with a daily capacity of 275,000 barrels. The tanker fleet included 14 steamships and 21 barges.

Will Stewart realized a lifelong ambition in 1923 with the establishment of the Provident Fund, adopted by the board on July 1. This retirement program for employees rounded out the company's benefits program, which already included medical and profit-sharing plans.

It was also in 1923 that a promising young petroleum engineer and geologist from Kentucky named Albert Chatfield "Cy" Rubel joined the company, beginning a long and beneficial association. A graduate of the University of Arizona, he had served in World War I as a captain in the U.S. Army Corps of Engineers, then spent four years looking for oil and gas in the southwest United States and Central America. Rubel managed to sell himself to Union's

Left: A chemist at Oleum ran tests on aromatic hydrocarbons, which Union began producing in the mid-1920s for sale to the paint and varnish industry. Opposite: By 1930, Union tank trucks in Hawaii kept a network of eight service stations well supplied.

Lyman Stewart was photographed just a few weeks before his death in 1923 at the age of 83.

exploration department as a bright young go-getter and eventually became Bill Orcutt's successor.

On September 29, 1923, Lyman Stewart died of pneumonia at the age of 83. His death had come only 18 months after his final victory in the Royal Dutch Shell takeover fight — a struggle that had weakened his already frail constitution. His friend and ally in the takeover battle, Isaac Milbank, had lived only five months after the victory. Seven weeks after Lyman Stewart's death, his brother Milton also died, not knowing that Lyman had preceded him to the grave.

Lyman Stewart's determination, verging on stubbornness, had infuriated some but had inspired many others. His single-minded dedication to acquiring oil properties and his vision of the role petroleum would ultimately play in the American economy made him both pioneer and pacesetter. On the day of his funeral, held at the Bible Institute of Los Angeles, business at all Union Oil offices was suspended.

Appraising Lyman Stewart's contribution to the industry and nation he loved, *Petroleum World* wrote: "The life of this revered veteran of oil…was the longest record of oil achievement which can be credited to any American. Sixty-four years he served petroleum, 24 in Pennsylvania, 40 in California….Long recognized as the father of oil in the Pacific Coast region, long given the honored title of 'dean of western oil men,' consulted by the oldest and the wisest and held in respectful awe by the younger element, Lyman Stewart had been the outstanding figure in California oil for 40 years."

At the time of Stewart's passing, business was booming. In December, Union's directors agreed to increase the capitalization to 1.25 million shares with a par value of $100, making Union Oil a $125 million company. In 1924, when Royal Dutch Shell sold its remaining interests in the company, Union's board voted to split the shares four for one, bringing the total number of shares outstanding to 5 million, with a par value of $25. In November, the company was listed for the first time on the New York Stock Exchange. The following year, the board offered 100,000 shares of stock to employees on a time-payment plan.

By 1925, Union Oil leased or operated 423 service stations. Its vehicle fleet consisted of 1,048 trucks and 856 automobiles. The *Union Oil Bulletin,* the company magazine introduced in 1921, reported: "The motorcar is no longer a luxury, but a necessity. The horse has practically disappeared from our streets and even from the farms. Motor-driven trucks have almost entirely superseded the railroad for short hauls. Thirty years ago, horseless carriages were prohibited from traveling at a speed greater than four miles an hour on the English public roads. America had similar laws much later than that. The motorcar and the petroleum industry are today dependent one upon the other."

Union Oil issued its first gasoline credit cards in 1925. Only a few thousand

WARNIN
DO NOT ATT
THIS HI

Top left: In 1926, musical Union service station operators and office employees in Seattle banded together, improvising a name from Aristo oil's advertising slogan. *Above:* Hugh A. Matier supervised a Union Ethyl low-gear test on a 35 percent grade in 1927. The car cleared the summit, a feat others — using ordinary gasoline — apparently failed. *Left*, a promotional tour of Yosemite.

of the handwritten paper cards, signed personally by the local district sales managers, were distributed. They were good for two months. In 1931, the term was expanded to three months.

The company marketed the "aristocrat of motor oils" — Aristo — advertised as not containing asphalt or any other nonlubricating substances that could cause build-up and engine wear. In ads for its nondetonating gasoline, Union described a 21-step refining process that resulted in more complete fuel combustion for smoother running engines and powerful performance. In 1926, the company introduced "the new super fuel" — Union Ethyl. Many companies began adding tetraethyl lead to their gasolines as a result of research completed early in the decade demonstrating its effectiveness as an antiknocking agent.

The company also courted the new commercial airline industry, which had begun in 1919. Aircraft design advanced rapidly during the 1920s, with the monoplane replacing the biplane. The cantilever wing and metal fuselage, which were developed in Germany during the war, improved on the flimsy wood and glue construction of earlier models. Union fuels and engine oils powered many an air race and demonstration flight, including the landmark trans-Pacific journey of the *Southern Cross* from California to Australia in 1928.

In 1926, a third-generation Stewart joined the company's board of directors. He was William L. Stewart, Jr., son of Union's president and already a veteran of the oil business from wellhead to terminal. A graduate of Stanford University

OUT TO PASTURE

"Please be advised that we have disposed of the three mules from the Dominguez District," Cy Rubel wrote to district accountant Stanley Clarke in 1928. Rubel, later president of Union Oil, was then a petroleum engineer complying with corporate reporting requirements as he gave away company assets. "I am unable to identify the mules in any more precise manner than this because, in the thirty-odd years that they have been working for the Union Oil Company, their names have changed as often as their drivers, and any name that I might give you for any individual mule would have very little significance. These mules were given to several people, to be used where I am certain that they will have a good home for the declining years of their life, and we can afford to get rid of them at any price, as their operating cost was about the same as for a five-ton tractor." Mules and horses did much of the work to help establish the oil industry, but mechanization slowly put them out to pasture. Four-legged transports were phased out of Union's product delivery operations in the early 1920s. Their fellow beasts in field operations followed as the company's vehicle fleet increased. As late as the 1960s, Union explorationists enlisted mules — branded 76, of course — to carry their gear into remote Central and South American jungles. Today, helicopters do much of the grunt work in rugged locations.

Christmas in 1923 at Will and Margaret Stewart's Pasadena estate, Rose Villa. Son Arthur (standing) worked his first summer for Union that year.

and the Massachusetts Institute of Technology, young Bill Stewart focused his interest on the research and refining end of the business. Eventually, he rose to become board chairman of a much larger, international Union Oil Company — although his grandfather might not have predicted so bright a future for him.

Like his father, Bill Stewart had started working for Union Oil during his summers off from school, first as a roustabout in the San Joaquin Valley oil fields, then as a pipefitter at the Wilmington refinery. He delighted in recalling the day in 1917 when Grandfather Lyman, showing a party of friends through the partially constructed refinery, introduced young Bill and asked his grandson: "How much did this property cost?" Bill didn't know.

"What's the payroll of the refinery?" asked Lyman. Bill didn't know the answer to that one, either.

"What is the refinery going to cost?" When Bill missed the third question, his grandfather led the party away in disgust, convinced that his uninformed grandson would never rise above the rank of pipefitter.

The year 1926 also brought the company's expansion into South America, through a partnership with Pantepec Oil Company of Venezuela, to explore an 880,000-acre concession in that country. In the United States, Union's research group launched the first gas-lift enhanced recovery projects, reinjecting natural gas into formations to boost crude and natural gasoline production.

In the midst of the company's enthusiastic growth, disaster struck. All phases of petroleum operations are vulnerable to the scourge of fire, but none has a greater potential for loss than the tank farms where millions of barrels of refined product and crude oil are confined in a relatively small space.

On the morning of April 7, 1926, an electrical storm swept in from the Pacific Ocean over the Union Oil tank farm in San Luis Obispo, California. Simultaneous bolts of lightning ripped into three covered earthen reservoirs, igniting 3 million barrels of oil. Within minutes another streak of lightning lit up a fourth reservoir, pushing the blaze totally out of control. Fire fighters couldn't get close enough to do anything.

Seventeen hours later, the burning oil overflowed into a fifth reservoir and

against a row of steel tanks. Fire-whipped winds blew embers onto the roof of a sixth reservoir, setting off another million barrels of crude, which engulfed more tanks. Before the conflagration was over, 15 huge steel tanks crumpled under the heat. Flames and smoke billowed as from a volcano for several days, attracting throngs of spectators.

The day after setting off the San Luis Obispo fire, the storm had moved 200 miles south and struck again — this time at Union's big tank farm near Brea in Orange County. The first bolt set off two reservoirs, which caused the oil to boil over into a third. A lake of blazing oil then flowed out and engulfed a small refinery. An army of 3,000 men enlisted from nearby oil fields battled the fires for days, finally throwing up earthen dikes that contained the oil until the flames burned themselves out.

In all, more than 8 million barrels of oil were destroyed, plus 21 steel tanks, miles of pipeline and fittings, and much adjoining property. Such coincidental disasters inflicted on widely separated facilities of the same company by the same storm defied the odds. But the insurance companies covered the loss, handing Union Oil checks for more than $9 million. The insurers called it the worst fire loss since the 1906 San Francisco earthquake and fire.

BUILDING THE WEST
The 1930s saw an enormous surge of public works projects in the West, including Bonneville Dam in Oregon, the Calaveras Tunnels to supply water to San Francisco from the Hetch Hetchy Reservoir, and the San Francisco-Oakland Bay Bridge. Union Oil supplied petroleum products for all of these projects, but the biggest by far was the effort to tap the waters of the Colorado River for hydroelectric power, irrigation, and residential use for a growing Los Angeles. The Union Oil shield was a familiar sight on trucks and equipment crawling over dusty construction areas during the building of the All-American Canal, the Metropolitan Water District Aqueduct, Parker Dam, and the mammoth centerpiece, Hoover Dam. A consortium of engineering and construction firms finished Hoover Dam almost two years ahead of schedule. It was dedicated as Boulder Dam (later changed back to Hoover) by President Franklin D. Roosevelt in 1935. To supply the project, Union set up a special organization and on-site installations. The company provided Union 76 gasoline for hundreds of trucks and automobiles, diesel fuel for tractors and scrapers, fuel oil for locomotives, as well as cleaning solvent and stove oil. The construction equipment also required 40 different lubricating oils and 23 types of grease.

Top right: In 1926, the year Union introduced its new ethyl gasoline, there were more than 400 Union service stations in the West.

Out of the flames and destruction of these two disasters came a renewed commitment by Union Oil to learn more about preventing fires and to improve methods of combatting them. A major step forward was the establishment of a "fire lab," which trained company personnel in the latest techniques and technology of fire prevention and control—a practice that continues today in an expanded and more sophisticated format.

When the first fire lab classes were held at the Los Angeles refinery in the late 1920s, smoke from the demonstration blaze attracted firemen from the immediate area anxious to see what was burning. They stayed to learn, and since then several hundred firemen from communities neighboring the company's refineries have participated in the program. Today, the company continues to share fire-fighting tactics with fire departments around the country.

If the defeat of Royal Dutch Shell chilled interest in taking over Union Oil, it did nothing to stop rumors. In 1926, the stock market got wind of a joint venture between Union and Atlantic Refining Company of Philadelphia. The companies invested more than $4 million in 250 sales depots in Australia and New Zealand. But when two senior Union executives were seen in New York, speculators thought they saw a merger in the works. Prices for Union Oil and Union Oil Associates stock went through the roof. In one day, more than 50,000 shares traded hands on the San Francisco Stock Exchange, and another 14,500 in Los Angeles.

Will Stewart tried to put an end to the merger rumors with a brief press statement denying that anything was afoot. But between 1925 and 1928, three independent California oil companies had been taken over by eastern interests—so the rumors about Union Oil persisted. Stewart issued periodic denials until speculators tired of the game.

As the end of the decade neared, Union Oil Company geared up for its fortieth anniversary celebration. It had more than 6,600 stockholders, and Union Oil Associates had another 3,850. Five thousand Union employees owned $2 million worth of stock through the Provident Fund. The company's crude production stood at 16 million barrels a year, and it was buying additional crude to produce the high volumes of refined products demanded by the voracious motoring public.

Union's financial success was dazzling, even in the face of the stock market collapse on Black Friday—October 28, 1929. In 1930, the *Los Angeles Times* noted that since Union Oil's founding it had paid out more than $164 million in cash and stock dividends to its shareholders. The company not only survived but prospered, despite its early years of factional strife and financial hardship, its occasionally bizarre management style, and its knockdown battles with hostile bidders. *Petroleum World* summarized the company's achievements:

"Union's growth, while not spectacular at any stage, borders on the phenomenal. In the past ten years, Union has discovered four of California's major oil fields — Santa Fe Springs, Richfield, Dominguez, and Rosecrans. In the manufacturing of oil, its pioneering has also been in evidence. It was one of the first to develop tubular stills. It has developed a direct fractionation of gasoline and serial fractional condensation. The company was also one of the first to use high-pressure cracking on a commercial scale. Major improvements in design for absorption towers and stills for recovering gasoline from natural gas are also credited to the company. The Santa Paula refinery was one of the first built in California; today the company owns seven. The company also built the first pipeline for tidewater transportation of oil, and was the first to move oil in bulk by tankers. It pioneered the use of oil for locomotive fuel."

Aftershocks from the 1929 stock market crash marked the beginning of the Great Depression of the 1930s. But even in an era of failing businesses and rising unemployment, Will Stewart was able to issue a cheerful report to Union Oil shareholders in early 1930: "The company's affairs are in a strong financial position and sound."

With the company's vigorous expansion in the 1920s, Stewart's message seemed to presage a smooth future for Union in the midst of growing economic turmoil and uncertainty in the country. But the rugged Depression years would not treat Union Oil gently. On June 21, 1930, within four months of his reassuring pronouncement, Stewart died at age 62 of a heart attack at his summer house in Hermosa Beach. The company would sorely miss his calm and firm leadership.

Will Stewart had literally been born into the oil business, learning it from the bottom up. He called himself "an old rig builder," referring to his early days as a roustabout. He had worked his way up as a pipeliner, salesman, and production manager.

During his 16 years as president, he had been a patient and skillful leader, accomplishing by persuasion what his father, Lyman Stewart, had achieved by sheer will and extraordinary vision. One of Will Stewart's outstanding contributions to the company was the industrial relations program, which was rooted in his concern for Union's workers. He was years ahead of his time with this program, as *California Oil World* noted:

"To W.L. Stewart may be attributed a systematic industrial relations activity. He had an intense interest in the problems of the employees. Men instinctively liked him, and he showed the same capacity as his father to enlist in the company's service capable, experienced workmen in all phases of the industry. He was

Opposite, portraits: E. W. Clark (top) became chairman when Will Stewart died in 1930. Will's sons Bill (center) and Art (bottom) were not sufficiently experienced for top executive posts. Opposite, bottom left: Union's Santa Paula refinery in 1926. Right: In a common Depression-era scene, a man buys an apple from one of the nation's unemployed, circa 1930.

quick to approve worthwhile effort and believed in giving his lieutenants scope to apply their talents. About his own duties he went quietly and unobtrusively, preferring always to encourage and direct rather than drive. He was amenable to suggestions at all times. Democratic, soft-spoken, kindly, he was nevertheless a man of decision, and Union Oil enjoyed a remarkable period of progress and prosperity under his leadership."

The company lost Will Stewart just when it needed him most. For the first time in its history, Union Oil was without the guiding hand of a Stewart, and now it was entering the worst years of the Great Depression. Although two Stewarts worked for the company at the time, neither was seasoned enough to be chairman or president. Bill was 33 years old and director of manufacturing. Four years earlier, he had been elected to the board of directors. His brother Arthur C. Stewart, 25, worked in the sales department. Art had graduated from Stanford as an engineer and attended Harvard Business School. He began at Union as a wiper in the engine rooms of company tankers, then started his sales career as a service station attendant on the fishing docks at San Pedro. Art had his father's flair for making friends and for selling.

On July 7, 1930, the board elected E.W. Clark chairman, filling what the directors viewed at the time as an interim, emergency position. E.W., as he was known to everyone in the petroleum industry, was a native of New Hampshire who had migrated to California in 1897. He had found work on the narrow-gauge Pacific Coast Railway, which ran north and south out of San Luis Obispo,

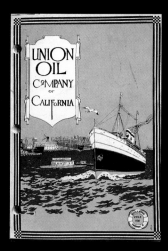

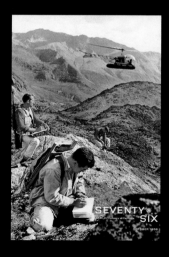

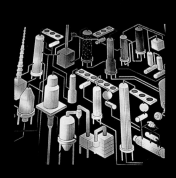

A LITERARY TRADITION

In March 1921, the first issue of the *Union Oil Bulletin* appeared. A trim 6-by-10-inch magazine, it was published every month by the Comptroller's Department. The *Bulletin* ran profiles of company personalities, news of employee tennis and golf tournaments, articles on company operations, and a page of jokes called "Refined and Crude." Within five months, the magazine had become so popular that it was distributed to all of Union's nearly 5,000 employees. For 20 years, the publication chronicled Union's growth as the industry boomed to produce products for an increasingly oil-driven society. In 1939, a new publication — which replaced the *Bulletin* — was issued. *On Tour* was launched as a tabloid but soon took on a 9-by-12-inch magazine format in response to its readers. The name referred to the oilman's working shift. The editors explained that "although it should properly be pronounced 'toor,' the petroleum industry has adopted it as just plain 'tower.'" In June 1957, the magazine was renamed *Seventy Six*, and incorporated *The Minute Man*, a dealer publication that dated back to 1929. In 1965, it absorbed *The Pure Oil News*. By the 1980s, *Seventy Six* had a circulation of 40,000, including employees, retirees, and other friends of Unocal around the world.

Press St. Clair faced the heavy task of leading Union Oil through the Depression. Below right: *As technology improved, drillers went deeper and deeper for oil in the 1920s and 1930s. Seventy-nine years after Drake drilled almost 70 feet to strike oil, a new record was set at 15,000 feet — almost three miles down.*

serving Union's oil fields in Santa Barbara County. Clark was manager of the little railway when he founded the Pinal Dome Oil Company in Santa Maria in 1901, purchased by Union in 1917.

When Union Oil and the Independent Oil Producers Agency laid the pipeline to carry products from the San Joaquin Valley to the sea in 1910, Clark became general manager of the pipeline operating company — Producers Transportation — by then a wholly owned subsidiary of Union. He went on to serve as Union's general manager before becoming executive vice president in 1921.

E. W. enjoyed sporty automobiles, which he drove like racers. He liked to visit the fields and isolated pumping stations to talk with the men on duty there. Although Clark had retired as executive vice president in 1929, he had remained on the board and on the executive committee.

At the same time Clark became chairman, the directors appointed Press St. Clair as company president. St. Clair had succeeded Clark as executive vice president in 1929. Born in Dutch Flat in California's Mother Lode, St. Clair was raised in Bakersfield, where he helped his father lay out the town's first gas main. Eventually, he became manager of the Bakersfield Gas & Electric Company, but the spectacular Kern River oil strikes lured him into becoming an independent oil producer.

St. Clair had become affiliated with Union Oil in 1909 when, as president of the Independent Oil Producers Agency, he negotiated an agreement making Union the agency's sales agent. He joined Union's board in 1919 and was elected a vice president in 1922. Both Clark and St. Clair had been instrumental in the formation of the American Petroleum Institute.

St. Clair's management style was a drastic departure from the soft-spoken, persuasive approach of the Stewarts. His dominating physical size — six feet, 220 pounds — was matched by a strong personality and explosive temper. He loved a fight and usually tried to control committee meetings by outtalking everyone else.

The new president faced a rugged task. Union, along with other oil companies in California, was producing more and more oil that was worth less and less as demand fell. California refineries poured out more than 850,000 barrels of product a day in 1930 for a market that absorbed less than 700,000. Storage facilities filled up, and producers began dumping their crude at below cost.

Union cut its drilling activity from 41 crews to 10. But the crews continued

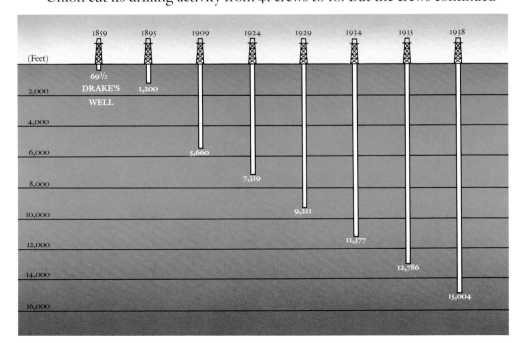

to drill for smaller independents, hitting richer oil sands than they had ever tapped before. Price wars broke out in 1930 as the petroleum industry rapidly fell into chaos.

Troubles in the retail market were related to hard times in the automobile industry, where the factory output of cars slipped from a high of 5.3 million vehicles in 1929 to less than half that figure by 1934. Gasoline had become the oil companies' most profitable product during the 1920s. But in the early 1930s, service stations often sold gasoline for less than the cost of production.

In 1931, a destructive six-month gasoline war nearly ruined the Pacific Coast market. Union's sales fell from a 1929 high of $89 million to $61 million in 1930, the first year of St. Clair's presidency. During the following two years, sales declined another $10 million.

Despite the tough economic climate, Union's directors managed to come up with $4 million to acquire from Amerada Petroleum Corporation a one-half interest in the 160-acre King lease in Kettleman Hills, one of the richest strikes in the San Joaquin Valley. Union paid another $2.25 million for a half interest in the Getty-Armstrong lease covering 1,260 acres on the north dome of Kettleman Hills. These purchases, plus acreage already held, made Union one of the top producers in one of the greatest California fields.

In 1931, Chairman Clark died of a heart attack. Always robust, the 73-year-old Clark had provided an effective balance to the dogged, desk-pounding St. Clair. No one seemed able to replace him. The veteran geologist Bill Orcutt, head of exploration, was highly respected and could have exerted power had he chosen to do so. But Orcutt refused to be drawn into controversies whipped up by St. Clair's outbursts.

St. Clair was determined to maintain the company's long record of paying dividends to its shareholders, even if it meant cutting expenses to the bone. In 1931, Union directors began to unload some of the company's financial obligations. They liquidated Union's Venezuelan interests, acquired in 1926. (Years later a small piece of the acreage — in the highly productive Lake Maracaibo region — returned to Union with the acquisition of The Pure Oil Company.)

The company cut back in other ways. The number of drilling crews in the field was reduced to six, just barely enough to keep up Union's commitments to leaseholders. The company reduced the payroll a million dollars a year by estab-

Above: R.D. Matthews (top), Welsh by birth and American by choice, used the "Spirit of '76" (painting by A.M. Willard) as his inspiration for what would become one of the world's best known advertising symbols — the sign of the 76. Below, a Union billboard, circa 1935, and a variety of specialty products sold at Union service stations.

Union's chief automotive engineer Earl Cooper touted a new unnamed Union motor oil in rigorous test drives. The oil, later called Triton, gave western oils an edge on eastern oils.

lishing the five-day workweek, three years before the New Deal pushed the idea.

In 1933, St. Clair sold the company's half interest in Atlantic-Union Refining Company. Although this relieved Union of certain financial commitments, it also meant giving up an interest in a growing chain of marketing outlets in Australia and New Zealand.

Sales volumes in the United States slumped. The new National Recovery Act code curtailed output, primarily through production quotas and import controls. Meanwhile, competitors captured Union's U.S. Navy business by selling oil at less than production cost. Union decided to compete not on the basis of price but of quality, in order to free the dealers from the ruinous effects of the continuing price wars.

Union's researchers came up with an improved gasoline with the highest octane that could be manufactured at the time. The company's marketers decided that it should have a distinctive name, and indeed gave it a revolutionary one — 76. The name, based on the "Spirit of '76" slogan referring to the American Revolution, was suggested by Robert D. Matthews, Union's executive vice president. A Welshman, Matthews had developed a love of American history when he studied it to qualify for his citizenship papers.

Union's 76 gasoline went on sale in January 1932, and the new name was an immediate success. In February, for example, it was well enough known that a letter simply addressed "76, Auburn, California" was promptly delivered by postal employees to the company's substation there.

Unfortunately, 76 also coincided with the highest octane rating that Union's refineries could then achieve. This proved a problem. The company's application to register the trademark with the U.S. Patent Office was rejected. The reason was that since "76" could be construed as referring to the octane rating, it could not be the exclusive property of Union Oil Company. Nevertheless, six western states agreed to register the trademark: California, Oregon, Washington, Idaho, Nevada, and Arizona.

Sales director Victor H. Kelly and Union's attorneys argued that the number referred to the famous revolutionary spirit of 1776, but they were unsuccessful. It was another 15 years before the U.S. Patent Office finally certified Union's trademark, the blue 76 on an orange background with the word "Union." So was born the famous trademark, now one of the company's most valued — although intangible — assets.

TRITON: A BETTER OIL
In 1934, Union Oil Company announced a new motor oil called Triton, to be sold for 30¢ a quart. It was one of the company's most successful innovations, marking a dramatic turning point in western oil producers' rivalry with eastern oils. Until that time, the quality of motor oils had been dictated by the quality of the crude that produced them, giving eastern refiners a great advantage. As a result, eastern lubricating oils won an inordinate share of sales on the Pacific Coast, almost half of an $80 million market by 1933. Finally, a Union research team came up with a process to produce high-quality lubricating oil from heavy western crude. Union mounted a spectacular marketing effort. In one grueling and well-publicized test run, Union's chief sales engineer, former racing champion Earl Cooper, and nine other drivers shuttled a new Studebaker President 8 up and down the coast. The car racked up 60,000 miles in 60 days and showed remarkably little engine wear. The new oil's name — Triton — was chosen from 50,000 submitted in a contest. Robert T. Willis, a research inspector at the Oleum refinery, won the first prize of $500. Triton was enthusiastically received by Depression-era consumers, who were trying to limp through hard times by getting the most out of their auto engines. After only four months on the market, Triton had won over 350,000 new users.

At the Oleum refinery, Union spent $2 million to build a lubricating oil plant. Researchers had been working for several years on a refining process to make a 100 percent paraffin-base lubricating oil from California crude. The need was critical because the increased horsepower and speed of automobile engines demanded lubricants that would resist oxidation. Pennsylvania crudes had, in fact, yielded such a motor oil and, by 1933, had grabbed almost half the $80 million West Coast lubricant market.

In 1934, Union's researchers perfected a process that used liquid propane to remove the asphalt and other substances from heavy western crude oils, producing an oil equal to or better than eastern oils. Standard Oil of Indiana and Standard of New Jersey had been working on a similar process, so Union pooled its propane-solvent patents with those of the two Standards in order to avoid a legal battle.

Union produced its oil, called Triton, in the new plant at Oleum. Backed with heavy promotion, this high-quality motor oil eventually helped Union increase its share of the market against eastern oils. Union researchers followed up the development of Triton motor oil by perfecting a new diesel-engine lubricating oil, known as Diesolife, which was as efficient in diesel-fuel engines as Triton was in gasoline engines.

In 1934 and 1935, Union spent more than $2 million for new marketing outlets for both bulk and retail sales. The company organized Union Service Stations, Inc., a wholly owned subsidiary, to take over and operate failing service stations of Union dealers caught in the Depression's financial squeeze. These

Top left: Dr. Ulric B. Bray (standing) and C.E. Swift demonstrated the precipitation of asphalt and wax from a lubricating oil stock with propane to show how Triton was produced.

Union trucks of the 1920s and 1930s:
<u>*Right,*</u> *a Leland truck, 1921.*
<u>*Center,*</u> *the Union terminal in*
Covina, California, circa 1925.
<u>*Bottom,*</u> *Union tank trucks of*
the 1930s.

outlets, along with the small number of demonstration service stations, formed the nucleus of a chain that ultimately would make the company a major factor in the West Coast retail market.

The company's oil production rose in the mid-1930s. In 1934, a Union crew in Kern County drilled an 11,377-foot hole, setting a record for the deepest in the world until that time. The Santa Maria field was discovered, and deep drilling was paying off at three more prodigious fields — Santa Fe Springs, Richfield, and Dominguez. By 1935, the company's production wells numbered more than 1,000, although 400 were shut in or restricted because of the glut of crude flooding the market. Union held almost 300,000 acres of promising or proven oil lands in the western states.

Union's directors felt confident enough about the company's prospects in 1936 to enlarge the employees' benefit plan, providing group disability insurance for employees to compensate them for loss of income during periods of sickness and off-duty accidents. R. D. Matthews pointed out that the payroll topped $15.5 million for the 8,928 employees. He added that the "maintenance of morale and more intimate contact and understanding within the organization is a prime factor in its progress and welfare."

In 1937, Union's drillers discovered the Rio Bravo field in the San Joaquin Valley with another deep well, completed at 11,302 feet and yielding 2,600 barrels of oil per day. The company was also producing in Texas and had sent geophysical crews on an extensive survey in California. Other crews explored in Colombia and Alaska.

Even as the company pulled itself out of the Depression, there was discord in the ranks. Under St. Clair's domination, team spirit had dissolved and managers pulled in opposite directions. St. Clair seemed unable to unite the executives or develop the cohesive plan of action that would be needed for real recovery. Union had lost its edge in manufacturing and, despite the introduction of new products, in marketing. St. Clair offered further belt-tightening to improve the situation, but the directors and many shareholders began to realize that a more creative approach was required.

Above: In 1937, Union's service station at the corner of Gayley and Lindbrook in Westwood, California, was described as "strikingly modern." Below left: In 1931, Union acquired acreage in Kettleman Hills, one of California's richest fields.

Part 2

1938–1964

The War Years

The Big Independent

Gearing Up for Growth

Reese Taylor:

MAN OF STEEL

Reese H. Taylor, who led Union Oil Company for nearly 24 years as president, chairman, and chief executive officer, was born in Los Angeles on July 6, 1900. Educated as a mechanical engineer at Cornell University and the University of California at Berkeley, Taylor returned home in 1922 and went to work as a helper in the structural shop of the Llewellyn Iron Works.

Taylor had to work twice as hard to prove himself there, he later explained, because his father was president of the company. In 1929, Llewellyn merged with Consolidated Steel Corporation, and in 1933, only eleven years out of college, Taylor became president of the expanded company.

A commanding figure at six feet three inches, Taylor built a reputation as a mover and a doer. For example, when the Metropolitan Aqueduct ordered siphons too large to be transported by rail from the East, Taylor stepped in and contracted to fabricate the giant tubes in Los Angeles. He had them delivered by truck and trailer, which required clearing all traffic from the highways to make room.

During construction of Hoover Dam, eastern companies thought they had locked up the fabrication of the transmission towers, which would carry cable from Nevada to Los Angeles. When Taylor came up with some novel engineering ideas, he won a sizable slice of the business for Consolidated.

In 1937, Taylor joined Union Oil's board of directors; he was nominated by William L. Stewart, Jr., grandson of the company's founder. The following year, the directors elected Taylor president, asking him to reinvigorate the company after the bleak years of the Depression.

Taylor took the oil industry in stride. Business was business, and there were certain rules and strategies that could be universally applied. He believed that quality was what mattered, and that people who sold only on the basis of price were shortsighted.

The Depression had taught him valuable lessons. As sales kept shrinking in the early 1930s, managements of some companies thought that price cutting—with resultant higher sales—was the key to better plant utilization.

Consolidated took another approach. "We decided not to reduce prices," Taylor said, "but to cut operating capacity and overhead instead. Within a short time, our company was one of the few in the steel-fabricating industry to eliminate unprofitable business and to use its capacity more efficiently. And it was not long before our bookkeeping shifted from the red side of the ledger to the black."

As a manager, Taylor could be tough and demanding, but he also had an uncanny sense of what was right and timely. Despite a reputation for bluntness, he had a deep regard for people. "The success of a corporation," he said, "depends on the individual and aggregate efforts of all its people, and the corporation's greatest responsibility is that of people—of human relations."

With the United States' entry into World War II in December 1941, Taylor accelerated the renovation of Union Oil facilities wherever possible. The company played a vital role in the war effort to help keep the armed forces supplied with petroleum fuels. Taylor himself was called to Washington, D.C., for six months in 1942 to head the Iron and Steel Divi-

Clockwise, from top left: Reese Taylor and Cy Rubel made an unstoppable team for two decades. In 1956, Reese Taylor spoke at the cornerstone ceremony of the new Union Oil Center—the "building that freedom built"—and welcomed new director Prentis Cobb Hale, Jr. Taylor made a young friend at a benefit baseball game he organized to raise $90,000 for the John Tracy Clinic for hearing-impaired children.

sion of the War Production Board. The following year, he set up a Fuels and Lubricants Section for the U.S. Army.

Taylor may have welcomed the double responsibilities that commanded his attention during the war years as some relief from personal tragedy. After a long illness, his wife, Kathryn, died in September 1943, leaving him to raise their three sons.

In Washington, Taylor was dismayed to find that many government representatives seemed to have a poor grasp of the basics of capitalism. This inspired him to launch a series of ads that used examples from Union Oil to explain how free enterprise worked. The campaign started out in Pacific Coast newspapers in 1943, but its popularity soon led Union to expand into national publications. Union used the free enterprise theme in its advertising for 20 years.

In late 1944, Taylor married the woman who developed the first free enterprise ads, Union's advertising manager, Margaret Corrie. Described as a dynamo by some who knew her, she had first worked with Taylor as his secretary at Consolidated. They had two children.

Under Taylor's firm hand, Union Oil Company developed a strong public identity, becoming known as a good corporate citizen and a champion of the American way. No one typified the company's presence in the community more than Taylor. He became highly visible, lending his support to a wide range of civic and cultural projects. Taylor preached public service: "It is essential to take a serious interest in the affairs of your community. In other words, be a good citizen." He wanted his city and region to be the best, just as he wanted it for Union.

"Man-hours are very precious things," Taylor said. "I know that at 22 every man feels this life will last forever, but it really won't. It's always later than you think." And so he filled his hours full. While building a great

petroleum corporation and traveling to Union's far-flung operations, he still found time to serve as a director of the Federal Reserve Bank of San Francisco from 1937 to 1959, one of the longest terms in the history of that organization.

Taylor served on the board of a number of business and charitable organizations, including two hospitals. At various times, he was a trustee of four different universities, and he served five terms as a director of the YMCA of Los Angeles. As head of the Music Center Operating Company, Taylor was instrumental in helping build the Los Angeles Music Center, and he also served as vice president of the Hollywood Bowl Association.

He was keenly interested in sports. A devotee of thoroughbred racing, he became president of the Los Angeles Turf Club. He was a strong supporter of tennis, helping to establish Perry Jones' Youth Tennis Foundation, which developed such champions as Jack Kramer. He was also a member of the Davis Cup Committee and of the Organizing Committee for the Eighth Winter Olympic Games at Squaw Valley, California.

Especially interested in baseball, Taylor involved himself closely in the effort to bring a major league team to Los Angeles. Once the Dodgers had moved west from Brooklyn in 1958, Union helped to build Dodger Stadium and then sponsored the team on radio and television. The company also sponsored broadcasts of football, hockey, tennis, thoroughbred racing, and sports educational programs. Taylor, however, adamantly refused to have anything to do with boxing.

In the end, Taylor had lived up to his own standards of a good manager. "A business," he said, "is a going concern that we are morally obligated to hand over intact, if not improved, to the next generation." The growth of Union Oil Company from 1938 to 1962 was a clear measure of Reese Taylor's success.

5

The War Years

When Reese Taylor stepped into the presidency of Union Oil in late 1938, the world was poised for war. Opposite: After the bombing of Pearl Harbor, government troops — in World War I helmets — were posted to guard oil fields, tank farms, and refineries. Concern about enemy sabotage ran high.

When Press St. Clair retired as Union's president in 1938, following a serious automobile accident, he left a company that seemed to be marching briskly out of the Depression. Earnings and production were on the increase, and St. Clair had recently reported that "both domestic gasoline sales and offshore shipment of crude were the highest on record." Union explorationists reached out into new territories, and deep drilling added millions of barrels to the company's reserves.

The situation, however, was not as bright as it might have appeared to outsiders. St. Clair's insistence on paying dividends during the Depression had, in fact, drawn down the company's financial reserves, now much needed for expansion. His emphasis on cost cutting and belt tightening had been accomplished at the expense of refining operations that were sorely in need of rebuilding and modernization. And despite increased sales, Union's position versus its competitors in both the West Coast and world markets had slipped alarmingly.

At the same time, St. Clair's explosive, desk-pounding style masked an inability to manage his own senior executives, who maintained their power over semi-independent fiefdoms within the company by ignoring the president. They went directly to the board of directors for approval of their own projects. As a result, the executives were not united behind any coordinated strategy for the company as a whole.

With St. Clair's retirement, these factional differences came to a head. Clearly, Union needed a strong and decisive hand at the helm. Some directors and many stockholders held high hopes for founder Lyman Stewart's two grandsons, Bill and Art, who had worked their way up to responsible positions in the company. Bill Stewart was vice president in charge of manufacturing. Arthur Stewart had demonstrated a strong aptitude for sales and was in the marketing department. Some internal cliques, however, opposed a new Stewart administration, and the Stewart family was no longer in a position to control the company — which they made no attempt to do, in any case.

Unable to agree on an inside candidate for president, the directors began to look outside the company. Director William S. Charnley finally ended the impasse. At a board meeting, he had a sudden inspiration. He is sitting at this table, Charnley thought and promptly conducted an off-the-record poll of the other directors. Nearly all agreed: Reese Taylor was the man.

Taylor, 38 years old and the president of Consolidated Steel Company, had been elected to the Union Oil board a year earlier. He had no experience as an

Left, the Los Angeles refinery. Reese Taylor instituted a rebuilding program at Union's refineries in 1939, none too soon given the demands that war placed on American industry. By the end of 1942, Union doubled its production of aviation gasoline. Below: In 1943, Taylor (dark hat) and Bill Stewart (right) inspected new facilities with Los Angeles refinery manager Percy H. Wilson.

oilman, but he was intrigued by the business — an indigenous California industry and not the western adjunct of an eastern industry, like steel. Needless to say, the announcement that Reese Taylor was to be the next president of Union took the oil business by surprise.

On his very first day at work — October 24, 1938 — Taylor began to give strong direction to the company. As someone remembered later, "things began to happen fast." Cy Rubel, director of production, was in his office early that day, working on a knotty exploration problem. When the intercom buzzed at 7:45, Rubel ignored it; but after the third buzz, he flipped the switch and said, "Who in the hell is it and what do you want?"

"This is Reese Taylor," a voice replied. "Where is everybody? I want to talk with somebody who can tell me something about the oil business."

For Union employees, that day marked the beginning of a new era. Managers quickly sensed that 7:45 now began the workday; before the week was out, they were arriving at their desks before Taylor reached his. The five-man executive committee — which for years had met once a week to decide on leases, purchases, and other urgent matters — took on greater importance, according to Art Stewart. The committee — made up of Taylor, Rubel, treasurer Harold W. Sanders, Bill Stewart, and Art Stewart — gathered every morning at ten o'clock to discuss the problems of the day. This gave Taylor the benefit of combined years of expertise in all facets of the oil industry.

Suddenly, decisions came faster. Field representatives were in a better position to compete for leases since they didn't have to wait so long for an okay from management. To speed the process even more, decision-making was passed down the chain of command to superintendents in the field, who were expected to understand their operations better than executives in the office.

Although Taylor pretended it was the start of his education in the industry (learning the oil business from "the top down," as he put it), he was well aware of the situation at Union. He knew how badly new facilities were needed; of Union's five refineries, only three — at Oleum, Wilmington (Los Angeles), and Bakersfield — actually turned out products.

Taylor had absorbed a great deal of inside information during his year as a director. He understood the politics of the company, including the penchant of some old-time managers to go their own way. Union's new president, armed with an agreement from the board allowing him to proceed without interference, simply ordered an end to these independent actions. Most department

heads cooperated and settled into the new routine. Others, like Robert D.
Matthews, resisted and were eased out.

Born and educated in Wales, Matthews had been brought into Union as a
young accountant by John Garrigues in 1913. Matthews survived Garrigues'
short tenure and went on to become Union's youngest director at the age of 27.
He first made his mark by modernizing Union's accounting practices. Later, he
became head of manufacturing operations, then head of distribution, and finally
executive vice president.

Under St. Clair, Matthews had adopted a high-handed style of operation,
going around the president and directly to the board to get approval for his
projects. He tried the same tactic with Taylor but overplayed his hand. Taylor
reminded the board that he had accepted the Union presidency with the understanding that he would have the power to eliminate inside factions. Then Taylor
called Matthews in and asked him to resign. Matthews and several of his supporters left the company early in 1939.

"We got a team under Reese," Bill Stewart said later. "That was a real revolution in the company."

The company was sorely in need of a revolution. It enabled Union Oil to
adjust to the significant changes that were occurring throughout the oil industry.
The hard-bitten, seat-of-the-pants characters of the oil patch were steadily being
replaced by college-educated scientists, engineers, and technicians. Petroleum
was becoming a high-technology industry.

By the end of the 1930s, explorationists had made most of the easy finds,
and inventive researchers came up with new ways to seek and drill for oil.
Innovative developments in drilling and well-logging technology, as well
as in reservoir management, enabled companies to squeeze more oil out of a
particular field. Not only could drillers probe deeper, routinely reaching depths
of 10,000 feet or more, but new devices and techniques allowed multiple well
completions from one site. Exploration, drilling, and production began to move
offshore into shallow coastal waters.

While economic conditions improved in the late 1930s, the oil business
endured yet another cycle of overproduction, intensified by the discoveries of
huge fields in East Texas. In Southern California, the opening of the prodigious
new Wilmington field added to the glut.

The real competition, however, began to occur in manufacturing. Consumers demanded higher octane, antiknock gasoline, while advances in airplane
engines created an expanding market for 100-octane aviation fuel. Refiners found
better ways to transform crude oil through the use of catalytic crackers, rearranging hydrocarbon molecules into high-value fuels and other products. The inven-

"Truth conquers all" was the motto over the entrance of the building at the Los Angeles refinery that served as the company's research headquarters from 1922 until 1951. In the 1930s, the first 76 gasoline and remarkable Triton motor oil were developed here. More powerful fuels and improved lubricants followed in the 1940s. When the structure was demolished in 1984, the cartouche bearing the motto was moved to the company's research center in Brea, California.

tion of polymer 66 (nylon) and synthetic rubber in the mid-1930s heralded the beginning of the petrochemical age.

A quick survey showed Reese Taylor how far Union had fallen behind. True, the research and manufacturing division, under Bill Stewart's direction, had been productive. Stewart's team of eager young technicians had come up with ways to make more power-packed gasolines and better lubricants, and had developed a remarkable new all-purpose, barium-based grease called Unoba, which replaced scores of specialized greases in the automotive and industrial fields. But the research staff itself was jammed into outdated laboratories at the Los Angeles refinery and other nearby rented space.

In fact, many of Union's facilities — upstream and downstream — sorely needed to be rebuilt. Nearly half of the company's 1,200 producing wells, most of them in California, were shut down, partly because of overproduction — but also because refining and transportation facilities proved inadequate to handle the potential output of crude.

As a measure of the company's lagging efficiency in manufacturing, Union refineries had to process 13 percent of California's crude in order to produce only 7 percent of its gasoline. A Chase National Bank analysis of 30 petroleum corporations revealed that, on the average, an oil company spent 16.6 percent of its

total investment on refinery facilities. With Union's investment at only 8.3 percent, the company was losing market share to rivals who had built modern catalytic cracking units.

Taylor asked Union's department heads to come up with estimates on the
cost of completely rehabilitating the company's facilities. The total came to $73
million—at least $30 million more than the Union treasury could raise, even
after cutting dividends and drawing on amortization funds. "We'll have to go to
New York for the thirty million," Taylor told the board of directors. Less than six
months after becoming Union's president, he went east to talk to investment
brokers— "to wildcat for millions of dollars."

Taylor visited Dillon Read & Company, the investment brokers who had
handled some of Union's previous financing. He discussed Union's financial situation with Dillon Read president James E. Forrestal, who, a decade later, would
become U.S. Secretary of Defense. Forrestal called in Frederic H. Brandi (later
president of Dillon Read and a Union director), and together they reviewed the
financial markets. Taylor asked not only for money to carry out Union's ambitious modernization program, but also for funds to redeem $10 million worth of
debentures and $8 million worth of bonds, due to mature early in 1942.

Forrestal suggested that Union take advantage of lower interest rates by
offering $30 million worth of 3 percent debentures. But, Forrestal pointed out,
"the trouble is that the eastern analysts don't know anything about Union Oil
and its potential. You'll have to tell them." Forrestal and Brandi organized a
series of meetings with 30 analysts and financial counselors. Union Oil's new
president told the story of the company's beginnings half a century earlier, of
how it had grown and prospered, and what its aggressive plans would mean for
the future.

Taylor's enthusiasm and conviction about Union Oil's prospects intrigued
the financiers, and Dillon Read structured a syndicate of 25 underwriters to handle the offering. Investors snapped up the $30 million worth of debentures
almost immediately. Taylor applied $20 million to retire prior obligations that
carried higher interest rates. The balance was added to the modernization fund
for the company's refining and transportation facilities.

Reese Taylor's rebuilding program, which got underway in 1939, marked
a significant turning point in the company's history. Union stepped out
of the defensive stance of the Depression years and moved forward
aggressively. One sign of the changing times was the replacement of the old
Provident Fund (started by Will Stewart on behalf of the employees in 1923) by
the Employees' Retirement Fund. Changed conditions in the late 1930s, along
with the enactment of the Federal Social Security Act, made a new plan administered by an insurance company more desirable. The assets of the Provident
Fund, including 213,350 shares of Union Oil, were distributed to employee members of the old fund.

The relentless search for more oil in new places continued, and Cy Rubel,
vice president for exploration and production, made a fateful decision in early
1939. He sent Union's veteran geologist Sam Grinsfelder to Texas to conduct a feasibility study of the entire region—including Texas, Louisiana, and
Mississippi. Grinsfelder was not long in reporting back. On May 19, he wrote to
Rubel sketching out the geological features of West Texas and the Gulf Coast
and assessing the prospects for finding and producing oil. Based on past performance, Grinsfelder said, West Texas oil was cheaper to find but of poorer quality
than Gulf Coast crude. But Gulf Coast oil, even with its higher exploration
costs, had a shorter payout schedule and was closer to marine terminals.

Grinsfelder estimated that it would cost $5,600 a month to maintain an

exploration office in Houston, and $2,300 to keep a branch office in Midland,
Texas. His recommendation: Drill on the Gulf Coast. He opened an office in
Houston with three geologists and a landman. The company should be prepared
for a few dry holes, he warned, but the first four wildcats struck oil.

By 1940, as Union began its second half-century, the company had moved
far beyond the most ambitious dreams of its founders. No longer family-owned,
Union belonged to more than 27,000 shareholders. Union's refineries processed
69,000 barrels of crude a day. The company's net crude oil production was
41,000 barrels per day. Although more than 500 wells were shut in due to the
persistent glut of crude on the West Coast, Union continued to add to its reserves
with the discovery of vast new pools under the Louisiana tidelands.

In December 1938, Union had launched its first new tanker in 16 years and
the largest to date — the 103,000-barrel *L.P. St. Clair.* Its sister ship, the *Victor H.
Kelly,* was launched in 1939. These tankers represented important economies in
transportation costs as Union continued to rebuild.

In marketing, vice president Art Stewart moved to consolidate and reorganize in 1940. The marketing area, which had shrunk during the Depression, was
expanded from the coastal states into Arizona, Utah, and Idaho. Union products
were sold in more than 5,000 retail outlets, including 470 company-operated
service stations.

Even though domestic sales volumes increased as the nation's industries
recovered from the Depression, low prices for gasoline and fuel oil cut into
Union's revenues. Union's export sales were also down, disrupted as Japan exercised its imperialistic ambitions against China and the Soviet Union. Company
sales dropped from $83 million in 1937 to $72 million in 1940.

The L.P. St. Clair's keel was laid in a Maryland shipyard in April 1938, and the tanker was launched eight months later. With a capacity of 103,000 barrels, it was the company's largest tanker — and the first built since 1922. _Center right:_ In March 1939, two months before he retired, Union chairman St. Clair followed a seafaring tradition when he presented his portrait to ship's captain Hans Halvorsen.

The New York Times.

Copyright. 1941 by The New York Times Company.

VOL. XCI No. 30,634.   Entered as Second-Class Matter, Postoffice, New York, N. Y.   NEW YORK, MONDAY, DECEMBER 8, 1941.   THREE CENTS NEW YORK CITY and vicinity

JAPAN WARS ON U. S. AND BRITAIN; MAKES SUDDEN ATTACK ON HAWAII; HEAVY FIGHTING AT SEA REPORTED

CONGRESS DEC... ...OKYO ACTS FIRST   ...AM BOMBED; ARMY SHIP IS SUNK

Meanwhile, the modernization of Union's manufacturing division continued in 1940. At the Los Angeles refinery, a new alkylation plant neared completion; it was designed to use sulfuric acid as a catalyst to convert by-product gases into blending stocks for the production of 100-octane aviation gasoline. A new polymerization plant at Oleum also converted by-product gases into gasoline blending stocks. Other state-of-the-art units were either in the engineering stage or under construction.

Taylor was a strong supporter of research: "Income appropriated for research is not spent," he declared, "it is invested." The board of directors agreed and authorized funds to build modern laboratories and strengthen the research staff.

As international conflict spread in Europe and the Pacific in 1941, Union refineries stepped up their output of 100-octane aviation gasoline to fuel the war planes that rolled out of the aircraft factories at an accelerating rate. On December 7 that year, the Japanese attacked Pearl Harbor, triggering U.S. entry into World War II. Union, like other oil companies, immediately became part of the war industry.

"We recognize the prior claim of the government upon all the petroleum products the company is capable of producing," Taylor said in a message to Union employees. "So long as the war lasts, supplying government needs must be the company's first responsibility."

Taylor spelled out clearly the company's priorities: "There are two great jobs confronting us. First, to meet the acid test of all-out war production to fulfill all of the demands being placed upon us. The second, to do such a good job in this respect that the American system of free enterprise will never again be threatened.

"The fact that mechanized warfare is dependent upon petroleum places great responsibility upon the oil industry," he said. "The government has asked us to quadruple production of 100-octane aviation gasoline during the next year. Vast quantities of petroleum fuels, lubricants, and technical products of all kinds are required by the armed forces and war industries. Union Oil is doing its utmost to aid the war effort and to carry its allotted share of the staggering task laid upon the nation."

Despite the wartime shortage of materials, Union was able to complete the refinery units already under construction. To boost production further, a small refinery, shut down for many years, was also reopened. By the end of 1942, the company not only produced more crude oil than ever before in its history, but Union refineries managed to double their production of aviation gasoline.

Manufacturing still couldn't keep up with demand for products, and other plants had to be built. In January of that year, Taylor had gone to New York again to raise another $15 million; the debentures were quickly sold by the same

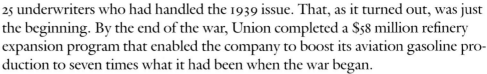

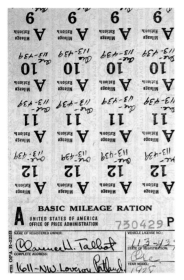

Above: Ration tickets for gasoline and other vital commodities were issued to U.S. citizens during the war. Opposite, below: A soldier strained against heavy fuel hoses to fill a storage tank; petroleum products accounted for 6.5 of every 10 tons of supplies the U.S. shipped to its troops overseas. Left: A P-38 Lightning fighter (top) flew escort for a B-17 bomber. Below right: A poster paralleled a soldier and a riveter to demonstrate the importance of industry efforts in support of the armed forces.

25 underwriters who had handled the 1939 issue. That, as it turned out, was just the beginning. By the end of the war, Union completed a $58 million refinery expansion program that enabled the company to boost its aviation gasoline production to seven times what it had been when the war began.

In 1942, Taylor temporarily slipped back into his role as a steel man. Because of his previous experience, he was called to Washington to head the Iron and Steel Division of the War Production Board. His tour of duty lasted only six months, but later in the war he was called again — as an oilman — to set up a fuels and lubricants section for the army.

Reese Taylor returned to private industry highly frustrated by his service in Washington, D.C. He was especially upset about what he perceived as government's lack of comprehension about the business world. "Businessmen have so much trouble in Washington primarily because the government people don't understand what makes business function," he declared.

Only a year earlier, Taylor had stated in his annual report to shareholders: "Threats of legislation prescribing federal control, or requiring divorcement of transportation and marketing operations, are disquieting influences....While the need of a certain degree of regulation is recognized, the management believes that the best interests of the public, stockholders, and employees will be served if business enterprises are permitted, and encouraged, to operate without unnecessary regulation."

Taylor decided he could help not only Union but business in general by explaining how free enterprise worked, and he proceeded to earmark a sizable portion of Union's print media advertising budget to do the job.

The first ad, which appeared early in 1943, explained that the free enterprise system maximized economic productivity, and that large corporations like Union Oil played a critical role in the overall economic prosperity of the nation. As more ads followed, the free enterprise message became so popular with the public that Union published the series in a book, *How and Why American Business Functions,* which ran through a dozen editions. The ads also helped sell products — a pleasant surprise to the Union marketing people who had resisted this institutional approach to advertising.

Meanwhile, the war consumed prodigious amounts of petroleum, both as fuels and lubricating oils, and in other forms: plastics, synthetic fabrics, and

GIVE 'EM

BOTH BARRELS

Top left: Rubber was recycled during the war, since rubber imports were disrupted. Top right: Union's storage tanks in Torrance, south of Los Angeles, were camouflaged against Japanese air raids — a genuine fear on the West Coast. Center left: In 1942, "Ike" sent Union employees a note of thanks in the midst of the North Africa campaign. Center right: New York schoolchildren showed off tin cans they collected for recycling. Right: Even before the U.S. entered the war, the armed forces were engaged in defensive maneuvers — often fueled by Union Oil products.

WOMEN ON THE HOMEFRONT
World War II scrambled the
social order in American industry. Women stepped into jobs
that had been generally held by
men. At Union Oil, young male
employees went off to distin-
guish themselves as officers,
fliers, and combat heroes. Many
women also served in the armed
forces, but many more stayed
home to do their patriotic duty
(and support their families) by
filling the jobs the men had left
behind. At Union 76 service stations, for example, the thinning
ranks of Minute Men were bolstered by smartly uniformed
women turned out in eight-day
training courses. A 1943 issue of
On Tour featured Margie Klotz,
a graduate of Union's first "Minute Maid" training class in 1942,
who was soon managing a
large station at the corner of
Crenshaw and Vernon in Los
Angeles. Lest she be thought
unfeminine, the article pointed
out that she still took time to
help her mother with house-
work and to go out on dates.
Other women replaced men as
barrel handlers, truck drivers,
loaders, lab inspectors, pipefit-
ters' helpers, and pumpers. While
most stepped aside for returning
servicemen at the end of the war,
the American work force would
never be quite the same again.

Top right: Remember the
Montebello! *became a Union*
slogan after the tanker was
torpedoed.

asphalt. A single armored division, for example, used 60,000 gallons of gasoline
daily to keep fighting.

Union's facilities, along with those of other oil companies, expanded to
meet the need. Transporting the oil to the front proved a tough, sometimes
dangerous job—particularly on the high seas. Slow-moving tankers, which more
often than not had to sail unescorted, were especially vulnerable with their
explosive loads. The Japanese attacked them in the Pacific, and German subma-
rines prowled the Gulf of Mexico, the Caribbean, and the Atlantic coastline,
sometimes sinking tankers within sight of shore.

After the attack on Pearl Harbor, Union's entire tanker fleet had been taken
over by the U.S. War Shipping Administration, which reassigned the tankers,
together with a score of government oil carriers, back to Union for operation.
Even before December 7, two Union tankers had been carrying British oil
between the Dutch West Indies and the Atlantic Coast; and three more had been
delivering petroleum products to the European Allies via the Soviet port of
Vladivostok and to American bases in the Pacific.

Within two weeks of the United States' declaration of war, Union felt the
enemy's fury. On December 21, 1941, the Union tanker *Montebello* finished loading at Avila on California's central coast and headed north toward Vancouver.
Two hours later, a Japanese submarine hit the tanker in the port side with a
torpedo. Surfacing, the submarine poured shells into the wallowing, smoking
ship as the tanker crew took to lifeboats. As the *Montebello* went down, its crew
pulled for shore under a hail of Japanese bullets. Miraculously, not a single crewman was wounded.

The crew of the tanker *Gurney E. Newlin,* commanded by Captain Herman
Dahlhof, was not as lucky. In 1943, it was torpedoed in the mid-Atlantic by a
German U-boat. Only 7 of the Union tanker's crew of 41 were saved.

The Union tanker fleet, augmented in early 1942 with two new 100,000-
barrel vessels, the *Paul M. Gregg* and the *A.C. Rubel,* sailed with distinction
throughout the war. Tankers bearing the big U insignia—for Union—on their
stacks kept the oil flowing to air corps fighters and bombers on island bases in the
Pacific and fed the tanks, trucks, and bulldozers of the army, air corps, and marines.

Union tankers also filled navy bunkers from Australia to Guam, Saipan,
Manila, Okinawa, Iwo Jima, and finally Tokyo. These ships maintained a vital
link between the refineries and high-speed navy tankers, which in turn refueled
combat ships on the move. It was this kind of supply chain that gave warships

the mobility to finally defeat the Japanese fleet. Admiral Chester W. Nimitz, in a personal citation to Union's tanker *La Placentia* for outstanding service in directly fueling combat ships at Majuro Atoll, called the American tanker fleet "one of our greatest secret weapons."

During the war, Union Oil people handled more petroleum than ever before. Beginning early in the conflict, in what became known as "Operation roll out the barrels," the company filled and secretly shipped up to 4,800 drums of gasoline a day from a special plant at Pittsburg, California, on San Francisco Bay. Altogether, Union people filled 862,000 barrels with 46 million gallons of gasoline to supply the critical landings in the Pacific.

By 1942, the company increased its crude oil production to more than 50,000 barrels per day, up from 41,000 in 1940. Grinsfelder's work in the Gulf Coast area had paid off with discoveries in the Vinton and Freshwater Bayou fields in Louisiana. Under the pressure of wartime demands, the company quadrupled the yield from these fields in a single year. In August 1943, Union wildcatters brought in their first discovery well in Texas — the forerunner of what was to become the highly productive West Texas Division.

As pressure for more oil mounted in 1944, Union's directors decided to buy the Glacier Production Company of Montana. Once again, Taylor had to raise money — this time $12 million in long-term loans from several banks — both to make the acquisition and for additional funds for general use.

Glacier was worth the price. Union acquired 90,000 acres of producing properties in what was at the time the most productive oil field in Montana. Glacier's new refinery and natural gasoline plant at Cut Bank, Montana, along with a distribution system, were also part of the package. As a result of this deal, Union gained an additional 2,700 barrels of crude oil a day from 172 wells and increased the company's potential reserves by 20 million barrels.

Another move to increase oil production did not turn out as well. In 1944, after lengthy negotiations with Paraguay, Union gained the rights to explore for oil in the 55-million-acre Chaco concession, an area half the size of California. Wildcatting this vast tract was an adventure for Union explorationists, who could reach the area only by airplane using overgrown landing strips left over from the Chaco War that Paraguay had fought with Bolivia in the early 1930s. But Union failed to find oil in commercial quantities.

Oil from producing fields was rushed to the refineries as fast as it came out

Top left: In June 1944, the Spirit of 76 *was christened. The B-17 cost $350,000 and was paid for by Union Oil employees' purchases of war bonds. The company magazine speculated about the plane's assignment, saying: "The wallop she packs will sound just as good against Hitler's chin as against Hirohito's." Above: Discoveries in Louisiana during the war years helped Union increase its production of crude oil.*

THE SECRET OF THE BARRELS

During World War II, invasions were highly mechanized with tanks, trucks, and jeeps gulping vast quantities of fuel. To keep them going required thousands of barrels of high-octane gasoline, rolled ashore from landing craft in the thick of battle. In 1943, the U.S. Army asked Union Oil Company to set up a secret barreling facility to help handle this huge demand. Two veteran Union engineers, R.C. Nichols and Fred C. Barr, supervised the design and construction of the plant in Pittsburg, California, along the eastern reaches of San Francisco Bay. J.V. Cox took charge of the new facility, which filled 4,800 barrels a day at peak levels. The empty 53-gallon barrels moved on conveyor belts to a five-acre stockpile area, then through inspection, filling, and capping stations. An innovative engineering feat, the barreling operation got the job done efficiently with a minimum of human muscle at a time when workers were scarce. Secrecy was critical, because the bursts of activity at the barreling plant presaged each of the historic invasions in the Pacific theater, including Hollandia, Saipan, Guam, Leyte, Luzon, Iwo Jima, and Okinawa. By the time the public (and most Union employees) learned about the operation at the end of the war, the Pittsburg plant site had been swept clean of every building, conveyor, pipeline, and valve, having filled 862,000 barrels with nearly 46 million gallons of gasoline.

U.S. forces used Iwo Jima as a base for raids against the Japanese, and the beach became littered with oil drums.

of the ground. Oil companies used all the equipment available; they had no choice but to work rigs to the point of collapse, since construction materials needed for repairs were diverted to war use. During one period, priority controls over critical materials, such as oil-well casing and pipe, forced Union to cut field development by half.

In Los Angeles, a giant "cat cracker" — a unique kind of catalytic converter that used new refining methods to increase gasoline yields — started up in mid-1944. With this and other new units at the Los Angeles refinery, Union was able to increase the production of urgently needed aviation gasoline fivefold over what it had been in 1942.

Rising 268 feet, as high as a 20-story building, the new cat cracker was impressive. The catalytic cracking process itself represented a revolution in petroleum refining. Unlike the prevailing thermal cracking method, which simply heated up the charge of oil so that each product could be drawn off as it vaporized, cat cracking passed vaporized oil over pellets of activated clay (zeolites) at extremely high temperatures. This not only efficiently produced a higher volume of more light-end products from a barrel of crude, it also delivered cleaner burning gasoline with higher octane ratings.

The zeolite pellets themselves were extremely porous, which meant they had an incredibly large surface area for their size. In fact, the 2.2 million pounds of pellets that made seven round-trips a day through the new cat cracker tower had a surface area equal to that of the entire state of California!

As the war came to an end in 1945, 330 Union employees were mustered out of the service to return home. Piles of abandoned oil drums on invasion beaches from Normandy to Iwo Jima and thousands of miles of pipeline constructed at record speeds were testimony to the herculean job done by oil company teams to keep the Allied forces moving. In his final victory report, Chief of Staff General George Marshall wrote, "No plane has failed to fly, no ship has failed to sail, for lack of oil."

76
UNION
76
UNION
UNION
IL DEALER
ROYAL TRITON
America's Finest Motor Oil

6

The Big Independent

Under Reese Taylor's leadership, Union grew to meet the demands of war and the economic boom that followed. Opposite: An early fifties service station in Pasadena, California, was one of a growing network of Union outlets throughout the West.

As World War II came to an end, Reese Taylor took stock of Union Oil's position and saw a company poised on the brink of spectacular growth. Union had greater crude oil reserves than when the war began; its pipeline systems were strategically located; its tanker fleet was back from wartime service. The company's refineries, upgraded to fulfill the enormous requirements of the armed forces, were prepared to meet the pent-up demand of an expanding civilian economy that had been operating under wartime restrictions for nearly four years.

Union had modernized its facilities at a cost of $58 million — funds obtained from bank loans and from Taylor's wildcatting for money through the sale of debentures. In mid-1945, a few weeks before the Japanese surrendered, Taylor's plan for restructuring the debt, which had earlier been approved by shareholders, was put into effect. On June 25, 1945, the company issued and sold 250,000 preferred shares and $25 million in 25 year debentures.

Taking advantage of low, postwar interest rates, the company retired its 1944 bank loans, obtained primarily to renovate the refineries, and the outstanding balance of debentures it had issued in 1939. With these actions, Taylor reduced Union's long-term debt by $13.7 million and increased the company's cash resources by $10 million.

One department had, of necessity, been neglected during the war years. Marketing had little opportunity to enlarge its operations while the government and the military were the company's prime customers. As the war ended, Art Stewart, vice president of marketing since 1940, launched an aggressive sales and service campaign. Union signs displaying the 76 logo sprouted in more and more locations around the western states. Stewart staffed his sales department with the best people he could recruit from leading universities, and those selected underwent intensive training in the research and refining departments before actually joining the marketing team. Union's annual sales increased 500 percent over the next decade.

Art Stewart also changed the company's relationship with its dealers. "Believing that an independent businessman operating his own station would have a more personal interest in the business and produce excellent sales results, we leased out the majority of the company's service stations," Stewart explained. "We retained only a few for personnel training and to test merchandising and operating procedures. Then we backed the independent operators with aggressive advertising and the finest of products." The leasing program provided

excellent business opportunities for servicemen returning to civilian life.

Among the products the independent Union Oil merchant had to sell were an improved Triton motor oil, a line of Unoba greases, and an improved aviation-type gasoline. Royal Triton, a new, purple-hued motor oil containing a detergent, became an outstanding success. It not only held up longer in car engines, it successfully counteracted rust, corrosion, and oxidation.

A new unit at the Oleum refinery increased the production of Triton and Royal Triton motor oils. This opened the way for Art Stewart's marketing department to push into East Coast markets — a satisfying irony for a West Coast company. While eastern motor oils had captured nearly 80 percent of the western lubricant market in the early 1930s, Union had fought back by developing a process for making a competitive western motor oil. By 1950, Stewart was able to report that Union's superior products — Royal Triton and others — were being sold not only on the East Coast but in every state in the nation, as well as in Canada, Cuba, and other countries.

In 1947, a survey of motorists in Los Angeles, San Francisco, Portland, and Seattle revealed that 82 out of every 100 gasoline buyers readily identified the 76 as Union's symbol. This was a larger percentage by far than were able to identify any other oil company's trademark, and it prompted Union's attorneys to make another attempt to register the 76 trademark with the U.S. Patent Office. This time they were able to convince patent officials, although certification took almost three years.

By 1948, Union produced more crude oil than ever before — more than 74,000 barrels per day. The refineries ran at full capacity to help maintain the

Art Stewart launched an aggressive sales campaign in 1946. Opposite: At a meeting for 76 dealers, Reese Taylor (in hat) called a quick conference with his sales management team—from left, Art Stewart, W.M. Sopher, George S. Smith, and Roy Linden. Opposite, below: Royal Triton 10-30, introduced in 1957, was one of several improvements on the original product. Below right: In 1947, Union's chief automotive engineer Earl Cooper gave Royal Triton a thorough test. His teams of drivers took just 30 days to rack up 30,000 miles on new stock model cars—like the Cadillac shown—with no oil changes.

company's 15 percent share of the western retail market. At the same time, drilling technology had advanced, and rigs had become more complex and expensive. A gusher, once a welcome symbol of success, was now an embarrassing indication of waste and incompetence. Oil wells, according to one driller, were brought in so carefully that he could go to work in his Sunday clothes.

In the old days, drillers had been proud of the way they could push a hole straight down. But slant drilling or "whipstocking," perfected in the mid-1930s, became the rule in the 1940s, with crews angling wells toward predetermined underground targets with great accuracy. From 6 to 20 wells could be spudded in from a single "island," the term used to describe an area where drilling sites were bulldozed or constructed.

Evolving technology brought about changes in the way Union conducted its drilling program. At one time Union owned and operated more than 40 "strings of tools," as drilling rigs were known in the early days. But with the cost of some huge modern drilling rigs ranging as high as $6 million, it became more economical in the 1940s to have the work done by independent contractors. Drilling, however, was still expensive. Contracting companies often charged thousands of dollars a day for their crews and equipment—so a scientifically drilled well could cost a million dollars or more.

Union's explorationists felt the pressure to keep dry hole costs to a minimum, and they proved highly successful. The company's reserves—depleted by record wartime production—increased by millions of barrels in the decade after the war. Using the latest seismic techniques, the explorationists used explosive charges to set off miniature, manmade "earthquakes" looking for possible underground indications of oil traps along the Gulf of Mexico and in West Texas, New Mexico, Oklahoma, Kansas, Montana, and North Dakota. In 1948 Union, with two other oil companies, began a seismic survey offshore the California coast between Los Angeles and Santa Barbara.

The bulk of the company's reserves were in California, and they had been found by the early wildcatters without benefit of modern scientific exploration technology. Amazingly, nearly 60 years after Lyman Stewart founded Union Oil Company, almost 40 percent of the company's production still came from the properties he had acquired.

Just as World War II ended, Union made a remarkable discovery, literally in its own backyard some 20 miles from the Los Angeles refinery. In 1903, Lyman

Above: Before the decade of the 1950s was out, Reese Taylor (left) chose Cy Rubel to succeed him as president. Left: When Union developed the Sansinena field east of Los Angeles after World War II, the company soundproofed its rigs and installed production equipment in low-lying areas to help pre-serve the rural character of the neighborhood.

Stewart's extraordinary nose for oil had led him to buy all mineral rights on the 3,400-acre Sansinena tract, which lay east of Whittier at the edge of the prodi-gious Los Angeles basin. Stewart had tramped over it, smelling oil and observ-ing it seep out of the hillsides. As usual, he made the purchase and told his fellow directors about it later.

Because of a lack of funds, the exploration department was able to drill only one well, which was abandoned after a series of accidents. In the ensuing 40 years, while Union was busy in other places, subdividers sold off surface rights on the tract, and the once wild and wooded landscape was covered with small farms, avocado orchards, and housing developments.

In the early 1940s, Union's exploration department wanted to drill a test well on the tract. The homeowners, however, were angered by the prospect of drilling and voted to prohibit oil derricks. Even though Union still held the mineral rights, any attempt to exercise them probably would have set off a long, drawn-out legal battle.

Union's geologists were divided as to whether a discovery was likely on the tract, but Cy Rubel took the optimistic view and prevailed. Before drilling began, Union's landmen called on the property owners, offering to pay

On July 12, 1952, the tankers
Victor H. Kelly and *Lompoc*
were unloading crude oil for
Union's Oleum (San Fran-
cisco) refinery at the outer
wharf in Carquinez Strait just
before noon, when a fire broke
out at a light-oil loading mani-
fold on the pier. The flames
moved swiftly under the wharf
and onto the *Kelly,* which was
nearly empty and about to sail.
Within 12 minutes, the tanker's
forward tanks exploded, damaging the *Lompoc,* which was half
unloaded. Oleum fire fighters
were joined by hundreds of
employees and other volunteers.
The burning vessels churned
away full astern, attempting to
break their mooring lines. The
Lompoc succeeded and, in open
water, was saved. After 16 hours,
the fires were out. Three of the
Kelly's crew were dead, including the captain, who had
collapsed with a heart attack.
Union honored 15 seamen for
their courage—among them,
67-year-old Torsten Fischer. A
retired Union Oil captain then
working as a docking master,
he took over command for
the *Kelly's* fallen master in
the midst of the disaster.
When forced overboard by fire,
Fischer swam to a tug and
returned to the inferno to help
pick up survivors. The losses
topped $3 million. When the
wharf was rebuilt, it was made
of concrete—not wood—and
was lengthened to accommodate two supertankers and five
barges at once.

Top right: The oil tanker
Victor H. Kelly *was lost in an
explosion and fire at the Oleum
wharf in 1952.*

royalties on any oil produced in the area—even though Union owned the
mineral rights outright. The exploration department promised to drill from
carefully selected islands hidden out of sight deep in the canyons and to
sheathe its drilling rigs to muffle the noise. Finally convinced, the homeowners withdrew their objections.

The first well, completed in 1945, was a duster, as were the next two. But
the fourth well tapped a reservoir of oil a mile beneath the surface. Field production rose to 5,000 barrels per day in 1952 and peaked in 1957 at more than
11,000—fully 10 percent of Union's total California production.

Cy Rubel's team carefully camouflaged the wells, locating the drilling
islands sparingly and whipstocking as many as 20 wells from each drill site.
When members of a women's club protested that the oil activity had ruined the
countryside, Rubel himself drove them through the Sansinena field. He offered
to buy a new hat for anyone who could spot an oil well, but none of the
women could claim the prize.

While the explorationists continued to find oil, the researchers developed an array of new fuels and other petroleum products—including
many for the burgeoning petrochemical industry. Union's profit margins depended more and more on wringing the higher value products and feedstocks out of a barrel of oil. Therefore, it was to the company's advantage to
find more high-gravity oil, which produced higher yields of gasoline and other
light-end products worth more than fuel oils in the marketplace. Unfortunately,
heavy California crudes—yielding a higher proportion of fuel oils—were still
the major part of Union's production.

In 1949, the company seized the opportunity to obtain a valuable source
of high-gravity crude oil with the purchase of the Los Nietos Company. Owned
by the five grandchildren of Edward L. Doheny, who briefly had been a Union
director in 1903, Los Nietos held valuable producing acreage in California,
Texas, and Canada. The company's daily production was 7,500 barrels of crude
oil and its reserves were estimated to exceed 46 million barrels.

Union also purchased the production from several leases held by Mrs.
Carrie Estelle Doheny. These lands in the San Joaquin Valley—mainly in the
Coalinga Nose, Pleasant Valley, and Guijarral Hills fields—gave Union another
6,000 barrels a day of high-gravity oil.

As the decade of the 1950s began, Union Oil was operating in a rapidly
changing market. In a dozen years, demographers predicted, California would

pass New York as the most populous state in the nation. The population boom in the western states brought with it a growing number of automobiles, airplanes, tractors, trucks, and diesel engines, all with ravenous appetites for gasoline and oil.

But while the demand for gasoline soared, the use of fuel oil declined. Industrial plants were converting to natural gas, some piped in from as far as Texas. Railroads had switched to diesels, and the navy cut back on its fuel oil purchases. With storage tanks filled to capacity, Union was forced to shut in more than 20,000 barrels a day of production. At the same time, it started shipping fuel oil to East Coast markets again. Competitors followed suit.

In 1950, Taylor reassured the company's more than 35,000 shareholders: "The current situation of oversupply is not new or unique. In the long pull, these situations tend to be self-corrective." The situation, in fact, corrected itself in a shorter time than Taylor might have imagined. Within weeks, the Korean War had begun, and the navy clamored for more fuel oil for ships.

The end of World War II had marked the beginning of the greatest oil search in Union's history. It continued into the 1950s to fuel the demands of an expanding industrial economy. Union's explorationists ranged the globe looking for new finds, traveling to Texas, Louisiana, Canada, Argentina, Central America, the Sahara Desert, and Alaska, among other areas.

To give company explorationists a technological leg up in their search for petroleum resources, Union bought the United Geophysical Company of Pasadena in 1950. United Geophysical had been founded by Herbert Hoover, Jr., who joined Union's board of directors with the purchase of his company. Hoover continued to direct seismic crews mapping underground formations from Borneo to Saudi Arabia.

Unexpectedly, the acquisition of United Geophysical made Union Oil a copper producer in a modest way when the company's geophysicists found a huge ore body in Pima County, Arizona. Union subsequently sold a majority interest in this strike to the Cyprus Mines Corporation and Utah Construction Company.

Through United Geophysical, Union operated its own seismic survey operations until 1954, when Hoover resigned to become undersecretary of state in

Above: Arabella Mays, aged 87, asked Union pipeliners to go around the oak tree she had played under as a child, and they complied. The line, completed in the mid-1950s, ran 225 miles from the San Joaquin Valley to Oleum. Left, a 1950s rush-hour traffic jam on the Hollywood (then Cahuenga) Freeway. Automobiles and the freeways that were built to accommodate them shaped the urban sprawl that came to characterize Los Angeles.

Left, a typical Union tank truck in the late 1940s. *Above:* In 1955, Union introduced two new higher octane gasolines — in designer colors: purple for Royal 76 and orange for 7600. Union service stations proliferated in the 1940s and 1950s: *top,* corner of Lakewood and Carson, Long Beach, California, 1955; *center,* corner of Portola and Woodside, San Francisco, 1948; *bottom,* Great Falls, Montana, 1946.

Left: Union helped pioneer off-shore California drilling as a participant in the CUSS 1 project in the 1950s. *Below:* During the 1950s, Union began to explore the open waters of the Gulf of Mexico. *Opposite:* A swamp buggy was the required transportation for oil hunters in bayou country. *Opposite, bottom:* Discoveries in the murky onshore channels and lakes of Louisiana made Union a major producer in the Gulf area.

the Eisenhower administration. At that time, the subsidiary was purchased by its officers, but Union continued to contract for its services.

Cy Rubel and his exploration group remained convinced that there were large untapped reservoirs under the continental shelf off the coast of California. But the Pacific Ocean proved to be a far more difficult drilling environment than the calm, shallow waters of the Louisiana bayous. In 1953, Union teamed up with Continental, Shell, and Superior oil companies to convert a huge freight barge into a floating platform, one that could ride out the strong tides and currents offshore California. Dubbed CUSS 1, after the initials of the owner companies, it was outfitted with a derrick, drilling rig, and crews' quarters.

The monster vessel was anchored over promising drilling sites pinpointed by seismic surveys. Under the direction of Union's Robert Bauer, CUSS 1 drilled a total of 300,000 feet of exploratory hole off the California coast. In the summer of 1957, it pushed down six wells in 54 days, some of them beneath 1,000 feet of water. While the results were positive, the climate for offshore drilling was not. The question of whether the state or the federal government controlled the rights to offshore oil remained unresolved, and leasing activities became snarled in red tape. The venture was dissolved.

Union bought out its partners and formed a subsidiary, Global Marine Exploration Company, to capitalize on the expertise that had been developed by the CUSS 1 project in marine engineering and architecture, and oceanography. Global Marine built several other giant floating drilling platforms that explored for oil throughout the oceans of the world. One notable customer, the Project Mohole Group, wasn't interested in finding oil at all. It simply wanted to drill deep holes all the way through the earth's crust to find out what lay underneath. In 1964, Union sold its 80 percent interest back to Global Marine, which in turn offered its stock for public sale.

Union found enough oil around the world to maintain its reserves at about 500 million barrels throughout the 1950s, despite increases in production to fuel the postwar economy. The company doubled its natural gas reserves from 1.1 trillion cubic feet in 1949 to 2.2 trillion in 1956, and doubled them again to more than 4 trillion cubic feet by the end of the decade.

The most spectacular discoveries were made in the Gulf Region, particularly Louisiana, where Union's luck at oil and gas finding had run out after the war. Dudley Tower, then operations manager for the Gulf Division, promoted dis-

LOU

TEXAS

EAST WHITE

VERMILION BLOC

G U L

trict geologist Ray A. Burke to area geologist in New Orleans in late 1952. Burke had made a few discoveries for Union in Texas since joining the company in Corpus Christi in 1951. In Louisiana, one of the first properties he studied was East Lake Palourde. Tower favored farming out the acreage since Union had drilled a 12,000-foot dry hole near the site in 1942. But Burke persisted, and Union crews drilled the first well to almost 15,000 feet for 250 barrels of oil a day. Four more high-producing wells followed.

The East Lake Palourde field was a turning point for Union's Gulf operations, according to Burke. "The discovery gave the organization confidence," he said, "and the backing we needed from headquarters in Los Angeles."

Union's luck held 40 miles northwest at Big Bayou Pigeon field in the Atchafalaya swamp. The first well, drilled to 13,000 feet, came up dry, but the second came in at 600 barrels a day, and so did five more. Discoveries followed at Caillou Island and North Freshwater Bayou, and development drilling extended many other fields.

In the early 1950s, Ray Burke looked far beyond the bayous. "I pushed for offshore exploration," he said. "I could see — and it took no great vision as a geologist — that the prolific coastal fields had to extend offshore."

Dud Tower and Z. Wayne Burkhead, chief geologist for the Gulf, also recognized the potential. But their boss, Cy Rubel in Los Angeles, was focused on offshore California. Burke made a presentation to Rubel in 1953 that included part of the Vermilion prospect offshore Louisiana. On a map, the shoreline can be difficult to pinpoint since the bayous gradually give way to open water. Rubel examined the map for a while before asking, "Isn't this offshore?"

When Burke replied in the affirmative, Rubel stood up and hit the desk with his fist to make his point. "I've said that our policy is to go offshore California." He reiterated his reasoning: Union had limited resources, and where it really needed big discoveries was near its refineries in California.

But Burke, determined not to let Union Oil pass up a prime opportunity, managed to include part of the Vermilion area in a seismic survey. Burke personally took the results to California. Sam Grinsfelder, vice president of exploration, liked what he saw — but the real test was Rubel. Cy looked the report up and down, Burke recalled, and then said, "Good-looking prospect."

In 1954, the federal government held its first lease sale in the Gulf, having

resolved disputes with Louisiana and Texas over boundaries between state and federal waters. Tower and Burke lined up an opportunity to drill the Vermilion prospect under a farm-in agreement with the company that held the acreage. The first well was drilled in shallow water about six miles offshore. Burke inspected the logs. "There was so much pay, I couldn't believe it," he recalled, but the well soon proved almost too hot to handle.

Near midnight on June 7, 1956, drilling crews encountered abnormally high pressure two miles below the surface. This increased steadily from 1,500 to 3,800 pounds per square inch. Then a lower flange on a blow-out valve gave way, and gas hissed up through the break, whipping out sand so fast that the blast cut through metal. The hiss soon mounted to a roar. By morning, the well was blowing wild. The platform had to be abandoned, and Union faced a major blowout—the "Wild Tiger."

Union called in Myron Kinley, famed for fighting well fires and blowouts. By June 11, his special equipment had been gathered and loaded on barges; but it was already too late to save the well, which had ruptured below the surface. Within a few days, the leaning derrick and platform were swallowed up in the sea-floor crater dug by escaping gas.

To prevent the gathering gas cloud from drifting where it could cause more harm, navy pilots air-dropped a tank of gasoline on the site and ignited it with tracer bullets. The Wild Tiger became an inferno. Union's company magazine, *On Tour,* described the scene: "The ocean-filtered vapors burned silently and spectacularly—tall central flashes and spirals of flame dancing amid a million lesser flares....High overhead, a private cloud, created by the fire's thermal updrafts, hovered over Block 26. And at a respectful distance a group of beaten but undefeated oilmen planned their next avenue of conquest."

Under the direction of Gulf Division drilling supervisors and engineers, led by Basil P. Kantzer and Edward E. Sands, Jr., a platform and derrick were erected in record time—37 days—a third of a mile from the fiery waters. Drilling had to be exact in order to intersect the Wild Tiger far below the surface and plug the well. The drillers were aiming at a target the size of a lamppost some two miles down and off at an angle. Drilling proved long and tedious, with the crews stopping frequently to check the course of the hole. No one wanted a second blowout, so every length of casing was tested to make sure it could withstand internal pressures up to 11,300 pounds. The relief well was cemented at a depth of 10,482 feet, just short of the target.

When drilling was resumed, a flotilla of pumping and cementing rigs stood by. Two hundred more feet, and the drilling mud ceased to circulate back through the casing to the surface—indicating that the drillers had reached the Tiger. They lost no time. In little more than an hour, 13 pumps forced 1,800 barrels of mud down the hole. During the following 36 hours, seawater was pumped down. Then came 3,500 barrels of mud, followed by more seawater, and finally 4,600 barrels of mud and 3,700 sacks of cement. The fire, although far less intense, continued to burn. After four days of pouring mud, water, and cement into the Tiger, gas was apparently still escaping.

The Union team was discouraged, but needlessly so. On November 20, the fire finally went out. The Wild Tiger gave a few burps of gas the next morning, but the fight was over. In reconstructing events, Union's engineers determined that the first mud pumped down the relief well may have done the job. The continued burning was attributed to escaping gas caught in surface sands, which was not depleted until a few days after the well had been plugged.

From the hastily erected relief-well platform, drillers whipstocked 15 more holes, every one a producer. The high-pressure reservoir that had blown out the

The Wild Tiger natural gas well burned for 162 days before Union crews could tame it. _Top:_ Seagulls circled over the flames that marked the site of the Tiger, while the relief well in the background was drilled to cut off the flow of gas far below the sea floor (diagram). _Right:_ In 1961, the Block 26 field was the company's leading gas producer.

Wild Tiger became the Gulf Division's most prolific gas field by 1961, with gross production of 162 million cubic feet of natural gas per day.

Elsewhere in the world, Union wildcatters pushed into ever more remote areas. They "shot" millions of acres in the jungles of Costa Rica and Peru with little reward. A few thousand miles to the north, however, Union wildcatters in the vast, flat expanse of arctic Canada had better luck. At first, until an all-weather road was constructed, the crews could work only in the winter when the muskeg—a deep boglike accumulation of moss and leaves—was frozen. In the summer, the muskeg turned spongy, swallowing up heavy equipment.

Union's first Canadian oil strike came in 1953 at Fairydell, in western Alberta. In 1956 the company's northernmost well, Red Earth 12-17, came in with 1,000 barrels a day of 38-gravity crude, setting off the greatest oil company land rush in Canada's history. In March, some 20 companies participated in a 200,000-acre reservation sale in Alberta's Peace River country near Red Earth.

While some explorationists roamed rugged frontiers, Union's geologists and engineers in California were not overlooking the possibilities offered by the company's oldest fields. Original production methods had left millions of barrels of crude oil underground, and Union began testing ways to push it out. Waterflooding had successfully flushed thick, sluggish crude out of the old Richfield area wells, and gas injection had revived production in the Dominguez field. Secondary recovery projects undertaken in 35 producing fields during the 1950s added 70 million barrels to Union's reserves.

The geologists were looking for new oil in old fields as well. One of the most remarkable strikes was at the Torrey Canyon field, where, after more than 60 years, ancient pumps still wheezed and nodded over shallow wells. Drilled at a cost of $3,400 each in 1889, the wells had never stopped producing oil. Scattered among these oldtimers were second-generation wells, continuous producers since they were drilled to 1,600 feet in 1910. Waterflooding had boosted the flow of crude from the lower zone. Then, in the late 1940s, new geological interpretations of the field data suggested to John Sloat, manager of exploration, that another oil zone might lie even deeper.

In 1950, Sloat and Clarence Froome, field superintendent, received the go-ahead to drill a deep well. Torrey Canyon No. 83 came in on April 30, 1952, at a depth of 9,000 feet for 526 barrels of oil a day and half a million cubic feet of gas. Subsequent deep wells were slant drilled from islands because of the mountain-

RESEARCH: AN EARLY PRIORITY
In 1891, Union Oil established the first petroleum laboratory in the West in a room at the Santa Paula refinery. The lab was set up to find methods to extract more products —including a nonsmoking kerosene—from California's malodorous crudes. Union's research got off to a slow start, set aside for more immediate priorities as the young company struggled to survive. In 1896, the breakthrough in kerosene refining was achieved not by a Union chemist, but by Eric A. Starke, employed by the Golden City Chemical Works in San Francisco. In the early 1900s, as advancing automotive and aviation technology demanded higher performance gasolines and lubricants, Union's research effort revived to play a critical role in the company's success. Some 60 years after the first small lab was opened, Lyman Stewart would have been pleased to see his grandson Bill break ground for Union's state-of-the-art facility in Brea, 25 miles southeast of Los Angeles. Completed in 1951, it housed a wide range of applied and basic research laboratories. Many important new products and technologies were developed, including a refining process— Unicracking—that produced nearly five barrels of high-value fuels from four barrels of feed-stock: alchemy, by the standards of Lyman Stewart's day. In 1982, the labs, home of the Union Science & Technology Division, were expanded and renamed the Fred L. Hartley Research Center.

Opposite, top: Union's wildcat discovery well at Red Earth in 1956 set off an oil company land rush in Canada's Peace River region. Opposite, center: Deep discoveries in Torrey Canyon in the 1950s renewed the field's status as a top Union producer. Left and opposite: Union opened its new research facility in Brea in 1951.

ous terrain. Costing up to $750,000 each, they were better producers than the deep discovery well, making Torrey Canyon again one of Union's top fields.

"We have everything in this field from the beginning of the industry," Froome boasted. Indeed, Torrey Canyon was virtually a textbook illustration of the story of oil — from seeps trickling heavy oil and tar reported as early as 1864 to the discovery of the deep oil zone some 90 years later. Data from the deep wells at Torrey Canyon led Union geologists to a new prospect two miles east where, at 3,000 feet, drillers tapped into the rich Oakridge field. Union's geologists began to take second looks at every old field owned or leased by the company.

Despite steady reserve additions, the western states still endured a famine of high-value gasolines and a glut of low-value fuel oils. Taylor, determined to correct the imbalance at Union, moved to upgrade manufacturing facilities once again, as he had in 1939. In 1950, the company broke ground for a $9 million catalytic cracking plant at the Los Angeles refinery. The massive new unit's capacity of 28,850 barrels a day boosted Union's cat-cracking capacity to 56,000 barrels per day, largest on the Pacific Coast. The new cracker went on stream in 1952, just in time to help meet the growing demands of the Korean War. Half of the fuel for planes, tanks, and other vehicles used in that conflict was supplied by California refineries.

The refinery also added a $6 million topping and distillation plant, which increased both the quantity and the quality of gasolines. At the same time, a new process removed unwanted sulfurs from the sour crudes and turned them into tons of marketable sulfur and agricultural ammonium sulfate. Other plants at the Los Angeles and Oleum refineries, and a small new refinery at Edmonds, Washington, converted the "bottom ends" (residue from crude processing) into asphalt for paving and roofing.

In 1955, the company's new refinery near Santa Maria, California, came on stream. Its twin coking units, along with the coker installed at Oleum a few years prior, raised the value of the company's heavy California crude oil by converting it to desirable gasoline feedstocks. Throughput of crude oil at the company's seven refineries in 1955 was 57.5 million barrels, or 164,000 barrels per day — a 7 percent increase over 1954.

Sixty years earlier, Lyman Stewart had wheedled $2,500 of the company's meager capital for the West's first petroleum laboratory in an effort to develop new and better quality petroleum products. In 1950, the ante was raised a bit as Reese Taylor approved an appropriation of $8 million to build a new research center at Brea, California. The first staff group moved from crowded quarters at the Los Angeles refinery to their new laboratories on September 1, 1951.

The original research lab — a room in the Santa Paula refinery —

Bill Stewart, who inherited his grandfather Lyman's enthusiasm for research, saw the culmination of a dream in Union's new research center. <u>Left:</u> During his tenure, Reese Taylor observed Union's corporate anniversary — October 17 — by inviting employees with 35 years of service or more to a special celebration; in 1952, events included a tour of the new research facility.

had included a work counter, some glass bottles and tubes, a burner, and a microscope. The new research facility — a complex of a dozen single-story buildings — contained laboratories, shops, offices, a library, and ample space for duplicating in miniature almost any working problem faced by Union people anywhere in the world.

Chief of the research staff of 300 men and women was Union's executive vice president — and Lyman Stewart's grandson — Bill Stewart. The research center had been Bill Stewart's dream for some 35 years, almost from the time he began working in the oil fields in the summer of 1915. The researchers themselves designed it, laying it out so that scientists and technicians could team up readily with operational groups from the fields, pipeline stations, refineries, and marketing outlets to focus on specific problems.

In a way, the laboratory was a reflection of the organizational structure of Union Oil Company. While a team in one area worked on formulating a better drilling mud, another in a different lab explored ways to recover more oil from depleted sands or to rearrange hydrocarbon atoms into more valuable products. Cy Rubel observed that "Union gets more from researchers than does any other company because our projects are all on the practical side. Each project is guided by a sponsoring group from the field or the refineries."

It didn't take the new research center very long to prove its worth. Not only did the work of the researchers result in more efficient petroleum production and refining processes, but within a few years, 40 other oil companies and chemical manufacturers were paying Union royalties for the use of its patented technologies.

THE GREAT PUMPKIN
In October 1952, the new
Hortonsphere storage tank at
the Union Oil refinery in Los
Angeles was getting a primer
coat of red-orange paint. People
couldn't help noticing how
much it resembled a pumpkin.
Paul K. Doyle, personnel supervisor, saw it every day as he
rode in with his car pool. Why
don't we paint it like a jack-o-
lantern, one of his fellow riders
suggested. With the reluctant
permission of the refinery
manager, Doyle enlisted one of
the operators — who had artistic
leanings — to design a face.
Then Doyle found a painter with
a boatswain's chair to do the
work — all for under $50. The
maintenance department set up
flood lights, and the world's
biggest jack-o-lantern lit up the
night sky. "It created quite a
stir," said Doyle. "The *Los
Angeles Mirror* gave us a full
front page!" Some of Union's
executives weren't sure they
liked the commotion, until
they realized that the "pumpkin" generated great goodwill.
News media across the country
picked up the story. *This Week*
magazine estimated that if the
tank were a real pumpkin, it
would yield close to 27 million
pies. The jack-o-lantern became
a fall tradition, with Union
employees handing out candy
to visiting trick-or-treaters on
Halloween. Doyle retired in
1980 as corporate vice president
of industrial relations.

By 1955, Union was vastly changed from the company Reese Taylor had
taken over 17 years earlier. And it was a far different company from Lyman
Stewart's struggling little 1890 enterprise. Stewart and Taylor had one thing in
common: They were both determined that Union Oil would continue to grow.
But where Stewart had a genius for finding and acquiring oil-producing properties, Taylor knew how to wildcat for dollars.

The headlong growth of the company in the 1950s demanded capital in
large chunks. In 1952, Taylor negotiated the sale of $35 million in con-
vertible debentures to help pay for new refineries and terminals. The
underwriters sold out the issue the first day it was offered to investors. In 1955,
when the company needed more capital for expansion, Taylor went back to
Dillon Read & Company, which agreed to head a group of underwriters of a
$60 million issue of debentures. Nearly all of the earlier issues had been exchanged
for common stock, reducing Union's debt. Taylor used $39 million of the new
money to retire loans and other obligations, and to buy back preferred stock;
that left $21 million for new capital outlays. The directors had already approved a
stock split, doubling the number of common shares to 15 million.

At the same time, Taylor was able to wring some cash out of certain assets.
He sold Union's fleet of six modern tankers and chartered the ships back into
Union's service. He had already sold the company's 630 railroad tank cars under
a similar leasing arrangement. These sales added $20 million to the company's
financial reserves.

In 1955, Union's 47,000 shareholders had a $354 million equity in the com-
pany. The book value of Union's assets was more than $500 million, and many
experts and analysts in the petroleum business estimated the company's actual
worth at something closer to $1 billion.

On October 17, 1955, the company's sixty-fifth anniversary, Reese Taylor
reflected on the progress of Union Oil and the industry to which it had contributed so much. "We are not ambitious to be the biggest oil company in the business," he said, "but we do like to be thought of as the best oil company. We are
still in our infancy in the uses of petroleum. In the next six decades, we will
accomplish far more than in the past six, provided we do not tax out of existence
the economic climate that enabled Union Oil to grow and thrive."

1.

2.

3.

4.

5.

6.

7.

THE CORNER STATION: 1913–1958
Union's network of service stations expanded rapidly from the first gas stand (1) in Los Angeles in 1913 (photo circa 1930) to more than 300 stations on the West Coast and in Hawaii by 1923. Modest wooden structures (2 & 5) soon gave way to more elaborate buildings that harmonized with their neighborhoods: (3) A twenties Honolulu station got a famous manager in 1933 — Olympic swimming medalist Duke Kahanamoku; (4) Carthay Super Service was adjacent to the Carthay Circle motion picture theater, scene of many dazzling premieres during Hollywood's heyday. Wherever the station, service was the priority (6). In the thirties, stations offered more pumps and more services (7 & 8). Gasoline was rationed during World War II (11). In the late forties, station canopies were longer and the 76 logo appeared in a circle (9). During the fifties, the company introduced higher octane fuels (10) and a sleek new prototype station (12).

8.

9.

10.

11.

12.

7

Gearing Up for Growth

Cy Rubel was named president of Union Oil Company in 1956. Opposite: The first Unicracker, which came on stream at the company's Los Angeles refinery in 1964, revolutionized refining.

Union Oil enjoyed a period of tremendous growth in the 1950s, with sales exceeding $400 million for the first time in 1956. To back those sales, the company's refining system was processing almost a third more oil than Union's 4,330 wells produced. Reese Taylor believed strongly in the company's future and in the free enterprise system that nourished it. Not only did he provide vigorous leadership for Union, he made sure that there was ample capital and crude oil for the company's ongoing expansion.

In 1955, Taylor approached his close friend W. K. Whiteford, president of Gulf Oil Company. Gulf had enjoyed outstanding success in finding new oil, especially in Venezuela and Kuwait, and had a surplus of both crude and cash — just what Union needed.

Since Union and Gulf served different geographical markets in the United States, Taylor proposed that Union purchase some of the surplus crude Gulf produced in Kuwait. Three 470,000-barrel supertankers commuted to the Middle East to transport crude oil to the huge new storage tanks and blending plants that had been added to Union's Los Angeles and Oleum terminals.

Taylor also proposed that Gulf lend Union some of its surplus cash: Gulf purchased 25-year debentures worth $120 million from Union with the agreement that Gulf could, at a later date, convert these debentures into Union common stock at prices ranging from $70 to $80 a share (Union's stock was then selling at about $50). If Gulf elected to convert, it could eventually own as many as 2.4 million shares of Union's stock, becoming the company's largest shareholder. The cash from Gulf enabled Taylor to retire the previous $60 million issue of debentures, a third of which were converted into common stock.

On August 1, 1956, Union's board of directors announced a series of changes in corporate management. Taylor became chairman of the board and chief executive officer to concentrate his efforts on managing the company's growth. The man who took over day-to-day management of the corporation as president was Albert Chatfield "Cy" Rubel, promoted from vice president for exploration and production. Rubel had overseen the discovery of more oil than had been found during any other period of Union's history.

Moving into the ranks of senior management as vice president was Fred L. Hartley, who had started as a trainee at the Oleum refinery in 1939 and moved up through the ranks in engineering, refining, and research. Hartley had been successful in selling Union's "Unifining" process, a remarkable advance in refining so-called sour (sulfur-laden) crudes, turning them into "sweet" feedstocks

that yielded relatively more light-end products for the marketplace.

Unifining (catalytic hydrodesulfurization) used beds of cobalt molybdate particles in alumina pellets to remove impurities from a variety of petroleum distillates. Unlike other catalysts, the cobalt molybdate particles could be used over and over again for long periods of time, thus making the process relatively inexpensive—less than one cent per barrel of oil processed.

Hartley, as manager of commercial development, took to the road to market the process. Refiners purchased licenses for more than a hundred Unifiners, which earned substantial royalties for Union.

The company also moved ahead to develop the oil shale resources it had acquired more than 30 years earlier. The technology to convert oil shale into crude oil had been developed in the 1940s. Union scientists, working under research director Claude E. "Speedo" Swift and process development supervisor Dr. Clyde Berg, had designed and built two pilot retorts at the research center at the Los Angeles refinery.

In 1955, Union's board voted to invest $5 million in the construction of a demonstration plant in a Rocky Mountains canyon near Parachute, Colorado. The plant started up in 1957. A conveyor carried shale ore to the plant, where a hydraulic feeder pumped crushed shale upward through a conical retort. The shale was heated as it moved upward, releasing oil and gas, which were drawn off at the bottom of the retort. The spent shale spilled out the top. The retort processed up to a thousand tons of shale per day, recovering half a barrel of oil from each ton of rock. Laboratory tests showed that Unifining could successfully process the crude shale oil, making it suitable for further refining and turning its high concentrations of sulfur and nitrogen into marketable by-products.

When the demonstration plant was shut down in 1960, Union's researchers

Opposite: In 1961, a Unifiner and gasoline reformer (left and right in foreground) were part of a $17 million construction program to boost octane-producing power at the Los Angeles refinery. Opposite, below: Union reexamined the economic potential of its oil shale holdings in Colorado when petroleum usage rose during and after the Second World War. Right: By 1961, Collier operated seven manufacturing plants in the western United States, including its original plant in Brea, California.

went back to their labs to improve the process. By changing the way in which the crushed shale was heated they were able to boost the yields, at least in the laboratory. But research was shelved for the next decade. A pilot plant using improved "Retort B" technology wasn't constructed at the research laboratory until the early 1970s, when conflict in the Middle East gave rise to new fears of oil shortages.

In the late 1950s, Union also owned a small mountain of tar sands near Santa Barbara. These sands, according to geologists, formed an oil reservoir that had been uncovered in past ages, allowing the volatile gas and light oils to escape. The residual tar, trapped in the sand, could be strip-mined to recover an estimated 50 million barrels of tar-sand oil. Despite the impressive potential of these two resources, neither shale nor tar-sand oil was economically competitive with crude from underground reservoirs.

Union's researchers in the 1950s found many innovative methods to process hydrocarbons, breaking down and rearranging the molecules in oil and natural gas into one salable new petrochemical after another. They were so successful that in 1952 Union set up Brea Chemicals, Inc., as a wholly owned subsidiary to manufacture and market some of these by-products.

By 1957, Brea Chemicals emerged as an important producer. Sales of ammonium nitrate and liquid aqua ammonia for fertilizer were booming. At the same time, Union purchased another successful petroleum by-products company in San Jose, California. Enterprising Robert T. Collier had built his business by using surplus petroleum coke from Union's Oleum and Santa Maria refineries. He made briquettes for fireplaces and calcined carbon for electrodes, which were used in electrochemical processes such as aluminum manufacturing. Collier Corporation and Brea Chemicals merged to form a $20 million-a-year Union subsidiary, Collier Carbon and Chemical Company.

In 1957, Taylor, like Lyman Stewart before him, was faced with a threat to the rights of California's independent oil companies. Union bucked several major oil companies in working to defeat a convoluted state ballot initiative known as Proposition 4. Its proponents tried to sell it as a conservation measure, but in fact it would have empowered a politically appointed state commission to unitize the pumping of oil from the state's producing fields. The result would have been the virtual confiscation of the independents' properties. In a bitterly fought election campaign, California voters were persuaded to defeat Proposition 4 by a wide margin.

On March 31, 1958, 1,200 employees moved into their offices in the new Union Oil Center, a $25 million complex on a bluff overlooking the Harbor Freeway in downtown Los Angeles. The center's 12-story office tower dominated the city's pre-high-rise skyline. Designed by one of the country's most respected architectural teams, William Pereira and Charles Luckman, it was a showpiece of

COMPANY HEADQUARTERS
When Union Oil Company of California was incorporated in 1890, the papers were signed in a new two-story building in Santa Paula, which became the corporate headquarters. In 1901, Union moved its corporate activities to the bustling business district of Los Angeles, occupying a five-story building at the corner of First and Broadway. The company expanded into offices in several buildings over the next few years. By 1908, the head office staff had grown to 46. They occupied a floor of the Security Building at Fifth and Spring. In 1912, the company signed a ten-year lease for several floors at Seventh and Spring. In 1923, Union consolidated its offices and moved its 600 headquarters employees into a new building on the corner of Seventh and Hope. The 12-story, steel-frame structure was elegantly faced with terra cotta brick. The *Union Oil Bulletin* described it as "a symbol of the majesty and might of California oil." Thirty-five years later, on March 31, 1958, the company moved again — this time with 1,200 headquarters employees — into the $25 million Union Oil Center on a bluff overlooking downtown Los Angeles.

Top: Excavation began at the site of the new Union Oil Center in 1955. Left: The building, completed in 1958, became a familiar landmark. Bottom left: Attending the cornerstone ceremony on October 17, 1956 — the company's sixty-sixth anniversary — were (from left) Union's Sam Grinsfelder, architect William Pereira, developer Del Webb, and architect Charles Luckman. Bottom right: A plaque commemorated Herbert Hoover's words of dedication.

Dud Tower (top) and Kenny Vaughan: Tower was Union's president from 1960 to 1962, when Reese Taylor took over the job again. In late 1963, Tower resigned and Vaughan succeeded him as senior vice president in charge of exploration and production.

1950s style. And, as befitted Los Angeles, it featured one of the West's largest underground parking garages. Said Reese Taylor: "This is the building that freedom built."

On April 26, 1960, Cy Rubel retired at the age of 65 after 38 years with the company. Taylor temporarily took over the president's role again until October, when the board announced that Dudley Tower would be Union's eighth president. Tower, an engineer trained at both UCLA and UC Berkeley, began his Union career in 1935 as a pipeline roustabout at the Dominguez field. He worked in exploration, as district engineer for Texas operations, manager of the Gulf Division, vice president of field operations, and finally executive vice president.

Union produced nearly 96,000 barrels of crude oil a day in 1960, and 354 million cubic feet of natural gas. Gulf operations were vigorous, producing more than half the company's gas — 200 million cubic feet per day — and 16,000 barrels of crude oil. "During the 1950s," noted Ray Burke, "we turned a small operation in the Gulf into a major oil and gas producer."

Gulf discoveries continued. Onshore, Union drilled its deepest well to date — 17,395 feet — to bring in the East Timbalier Bay field in 1959. In 1960, the discovery well at the Lake Pagie field came in at 8 million cubic feet of gas per day. Offshore, development of the prolific Vermilion blocks and other areas continued to yield new production of both gas and oil.

Encouraged by its offshore successes, Union was a major player in the federal lease sales for offshore blocks in 1960 and 1962. In both sales, Union was a 50 percent partner with The Pure Oil Company of Palatine, Illinois, which had pioneered offshore drilling in the Gulf in 1937. Two major fields resulted from the 1960 lease sale: Ship Shoal Block 208 and South Marsh Island Block 49. Union and Pure would become partners in a much larger sense in 1965 when the companies merged.

During the early 1960s, bolder companies — including Union — began to explore prospects in deeper waters. The Ship Shoal and South Marsh Island properties were in about 90 feet of water — shallow by today's standards, but deeper than was common for offshore operations at the time. And Union was preparing for even deeper ventures.

Kenneth C. Vaughan, vice president in charge of the Gulf Region, asked Thomas W. Stoy, Jr., Charles M. Schwartz, and Hale B. Ingram to investigate the possibilities. They prepared a report, called "Operation Bluewater," recommending the daring move into waters as deep as 300 feet. (In the Gulf, shallow green waters near shore give way to deeper blue waters further out.)

"We were swimming with the big boys on that one," Stoy said years later, after the company had set platforms in more than 900 feet of water and had done exploratory drilling in depths approaching 2,000 feet.

Some of the strikes in the Gulf turned out to be enormous natural gas producers. While Union's first Gulf gas well drilled onshore at Freshwater Bayou in the early 1950s was not an entirely welcome find, the situation had changed ten years later. By then, natural gas was a fuel in great demand, and Union had discovered two dozen new gas fields. A gas well, especially along the Gulf Coast where there was an extensive pipeline system to carry the gas to markets, was often preferred by Union's explorers to an oil well.

Both oil and natural gas were getting more expensive to find. In one year, Union paid more than $14 million for the right to drill on federal or state offshore blocks in the Gulf of Mexico. Wells ran from 10,000 to 17,000 feet deep and cost upward of $500,000 each, but the payoff could be substantial.

Far to the north, Union's Canadian fields were also successfully producing gas and oil. By 1961, Union had drilled 175 exploratory wells in Canada, bringing in 22 oil and 21 gas fields. Wells in northern Alberta and British Columbia delivered nearly 3,000 barrels of oil and more than 10 million cubic feet of gas a day to pipelines linking the fields to Canadian population centers.

Union's Canadian Division, organized in 1949, had become a sizable oil company in its own right in the 1950s. Canadians felt they ought to have a share in this enterprise so, in 1961, Union's directors voted to transform the division into Union Oil Company of Canada, Limited. Union Oil of California swapped its Canadian oil wells, facilities, and land leases for 3 million shares, representing 83 percent of the new company. Canadian investors quickly snapped up the remaining 17 percent of the shares.

Canadians joined Americans as directors and officers of the company. Union Oil of Canada expanded by buying smaller oil producers, and its output leaped to more than 12,000 barrels of crude a day by 1965.

In 1959, Union discovered Alaska's first natural gas field, in partnership with the Ohio Oil Company (which became Marathon in 1962). Drillers were looking for oil beneath the Kenai Peninsula when the well blew out at 4,232 feet as a wild "gasser." They struggled to get the well under control and then continued to drill almost three miles down, the deepest hole in Alaska. They failed to find oil but proved up the gas field.

The field was only 80 miles south of Anchorage, where about half of Alaska's population was concentrated, but the distance was marked by forests, rugged hills, and Turnagain Sound in Cook Inlet. The sound stymied pipeliners as they tried to put down a line to carry Kenai gas to consumers in Anchorage. Powerful currents, 35-foot tides, and the seabed of abrasive glacial silt made the pipeline-laying job one of the toughest in petroleum history.

Work was suspended when the winter storms began in late 1961, and the pipeliners positioned themselves for another try in the spring. They towed a "Louisiana cruiser" from the Gulf of Mexico through the Panama Canal and up the West Coast to Alaska. The cruiser was a huge barge with facilities for welding, x-raying, wrapping, and coating pipe, which was then fed out a long stern boom known as a "stinger." As the pipe touched the bottom of the sound, hydraulic jets dug a bed for it in the silt. Turnagain's massive tides did the work of filling in the trench. Then, as insurance, the pipeliners laid a duplicate line across the sound in 11 days. Residents of Anchorage began cooking and heating with natural gas in 1962.

Union continued to search for oil in Alaska, too. Seismic work in the Cook Inlet, offshore the Kenai Peninsula, had revealed some tremendous structures with oil-bearing potential. The executive committee in Los Angeles at first turned down the exploration group's request to bid on the acreage, but the persuasive Ray Burke, who became Union's director of exploration in 1961, provided additional evidence of the prospect's potential. Union requested that Alaska—a state only since 1959—hold a lease sale. In 1962, Union, again in partnership with Marathon, purchased drilling rights that would make it the state's leading oil producer for several years.

"Our success can be attributed in large part to the fact that we were in quite early, took a strong front position, and retained it," recalled Dr. Harold M. Lian, who was Union's chief geologist in Alaska when the strikes were made. "There are many rewards for that—for being daring and taking some risks." In 1963, before drilling began in the inlet, Lian was summoned to Los Angeles by Burke, by then vice president of exploration, to help in an expanding worldwide search for oil.

In 1958, Union wildcatters had found oil in Argentina, but that country's new government promptly canceled the company's concession. About the same

Ray Burke was named vice president of exploration and production in 1962. He joined Union in 1951 and played a key role in the company's growth in the Gulf Region—and later in its international expansion.

In March 1958, Union geologist Alfonso M. Escalante was hacking his way through the dense jungle on Union Oil's concession E-19 in the Department of Petén, Guatemala, when he made a remarkable discovery—and it wasn't oil. That night in camp, by the light of a gasoline lantern, he entered in his field notes: "Today, while cutting trail six kilometers southeast of camp, we uncovered the ruins of an ancient Indian city." What Escalante and his crew had found were the remains of two pyramids, several other buildings, and four elaborately carved limestone *stellae* (half-ton blocks). The ruins, spread over about 40 acres, were not far from the now-famous Mayan city of Tikal, then being excavated. Within the year, Escalante was transferred to Argentina; J. Erick Mack, Jr., another young Union geologist on his first assignment, replaced him. Mack found more ruins. "Tikal was at one end of a series of Mayan settlements, and Chichen-Itza in the Yucatan Peninsula was at the other," he explained. "Our field parties were made up of 30 men or so, so as we mapped the rocks we came across some of the ruins." The finds were reported to the Guatemalan government. Archaeological studies have since revealed much about the complex Mayan civilization, which flourished from the third to the eighth centuries. Escalante went on to explore in Patagonia and other areas in Latin America before joining Union's domestic Oil & Gas Division. Mack participated in the discovery of the Moonie field in Australia, and later was exploration manager for Latin America; he eventually joined the Geothermal Division.

Top right: In 1960, Union drilled a third well in its new Kenai gas field in Alaska.

time, Union had expanded into the eastern hemisphere, exploring the Spanish Sahara with a Spanish partner. That venture proved to be not only unprofitable, but high-risk in a very personal sense for the people involved—the first seismic crew in the area was kidnaped and held for ransom by bandits.

Persistence, however, paid off in Australia. On December 17, 1961, Union and its partners, Kern County Land Company and the Australian Oil and Gas Corporation (AO&G), brought in 5,800-foot Moonie No. 1 in Queensland for 2,200 barrels per day of high-gravity crude. As the first commercial oil discovery in Australia, the Moonie field was cause for national celebration.

Until that time, Australia imported all the oil it consumed—250,000 barrels daily. Oil companies had spent millions of dollars on more than 600 dry holes. In 1959 Sam Grinsfelder, just before his retirement, had negotiated a deal to explore 40 million acres of grazing land and desert in Queensland and New South Wales. Union was the operator, providing the seismic and drilling crews and running the play. AO&G had 20 percent of the operation, while Union and Kern (each with 40 percent) put up all the money. The Australian government agreed to subsidize some of the exploration costs through refunds to the oil companies.

After the discovery, Union drillers rounded out the Moonie field with a dozen new wells, all but one of which were producers. The company followed up quickly with 25 more holes—all dry—in other areas of the vast concession, which was as large as the state of Oklahoma. But in the Alton area of the Surat

Left: Union and its partners made the first discovery of oil in commercial quantities in Australia in 1961. Opposite: Wells in the Las Cienegas field, located in the heart of Los Angeles, were covered to muffle the sounds of drilling.

Valley north of Moonie, Union drillers brought in a well that flowed on test at the rate of 480 barrels per day of high-gravity crude and then followed up with a series of equally promising wells. To the north, another crew tapped a third potential reservoir, known as the Conloi field. Union and its partners laid a 10-inch pipeline from the Moonie field to the nearest coastal city, Brisbane. There, the crude was fed into tankers for the 500-mile voyage south to the Australian refineries at Sydney.

On March 6, 1963, Queen Elizabeth II and Prince Philip, Duke of Edinburgh, dedicated a monument at Brisbane commemorating Australia's first oil strikes. The Queen personally commended Union's Cy Rubel, Bill Stewart, Ray Burke, and their colleagues.

The Australian discoveries enjoyed high visibility but, closer to home, finds larger than Moonie sometimes went unnoticed—and literally unseen. Union's wildcatters had amazing success with onshore exploration in Southern California in the early 1960s. Under the Hacienda Country Club golf fairways, southeast of Los Angeles, they drilled more than two dozen producing wells, situating the pumps out of sight behind shrubbery and in low-lying areas.

One of the largest fields discovered in California during the 1960s—the Las Cienegas field—sat practically in the middle of Los Angeles, only 20 miles from Union's refinery. In the early days, from 1890 to 1912, there had been considerable drilling in the Beverly Hills and mid-Wilshire districts west of downtown. At that time, the area was open country with few houses or buildings, but between world wars it was heavily developed. As early as 1955, Rubel and Grinsfelder had decided the area was worth another look, and they gave the task to the geologists and landmen.

The assignment was not easy. There was little open land where seismic studies could be conducted. But the explorationists determined that the work could be

done effectively along Exposition and San Vicente boulevards, next to the old Pacific Electric Railway right of way. Preliminary tests proved intriguing, and Union's crews followed up by drilling shallow core holes to 1,500 feet, using a compact, soundproofed rig. Crews worked only during the daytime to avoid disturbing the residents—drilling behind billboards, on vacant lots, and on supermarket parking areas.

Meanwhile, the landmen were busy preparing to lease 7,000 acres in the mid-Wilshire area of the city. More than 100 landmen were assigned to cover the 30,000 lots involved. The area included some tough neighborhoods frequented by drug dealers, pimps, and prostitutes. Union's landmen, who made most of their contacts at night, sometimes found it necessary to hire bodyguards.

Other companies soon sniffed out Union's intentions and began to compete for rights, but in the end Union held about 70 percent of the leases. Because some owners had signed leases with more than one company, rival companies claimed 40 percent—which left 10 percent of the leases in dispute. The leases were eventually awarded to the company that first recorded them.

In 1961, after lengthy testimony in numerous hearings and with the approval of several city offices—including the planning commission, the planning committee of the city council, the city council itself, and finally the mayor—Union drillers were set to put down a hole on a 260-acre site near the corner of Western and Adams.

John E. Kilkenny, chief geologist of the Pacific Coast Division, worked on the project from the beginning. "The first well—a straight hole—was dry, as were a redrilled hole to the west and another to the north," he recalled. "Finally, a redrilled hole to the south found basement granite with oil shows at a shallow depth. We continued drilling in the basement rock at a high angle from vertical until we again encountered sedimentary rocks with oil shows."

Union's crews had drilled down 3,500 feet looking for a reservoir that lay at 2,500 to 3,000 feet. They clipped the edge on the way down and found other oil shows below the reservoir, but it was too shallow for them to reach by slant drilling from their original location. "It must have been the first time in exploration drilling history that an oil field had been found by drilling underneath it," noted Kilkenny.

With this discovery, Union was able to get further approval from the city for another drill site located directly over the field. The property belonged to the Roman Catholic Church, and the bishop blessed the first well at a spudding-in ceremony. The next day, said Kilkenny, drillers hit oil sand.

The Las Cienegas discovery well flowed high-gravity crude. The field, with its wells slant-drilled from sites that were camouflaged to look like home properties, may have been the only oil field with street addresses—4848 West Pico and 2126 West Adams. More than 20,000 lot owners shared in the royalties. Five other prolific oil deposits were also found in the area. Union eventually drilled 78 producing wells, and by 1988 the field had produced more than 57 million barrels of oil and 50 million cubic feet of gas.

In the early 1960s, the company geared up to begin an exploration program off the California coast. While seismic surveys were encouraging, the ownership of offshore territories was still controversial. The problem was complicated in Southern California by the existence of offshore islands, a situation the U.S. Congress had not fully clarified in legislation giving states the rights to any oil found within three miles of shore.

Nevertheless, Union's directors allocated the money to explore offshore Santa Barbara. For the time, the cost was considerable; Union paid the state of

California a bonus of $3.6 million for the right to drill on 11,500 acres in three parcels. Explorationists brought in the *George F. Ferris,* a 6,000-ton barge with four 275-foot legs sticking up 200 feet above its decks. This was an early "jack-up" rig, so called because once its legs were lowered, the platform was jacked up above water level. The *Ferris* carried a 145-foot drilling tower, 80,000 gallons of diesel fuel, 100,000 gallons of fresh water, and ample living quarters. It drilled eight costly dry holes before the effort was suspended in 1965.

Offshore Huntington Beach, Union bid almost twice as much — more than $6 million (just beating the next highest bid) — to drill on a 2,000-acre parcel seaward of a productive onshore field. But this one paid off. When a drilling barge found oil, Union's management approved another $2.3 million for a permanent drilling platform. A giant, prefabricated rig was towed in two sections from Houston through the Panama Canal and erected at the site. Platform Eva, Union's first development offshore California, was a $10 million venture by the time the first barrel of oil was pumped on January 17, 1964. Within a year, daily production was 8,000 barrels and increasing steadily. (Eva took its name from *Little Eva,* a houseboat that served as headquarters for the crews that drilled Union's first successful wells in Louisiana.)

Platform Eva was a bright start for a year in which Union's oil and gas operations in Alaska and the Gulf of Mexico would have to weather major natural disasters. On Good Friday, March 27, 1964, a violent earthquake struck the Alaskan coast. Union's rigs and pipelines withstood the shaking, but Anchorage, Valdez, Whittier, and other communities were in shambles. Union lost wharves, docks, storage tanks, warehouses, and other marketing facilities.

Union's 50 employees and their families came through the disaster without injury, although many of their homes were damaged. Union people in Seattle quickly set up a disaster fund to which hundreds of employees throughout the company contributed generously.

Within 24 hours of the quake, Union trucks began delivering gasoline and heating oil to Anchorage from the company's few undamaged tanks. Unfortunately, little time remained to rebuild storage facilities to carry the Alaska market through the next long winter. Tanks, pipelines, and pumps — fabricated as far away as Pittsburgh — were loaded in pieces on flat cars, which in turn were loaded onto seagoing barges in Seattle to be towed to Anchorage. From there they were shunted by rail to the tank farm sites, where welders joined the parts together before the first winter storms arrived.

The rush to fill the new storage facilities with a winter's supply of products caused another disaster. In mid-October, the Union-chartered tanker *Santa Maria* — loaded with gasoline, heating oil, and other products — collided with another vessel in Cook Inlet, only a mile from the Anchorage waterfront. Residents watched from shore as flames engulfed the tanker. One crewman was lost. However, a rainstorm helped smother the flames, and the crew was able to save the tanker and all but 7,000 barrels of its 117,000-barrel cargo. The *Santa Maria* was towed to Seattle for repairs.

Because of the accident, filling Anchorage's storage tanks fell behind schedule and became an emergency operation. The tanker *Lompoc* took over the job, arriving on its final voyage early in December shrouded in ice. Winter had taken over Cook Inlet, and the *Lompoc* not only had to slog through ice, but through a dense fog as well.

On December 18, long after the tugs had been frozen fast for the winter, the tanker managed to push its way up to the wharf. In the bitter cold, it took four hours instead of the usual 45 minutes to pump the gasoline out of the tanker's stern compartments. But the cargo of heating oil couldn't be pumped — the wharf's heating oil pipeline had frozen solid. When steam failed to thaw it, a welding crew worked all night to construct an alternate line. The next morning, the *Lompoc*'s keel rested dangerously close to bottom as the tide went out four feet lower than usual. Fortunately, the heating oil was removed just fast enough to keep the ship afloat.

While Alaska recovered from the earthquake, Union's Gulf operations braced for Hurricane Hilda. Tropical storm warnings were issued September 29,

Right: In October 1964, the tanker Santa Maria *was carrying winter fuel supplies to Union facilities in Anchorage when it collided with another vessel; rain helped douse the fire, saving the ship and most of its cargo.*

HURRICANE HILDA
The first warning came on the morning of September 29, 1964: Tropical Storm Hilda was forming in the Caribbean. The storm moved northwest, picking up force. By early Saturday, October 3, it crossed into the oil-producing areas offshore the Louisiana coastline, packing winds up to 160 miles per hour and whipping the waves to 60-foot crests. On a 12-hour sweep north through the Gulf's most prolific oil and gas areas—Eugene Island, Vermilion, South Marsh Island, Ship Shoal, and South Timbalier—Hilda downed 13 offshore platforms and damaged many more. The storm lost strength over the mainland, but still felled trees, cut power lines, tore off roofs, and flooded lowlands. When it was over, the oil industry had sustained $50 million in damage. Union estimated its losses at $2 million, more than half for the destruction of a platform on Eugene Island Block 276. Hilda was the first hurricane to hit the offshore platforms, most of which were set after Flossie's destructive passage in 1955. Union shut in its production in the path of the storm, and no wells blew out. No platform workers were injured, since all had been evacuated—or "brought to the beach"—before the storm hit. But once Union's engineers understood the devastating possibilities of hurricane-force winds and waves, they were able to strengthen the platforms and improve their design.

1964. Union evacuated its platforms and shut in both offshore and coastal production over the next three days. On October 3, the storm began a 12-hour sweep through the Gulf's most prolific production areas. It was the first hurricane to make so direct a hit since extensive oil and gas development had begun offshore in the late 1950s.

Hurricane Hilda downed 13 offshore platforms, including one Union platform on Eugene Island Block 276. When it was over, the oil industry had sustained $50 million in damage; Union estimated its losses at $2 million. After this first experience with 160-mile-per-hour winds and 60-foot waves, Union strengthened its platforms and raised the decks to reduce battering by storm waves.

As Union's oil and gas operations expanded, the company's researchers were preparing to introduce a revolutionary development in refining technology—Unicracking. The process was the result of a decade of intensive research and engineering involving two dozen Union scientists working first under Fred Hartley and then under Dr. W. E. Bradley during their respective tenures as vice president of research.

In a planning meeting in 1954, economics experts had predicted that the market for fuels would change dramatically in the 1960s. The demand for high-value, top-quality gasolines and jet fuels would soar, while the market for fuel oil would decline. At the time, Union refineries produced the equivalent of 55 barrels of fuel oil from every 100 barrels of crude. The planners urged the researchers to find a way to convert more of the crude to high-grade gasoline, diesel fuel, and jet fuel.

A process called "hydrocracking" looked the most promising. This "cracked" (broke down) hydrocarbon molecules under pressures ranging to 10,000 pounds per square inch. Since huge tanks that could withstand this kind of pressure were impractical, researchers looked for other approaches. They found a remarkable new catalyst that did the job at a lower pressure. Results were excellent from both laboratory bench-scale experiments and scaled-up ten-barrel-per-day pilot

Top left: Union's Platform Eva, offshore Southern California, came on stream in January 1964.

plant runs. Union's researchers named their new process Unicracking.

Reese Taylor, in a letter to employees on April 1, 1960, explained how it worked: "This new process is based on a novel catalyst that causes hydrogen to react with the feedstock under relatively mild conditions of temperature and pressure. Complete conversion of feed to gasoline can be achieved in the new process with a yield of about 115 volume percent."

In other words, the Unicracker's volume output was greater than its input—in effect converting 100 barrels of feedstock into 115 barrels of gasoline or other high-value products. And it was high-quality output "with no residue," reported John W. Towler, senior vice president. In November 1962, the directors approved the expenditure of $22 million to build the first Unicracker at the Los Angeles refinery.

The process was not quite perfected, however. "In the pilot plant, the first catalyst just fell apart on us," said Dr. Rowland Hansford, who had led the catalyst research since the project's inception. "It crumbled into a fine powder. This was terrible! We were already committed to building a Unicracker at the Los Angeles refinery. Unless we could solve our problem, we might wind up with a very expensive shell of a unit and nothing to make it work."

Hansford's team bullied their way to a conclusion. It took 50 people six months to solve the problem of finding a bonding agent strong enough to hold the catalyst together without interfering with its work. "Rowland stuck it together with aluminum oxide," recalled Cloyd P. Reeg, then the group leader in process development. "The result was a very rugged catalyst."

Standard Oil of New Jersey had been working on a similar process, and the two managements decided to pool patents and license the process to other companies on a royalty basis. Union's Unicracker came on stream in 1964, and the process exceeded expectations. Within a year, ten units were being built by other oil companies.

By 1965, there were 76 different blends of 76 Union (later transposed to Union 76) gasolines tailored for optimum engine performance in a wide range of climates. These were mixed by a new electronic blending system that replaced the old cumbersome batch process of mixing gasoline in huge tanks. The new system blended up to ten different stocks at one time and fed them directly into a

The development of Unicracking took years, with teams of dedicated scientists working on different aspects of the project to make it work. In 1960, Unicracking researchers gathered around while K. W. Sache ran a catalyst experiment. The men included refining research manager Hal Huffman (with striped tie) and Cloyd Reeg (right foreground), group leader, process development.

Above: Ads in the 1960s emphasized the speedy service of Union's "Minute Men." *Top left:* Union's new marine fuel dock in San Diego built in 1961 was part of a great expansion of the service station network. *Top right:* Union's Dodger Stadium station did a brisk business. *Left:* The "Sparkle Corps" of white-gloved women inspected stations for cleanliness. In the background is the Space Needle built for the 1962 Seattle World's Fair; Union supplied lubricating grease for the needle's rotating restaurant and other mechanisms.

pipeline to the storage tanks. It could operate at a rate of 5,000 barrels per hour and was controlled from a keyboard console.

Fred Hartley guided a revolution in retail marketing in the early 1960s, after his success in selling the patented Unifining technique caught the attention of Reese Taylor. "You should be heading up all of our marketing," Taylor told Hartley one day in December 1959. "This would be a radical change from your engineering and research work, so take your time in making a decision." After an hour's discussion, Taylor said, "Well, let's have your decision."

"That's how I became a marketing man," Hartley recalled. He spent months on the road, learning marketing from dealers and customers. Under Hartley, hundreds of Union stations were refurbished and hundreds of new stations were built. Union credit cardholders numbered more than a million. The company emphasized service; one aspect of that was embodied in the women of the "Sparkle Corps," who checked stations for cleanliness and other customer comforts.

"Our marketing philosophy was simple," explained Hartley. "Instead of distributors of commodities, our dealers became merchandisers. In addition to gas and oil and services to motorists, we offered a line of sales impulse items carrying the 76 Union label. Our goal was to sell profitably—rather than to increase volume just for growth's sake."

As the company grew, so did the size and number of its subsidiaries. To handle the booming demand for petroleum products in the Far East, the Unoco company was launched in January 1962, with F. K. Cadwell as president. Unoco Limited, a wholly owned subsidiary based in Hong Kong, with branches in Singapore, Tokyo, Manila, and London, sold crude oil and petroleum products throughout the Far East and other world markets.

Union had been trading in Asia since 1906, when Will Stewart made Union's first sale of fuel oil and refinery products in Japan. After 1933, Union's outlet was Maruzen Oil Company, which built a small refinery near Osaka. Following World War II, Maruzen grew spectacularly under the leadership of its president, Kanji Wada, and with the technical and financial help of Union. Maruzen engineers, technicians, and marketers came to the United States to study at Union facilities, and Union sent teams to Japan. By the 1960s, Maruzen had become the third largest petroleum company in Japan; in 1963, Union purchased a 33 percent interest in the company for $15 million, obtaining 180 million shares of newly issued Maruzen stock.

In 1961, Taylor announced that Gulf Oil Company had agreed to sell back at par the $120 million worth of debentures it had bought in 1956. Had Gulf chosen to exercise its right to convert this debt to common stock, it would have owned approximately one-fourth of Union's shares. The money to pay Gulf came from two new issues of 40-year debentures sold to the public.

Not all parties were as unmeddlesome as Gulf. Early in 1960, an unknown organization began to purchase large blocks of Union shares on both the New York and Pacific Coast stock exchanges. Efforts to identify the purchasers failed. Finally, Reese Taylor cleared up the mystery. In a letter to stockholders on June 1, 1960, he wrote:

"Several days ago we received word that Phillips Petroleum Company had reported to the Securities and Exchange Commission in Washington, D.C., that it had purchased and now owned in excess of one million common shares of Union Oil, or slightly over twelve percent of the total outstanding. This is the first knowledge that your board of directors or management had of Phillips' acquisition of stock, as the shares had been purchased in other names and in such a manner as not to disclose the identity of the real owner. More recently, Phillips advised your management that it had purchased these shares solely as an invest-

CELEBRITY DEALERS
The retail network expanded rapidly during the 1950s, and some of the new dealers were celebrities. Amiable actor Ben Alexander (above) bought his first Union station in 1946 and later acquired three more. In a 1958 ad for the company, Alexander said: "I've always made it a point never to go into a business until I had learned it thoroughly. At the service station, I worked right along with the boys. I can lube a car or wash a windshield with the best of them." Not content to just sell gasoline, Alexander was also a successful car dealer. His experience as an independent businessman in the City of the Angels may have helped prepare him for his most famous role. He played Officer Frank Smith, dependable sidekick to Jack Webb's Sergeant Friday, on the original *Dragnet* television series from 1952 to 1958. Another celebrity Union dealer was 49er running back Joe "The Jet" Perry, who purchased a station at the corner of Ellis and Taylor in San Francisco in 1959. On opening day, teammates Hugh McElhenny and Y. A. Tittle showed up to don Minute Man uniforms, clean a few windshields, and check tire pressures. In Los Angeles, famed Rams fullback "Tank" Younger took over a station at the corner of Western and Santa Barbara (later Martin Luther King Boulevard). His motto: Tank up with *Tank*. Keep your car *Younger*.

**U.S. MOVES TO BLOCK
SALE OF UNION OIL CO.**

Tours White House

**Mamie Hostess
To Jacqueline**

LOS ANGELES EVENING

HERALD EXPRESS

United Press International   Associated Press   Dow-Jones
1111 S. Broadway, L. A. 54   Phone RI. 8-4141

SUNSET
Race Results
Complete N. Y. Stocks

VOL. XC   Four Sections   10 CENTS   FRIDAY, DECEMBER 9, 1960   S   NO. 221

ment, because of its confidence in their intrinsic value, and had no purpose or intention to seek any merger or consolidation."

Phillips continued to purchase Union stock until, by November 30, 1960, it had brought its total holdings to 1.3 million shares—15 percent of Union's outstanding shares—making it the company's largest stockholder.

Meanwhile, Taylor became concerned and urged the U.S. Department of Justice to take antitrust action. When the government proved reluctant, Union decided on the highly unusual step of filing its own antitrust lawsuit. The basis was "incipient competition," meaning that the two companies were already in significant competition and headed toward more. Claude S. Brinegar, who had joined Union as an economic analyst in 1953 after completing his doctoral studies in economic research at Stanford University, was assigned to gather evidence to support Union's claim.

"Both companies had retail operations in Spokane and Salt Lake City, and I sent people there to count the stations and gather sales data," he recalled. "Less obvious at first was the competition for fertilizer sales in California's Imperial Valley, but Phillips and Union both had growing shares of that market."

The Justice Department joined Union in its lawsuit in December 1960. "That's when the judge began to take us more seriously," noted Brinegar. On January 13, 1961, a Los Angeles court issued an injunction against Phillips to restrain the company from acquiring additional shares of Union Oil stock and from voting the shares it already held. The Phillips raid was essentially over.

In June 1963, shipping magnate Daniel K. Ludwig, president of National Bulk Carriers, Inc., purchased the block of Union shares held by Phillips. The antitrust action was dropped. Ludwig—elected a director in July 1963—was Union's largest shareowner, holding more stock than even the Stewart family.

Early in 1962, Taylor perceived that Union might be getting too big for its organizational structure. Production and sales volumes had more than doubled in the preceding decade, and the company had pushed out in all directions. Taylor asked company officers and outside experts to study the situation. After reviewing their recommendations, he announced a major streamlining. Basic operational activities would be regrouped into profit centers: Exploration-Production, Refining-Marketing, Unoco Overseas Sales, and Collier Carbon and Chemical. Each profit center would be nearly autonomous—with its own monthly profit-and-loss statement—under a senior vice president reporting to the president.

In 1963, Daniel K. Ludwig bought the more than 1.3 million Union Oil shares held by Phillips Petroleum, making Ludwig Union's largest shareholder.

Civic and Industry Leader Succumbs

Reese H. Taylor, president of the multi-million dollar Union Oil Co. of California and chairman of that firm's board of directors, died suddenly today at Good Samaritan Hospital.

The prominent civic leader, sportsman and business administrator would have been 62 on July 6.

Doctors listed the cause of death as acute pancreatitis, an affliction of the pancreas, the abdominal gland which controls blood sugar.

Taylor succumbed at 5:25 a.m. With him at his bedside was his wife, Mrs. Margaret Corrie Taylor.

AILING 2 WEEKS

Her mate had been seriously ill for two weeks, but associates said he had been actively planning future business ventures. His death came as a shock to them.

The memory of Taylor's life will serve as a testimonial for those who advise: If you want something done, get a busy man to do it.

VE LIFE

Fred Hartley was appointed head of the Refining-Marketing Division. Dud Tower, who had fallen out of Taylor's favor, resigned as president of Union Oil but remained until 1963 as senior vice president of the Exploration-Production Division. The board of directors asked Reese Taylor to reassume responsibility as president and chief executive officer.

Scarcely six weeks later, on June 22, 1962, Reese Taylor, the strong man at the Union helm for 24 years, died of pancreatitis at the Hospital of the Good Samaritan in Los Angeles. "His was an outstanding and useful life of lasting achievement as well as of warm friendship," the board of directors eulogized. "He was a giant among men, and one of the great leaders in the petroleum industry, noted for his business statesmanship, courageous action, and enlightened farsightedness."

The board turned to familiar figures to take command of the company. They sent out a hurried call for Cy Rubel, who was enjoying a leisurely fishing trip off Vancouver Island, British Columbia. A Canadian coast guard boat caught up with the retired Union president in Prince Rupert as he put in for supplies.

"When I finally reached a shoreside phone and received the shocking news, I was urged to return immediately," Rubel said later. He and his wife refueled their boat and left before dawn for Ketchikan, Alaska. From there, a chartered seaplane flew them to the nearest airport on Annette Island. "Mrs. Rubel and I made a quick transfer to a Union Oil plane," Rubel recalled. "We reached Los Angeles around midnight, still in our dirty, smelly fishing togs."

When the directors asked Rubel to resume the presidency, he agreed under two conditions: He was to be both president and chief executive officer, and he must have the unanimous backing of the board. At the same time, Bill Stewart was called out of retirement to serve as chairman of the board. Since Rubel had continued on as a director and a member of the executive committee, and Stewart was still a director, both were up-to-date on the company's problems and prospects.

Rubel put an early end to rumors that he would be a caretaker: "I am not an interim president," he stated. "I am and will be an active, operating president — and if you don't think so, just watch. Bill Stewart and I will work together closely as we have for so many years."

To the executive committee, Rubel declared, "Reese left us a financially sound and operationally progressive company. The basic policies he established will be continued. To carry them out aggressively and successfully will involve the united effort and full cooperation of everyone. This will be a team effort. As a team, we are going to make Reese's planned program work."

Taylor's "financially sound and operationally progressive company" had been no small achievement. Union was now a big league oil company with more than one-half billion dollars in shareholder equity. It had 7,000 employees, $600 million in annual sales, $45 million in earnings, 546 million barrels in liquid hydrocarbon reserves, and 5.3 trillion cubic feet of natural gas reserves. Moreover, Taylor had shaped the personality of the company with his championing of free

Left: Directors Harold W. Sanders (starting second from left), Art Stewart, and Bill Stewart, shown at Union's annual meeting in 1962, were members of the executive committee that helped "educate" Reese Taylor in the oil business after he became president in 1938. *Below left:* Huge 76 logos, each weighing more than 1,600 pounds, were installed atop the scoreboards at Dodger Stadium in 1962.

enterprise, and by making the company an active participant in civic affairs wherever it did business.

Only a year after Reese Taylor's death, the board had to issue another eulogy. On August 30, 1963, Bill Stewart died in the same hospital as Taylor. Of the grandson of Union's founder, the board said: "During his thirty-seven years of loyal and dedicated service as a member of the board—longest in the company's history—his uncompromising integrity, unswerving devotion, and warmhearted sense of fairness left an indelible imprint in helping to shape the destiny of the company through its years of greatest growth and progress."

In 1964, Atlantic Refining Company suggested a possible merger with Union Oil. Such a merger, with Atlantic in Philadelphia, would have created a nationwide integrated oil company with annual revenues exceeding $1 billion. After discussions were under way, however, Atlantic acquired Hondo Oil, making Hondo's chief executive, Robert O. Anderson, a major Atlantic shareholder. He apparently did not favor a merger with Union Oil, and the talks were called off. (Anderson would later head ARCO, formed by a merger of Atlantic with the Richfield Oil Company of California in 1968.)

The Atlantic merger talk and the Phillips raid focused the attention of analysts and investors on Union Oil. What they saw was a "sleeper"—a harddriving, profitable oil company with topflight producing, refining, and marketing facilities in the country's fastest growing area. Union stock soared in three years from $40 to over $100. In late 1964, the directors voted a three-for-one stock split.

Union Oil was owned by some 70,000 shareholders living in all 50 states and 36 foreign lands. Behind each share of stock was a reserve of 35 barrels of oil or its equivalent in natural gas. Reserves of both oil and gas were the highest in Union's history, and in a 1964 report to employees, Rubel promised a substantial improvement on that position.

Crude production totaled 125,000 barrels per day, and gas output topped 600 million cubic feet per day. Newly enlarged tankers cut the cost of transporting Middle Eastern crude to Union's refineries. The Unicracker increased the output of high-value products. Sales volumes had increased by one-third since 1960.

Below: The first time Los Angeles refinery employees painted a storage tank (vaporsphere) as the world's biggest baseball was in 1965—the year the Dodgers beat the Minnesota Twins in a seven-game World Series. The world champion Dodgers were so honored again in 1981 (shown) when they beat the Yankees 4-2 and once more in 1988—L.A. over Oakland, 4-1. Below right: Union sponsored the popular Skyride at the Seattle World's Fair in 1962 and took the opportunity to introduce an illuminated version of the 76 globe.

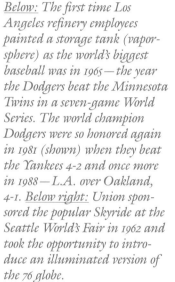

The subsidiaries were thriving. Union Oil of Canada, for example, reported net earnings of $1.2 million in 1964—more than five times its 1963 earnings. T. Craig Henderson, president of Collier Carbon and Chemical, had seven plants turning out petroleum by-products. The outlook appeared so promising that Union's directors allocated $140 million for capital expenditures in 1965.

With such bright prospects ahead, Rubel decided that the time had come to turn the helm over to a younger president. At his urging, the directors chose Fred L. Hartley as Union's ninth president on August 31, 1964. Rubel was elected chairman of the board. Having led the company through two years of record growth and earnings after the abrupt ending of his first retirement from Union Oil, he looked forward to his second. "I don't intend to be the Archie Moore of the oil industry," he said.

Hartley became chief executive officer on December 28, 1964. Rubel retired as chairman of the board the following April and devoted much of his time to politics. He worked on Barry Goldwater's unsuccessful presidential campaign in 1964 and advised his close friend Ronald Reagan to run for governor of California.

After Rubel's death on May 31, 1967 at age 72, the governor eulogized him as a loyal supporter and confidant. "Cy never put a string on service," Reagan said. "He held true to one statement he made consistently—he never wanted anything but good government."

Hartley, whom Rubel had chosen to lead the company through some of its most successful and challenging years, said: "Cy Rubel was an inspiration to all who knew of his efforts and leadership to elevate the character of man and the quality of our society."

Reese Taylor talks with a shareholder at his last annual meeting in 1962.

Part 3

Fred L. Hartley:

VISIONARY ENGINEER

One year after Reese Taylor had been tapped for the presidency of Union Oil, Fred Lloyd Hartley joined the company at the refinery in Oleum, near San Francisco. Few would have guessed that the fresh-faced, 22-year-old trainee was presidential timber.

"I was the only descending passenger when the train stopped at a lonely station in the countryside near the refinery," Hartley recalled. "I had $25 in my pocket and a suitcase mostly filled with dirty clothes accumulated during the several days of the train ride. No brass bands, no welcoming committee, no friends. And then they put me — a bright young college graduate — to work on a labor gang, hoeing weeds and cleaning out dirty tank cars. I think that's where I learned the basic philosophical tenet that has guided me in my life since: Be enthusiastic!"

Hartley, however, had shown considerable enthusiasm before then. The Great Depression was on in 1934 when he finished high school in Vancouver, British Columbia, and he needed money for college. He drove a truck for his father during the day and worked odd jobs at night at a local drive-in restaurant. He spent the next five years at the University of British Columbia earning the equivalent of a master's degree in chemical engineering.

During his first two summer breaks, Hartley worked his way up from dishwasher to steward on a cruise ship running between Vancouver and Skagway, Alaska. The third summer he joined a five-man team working for the Canadian Topographical Survey. Traveling by horse and canoe, they surveyed about 600 square miles in the Yukon Territory. In 1938, he spent his final summer break from college

working as a draftsman and junior engineer for Standard Oil Company of California's Canadian subsidiary.

As graduation approached in the spring of 1939, Hartley was recruited by Union Oil. His early assignments would test his mettle: One was to chisel rock-hard residues from the bottoms of furnace stacks. He earned 75 cents an hour.

"I tackled that job like it was one of the most important in the refinery," he said. "I worked hard — and with enthusiasm, although I must confess that at times it was very difficult to muster that feeling."

Two months later — and not a day too soon — he was assigned to the inspection lab to run chemical tests on petroleum products. In September, he was promoted to junior research engineer at the Los Angeles refinery. As such, he helped design and operate a variety of petroleum processing plants.

Hartley's career was launched. He felt confident of his future in his new country. While proud of his Canadian heritage, he often referred to himself as "an American by choice."

Hartley's college sweetheart, Peggy Murphy, graduated in June 1940 with a degree in physics and mathematics. In November, she joined Fred in California and they were married. Their children, Margaret Ann (Marnie) and Fred, Jr. (Jack), were born in 1956 and 1958, respectively.

By December 1941, when America entered World War II, Hartley was in charge of starting up Union's new hydroformer at Oleum, urgently needed to manufacture aviation fuel for the war effort. Neither the Canadian nor the American armed forces drafted Hartley. His skills were deemed more valuable on the home front.

Clockwise from top left: Fred Hartley conferred with President Gerald Ford during a tour of The Geysers in 1975. Hartley posed in front of Union Oil Center in 1976. Among numerous honors, Hartley was named California Manufacturer of the Year in 1977. He represented the United States at EXPO 86 in Vancouver, Canada, as U.S. ambassador and as commissioner-general to the U.S. exhibition. Hartley received his diploma from the University of British Columbia in 1939. By 1941, the young research engineer was building a great career.

"I'm sure there were others in the company at least as qualified as I was," Hartley recalled. "But I never have and never expect to take a back seat to anyone for an enthusiastic approach to a project. By enthusiasm I mean keen interest and desire and belief in what I'm doing."

Union's hydroformer technology had been purchased from another company. While it was supposed to be a proven process, Union bought a bill of goods, according to Hartley. "We had a hell of a time making the plant run," he recalled.

Hartley's enthusiasm didn't flag, however, and he earned a reputation for getting the job done. "It was the first opportunity I had to show I was capable of running an operation, working with the men and the [labor] union, solving technological problems, and keeping up the drive," he explained.

When the war ended in 1945, the hydroformer had to be junked, but the experience had lasting value for Hartley. He understood, on a nuts-and-bolts level, the importance of developing the company's own technology. In later years, emphasis on technological innovation would be a central theme in Hartley's corporate strategy.

In 1944, Hartley moved to the headquarters office in Los Angeles as manufacturing process supervisor in charge of process engineering design for all of Union's new plants. He was promoted to general superintendent at the Los Angeles refinery in 1950.

After a serious fire at the refinery in July 1951, Reese Taylor, Union's president, surveyed the scene and asked Hartley about the causes. Hartley, always direct, told Taylor that Union had built its modern high-pressure plants in the worst possible place—among old tank farms and piping systems.

Taylor, equally direct, took the problem to higher levels of refinery management. Hartley was caught in the backfire. His position at the refinery became increasingly untenable and, in 1953, Taylor arranged Hartley's transfer to the research department.

There, Hartley started up what soon became a highly profitable enterprise for Union—the sale and licensing of Union technology to other companies. In 1955, he was put in charge of research. In 1960, he took over marketing of refined products and made significant changes to revamp and strengthen operations. He was also elected to the board of directors in 1960. In 1962, refining activities were added to his responsibilities.

Hartley was elected president and chief executive officer in 1964, and chairman of the board in 1974. In 1976, he experienced a great personal trial—a coronary artery bypass operation. He recovered quickly and was back to work within weeks.

Hartley's vision and enthusiasm took Union from regional to international stature within a few years of his assuming the presidency. The 1970s and 1980s brought some of the most dramatic events in the oil industry's history: a virtual explosion in technological development, the rise of OPEC, recurring energy crises, and a destructive wave of corporate takeover raids.

The dedication, ingenuity, and strength of character Hartley brought to the company made him the effective and forceful chief executive Unocal would need during these tumultuous and challenging years.

8 Creating an International Oil Company

Fred Hartley took over a company that was poised for expansion. Opposite: After merging with The Pure Oil Company, Union Oil had a national marketing presence. Pure Oil stations, such as this one at 1525 Church Street in Decatur, Georgia, received a new look.

F red L. Hartley took charge of a strong regional oil company in 1964. "I was a witness and, in my own part of the company, a participant in the dynamic change and growth of the Taylor years," Hartley recalled. "When I finally came to the same job, he and Cy Rubel had left the company with a tremendous momentum operating at full speed ahead."

Hartley was equal to the challenge. He led the fast-moving company into one of its most productive periods. Hartley guided Union through a merger that virtually doubled the company's size and strength. "I did not become chief executive officer of Union Oil to see it remain a regional oil company," he noted.

During the next five years, the Union Oil Company expanded its oil and gas operations into new frontiers in America and overseas. Before the decade closed, Union was a major player in the booming oil fields of Alaska, the Middle East, and Indonesia, and had established a foothold in other important regions, including the North Sea.

Hartley, recognizing the potential of alternative energies, pushed development of the company's geothermal resources. Refining and marketing operations were upgraded, and new technologies were developed to keep the company competitive in the marketplace. Chemicals manufacturing and marketing became a larger segment of the company's business.

Hartley knew that continued growth was imperative to maintaining the company's momentum. America was energy hungry, and the country's appetite for fuels and other hydrocarbon products kept increasing.

While Union had a strong presence in domestic exploration and production, the United States was a maturing oil province. For new major discoveries, oil companies began looking at unexplored areas offshore and overseas. The companies anticipated operating in tougher physical and political environments. The successful competitors in the world oil market of the future would be those with a broad financial base capable of supporting global exploration and long-term research into new technologies.

The world was changing. U.S. oil imports from the Middle East rose rapidly. To adjust to this contingency, two of Union's tankers — the *Lake Palourde* and the *Torrey Canyon* — had been "jumboized" in 1964, almost doubling their capacities. Union Oil was ready to jumboize, too.

Meanwhile, The Pure Oil Company headquartered in Palatine, Illinois, came under attack. In June 1964, a syndicate led by the brokerage firm of Loeb, Rhoades and Company offered to buy out the company. Pure Oil president

Robert L. Milligan was galled by this power play, which came at a time when Pure was most vulnerable. First-quarter earnings were off 45 percent from 1963, showing the worst results in 20 years — and the situation was not improving rapidly. Gasoline price wars had taken a toll; an unusually warm spring had cut into heating fuel sales; and Pure had not had time to reap the rewards of developing its extensive new natural gas strikes.

Loeb, Rhoades' representatives had assured Milligan months earlier that their stock purchases were for investment purposes only (a phrase that echoed down the years to the hostile takeover situation Union faced in 1985). Then they changed their tune. It was obvious to Milligan that the purchasing syndicate stood to gain an immense profit from the holdings of Pure's shareholders. By borrowing $500 million against Pure's reserves, the syndicate could pay off the principal and interest in ten years — and still own half the reserves.

Soon, other organizations took an interest. A second offer and then a third followed the Loeb, Rhoades bid. Pure's directors were relieved of the necessity to make an immediate decision, since they would need time to consider each offer. Milligan wrote to shareholders, explaining the situation and noting that the company had commissioned a study to evaluate its oil and gas reserves.

A study was essential to help management determine the company's worth. More importantly, it bought time for Milligan — valuable time that he used to explore the possibility of merging with another company. Out to get a better deal for Pure's shareholders and employees, he knew the employees would be better off working for a strong corporate organization — a much brighter prospect than working for an "oil" company stripped of its reserves. Stockholders, too, would stand to gain more from a merger. They would not have to pay capital gains tax if a merger involved a tax-free exchange of stock from one company to another. They would be able to preserve their investment in an oil company, and if it were done right, the investment would be in a stronger company.

On October 19, 1964, the study results were issued: Pure had crude oil reserves of 539 million barrels and natural gas reserves of 2.65 trillion cubic feet. The first three offers for Pure had been withdrawn in September, but new offers were bound to follow soon. However, Milligan had formed his own plan.

Late in 1964, Milligan and Hartley briefly explored the potential benefits of merging their two companies. It would create a strong oil company too

Below: In the 1920s, Purol tank trucks served a marketing territory that stretched, albeit thinly, from Washington State to New England to Florida. Later, Pure Oil consolidated its markets east of the Mississippi. Bottom left: On December 18, 1914, the discovery of oil at Cabin Creek, West Virginia, led to the formation of Pure Oil. Bottom right: The "Hot Shot Boys" were drillers at Pure's Van field in East Texas, circa 1930.

Right: After the 1965 merger, the addition of more than 13,000 Pure service stations gave Union Oil a network of some 17,000 retail outlets in 37 states.

● Pure Marketing Areas
● Union Marketing Areas

big to be easily absorbed by rivals or carved up by financial syndicates. Pure's marketing operations in 25 states east of the Rockies would complement Union's western marketing organization. Since the marketing areas did not overlap, a merger would not reduce competition in gasoline sales in either region. Yet, localized gasoline price wars, which subjected regional marketers to frequent drubbings on the bottom line, would have less overall effect on the new, bigger company. Price wars, the result of industry efforts to market relatively cheap and plentiful supplies of crude oil, persisted throughout the 1960s.

Thus, if Union and Pure merged they would form a national organization with a depth and balance that neither could achieve as a regional entity. Such a merger would stimulate competition, providing a stronger player both in the consumer market for petroleum products and in the worldwide scramble for exploration acreage.

By January 1965, Milligan was ready to act. He called Hartley, and they reviewed the broad outlines of a formula for merging Pure Oil into Union Oil through a new issue of Union Oil convertible preferred stock. Hartley assigned Charles F. Parker, Union's senior vice president for finance, and Claude S. Brinegar, manager of economics and corporate planning, to make a detailed study of the potential terms of the proposed consolidation. They confirmed that the possibilities for mutual stockholder benefit were highly promising.

On January 29, when the Pure Oil board of directors authorized Milligan to proceed with merger negotiations, offers and expressions of interest began to pour in from all corners—one from as far away as Belgium. Four offers turned out to be serious; Union's offer was preferred by the majority of Pure's directors.

Hartley and Milligan continued their negotiations as quietly as possible. Shareholders of both Union and Pure would be unsettled if rumors circulated before the actual terms of the merger could be announced.

Headlines in financial columns, however, soon touted the "battle of the giants." Trading in Pure Oil shares was suspended briefly on the New York Stock Exchange. Dissident Pure shareholders threatened lawsuits to scuttle the merger unless Union upped its bid.

One Union director, shipping magnate Daniel K. Ludwig, adamantly opposed the merger. (Some have speculated that he had merger plans of his own.) In any case, Ludwig called Hartley soon after the February merger meetings to

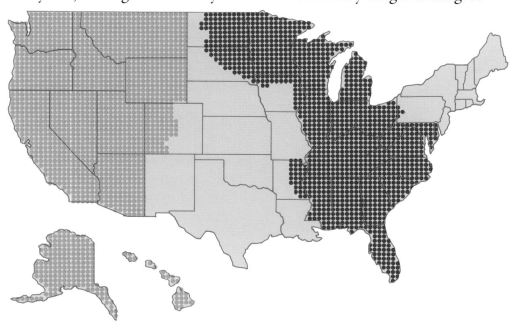

propose selling his stock to Union. In 1963, Ludwig had purchased the Union
Oil shares that Phillips Petroleum Company had accumulated in its attempt
to take over Union. Ludwig held some 4 million shares worth approximately
$146 million. A buyout would be a big bite for Union on top of the $650 million
merger, but the board voted to accept the offer on February 11. Ludwig resigned
as a director, having served less than two years.

In order to buy out Ludwig, Union needed to borrow $125 million quickly.
Charlie Parker and Leroy B. Houghton, Union's treasurer, were assigned to the
job. February 12 was Lincoln's Birthday, a bank holiday in most states. Parker
and Houghton spent the day on the phone tracking down the heads of 17 of the
country's largest banks at their homes, on golf courses, and at parties. By day's
end, Union had authorizations to borrow $180 million in five-year loans—a clear
demonstration of confidence in Union Oil's management.

Both the Pure and Union boards approved the merger in April. Dissident
Pure shareholders geared up for a proxy fight, bombarding the nation's financial
editors with press releases attacking Pure's management. Meetings to vote on the
merger were scheduled for July 2; Pure shareholders would gather in Columbus,
Ohio, and Union shareholders in Los Angeles.

On May 27, a few hours after comprehensive proxy statements had been
mailed to stockholders, Union and Pure representatives were finally free to speak
out in answer to their critics. Milligan and Parker (Hartley was out of the country) called a joint press conference in New York.

"Truly, here is a case when two plus two equals five," Milligan said of the
merger. "If there is a proxy fight, we're ready for it," Parker declared.

During the next several weeks, teams of Union and Pure officers met with
Pure shareholders to explain how the merger would enhance their earnings and
the value of their holdings. These personal contacts proved highly successful.
Claude Brinegar and John Spence, Pure's vice president and secretary, picked up
proxies in New York for 1.3 million Pure shares alone during just two days.

In July, more than 77 percent of Pure's shares were voted to accept the Union
merger offer, representing an overwhelming majority of the total shares voted.
As it turned out, only 59 Pure shareholders—holding less than 1 percent of the
outstanding shares—dissented. Union shareholders also voted overwhelming
support for the merger. U.S. antitrust officials ruled that they would take no
action against it. And so, the largest merger to that time in the history of the

*Top left: In 1927, Pure was the
first major oil company to stan-
dardize its service station design
with the introduction of the
cottage stations. Above: The
Union-Pure merger was accomplished by an exchange of stock
certificates. Opposite, center and
bottom: Famed aviator Wiley
Post helped develop a pressure
suit for high-altitude flying.
During his Pure Oil–fueled
flight in 1934, he confirmed the
presence of the jet stream above
30,000 feet.*

Right: On Union Oil's seventy-fifth anniversary in October 1965, the board of directors met in the company's original head-quarters in Santa Paula, California. Seated (from left), directors Arthur C. Stewart, Fred L. Hartley, and Donold B. Lourie. Standing (from left), directors Charles B. Thornton; Robert DiGiorgio; John W. Towler; Kenneth C. Vaughan; Reed O. Hunt; Fred D. Fagg, Jr.; William H. Doheny; Charles F. Parker; corporate secretary Robert F. Niven; and general counsel L.A. Gibbons. Absent were directors Prentis C. Hale, Robert L. Milligan, and Henry T. Mudd.

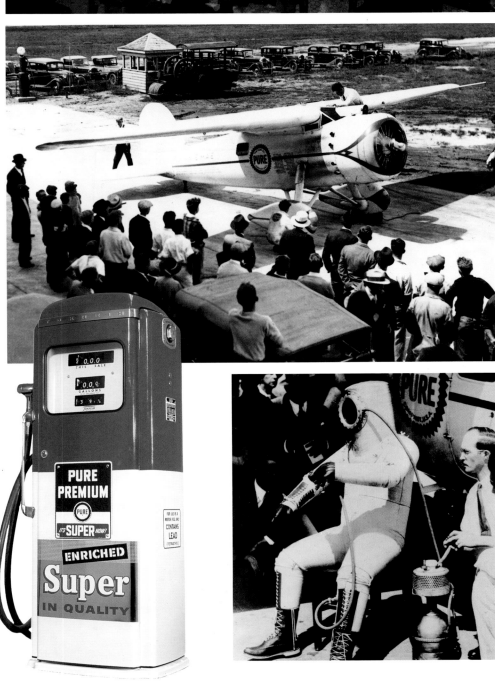

U.S. oil industry was achieved. With $1.7 billion in assets, the new Union Oil became the ninth largest company in the industry. Reserves totaled more than 1 billion barrels of crude oil and natural gas liquids, and nearly 9 trillion cubic feet of natural gas. The company had 10 million acres of land in the United States and Canada to explore, and another 48 million acres abroad. Product sales averaged 360,000 barrels a day.

In statements to the Department of Justice, Hartley noted that Union Oil Company aspired to be "not another Goliath in the oil industry, but a bigger David." Just adding up the numbers, however, wouldn't make the merger a success. The biggest challenge for this new "David" lay ahead. Claude Brinegar was assigned to lead the effort to forge a true "Union" of the two oil companies. The process would take six years.

Exploration and production activities were quickly and smoothly combined. Research was consolidated at Union's laboratories in Brea, California. Pure subsidiaries became Union subsidiaries.

It would take a much longer time to reorganize Pure's refining and marketing activities headquartered in Palatine, and to change Pure's public image over to Union 76. (The Palatine postal address was changed in the mid-1970s when the headquarters site was included in an area incorporated by the neighboring village of Schaumburg.)

Many Pure employees felt uneasy. "They weren't sure about their futures," Brinegar recalled. "Consequently, they were very cautious. They often wanted to check with their potential bosses in Los Angeles before they'd do anything."

This reluctance to act could hurt business, so Brinegar constantly assured people — both in the head office in Palatine and in the field offices — that changes would not happen overnight. Each situation would be assessed in an orderly and studied fashion. Merging operations might take days, weeks, or months; but Union employees were not going to stream over the Rocky Mountains to invade the Pure Oil offices in Palatine.

Despite assurances, it was understood that some jobs would become redundant once the companies were merged. Pure had a far more complicated executive hierarchy than Union's — almost an extra layer of management.

"As I look back now and reflect on the integration of the Pure system into

Top: Claude Brinegar, who joined Union as an economic analyst in 1953, led the company's effort to absorb Pure Oil operations. He became president of the Pure Oil Division in 1965 and president of the new Union 76 Division in 1968. Above: Bob Milligan, president of Pure Oil from 1954 to 1965, served as a Union director and chairman of the Pure Oil Division and subsequently the Union 76 Division from 1965 until his retirement in 1971. Left: A manufacturing plant at the Dollarhide field (acquired in the Pure merger) in West Texas removed liquids from natural gas produced with the field's crude oil.

In 1958, Pure purchased 250 acres of corn and soybean fields near Palatine, Illinois, where the company opened its new headquarters building in 1960. The area was later annexed by the village of Schaumburg.

ours," Brinegar said, "I realize we evolved certain management techniques that are common now. We appointed task forces to handle special assignments — with people having a special job for a while and then going to another assignment. We used this approach extensively for almost three years."

The task-force strategy seemed particularly appropriate in the merger situation, since it involved teams of employees from both Pure and Union working together to effect solutions. Each team reviewed certain areas of operation to determine which jobs were necessary and which were redundant. Tough decisions were made about who to keep and who to transfer; some employees were offered early retirement or another settlement.

In October 1965, Pure's refining, marketing, and petrochemical operations were organized into a new profit center, the Pure Oil Division, with Brinegar as president and Milligan as division chairman. By early 1967, Pure's corporate activities had been moved from Palatine to Los Angeles. Union's accounting methods and other administrative procedures had been introduced, resulting in more cost-effective operations. Plans were under way to replace Pure Oil signs with Union 76 signs at the company's 13,000 retail outlets in the East.

Many talented Pure employees made significant contributions to the success of the expanded Union Oil Company in the ensuing years. William S. McConnor became a corporate senior vice president and president of the Union 76 Division. He was succeeded in 1986 by another former Pure employee, Roger C. Beach. Thomas B. Sleeman became a corporate senior vice president and president of the Chemicals Division. All three men were elected to the board of directors. Dr. Carel Otte became president of the Geothermal Division.

Jack Vance, managing director of the Los Angeles office of McKinsey and Company, management consultants, had been involved with Union's operations from the early 1960s. In summing up the merger some ten years after the fact, Vance said: "If you look at Union Oil, it was a question of survival. Union had to become a national, integrated oil company with sufficient resources to remain competitive and grow. The merger, then, was fantastically important to the company's future. That it was completed so successfully was a clear demonstration of good management strategy....Claude directed one of the cleverest strategic digestive processes that I've ever seen done."

Six months after the merger was approved by shareholders, Hartley announced the formation of the Union International Oil & Gas Division. Ray A. Burke, vice president of exploration and production, was chosen to head

Above: Union and three partners discovered the huge Sassan
field offshore Iran in 1965. *Left:*
Pure Oil and three partners acquired a 28,000-acre concession
in Venezuela's Lake Maracaibo
in 1956. The following year, they
brought in a discovery well at
nearly 2,500 barrels per day.

up the new division. At the same time, Burke was elected corporate senior vice president, and a member of the board of directors and the executive committee.

"The decision to create the International Division," Hartley explained, "reflects our belief that oil and gas discoveries of the future are more likely to be made overseas, and in most cases offshore, where exploration techniques have reached a high state of development."

The new, bigger Union had the resources to be a much more aggressive player in the worldwide search for hydrocarbons. It could take on several major projects at the same time — committing the hundreds of millions of dollars necessary to explore in distant and difficult climes.

The company had been laying the groundwork for many of these international plays for years before the merger. Management had long recognized the need to improve Union's marketing position by producing more and buying less foreign crude to fulfill Union's import quota. (In 1959, President Dwight Eisenhower instituted limits on oil imports to protect against import dependence and to stimulate the domestic oil industry.) Opportunities were expanding for companies that could bring essential technological expertise to foreign countries, particularly developing countries in need of energy resources to support growing populations.

At the annual meeting held in April 1966, Burke reported to shareholders that Union was conducting exploration activities in some 15 countries throughout the world. "We have production…in Australia, Venezuela, and Canada," he said, adding that net production from these areas amounted to about 35,000 barrels of oil a day. That figure rose dramatically during the next decade as discoveries in the Middle East and Southeast Asia were developed.

In remarks at the same meeting, Hartley explained that the demand for energy from petroleum historically increased at a faster rate than the growth in populations using that energy. The free world's daily consumption of 25 million barrels of petroleum products a day in 1964, he noted, was expected to rise to 35 million barrels per day by 1970.

"No wonder oil companies are looking for raw materials in such difficult

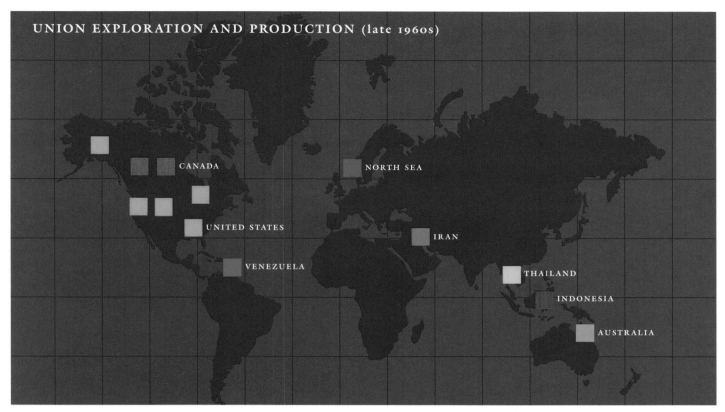

UNION EXPLORATION AND PRODUCTION (late 1960s)

CANADA

NORTH SEA

UNITED STATES

IRAN

VENEZUELA

THAILAND

INDONESIA

AUSTRALIA

After merging with Pure Oil, Union Oil had a wider international reach. The map shows both producing areas and exploratory prospects that yielded major discoveries.

places as the North Sea, Alaska's Cook Inlet, offshore waters, and even under people's houses here in Southern California!" Hartley said.

"No wonder we are also thinking of eventual oil production from shale oil, tar sands, and possibly coal," he continued. "Even with the advent of nuclear power, solar energy, and fuel cells in the future, we expect a continuing growth in consumption of oil and gas for a long time to come."

The discovery of gigantic onshore oil fields in the Middle East had brought oil explorers running in the 1920s and 1930s. In the early 1960s, the state-owned National Iranian Oil Corporation (NIOC) began conducting marine seismic surveys in the Persian Gulf. NIOC needed funds to finance the surveys, so it stipulated that only those companies that helped underwrite them would be eligible later to bid on the prospects.

Union was one of 26 foreign oil companies that persisted in the effort to the bidding stage. NIOC would be a 50 percent partner in any venture and would be liable for its half of the expenses only if commercial production were established, defining commercial as more than 630,000 barrels lifted from a field.

The Persian Gulf play was an expensive proposition, so the foreign companies formed joint ventures in order to finance their bids. Union and three partners, each with a 12.5 percent share, contributed to a $25 million bonus to secure the drilling and production rights on three prime blocks. The agreement with NIOC was signed in February 1965. Union and its partners formed the Lavan Petroleum Company to conduct operations.

Burke wanted to drill first on the block closest to Abu Dhabi's waters, but the other joint-venture representatives were hesitant. A boundary dispute could complicate matters. So Burke flew to London to consult the British Admiralty's mapping division, which had developed the precepts by which such offshore boundaries had been established in similar situations around the world. The admiralty's opinion, issued within two months, gave the joint-venture partners the confidence to proceed. Lavan drilled in the Sassan block and, by December 1965, they knew they had something. The Sassan field was subsequently rated by the *Oil & Gas Journal* as the thirty-ninth largest in the free world, with crude oil reserves exceeding 1 billion barrels. Development of the field, however, presented enormous difficulties. Summer temperatures in the Persian Gulf can reach 120 degrees F. with humidity at 80 to 90 percent. The prevailing *shamal* wind rises to gale force for days at a time, blowing sand and sharply reducing visibility.

More than once during the development of Sassan, surging seas severed the 22-inch pipeline crews were laying to connect the field to production and shipping facilities on Lavan Island. Once, the supply barge capsized. Retrieving pipe and equipment from the sea floor was no easy task, since the pipeline was laid at a record depth for the time — 306 feet at one point.

The joint-venture partners' persistence and ingenuity eventually paid off. The first shipment of Sassan crude oil was made in November 1968 and totaled 506,000 barrels. Union's one-eighth share in production averaged close to 15,000 barrels per day in 1969.

As if such extreme climatic conditions were not enough, U.S. oil companies operating overseas faced growing political challenges as well. The companies had to develop new negotiating skills in order to satisfy the needs and demands of their host countries while continuing to operate profitably for their investors.

Union's development history in Indonesia provides a good example of this new and more complex international business environment. Henry L. Brandon first arrived in Jakarta on August 5, 1960. A lawyer who functioned as a roving landman for Union's international oil and gas operations, he played a key role in developing the prototype production-sharing contract with Dr. H. Ibnu Sutowo, president of Permina, one of several Indonesian state oil and gas companies that merged in 1968 to form Pertamina.

Indonesia, emerging from 400 years of colonialism, had won its independence from the Netherlands in 1949 after four years of bitter struggle. In the early 1960s, the Indonesians again battled the Dutch — this time over control of West Irian (Netherlands New Guinea). In 1962, the Dutch relinquished control of West Irian to the United Nations, which in turn gave it to Indonesia in 1963. Obviously, Indonesian President Sukarno would not be interested in any association that remotely resembled a continuation of foreign domination.

"When I arrived, General Sutowo had started talking about production sharing," Brandon recalled. This was a new type of arrangement in which Indonesia would allow foreign-owned companies to share in the production of its resources in return for capital and know-how. Indonesia would retain ownership of the resource.

Brandon covered a lot of miles commuting between Jakarta, where Union had a negotiating team, and company headquarters in Los Angeles in the effort to reach an agreement that both Union and the Indonesian government would find acceptable and profitable. Finally, Brandon presented a 30-page document to the Indonesians. They asked him to cut it down, which he did — but several years passed before Union signed such an agreement. Union and other foreign oil companies put their interests on hold while Indonesia struggled through a Communist uprising in 1965, which was quickly suppressed but then followed by months of bloody rioting and retaliation.

In 1967, General Suharto emerged as the country's new leader. Union and many of its competitors resumed their interest. "Two other companies signed production-sharing contracts before we did," Ray Burke recalled, "but we had laid all the groundwork five years earlier."

Hank Brandon returned to Jakarta in 1967 and was joined there by Charles M. Schwartz, head of company operations in Australia. Schwartz's negotiating team included Richard J. Stegemeier, who had just been transferred to Queensland to manage production operations at Union's Moonie and Alton fields.

Opposite, top: Union drilled the Attaka discovery well offshore East Kalimantan, Indonesia, from the Wodeco VI *drilling ship in 1970, ten years after company representatives first contacted Indonesian officials for drilling rights. Center: During his tenure in Southeast Asia, Dick Stegemeier held many visas. This one was valid for four months in Indonesia. Opposite, bottom: Stegemeier grew a beard in the tropics and, on a wager with Fred Hartley, kept it until Union discovered oil in Indonesia.*

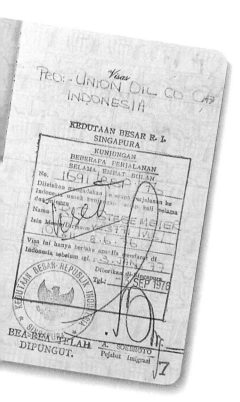

Right: Stegemeier and Henry T. Snow (third and fourth from left) met with local officials in East Kalimantan about drilling, circa 1970.

A few years earlier, Stegemeier had been instrumental in Union's negotiations with the Tokyo Gas Company. At that time, Union had been considering participation in a project to liquefy and export natural gas to Japan from the Kenai field in Alaska. Union eventually pursued a different option for the Kenai gas, but the experience proved invaluable for Stegemeier.

Brandon was sidelined by hepatitis before negotiations were concluded, but Schwartz's team, which also included John Zender, manager of exploration, carried on. "We were really a good team," Stegemeier recalled, "with a balance of expertise in exploration, production, geology, and geophysics."

Union signed two production-sharing contracts with Pertamina in 1968: one for an area offshore north Sumatra, and the other for areas both on and offshore East Kalimantan. "The contract we negotiated for northwest Sumatra," Stegemeier noted, "set the stage for the modern production-sharing contracts under which all of our operations in Indonesia have been conducted. We use that same type of contract in other parts of the world."

Also in 1968, Union took on the unusual role of rice exporter to help the country secure badly needed supplies. Traditionally, oil companies in Indonesia included as part of their wages to employees rations of basic commodities: rice, sugar, and kerosene. Loss of these rations would have been devastating to the Indonesian workers. But the country's rice crop was much below normal in 1968, and the government could not borrow money to import rice. Until the new Indonesian regime under President Suharto gained the respect of traditional lenders, the government was forced to improvise. So Sutowo, on a trip to Los Angeles, relayed a request for Union Oil's support to Ray Burke. Union took the opportunity to demonstrate its confidence in the new government as well as in the country's oil potential.

Burke gave the job to Union's purchasing department, and a load of California rice was soon on its way to Indonesia. "It was widely known in the country that Union did this," Stegemeier said, "and the people have never forgotten our humanitarian effort." The Indonesians also never missed a payment on the loan.

Drilling efforts on the Sumatra properties proved disappointing. The story for offshore East Kalimantan turned out quite differently, but it was almost two years before the first well was drilled. Seismic exploration revealed a large structure that straddled the line where Union's acreage bordered the contract area of a Japanese firm, Japex (subsequently Inpex).

"When we see a structure crossing property lines," Stegemeier said, "we usually talk to the other side about sharing the costs fifty-fifty." In the United States,

this is common practice and is done under "unit" agreements. But unitization proved to be a new concept to Japex's executives.

"So we decided to go to Tokyo," said Chuck Schwartz. Sam A. Snyder, associate legal counsel, flew in from Midland, Texas, to draw up the legal documents that would satisfy the American, Japanese, and Indonesian parties to the contract. Under the final agreement, Union and Japex agreed to split costs and profits equally with Union as operator.

"We had a rig en route to Indonesia while we were negotiating," Schwartz recalled. "Within a week of signing the agreement, we were drilling. The first well tested at a rate of 11,300 barrels a day."

That well marked the discovery of the Attaka field in August 1970. "It was a magnificent oil field and beautiful oil—sweet, no sulfur, light, high gasoline content," said Stegemeier, who sent news of the discovery in a coded short-wave message to Sydney for forwarding to Los Angeles. Just 27 months later, Stegemeier, who was promoted to vice president and manager of operations in Indonesia following the Attaka discovery, opened the valve on Union's first producing well in that nation.

Early estimates projected Attaka's lifetime production at 250 million barrels of crude oil. The field has since produced more than 425 million barrels and continues to produce at over 40,000 barrels a day. "It has far exceeded all of our expectations," said Stegemeier.

In 1962, when Ray Burke was newly appointed as vice president of exploration and production, he made his first trip to Indonesia to meet Brandon and Indonesian dignitaries. He also visited Thailand. Two years earlier, Union's John Hazzard and Stan Wissler had evaluated petroleum possibilities there and recommended the company's involvement. Burke talked with key government ministers and found them eager to examine their country's oil and gas potential.

Burke and Brandon felt that Union could begin exploration activities under the country's existing mining law but assisted the Thais in finding the expertise they needed to develop a petroleum law. In 1962, Union was the first oil company awarded exploration rights in the kingdom of Thailand with an onshore concession on the Khorat Plateau. Richard D. Stewart, who set up the company's first office in Bangkok, lost no time in applying for a concession in the Gulf of Thailand in 1968 when the government opened up the offshore area to exploration. Union's Gulf holdings later proved highly productive.

While Burke was involved in working out the final details of production-

A GIANT STEP

In 1937, one obstacle confronted drilling crews eager to tap the rich resources buried beneath the Gulf of Mexico—water. That year, Pure Oil and Superior Oil made history by drilling the first open-water well. The Gulf of Mexico State No. 1 was located a full mile from the Louisiana shore—a short distance by modern standards, but a major hurdle in 1937. The roots of offshore oil exploration can be traced to late nineteenth-century slant-drilling efforts and early twentieth-century projects in the shallows of Lake Erie and along the California coastline near Santa Barbara. The Pure-Superior well was off-shore from wild coastal marshes. Drilling crews endured daily boat rides to and from work over choppy waters, 13 miles each way. There was no radio communication. In foggy weather, the boat crews navigated by the sound of the rig. The wooden rig, although it stood in only 14 feet of water, had to be specially treated with creosote to protect it from the corrosive effects of saltwater. Heavy equipment was transported on flat-topped barges that sometimes needed a tow from the chartered shrimp boats carrying the crews. The first well, completed in early 1938, flowed at 200 barrels of oil and 200,000 cubic feet of gas a day. The platform was enlarged and ten more wells were drilled. Unocal and others have since pushed 100 miles and more offshore, drilling in water depths greater than 1,000 feet.

Left: Pure was a 50 percent partner in drilling the world's first open-water well, spudded in 1937 and completed in 1938 in the Gulf of Mexico. Opposite: In 1964, the North Sea was divided into sectors in order to expedite oil and gas exploration and development.

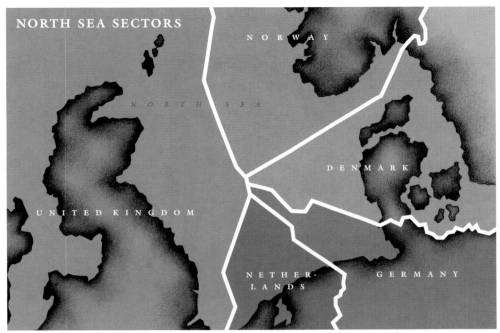

sharing agreements with Indonesia from company headquarters in Los Angeles, he also directed efforts in other parts of the world. The North Sea looked especially promising.

Groningen, a huge natural gas field, had been discovered on the Dutch seaboard in 1959; but offshore development had been slowed by jurisdictional disputes. In 1964, the five countries bordering the sea agreed to divide it into Norwegian, British, Dutch, German, and Danish sectors for purposes of oil and gas exploration and development. Union's participation in seismic surveys of the area yielded information that sent Burke and Sam Snyder to the Netherlands in 1967.

They were looking for potential partners for a joint-venture exploration effort in the Dutch sector. They selected Nedlloyd (then the Nederlanden Steamship Company) because, according to Burke, "we believed their long and successful history in the shipping business reflected an understanding of risk and a willingness to take risk."

The Union-Nedlloyd partnership proved a sturdy one. The first offshore well, drilled in 1968, found natural gas — not in commercial quantities but enough to encourage the explorationists to keep looking. Eleven years later, the first two discoveries of oil proved commercially viable.

The merger with Pure had brought not only the broader financial base Union needed to improve its international position, but also some foreign properties with significant production — notably in Venezuela and Canada. In 1965, Union's production from holdings in Venezuela's prolific Lake Maracaibo area yielded net production of 5,000 barrels per day. The daily production from former Pure holdings in Canada was 11,000 barrels of crude oil and 1.2 million cubic feet of natural gas. Late in 1965, Union Oil Company of Canada issued approximately 1.2 million shares of common stock to Union Oil Company of California in exchange for Pure's Canadian properties.

Three years after the Union-Pure merger, the company's investment in the Persian Gulf began to pay off, and Union was on the brink of major discoveries in Southeast Asia. During those three years, the company's reserves and production rose steadily. While the foreign developments were important, Union Oil also had strong domestic oil and gas operations.

In 1965, U.S. oil and gas operations for Pure and Union had been quickly consolidated under Kenny Vaughan, senior vice president of exploration and production. "Our experience was gratifying in that it was a very easy maneuver,"

The THUMS project won numerous awards for its design. Built within a mile of the shoreline at Long Beach, California, its rigs were disguised to resemble buildings. Landscaping hid other equipment from view. Union held its interest in the project for 24 years, selling it in 1989.

said Joseph W. Luckett, Jr., who, in 1965, was in Denver as Pure's regional general manager for exploration and production.

Luckett recalled staff meetings when Vaughan outlined the overall plan for merging operations. "We attempted to crossbreed the organizations — get the Union people into what had been old Pure territory and vice versa," he said. The idea was to unify operations — and to discourage the formation of potentially divisive Pure and Union cliques. The continued success of domestic exploration and production was of the highest priority.

Ray Burke noted: "We recognized that it would be important for our company to make a more concerted effort to expand its energy resource base beyond the United States, but this didn't mean that we were de-emphasizing domestic exploration. We continued what I would call a total outlook for exploration in the U.S. While many other companies were moving out, we maintained district offices in all of the key exploration areas of the U.S. — anticipating the day when the price of crude oil and natural gas would go up."

But at home, as well as abroad, the oil search focused on offshore areas. One major development was a sure thing — a rarity in the oil business. The East Wilmington field, a giant onshore reservoir that underlies the city of Long Beach, was known to extend offshore. A contract to develop it was awarded on competitive bid in 1965 to five companies. The operation became known as THUMS, an acronym for the five equal partners: Texaco, Humble (which became Exxon), Union, Mobil, and Shell.

The city of Long Beach and the state of California retained 96 percent of the profits. That was agreeable to the oil companies, since the presence of the reserves had been confirmed. It was just a question of getting the oil out of the ground.

In fact, the major risk to be considered in the project was the nature of public response to oil development so close to the beach. Plans called for the THUMS production facilities to occupy four manmade islands less than a mile from shore, so the oil companies took a unique approach to construction. Derricks were covered to look like modern buildings, and the islands were landscaped with plants and waterfalls. The project has won numerous awards for environmental and scenic adaptation.

Farther north and farther offshore, Union was involved in exploring the Santa Barbara Channel. In February 1968, Union and three equal partners had made successful bids for federal leases on more than 46,000 acres in this highly prospective area. That summer, three exploratory wells found commercial quan-

ICE-PROOFING A PLATFORM
"Why don't we build a mushroom?" suggested Richard W.
Yarbrough of Union's Oil &
Gas Division. So was conceived
the industry's first monopod
offshore platform. Yarbrough
was meeting with consulting
engineers seeking an innovative
platform design that could
stand up to the harsh offshore
environment of Alaska's Cook
Inlet. The monopod would
have only one large support
(like a mushroom), making it
less vulnerable to damage from
huge chunks of ice often carried on the inlet's rushing
tides. A total of 32 wells could
be drilled through the leg,
which measured 24½ feet in
diameter. Since the one-leg
design required less steel in
its construction, the platform's
$12 million price tag was 20 per-
cent less than a conventional
four-legged counterpart. The
monopod was installed in the
Trading Bay field in 1966. Since
the configuration could not be
economically adapted to water
depths greater than 100 feet or
to accommodate more than 32
wells, the platform continues
to hold a unique place in the
Cook Inlet—an ingenious
solution to a singular problem.

*The monopod provided a novel
solution to the problems of operating in Alaska's Cook Inlet.*

tities of oil on Block 402. Platform A was set in the fall to produce the oil, with Union Oil Company as operator.

Even farther north, Union explored the icy waters of Alaska's Cook Inlet. Drilling in the inlet proved treacherous, with tides surging as much as 30 feet, currents exceeding six knots, and large blocks of ice battering everything in their path during the long winter.

Nevertheless, four new oil fields were discovered in 1965 and 1966. Union Oil held substantial interests in three of them: Granite Point, Trading Bay, and McArthur River. From virtually no production in 1965, the Cook Inlet was providing over 12 percent of Union's total supply of domestic crude oil by 1969. The company was the biggest producer of crude oil in Alaska, a position it would hold until oil from the Prudhoe Bay discovery would begin flowing south through the Trans-Alaska Pipeline System in 1977.

The Cook Inlet's sweet, low-sulfur crude was an ideal feedstock for high-quality gasolines, lubricating oils, and fuel oils. It was easily transported to Union's West Coast refineries. But using the company's extensive natural gas reserves on the Kenai Peninsula—estimated at more than 1 trillion cubic feet by 1965—presented a tough challenge. Pipelines reached limited markets. While other oil producers used some of the gas to repressurize their fields, and the city of Anchorage took some for residential use, Union sought larger potential markets.

One alternative was to liquefy the natural gas and ship it to Japan or other foreign markets, and Union explored this option with its joint-venture partner in the Kenai field, Marathon Oil Company. (U.S. markets were out of the question since the prices allowed by the Federal Power Commission for interstate gas were lower than the cost of producing and delivering liquefied natural gas.)

As negotiations proceeded, however, Union judged the liquefied natural gas project to be economically infeasible, and the company pursued another option. The natural gas could be used as feedstock to produce ammonia and urea, basic

nitrogen fertilizers. The products could be sold through Union's wholly owned subsidiary, Collier Carbon and Chemical Corporation.

Collier had built up a strong position in the West Coast fertilizer market. In 1961, it had acquired the Pacific Guano Company, with seven outlets in California. Pacific then expanded through further acquisitions in the western United States and Illinois. Following the Union-Pure merger in 1965, Pacific took over operations of the Pure Gas and Chemical Company headquartered in Denver. The expansion prompted a name change for Pacific to the PureGro Company.

In 1966, Collier signed contracts for a 1,500-ton-per-day ammonia plant and a 1,000-ton-per-day urea plant to be built near the Kenai gas field. Completed in 1969, the plants were designed to use more than 60 million cubic feet of natural gas per day.

Alaska was a frontier for Union Oil in the 1960s, but the company was also active in more traditional oil country. The combined holdings of Union and Pure provided strong positions in the Gulf Region, both onshore and offshore, and in California and Oklahoma.

Union had set up its first office in the Gulf Region in Houston in 1939. The year before, Pure had been a partner in the first well drilled in the Gulf. Although it was located only a mile offshore, it opened up an important new source of petroleum for America.

By the 1960s, both companies had extensive holdings in the region. Union played an active role in federal lease sales of Gulf offshore properties in the sixties. By 1968, Union was the second biggest producer of natural gas in the Gulf. And, thanks to the merger, it could handle its growing crude oil supplies in the region more efficiently.

Before the merger, Union's Gulf crude was sold or traded for crude supplies in California to feed the company's refineries in Los Angeles and San Francisco. Pure, however, was crude deficient. Texas put a ceiling on how much production was allowable from oil wells. Pure could not produce enough to supply its own refinery in Smith's Bluff, Texas.

That all changed beginning in 1965, when Union's growing Louisiana production made up the deficit in crude supplies to the Smith's Bluff refinery. By 1968, the Gulf Region was gearing up to meet demands of the company's new refinery under construction near Chicago.

During this time, Union's properties onshore California and in midcontinent

Above: In 1974, Union began construction to expand its ammonia and urea manufacturing complex in Alaska; modular units were shipped by barge from Washington State to Kenai. *Below:* The original Kenai fertilizer plants, completed in 1969, were designed to use more than 60 million cubic feet of natural gas per day as feedstock.

A HOT PROSPECT

In 1847, William Bell Elliot was hunting grizzlies in the rugged Mayacamas Mountains north of San Francisco when he came across a place he dubbed the "gates of hell." Fumaroles dotting the landscape emitted clouds of steam. Although access was difficult, some saw commercial potential. By the 1860s, The Geysers mineral hot springs resort was in business. Its impressive guest list included Theodore Roosevelt, Jack London, John Muir, and Giuseppe Garibaldi. In 1922, following the example of Prince Piero Ginari Conti, John Grant drilled steam wells into fumaroles at The Geysers to generate electricity. Conti's work in Larderello, Italy, in 1904 had resulted in the world's first electrical power station run on geothermal steam. In the western United States, however, geothermal energy could not compete with cheap hydroelectric power until the 1950s. Then the Magma and Thermal power companies were formed and signed their first sales contract with Pacific Gas & Electric Company. In 1960, the first power plant at The Geysers went on stream. At that time, Pure Oil was looking to diversify. A chance meeting with a Magma shareholder sparked Dr. Carel Otte's imagination and led to the formation of Pure's Earth Energy subsidiary. After the Union-Pure merger in 1965, the new Geothermal Division developed the technology to rapidly expand commercial energy production at The Geysers.

Top right: In 1967, geothermal wells were vented to test production rates. The Geysers may have looked like the "gates of hell" to early explorers, but later entrepreneurs saw a valuable resource with great potential for commercial energy production.

areas continued to be steady producers. In late 1965, Hartley gave this status report on Union's production in its home state: "In California, we have been successful in reversing a long downward trend in crude oil production. So far this year we have averaged 69,000 barrels a day of crude and gas liquids, our highest rate since 1957 and an increase of 16 percent over a similar period last year."

California also held promise of a new source of energy for Union Oil: electricity generated from superheated water or steam contained in underground reservoirs. With the Pure merger had come a group called Earth Energy, headed by Dr. Carel Otte. In 1965, Otte's group shifted its attention away from California's Imperial Valley, where geothermal resources had been a promising source of potassium chloride. A major potash discovery in Canada and the technological problems of mining the Imperial Valley resource made the project less attractive.

But Otte had begun to investigate another geothermal area north of San Francisco, and he received the backing of Union's executive committee to continue with the acquisition of geothermal leases. In 1967, Union signed a contract with two companies operating in The Geysers area—Magma Power and Thermal Power. They merged their holdings with Union's, giving Union 50 percent and the role of operator.

In September, Earth Energy became the Union Geothermal Division—starting what eventually became the world's largest geothermal project to generate electrical power from steam. In announcing the project, Hartley said: "This is Union's first move into the commercial use of a form of energy other than petroleum or natural gas. We are most optimistic about its potential as a means of producing dependable and economical electric power."

During the first three years following its 1965 merger with Pure, Union Oil Company invested more than $1 billion in capital projects. Roughly half was spent on exploration and production; most of the balance went to upgrade and integrate the company's downstream operations—refining, marketing, and transportation.

The formation of a separate Pure Oil Division shortly after the Union-Pure merger recognized the differences in the marketing operations of the two companies. For the next several years, Claude Brinegar, the new division's president, and his team worked to integrate Pure's refining and marketing operations into Union's.

"We think of The Pure Oil Company today," Hartley noted in late 1965, "as having opportunities for profit growth much the same as our western refining and marketing division had in the past. And we're taking much the same approach with The Pure Oil Company as we took in the West. The object is to improve our combined operations."

Union's refining and marketing operations on the West Coast had undergone a program of cost cutting and streamlining in the early 1960s. At that time, all of the domestic oil companies were taking a beating because of gasoline price cutting. Hartley, who became senior vice president in charge of marketing in 1960, had seen the need for some painful business decisions. He called on management consultants from the firm of McKinsey and Company to help analyze marketing operations. Costs would have to be cut to maintain profit margins. Goals were set, and responsibility for achieving them was accepted by key personnel.

Union was producing more gasoline than it could sell profitably, given the gasoline price wars. So Hartley insisted that refinery output of gasoline be reduced to levels where it would support but not exceed retail sales. Unprofitable gasoline stations were closed.

In an interview published in *Fortune* magazine in 1967, Hartley underlined the point about putting profitability ahead of sales volume in this way: "At one time, we would have sold a five-gallon can of gasoline and delivered it to the Himalayas. We don't do that kind of thing any longer."

In 1965, Pure was in much the same situation — overproducing and then having to dump gasoline at cheap prices. And it was buying crude oil to do it, since its own supplies could not fill the demands of its refineries.

Using the task-force approach, teams of Union and Pure people determined how and where to change and streamline operations. The retail network was included: Operations in unprofitable locations were moved, sold, or closed; new locations were scouted.

Between 1965 and 1972, U.S. demand for gasoline increased 39 percent. Construction of service stations was booming by the late sixties, and Union had an active building program. The auto/truckstop system that Pure had developed was also expanded. These large facilities cater to the needs of interstate truck drivers and tourists alike, providing automotive services and the added amenities of stores and restaurants.

Above: In the late 1960s, Union began a program to upgrade its refining and transportation systems. This included installation of a 30,000-barrel-per-day Unicracker at the San Francisco refinery. *Opposite, top and map:* In 1968, Capline was completed; the pipeline carried Gulf crude and imports to the Midwest for refining. *Below:* Union built a new midwestern refinery outside Chicago between 1968 and 1970.

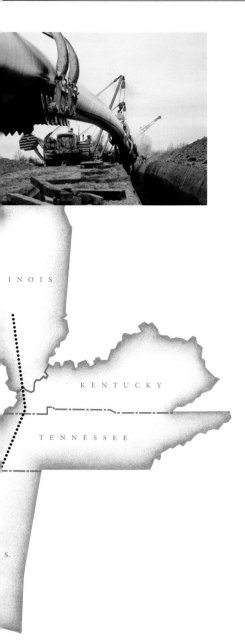

At Union's annual meeting in April 1967, Hartley told shareholders: "We are conducting a major economic and engineering survey covering the refining and distribution requirements of the company, particularly the Pure Oil Division. We want to determine how we can compete more strongly in that area. Ultimately, we expect to construct a large refinery in the Middle West."

The decision was made to build the new refinery on Pure's property in Romeoville, Illinois, near Chicago. "It became clear," Brinegar recalled, "that we could not profitably rebuild [Pure's] Heath or Toledo refineries, and the Lemont refinery [in Romeoville] was really at the end of its economic life. If we kept those three small refineries going it would be a holding action with high costs."

The new Chicago refinery was designed to process 140,000 barrels of crude oil a day (capacity was later boosted to 153,000 barrels). The $220 million expenditure needed to build it was, at the time, the biggest in Union Oil's history. Three years passed from groundbreaking to start-up in 1970.

At the annual meeting in 1967, Brinegar also reported that Pure and seven other companies had joined together to build a 40-inch-diameter pipeline — Capline — from Louisiana to Illinois. Pure's share was 13.2 percent.

Capline extends from St. James, Louisiana, to Patoka, Illinois, just east of St. Louis, Missouri. When it was first built, it was the nation's largest common-carrier crude oil line and was later second only to the Trans-Alaska Pipeline System. From an initial load of 420,000 barrels a day, Capline peaked at more than 1 million barrels a day in the early 1980s.

A second common carrier, in which Pure also had an interest, connected Capline to the new Chicago refinery. Brinegar described the pipeline projects as examples of the benefits "that have made the merger such a success."

He added: "Pure's Midwest refinery system has long needed assured supplies of quality crude oil, while Union's expanding production in Louisiana has been searching for a long-term market. The merger brought these needs together, and Capline provided the solution."

Included in the facilities at Chicago were units to provide a substantial volume of solvents and aromatics for the American Mineral Spirits Company, one of Pure's divisions since 1961. The company had been in business since 1923, with Pure as its majority shareholder since 1946.

AMSCO's management was eager to expand but had been stymied by Pure's reluctance to produce sufficient quantities of either solvents or the BTX aromatics: benzene, toluene, and xylene, which are polymer building-block chemicals. Union took a fresh look at the situation and supported AMSCO's enthusiasm for the possibilities of expanding markets for both solvents and emulsion polymers. Union's judgment was rewarded. The subsidiary soon began to demonstrate the highly favorable return-on-investment performance of solvent production.

Union also authorized the subsidiary's management to determine how the business of manufacturing and marketing emulsion polymers should be developed. In 1966, AMSCO purchased its first emulsion polymer plant, located in Charlotte, North Carolina, and hired a marketing vice president with experience in these products.

Union researchers were challenged to develop superior emulsion polymers. By 1968, Dr. Joseph Walker—associate research director and formerly Pure's acting director of research—and his group produced a breakthrough in latex paint emulsion technology. The new product proved exceptionally durable and flexible. Subsequent development created a family of vinyl acrylic emulsions suitable for use in a wide variety of paints.

While the Chicago refinery was under construction, the entire refining

system—east and west—was undergoing varying degrees of renovation, including some new names. At the end of 1968, the Oleum refinery became the San
Francisco refinery to give it a clearer geographical identification with the nearest
major city. The Smith's Bluff refinery in Texas was renamed the Beaumont refinery.

In 1968, Union announced plans to upgrade its western refineries, particularly San Francisco, which was getting a 30,000-barrel-a-day Unicracker. This
substantially increased the refinery's production of gasoline and jet turbine fuel.
The new Unicracker was the twenty-first constructed since Union Oil introduced
the process commercially at its Los Angeles refinery in 1964. Unicracking, Hartley
said, had proved "even better than finding a four-million-barrel-a-year oil field
right under the refinery, because it gives us flexibility of products in an ever-
changing market."

Another new Union technology was the Unisar process, which removes
aromatics from jet fuel and paint solvents, thus improving quality and
reducing the amount of vapors these products release into the atmosphere.
Unisar technology helped Union comply with air pollution regulations that
placed stricter limits on the amount of solvent vapors that could be released into
the atmosphere. The first commercial Unisar plant was installed at the Beaumont
refinery in 1969, and a second was completed at San Francisco in 1971.

The Beaumont refinery was designed to process the sweet, low-sulfur crudes
that were characteristic of Texas production—as well as those imported via the
Gulf of Mexico from Africa, the North Sea, and other overseas areas. The Chicago
refinery was built to be flexible; it could handle any type of crude oil, including
the syncrude that might one day be produced from Union's extensive oil shale
holdings in Colorado.

The West Coast refineries were also flexible, but particularly geared toward
the sour, high-sulfur crudes typical of much of California's production. The principal objective of renovating the California refineries was to increase the efficiency
of gasoline production and reduce the amount of nonsalable residual materials
left over at the end of the refining process. Substantial investments were also
made in emission-reduction facilities.

The integration of Union and Pure operations to form a stronger organization was symbolized by the company's new corporate image. In September 1967,
a corporate identification program, developed by industrial designers Lippincott
& Margulies, was introduced to customers, shareholders, and employees.

Right: The first commercial Unicracker was worth more than finding a 4-million-barrel-a-year supply of crude under the Los Angeles refinery, according to Fred Hartley. *Below:* The Smith's Bluff refinery (catalytic reformer) near Beaumont, Texas, was acquired with the Union-Pure merger in 1965. *Inset:* Claude Brinegar (second from left) and Charles Parker (right) attended an auto race that Pure helped sponsor. *Bottom:* Pure's racing interests began in 1915, when the first three autos to finish a 500-mile derby in Minneapolis–St. Paul ran on Pure gasoline.

The program included a new corporate logotype and marketing symbol; new package designs, stationery, and forms; and new signage for service stations, offices, and vehicles. The Union 76 brand replaced a collection of brand names that had been developed individually over time, among them Union's Minute Man service and tires, Union's Royal Triton motor oil, and Pure's Firebird gasoline.

The corporate identity program helped unify the new company. When applied to Union service stations in 37 states in the West and Midwest, the Sign of the 76 became a familiar beacon symbolizing quality and service to the motoring public.

But the new signs didn't go up overnight. "We feathered the change into the Union Oil family as part of the normal station maintenance painting cycle," noted Brinegar. "That way, the public could get used to our name gradually, and we could spread the cost over a period of time."

Pure signposts were left standing at stations after the buildings had been painted in Union's colors and the building signs changed. Once the customers had a chance to associate Pure and Union, the Pure Oil signs were replaced by Union 76 spheres. Even the company's credit cards carried both Pure and Union logos for a time. The gradual shifting of Pure stations to Union 76 stations was accomplished by early 1970.

In the fall of 1968, Claude Brinegar was named president of the newly formed Union 76 Division with responsibility for domestic refining, marketing, and distribution activities — east and west. He was also elected a corporate senior vice president and a director. The Pure Oil Division of the company ceased to exist, marking the completion of the major phases of the merger.

The merger years provided challenges that tested and strengthened the new Union Oil Company. From 1965 through 1968, the company showed steady increases in earnings from operations and in replacement of reserves of both oil and natural gas. But as Union adjusted to its new size and took advantage of the opportunities the merger offered, America's business and social climate was growing more complex. The 1960s was a decade of social turmoil marked by civil rights and antiwar protests. The 1970s would be characterized by economic and regulatory upheaval.

"From an economic standpoint, the environment in which we do business is unstable," Hartley stated in early 1969. "While costs in every sector are rising — including labor, materials, taxes, and interest rates — product prices remain largely unchanged, thus involving us in a serious cost-price squeeze. Maintaining and increasing our level of earnings under these conditions is a challenge to our ingenuity and a spur to cost-conscious management."

Adding to the challenge would be the tangle of legislation spawned as government tried to respond to a growing public consciousness of environmental values. In the late 1960s, Union was involved in two disastrous accidents that heightened concerns about the environment.

On March 18, 1967, the *Torrey Canyon,* one of the Union supertankers that had been jumboized in 1964, ran aground on the Seven Stones Reef off southern England. The cause was later set to navigational error. The ship, only 100 miles from port in Wales after a journey from Kuwait of more than 11,000 miles, began to spill its cargo of 880,000 barrels of crude oil into the sea.

In the first six days, as much as a quarter of the oil spilled and was blown south, away from the Cornish coast. Then the wind changed, and oil soon appeared on the beaches. In early April, oil began rolling onto the shores of Brittany in France. Loss of seabirds was estimated at 40,000 to 100,000. In Cornwall and Brittany, intertidal life was devastated — more by detergents used to disperse the slick than by the oil itself. In Brittany, valuable oyster beds were of particular concern, but only one oyster river was hit. While areas affected only by oil recovered

Below: Union's 76 symbol has been redesigned many times over the years. An updated version (lower right in chart) introduced in 1967 replaced other marketing symbols, including Pure's Firebird. Opposite: When the Torrey Canyon (top right) was enlarged in 1964 (top left and drawing), its stern was severed and attached to a bigger hull. This increased the tanker's capacity to more than 850,000 barrels of crude oil.

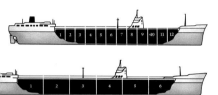

within a few months, a normal balance of life returned more slowly to shores also touched by detergent.

The *Torrey Canyon,* under long-term charter to Union from a Liberian company, had been subchartered to the British Petroleum Company for the voyage. Once salvage efforts had proved unsuccessful, the British bombed the tanker to burn the remaining crude oil, estimated at 150,000 to 300,000 barrels. Several weeks later, gales and heavy seas dislodged the wreckage from the reef and sent it to the bottom.

Union was covered by insurance for both the loss of the $17 million ship and the $7 million spent for cleanup and other costs. After the disaster, however, Lloyds of London eliminated coverage on oil spills and ocean pollution. Tanker operators, including Union, formed private insurance groups.

Union had cooperated in efforts to minimize the spreading of oil from the *Torrey Canyon* and to clean up the beaches. Soon after the disaster, Hartley reiterated the company's position: "It continues to be company policy to comply with and, wherever feasible, to exceed the regulations established by governmental agencies charged with pollution control....It is Union Oil Company's policy, intent, and desire to be a good and responsible neighbor in all areas in which we and our subsidiaries have operations."

Less than two years later, however, disaster struck again. Another oil spill — this one off the highly populated coast of Southern California — involved much less oil but a greater uproar. Union had drilled four development wells from Platform A on Block 402, which covered some 5,000 acres in the Santa Barbara Channel. On January 28, 1969, as the fifth well neared completion, a powerful stream of drilling mud and gas shot through the drill pipe high into the derrick. Within a quarter of an hour after the blowout, the drill pipe was dropped back into the hole and the wellhead sealed.

But this was no ordinary blowout. Gas and then oil bubbled up to the ocean's surface several hundred feet from the platform. Oil, trapped in the well bore under tremendous pressure, erupted through shallow open fractures and seams in the sea floor. Over the next 11 days, some 15,000 barrels of mud (about 8 million pounds) were pumped into the well bore to stop the flow of oil. The mud was replaced with cement in the following days to permanently seal off the well.

The oil formed a huge slick floating off Santa Barbara. Efforts to disperse it and contain it with log booms were overpowered by heavy seas. The oil moved onto the beaches. High tides and strong winds sprayed it on sea walls, cliffs, and homes.

The season had been particularly devastating in terms of weather for the

Santa Barbara area both before and after the spill. Storms and floods had taken lives and destroyed property. In fact, much of the debris hauled away by workers cleaning up the oil had been deposited on the beaches earlier by the storms. No wonder then that by July 4, the holiday crowds found many of the beaches in better condition than they had been before the spill.

As soon as the oil was removed, fish and bird populations began to recover. The birds had fared the worst. An estimated 3,600 died after swallowing or being coated with oil. Union's research department set up a bird-cleaning center, but less than 10 percent of the 1,600 birds treated survived.

Given the nature of the spill—straight from the reservoir—estimates as to the amount of oil involved varied widely. Published reports ranged from 20,000 to 77,000 barrels. Some estimates were based on the size of the oil slick. Later estimates took into account the flow rates of wells completed from the reservoir.

The spill affected a popular resort beach close to the media capital of the West Coast. It received a lot of coverage both in print and on television. Pictures of struggling, oil-coated birds were seen around the world. Public response was negative and in many quarters escalated to outrage when Hartley was widely mis-quoted as saying: "I'm amazed at the publicity for the loss of a few birds."

What he actually said was: "I think we have to look at these problems rela-tively. I am always tremendously impressed at the publicity that the death of birds receives versus the loss of people in our country in this day and age. When I think of the folks that gave up their lives when they came down into the ocean off Los Angeles [in a plane crash] some three weeks ago—and the fact that our society forgets about that within a 24-hour period, I think relative to that the fact that we have had no loss of life from this incident [the oil spill] is important."

This statement was made during Hartley's voluntary appearance before Senator Edmund Muskie's Public Works Committee on air and water pollution on February 5, eight days after the spill. Hartley went on to describe the efforts by Union and its partners in the cleanup and response to damage claims.

The misquote first appeared in the *New York Times,* then was picked up by

S A N T A   B A R B A

Left: The massive cleanup effort after the Santa Barbara oil spill was complicated by many tons of storm debris deposited on local beaches before the spill. Opposite, top: Union employees and vol-unteers treated some 1,600 birds that had swallowed or been coated with oil, but less than 10 percent survived. Opposite, bottom: Fish populations recovered quickly. Platform A, like other offshore platforms, soon became an arti-ficial reef providing a haven for marine life.

ANTA BARBARA

⊙

⛏ PLATFORM A

A   N   N   E   L

the *Wall Street Journal,* the *Washington Post,* NBC News, and *Time* magazine. Jerry Luboviski, then director of corporate communications for Union, personally pointed out the error to the appropriate editors. Retractions were printed in publications across the country, and Union ran a full-page newspaper ad in an effort to get the truth out. The truth, however, often fades in the heat of emotion. Public perception cannot be "retracted," and misunderstanding persists.

Once the spill was controlled and appropriate responses were set in motion, attention focused on preventing further seepages. Dr. Lee DuBridge, science adviser to President Nixon, established a special panel of distinguished scientists and engineers, who recommended that drilling continue. Their report made it clear that the reservoir from which the spill had occurred should be depleted as rapidly as possible to reduce subsurface pressures. By year end the seepages were minimal, far less than the centuries-old seepage in state-owned waters off nearby Coal Oil Point. Tents were constructed over the fissures on the sea floor near Platform A to gather the small amounts of crude oil that continued to seep up into the water.

The spill led to an industrywide review of offshore drilling and production operations. Procedures were tightened up and new technology developed to minimize the risk of future platform spills. Since 1969, the industry's record of operations in the channel has been excellent. University of Southern California researchers, in a study commissioned by the Western Oil and Gas Association, concluded that there had been no permanent damage to the environment.

But public ire had been roused. The psychological impact of the spill endured long after the oil itself was gone. Strong public opposition has kept oil exploration and development offshore California to a minimum. By many assessments, the Santa Barbara Channel oil spill was the major event that helped coalesce environmental protection groups into a powerful lobby. The timing was right, and the media coverage assured a broad, emotional public response.

The environmental movement has focused needed attention on issues involving air, water, and food quality, as well as preservation of wilderness resources. But it has also contributed to a burdensome and often conflicting tangle of federal, state, and local regulations that have hampered economic growth, including vital energy development. Much of this legislation was enacted during the 1970s, as Americans tried to strike a balance between environmental and economic values — and were forced to face a new world power, the OPEC cartel.

9

Energy, Environment, and Politics

President Richard M. Nixon signed the nation's first comprehensive piece of environmental legislation in early 1970. Opposite: Union Oil introduced low-lead regular gasoline in May 1970. The new product helped reduce atmospheric lead emitted by the increasing numbers of automobiles jamming highways and adding to air pollution in cities such as Los Angeles (insets).

The environment received little attention during the Nixon-Humphrey presidential campaign of 1968. But clean air, clean water, solid-waste disposal, and the preservation of scenic values were areas of growing public concern and legislative action during the 1960s. The media blitz surrounding the Santa Barbara oil spill, which occurred only eight days after Richard M. Nixon was inaugurated on January 20, 1969, provided a strong national focus around which various environmental groups could rally.

Dr. Carleton B. "Bud" Scott, Union's liaison with government agencies on issues related to the spill, noted that "the gun was loaded, and [the spill] triggered it. If it hadn't been that event, it could have been anything else."

The new administration and the legislature in Washington, D.C., were quick to respond. By the end of 1969, Congress approved the nation's first comprehensive piece of environmental legislation. President Nixon signed it on New Year's Day, 1970. "It is particularly fitting that my first official act of the new decade is to approve the National Environmental Policy Act [NEPA]," the President observed. "The 1970s absolutely must be the years when America pays its debt to the past by reclaiming the purity of the air, its waters, and our living environment. It is literally now or never."

NEPA established a Council of Environmental Quality with responsibility to review federal environmental programs to make sure that they "use all practicable means…to create and maintain conditions under which man and nature can exist in productive harmony and fulfill the social, economic, and other requirements of present and future generations of Americans."

The environmental policy act contained a clause requiring the federal government to consider environmental values prior to launching its projects. Thus was born the environmental impact statement.

"NEPA has turned out to be a good statute," said Bud Scott, who was appointed Union's director of environmental sciences in 1972. He found that, used appropriately, environmental impact statements could be good planning tools for industry.

NEPA, however, was just the beginning. On February 10, 1970, Nixon sent a strong message to Congress urging the legislators to consider environmental quality issues. In July, the President proposed formation of the Environmental Protection Agency (EPA), which was established in December to function as the monitoring, research, standard-setting, and enforcement arm for the government's pollution abatement programs.

President Nixon's programs were presented amid rising public concern. On April 22, "Earth Day" events and demonstrations across the nation focused attention on environmental issues. In December, *Time* magazine designated the "environment" as 1970's issue of the year.

The politics of the environment boiled over in 1970, resulting in a flood of government regulations. The pace of new environmental legislation was relentless, and keeping up with it soon became a full-time job. The three-person staff that started Union's Environmental Sciences Department in 1972 quadrupled in four years. The department continued to grow throughout the decade, dealing primarily with the EPA. In addition, there was a growing number of state and local environmental agencies creating their own regulations.

In 1970, the Council on Environmental Quality (CEQ) issued its first annual report, including a chapter on citizen participation that described hundreds of local, regional, and national organizations with environmental agendas. In the CEQ's 1973 annual report, the citizen-participation chapter was three times longer and listed twice the number of organizations, many of which were oriented toward legal action.

The proliferation of agencies and regulations could not banish environmental pollution overnight. Nor could the problems be solved outside the context of the national economy. But because of the emotion surrounding the issue, that's what legislators often tried to do. Focusing narrowly on the environment, they set aside economic issues—this in a time of declining productivity and runaway inflation fueled by the country's continued involvement in the Vietnam War. (Although a cease-fire agreement was signed in 1973, American troops were not evacuated until 1975.) Inflation hit 6 percent in 1970—shocking then but mild in comparison to the double-digit rates that would prevail at the end of the decade.

"Inflation continues to dominate the domestic economy of our country," Fred Hartley noted in 1970. "In spite of the indisputable facts and the pleadings I and many others have made to those in authority in Washington, they have continued to pursue their ridiculous economic policies....It is essential to stop the snowball of wage increases in excess of productivity increases—and the resultant price increases in excess of fair value." The company's new Chicago refinery, for example, would have cost 35 to 40 percent more had its construction begun rather than ended in 1970.

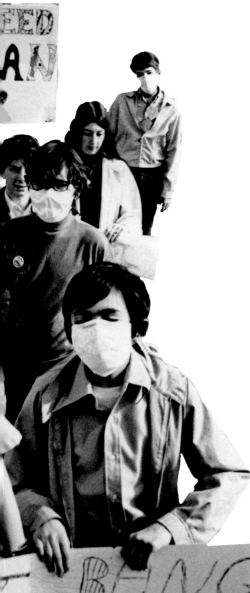

The industry also faced sharp increases in federal income taxes in 1970, largely because the Tax Reform Act of 1969 reduced depletion by 5.5 percentage points and instituted a minimum tax. The depletion allowance, which had been set at 27.5 percent by Congress back in 1926, dropped to 22 percent—and it was effectively less than that given the new tax structure.

Percentage depletion, provided in the form of a tax reduction, gave oil companies and other mineral producers credit for the loss of nonrenewable resources. The intent was to allow resource companies more capital to invest in continued exploration. The government's action to reduce this incentive for oil companies came at a time when exploration costs were rising in the difficult frontier areas in the Arctic and in deeper offshore waters.

Higher taxes and inflation were the major reasons for the 17.5 percent decline in Union Oil's earnings in 1970, despite record-high revenues and record levels of operation. The company reduced its capital expenditures that year to about $300 million in response to the economic situation. Annual expenditures had been much higher during the previous five years, as Union invested $1.25 billion in capital projects in order to integrate Pure Oil into its operations and upgrade facilities. Expenditures had peaked at $500 million in 1968.

In 1971, President Nixon acted to stem inflation by instituting a wage-price freeze nationwide. In the petroleum industry, the freeze served to discourage domestic exploration. The lids placed on crude oil and refined product prices also discouraged increased imports, even though federal import quotas had been relaxed in 1970. The price and shipping costs of imported oil were rising, making it economically impractical for refiners to use imports to make up for domestic shortages.

Increasingly severe environmental regulations exacerbated the difficult economic situation in the petroleum industry. Growing pessimism about the state of the environment was transformed into an overly optimistic view of how quickly—and at what cost—technology could solve the problems. Some lawmakers seemed to believe that they could legislate technology.

In 1972, Hartley testified before the Senate Subcommittee on Air and Water Pollution: "It is my opinion that lawmakers do not fully realize the very difficult technical task of developing control systems within the time period and within the limitations imposed by the Clean Air Act amendments of 1970. Most major

Pure Oil's Firebird marketing symbol, retired after the merger with Union Oil, was drafted by helicopter pilots of the Armed Platoon, Company A, 501st Aviation Battalion in Vietnam. The pilots, who provided cover and air strikes for ground troops, called themselves the Firebirds. When Pure Oil distributor Jess Sheffield of Ozark, Alabama, heard about it, he sent Firebird decals and shoulder patches to the platoon's base in Bien Hoa.

technical developments are more evolutionary than revolutionary. Certainly we didn't try to put a man on the moon with the first rocket."

The Clean Air amendments were the congressional response to President Nixon's environmental message of February 1970. (The Air Quality Act of 1967, which replaced the first Clean Air Act passed in 1955, is still commonly referred to as the Clean Air Act.) The President had requested new, significantly lower auto emission standards for 1973 and 1975. He got more than he asked for. The amendments set standards and timetables that could not be met given the state of the technology. Extensions were granted, but not until the problems had been raised and disputed repeatedly by representatives of industry, the Environmental Protection Agency, and the judiciary. Similar problems arose with the Federal Water Pollution Control Act amendments that were passed at the end of 1972 over the President's veto.

While NEPA was a landmark in federal environmental legislation, the state and local governments in California — Union's home state — had long been active in regulating industry. Air pollution had been all too obvious a problem in the Los Angeles basin since World War II. In the early 1950s, Union had made its first major pollution-control expenditure — a $1.8 million sulfur recovery plant at the Los Angeles refinery. That original plant recovered 90 to 95 percent of the sulfur in the refinery's emissions, keeping the company in conformance with state and local regulations for more than 20 years. To meet new, stricter Los Angeles County regulations in 1973, Union had to remove 99.9 percent of the sulfur in its emissions. The company spent about $11 million for that purpose.

"I want to impress upon you the tremendous cost of the last increments of control," Hartley told the subcommittee. "Admittedly, today's $11 million are inflation dollars, but it is still a very disproportionate figure for the last 10 percent of control compared to $1.8 million for the first 90 percent....The ultimate in control ends up being a great burden on the consumer," he said.

In conjunction with the Ralph M. Parsons Company, a major engineering contractor, Union codeveloped the commercial technology to meet the new sulfur requirements. The Beavon Sulfur Removal process was named for the man who conceived the idea, David K. Beavon, Parsons' director of process operations. The technology was proved at a pilot plant at Union's Los Angeles refinery in 1971. In August 1972, construction began on two commercial sulfur removal plants and related facilities at the refinery. By the time the plants were completed a year later, Union had sold the rights to use Beavon Sulfur Removal technology to six other oil companies.

Because of its early environmental controls, California boasted the nation's cleanest industrial base by 1970. The state's refineries were leaders in antipollution technology. When Union decided to build a new refinery near Chicago, its experience in California made that midwestern facility a landmark in environmental controls. It was well able to meet the standards imposed by a tough Illinois state law on air and water pollution that was signed on the day of the refinery's dedication, June 29, 1970.

The refinery showcased state-of-the-art systems and techniques. Some $37 million of the total cost was related to air and water quality. Smoke, dust, and chemical gases released to the atmosphere were at minimum levels. Water returned to the Chicago Sanitary and Ship Canal was cleaner than the water taken into the refinery.

To prove the point about water quality, Claude Brinegar, president of the Union 76 Division, drank a sample of the effluent water discharged from the

Union's Robert H. Bungay (left) and John R. Pownall (center) explained automated process controls to Lee DuBridge, President Nixon's science adviser, at the dedication of the new Chicago refinery. Right: The refinery was completed in 1970. Below: Almost 600 people jammed the cafeteria for opening ceremonies. Speaking, (left to right) were Fred Hartley; Claude Brinegar; Richard B. Ogilvie, governor of Illinois; Lee DuBridge; John F. O'Hara, mayor of Romeoville; and Kazuo Miyamori, president of Maruzen Oil Company.

refinery. Illinois Governor Richard Ogilvie joined him. The governor, in his remarks at the dedication, said: "The massive commitment which you have made at this refinery to preserving the quality of our precious natural resources of air and water provides an example for other industries to emulate."

Despite controls on industrial sources of emissions, Southern California's smog problem persisted. This was not the industrial smog that commonly occurred in eastern smokestack cities on damp winter days. (The term *smog* — combining "smoke" and "fog" — was coined in England at the turn of the century.) The Los Angeles variety of smog was different. Research in the early 1950s identified the major contributor to the smog problem as automobile emissions. Nitrogen oxides, unburned hydrocarbons, and other by-products of combustion, released by the skyrocketing numbers of cars on the city's streets, were trapped under an inversion layer in the atmosphere; sunlight triggered photochemical reactions that formed smog.

Cleaner burning gasoline, developed to make engines run better, helped reduce some of the harmful emissions. The Unionfining process, introduced as Unifining in 1953, was a catalytic process that removed sulfur, nitrogen, and olefins from gas-oil stocks. In the 1960s, Union's Unicracking and Unisar processes further improved the quality of automotive and jet fuels, and other refined products.

The problems being created by automotive exhaust emissions, however, had to be addressed directly, and California was the first state to do so in the 1960s. As it turned out, photochemical smog was not unique to Los Angeles. Denver, Phoenix, and other cities with growing numbers of automobiles and a certain set of climatic conditions were also suffering. In 1968, federal regulations applied California's auto emissions standards to the rest of the nation.

Meanwhile, the auto industry worked on the development of technology to clean up exhaust emissions. Catalytic converters installed in auto exhaust lines were a promising alternative. However, researchers found that lead in gasoline impaired the function of the catalysts that were central to the converter technology.

In February 1970, Edward Cole, president of General Motors, held a series of meetings with representatives of individual refining companies to discuss the problem of lead in gasoline. Cole asked the refiners to produce unleaded gasoline, although he realized it would be difficult and costly to maintain research octane ratings of about 94 for regular and 100 for premium without using lead.

To compensate, General Motors specified reduced compression ratios in new engines to accommodate lower octane fuels. California, joined later by the Environmental Protection Agency, adopted a standard of 91 research octane for new cars running on unleaded fuel. A 91 research octane rating compares with an 87 research-motor rating. (That is, there are two methods for determining octane: research and motor. The motor method is a more severe test for the gasoline, so motor octane ratings are several points lower than research ratings. In the early 1970s, research octane ratings were used on gasoline pumps. Since the mid-'70s, pumps have commonly reflected an average of research and motor ratings. Hence, a 91 octane rating at the pump in the early 1970s would equate to an 87 rating after about 1975.)

Many refiners had anticipated the need for unleaded gasoline, not because of catalytic converters but because of rising concerns about lead pollution in the air. Refiners had been adding tetraethyl lead compounds to gasoline since the discovery in the 1920s that they boosted octane ratings. As Detroit turned out more powerful, higher compression engines, lead in gasoline proved an effective, low-cost solution to the problem of engine knock.

As early as 1966, Hartley had told Union's board of directors that unleaded

Opposite, top: Unionfining technology — a hydrogen treatment process that removes sulfur, nitrogen, and other contaminants from a variety of petroleum products — helped make the Chicago refinery state-of-the-art in its environmental controls. Opposite, bottom: During the 1970s, domestic price controls kept down the cost of petroleum products in the United States. Calls for energy conservation went largely unheeded until the price shocks of 1979 and the subsequent phaseout of price controls.

1948 — United States becomes net importer of crude oil.

1959 — President Eisenhower imposes quotas on oil imports.

1960 — Organization of Petroleum Exporting Countries holds first meeting in Baghdad, Iraq.

1971 — President Nixon's wage-price freeze includes controls on crude oil prices.

1973 — U.S. oil imports reach 35 percent of demand. Arab oil exporters embargo U.S. shipments. OPEC prices triple, but controls keep domestic prices low.

1976 — U.S. crude oil production drops 11 percent from 1973.

1977 — Annual imports reach 46 percent of demand.

1978 — Revolution in Iran. Oil prices double. Consumption of refined products hits all-time high.

1981 — President Reagan lifts price controls on domestic crude oil.

1986 — OPEC increases production. Oil prices collapse.

1989 — Annual imports reach 46 percent of demand. In July, monthly imports top 50 percent for the first time since July 1977.

1990 — January imports total 54 percent of demand.

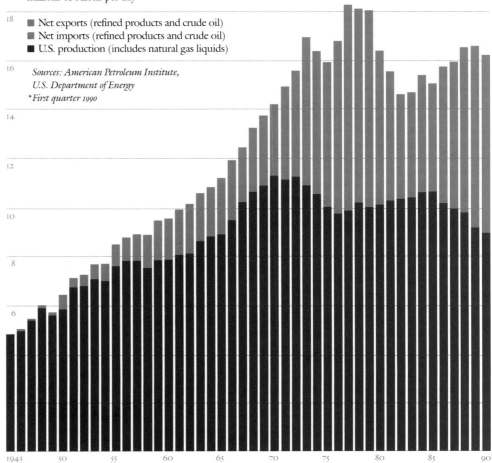

U.S. DEMAND FOR PETROLEUM
millions of barrels per day

■ Net exports (refined products and crude oil)
■ Net imports (refined products and crude oil)
■ U.S. production (includes natural gas liquids)

Sources: American Petroleum Institute,
U.S. Department of Energy
*First quarter 1990

A HELPING HAND
In the late 1960s, Union's management approved an aggressive
approach to identifying and treat-
ing the alcoholic employee. In
1969 Dr. Richard Call, then company medical director, set up a
program. John Newton played a
key role in developing and direct-
ing it for 20 years until his retirement in 1989. The program,
expanded in the 1980s to include
other forms of chemical dependency, was one of the first and
became a model for other corporations. Modes of treatment were
designed to be flexible, geared to
the needs of the individual and
his or her family. The aim was
to help employees regain their
productivity, their worth to the
organization as well as to themselves and their families. In the
program's first 20 years, more than
2,000 people were treated successfully, representing almost 90 percent of those who went through
the program. John Newton also
worked with the Los Angeles
Dodgers and other sports organizations to develop similar programs. By conservative estimates,
7 to 10 percent of American workers suffer from some form of chemical dependency. Treatment is
difficult, because those afflicted
typically deny their addiction.
Newton, himself a recovering
alcoholic, attributed the success
of the company's program to strong
management support and the principles of Alcoholics Anonymous.

gasoline would be required in the next decade, and the company was prepared
to introduce it in the fall of 1970. But new information came to light suggesting
that lead served not only to increase the octane rating, but also to protect the valve
seats in engines. Removing lead could increase engine wear.

There was another problem with unleaded gasoline: the cost to the consumer. Additional processing was required to manufacture unleaded gasoline
with sufficiently high octane ratings. This increased the cost to the consumer by
several cents a gallon, pushing the price higher than that of leaded premium in
some cases.

So Union developed an alternative, becoming one of the first companies to
introduce "low-lead" regular gasoline. In May 1970, Union introduced 93.5
research octane Low-lead Regular 76 gasoline in California. By fall, the gasoline
was also available in Arizona, Hawaii, and Nevada. Since low-lead was developed
as a transitional fuel, to be phased out once new cars were equipped with catalytic converters, it was not introduced in the company's eastern marketing region.
There, Union sold primarily to marketers, who in turn distributed products to
individual dealers, creating enough logistical complexity to make a low-lead
introduction impractical.

Low-lead Regular 76 contained half a gram of lead per gallon, 80 percent
less than the leaded regular it replaced. On average, it was priced one cent more
per gallon than Union's previous regular gasoline. Most cars using leaded regular
would operate efficiently on Union's low-lead. Meanwhile, low-lead gasoline
helped reduce the amount of lead released into the atmosphere while protecting
engine life in cars designed to operate on leaded gasoline.

Union's marketing strategy was to offer two grades of gasoline in the West:
leaded premium and low-lead regular. Most competitors offered a third unleaded
grade, some at the considerable expense of installing a third set of pumps at their
stations. By sticking to only the two grades, the company avoided an expense of
about $80 million.

Union offered low-lead in the West until the summer of 1974, when Detroit
introduced its 1975 models equipped with catalytic converters. At that time,
Union stations across the country continued the two-grade strategy, offering an
unleaded regular that served the needs of new cars on the road and a leaded
premium for older models.

Union was well equipped to produce unleaded gasoline. During the 1960s,
the company increased its production of high-quality gasoline blending stocks.

*Top left: Fred Hartley, flanked
by research vice president Dr.
W.E. Bradley (on his right) and
Claude Brinegar, called a press
conference in May 1970 to
announce the introduction of
low-lead regular gasoline in
Union 76 stations throughout
California and Nevada.*

In 1973, Dr. C.B. "Bud" Scott, Union's director of environmental sciences, thumbed through volumes containing the environmental impact statement required before construction could begin on the Trans-Alaska Pipeline System.

And, in the 1970s, it increased reforming capacity, the key element in producing unleaded gasoline. Reforming is a chemical process in which light crude oil components are combined to form high-grade feedstocks. Union's new Unicracker-reformer complex at the San Francisco refinery was completed in 1971. The refineries in Beaumont (Texas) and Los Angeles expanded their reforming capacities in 1973 and 1975, respectively.

With unleaded and low-lead fuels on the market, the Environmental Protection Agency continued to look for ways to enforce a graduated reduction of the overall lead content in gasoline. In a 1972 speech in Dallas, Hartley suggested the establishment of an average amount of lead per gallon below the current average. Each refiner would determine how to distribute the allowable amounts of lead among various grades of gasoline to meet the EPA average.

Union's plan would give refiners the flexibility they needed for the most efficient operation. It would allow them to pool leaded and unleaded grades for purposes of determining allowable lead levels. Initial EPA proposals would have focused only on leaded grades, creating a situation in which refiners producing a high proportion of leaded fuels would use higher total amounts of lead than refiners producing a high proportion of unleaded or low-lead fuels.

"Our argument to the government was that we should control the total amount of lead going out of the refinery," said Joseph Byrne, then vice president for Union's western marketing region. The EPA regulations, which were finally issued in 1976, closely resembled Union's recommendations.

In 1973, Bud Scott summed up the problems facing American industry because of the stronger emphasis on environmental cleanup: "There are three main points," he said. "Point one is technology. We — by we, I mean all companies — are having trouble coming up with the technology to comply with the environmental regulations, no matter from what level they may be generated. Two, once we do develop the technology, we need to know how we are going to pay for the hardware. Finally, there is a collision course between the environment and energy that must be resolved."

By "collision course," Scott referred to contradictory trends in the United States: rising energy demand versus increasingly severe regulatory obstacles to efficient energy production.

Environmental controls were just one of many complex factors affecting the U.S. energy situation in the early 1970s. America was approaching an energy shortage, as demand outpaced supply. In a speech in 1973, Hartley called it a crisis between "supply and desire" in reference to Americans' continued guzzling of low-priced fuels.

Prices were low, demand was up, imports were up — and the major oil-exporting nations, particularly in the Middle East, were beginning to set higher prices for their oil. Soon, these factors would come together in the 1973 oil price shocks.

By 1970, the United States, home to 6 percent of the world's population, was consuming one-third of the world's commercial energy, including 32 percent of its petroleum production. During the 1950s, U.S. gross energy consumption had risen 23 percent. During the 1960s, the rate of increase more than doubled — to 52 percent. The per capita increases in energy use were even more startling: over 35 percent in the 1960s compared with only 4 percent in the 1950s.

"It has reached the point where we are using too much oil and gas, surprising as that statement may seem for an oilman to make," Hartley said.

Both industrial and consumer consumption of energy were encouraged by low prices. Gasoline sold for less than 30 cents a gallon. American drivers were still more concerned with power than fuel efficiency. There were more cars being

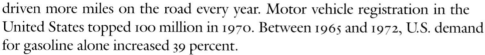

Left: On May 16, 1971, Peggy Hartley christened the 70,000-ton tanker Sansinena II. *After sea trials, the ship — with a capacity of 560,000 barrels of crude oil — began carrying Cook Inlet crude from Alaska to Union's California refineries.* Above: *Union had planned to use its original* Sansinena *(shown loading crude from the Attaka field in Indonesia) for the Cook Inlet run. However, even though the tanker had been built in the United States, Union was refused the necessary waiver allowing vessels registered abroad to be reinstated for domestic trade.*

driven more miles on the road every year. Motor vehicle registration in the United States topped 100 million in 1970. Between 1965 and 1972, U.S. demand for gasoline alone increased 39 percent.

Meanwhile, the skies were filling up with commercial jetliners, including the new jumbo jets. The 8 billion gallons of highly refined kerosene-type turbine fuels needed to keep the fleet in the air in 1969 was expected to double by 1975.

In the industrial sector, natural gas was priced so low that it cut into markets for coal and fuel oil. Natural gas prices had been regulated at the wellhead by the Federal Power Commission since 1954. A complicated system had been developed that set natural gas prices lower than crude oil prices on an energy-equivalent basis. The industry argued that such low prices would discourage exploration and that natural gas reserves would fall. It took years for those outside the industry to acknowledge the situation.

In its 1970 annual report, President Nixon's Council of Economic Advisers said: "Not only have prices been too low for desired consumption to be met, but they appear also to have retarded the development of new gas supplies. The only satisfactory solution to this problem is to allow the price, at least for new gas not previously committed, to approach market-clearing level."

After years of frustration, during which the industry's arguments were rejected, Hartley quipped: "I feel like the man who had his tombstone engraved with the words, 'I told you I was sick.'"

The proliferation of environmental legislation created still more demand on U.S. energy supplies. New equipment installed to control pollution used up energy in both construction and operation. Pollution control devices on cars tended to reduce gasoline mileage. Cleaner burning fuels, including some that might have been gasoline stocks, were diverted to industrial uses in order to meet air quality standards — particularly as dwindling natural gas supplies were earmarked for residential heating and cooking.

Halfway around the world, other events were taking place that would soon

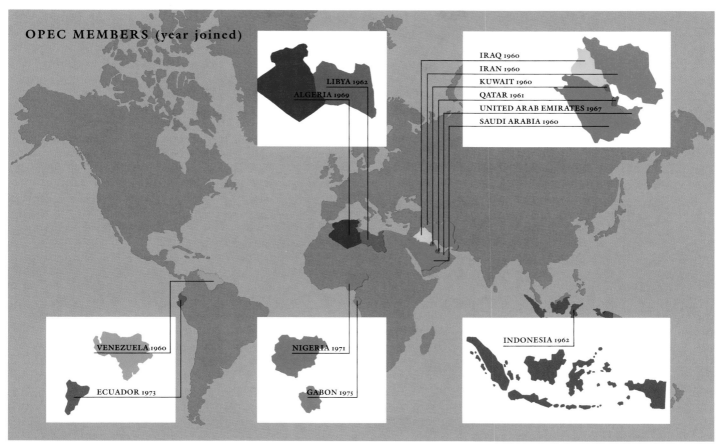

OPEC MEMBERS (year joined)

LIBYA 1962
ALGERIA 1969

IRAQ 1960
IRAN 1960
KUWAIT 1960
QATAR 1961
UNITED ARAB EMIRATES 1967
SAUDI ARABIA 1960

VENEZUELA 1960
ECUADOR 1973

NIGERIA 1971
GABON 1975

INDONESIA 1962

In September 1960, represen-tatives of Iraq, Kuwait, Saudi Arabia, Iran, and Venezuela met in Baghdad. They voted to demand that oil companies try to restore higher prices (and higher government revenues). They also formed the Organiza-tion of Petroleum Exporting Countries (OPEC) to unify their policies and protect their interests. By 1975, 13 countries were OPEC members, and they controlled more than half of the world's oil production.

shock the world energy market. In 1970, the government of Libya, a major oil exporter, cut its production. At the same time, Syria refused to allow repair of the vital trans-Arabian pipeline, which carried oil from Persian Gulf fields to the Mediterranean for export. Oil tankers were forced to go the long way around Africa to bring oil to the West, and shipping rates went up. The price of Middle Eastern oil imports in the United States rose some 75 cents a barrel higher than domestic crude oil prices.

After the Suez Canal crisis in 1956, when Egypt cut off that vital oil supply route, the United States had instituted oil import quotas to stimulate the domes-tic industry and assure a secure energy supply. In the 1960s, the quota system became riddled with loopholes favoring special interests. While Union favored reform of the system, the company supported its continuation in the early 1970s when there was pressure to eliminate it.

"Opponents of the oil import program theorize we should import more 'cheap' foreign crude and give the consumer the benefit of lower prices," Hartley said in August 1970. "We and others in the oil industry warn that foreign crude is cheap only as long as the producing nations allow it to be—that our best, cheapest source of oil is a strong domestic industry. Today's events are proving us correct."

Libya had succeeded in getting increases from major international oil com-panies in both tax rates and posted prices of oil. Persian Gulf producers followed suit, and these actions set a precedent for the Organization of Petroleum Exporting Countries. OPEC had been created in 1960 by Venezuela, Iran, Saudi Arabia, Iraq, and Kuwait. They wanted to unify their oil policies and resist price cuts for their crude imposed by major international oil companies. But the world energy situation changed dramatically during the 1960s. Energy supplies that had been in surplus in the late 1950s were being rapidly consumed by an increasingly industrialized world.

In 1970, the U.S. government relaxed import quotas. By 1971, the world

Top left: Construction of Collier's ammonia and urea plants in Alaska in the late 1960s more than doubled the Union subsidiary's capacity to produce nitrogen fertilizers and prepared it for the growth of the West Coast market in the 1970s. The reformer (shown) converts natural gas to hydrogen, which is then combined with nitrogen to produce ammonia. Above: Completion of the Trans-Alaska Pipeline System was delayed for years by environmental considerations. Congress expedited construction to increase domestic production in 1973 after the Arab embargo of oil to the United States.

surplus was disappearing. Meanwhile, OPEC had grown to include Qatar, Libya, Indonesia, the United Arab Emirates, Algeria, and Nigeria. (Ecuador joined in 1973, and Gabon in 1975.) OPEC negotiated with the international oil companies to gain a growing share of oil revenues for its members.

In 1972, Hartley again warned of the consequences of growing U.S. oil imports, which cost less than $5 billion in 1970 and were projected to increase sixfold by 1985. "As a major importer out of necessity, with no bargaining power and with no other alternatives short of a reduced standard of living," Hartley noted, "the United States would be forced to pay any price demanded by the producing countries."

Hartley's words proved prophetic, but few were listening in 1972. Even as the nation consumed greater amounts of energy and increased its imports, the domestic industry was severely hampered in its attempts to develop new sources of crude oil. After the 1969 oil spill from Union-operated Platform A in the Santa Barbara Channel, drilling had been resumed in order to deplete reservoir pressures—as recommended by the President's special advisory panel. Platform B was installed in 1970 to further develop the Dos Cuadras field. But the reaction to the spill was so strong that the third stage of development, Platform C, could not be installed until 1977, after years of litigation.

Exploration off the nation's eastern and western coastlines and in other highly promising areas was curtailed. Even the prolific producing areas so well established in the Gulf of Mexico were affected. In January 1972, a federal court canceled the leasing of 78 wildcat tracts offshore Louisiana in response to a suit brought by three environmental groups. Bids were returned unopened to the bidding companies.

As noted in Union's annual report published that spring: "It is incongruous that the very same environmental groups who have campaigned vigorously to reduce or halt the burning of fuel oils and coal because of the resulting pollution, have now successfully blocked a major lease sale in an area of high potential for new, clean-burning natural gas."

Year-end results for 1971 had shown that U.S. reserves of crude oil and natural gas were declining, and that crude oil production was down from 1970. Yet development of the huge Prudhoe Bay field—with reserves estimated at 10 billion barrels of crude oil—was delayed during this period. The Prudhoe Bay field was discovered on the North Slope of Alaska in 1968. The federal lease sale for North

POPCORN SULFUR
"We took sulfur and puffed it—
blew it up like a balloon," said
Unocal Science & Technology
consultant Donald C. Young,
who helped develop "popcorn"
sulfur. Since 1971, this innovative product has helped farmers
make their soils less alkaline and
more permeable, better able to
soak up moisture and nutrients.
For Unocal, the product helps
dispose of a waste by-product
of refining. Hydrogen sulfide
gas, released during crude oil
processing, is removed from
refinery emissions. The resulting sulfur has long been turned
to agricultural use. In its powdered form, however, it is difficult to handle and creates
problems of "dust pollution."
Unocal's popcorn-shaped sulfur
pellets, produced at the company's Santa Maria and Stockton
facilities in California, are easy
to handle. The pellets are less
flammable than powdered sulfur and provide a broad surface
area for reaction of the sulfur
with soil. Thus, Unocal trans-
forms a potential air pollutant
into a useful fertilizer.

*Top right: Popcorn sulfur is
produced by forcing water, air,
and molten sulfur through a
special nozzle.*

Slope prospects the next year brought in more than $900 million; Union's invest-
ment amounted to $76 million.

The company also purchased a small interest (less than 2 percent) in the
Trans-Alaska Pipeline System (TAPS) in early 1970. In August, the seven owners
of TAPS formed the Alyeska Pipeline Service Company to assume responsibility
for design, construction, operation, and maintenance. The proposed pipeline,
stretching 800 miles across the vast Alaskan wilderness, would bring crude oil
from the North Slope south to the deep-water port of Valdez. An unprecedented
22 million man-hours went into studies for the design and construction of the
pipeline, including studies of the wildlife, rivers, soils, permafrost, and potential
for earthquake damage.

Americans needed the oil. Alaskans needed the jobs. Alyeska had prepared
itself to do the job safely, with environmental concerns being an overriding consideration in design and construction. But impassioned opposition from environmental groups won court delays.

Finally, in late 1973, after the Arab oil embargo had begun, Congress passed
a bill expediting the pipeline's construction. Originally set for completion in
1972 at just under $1 billion, the pipeline eventually cost more than $9 billion—
with a significant part of the increase attributable to the years of delay. Oil didn't
begin flowing south until 1977. With no means to move oil from the North Slope
to markets in the Lower 48, Union drilled only one exploratory well on its
North Slope acreage between 1969 and 1973.

The economic pressures on the company were growing. Given the earnings
decline in 1970, some of Union Oil's directors considered selling the fertilizer
operations of the company's Collier Carbon and Chemical subsidiary. It would
have been a major divestiture, since fertilizers constituted more than two-thirds
of Collier's business. But the fertilizer market was temporarily depressed, and
start-up problems at the company's new plants in Kenai, Alaska, were causing
unanticipated expenses.

Hartley and Craig Henderson, Collier's president, took the long view—
even in those difficult and uncertain years—and successfully argued against the
sale. Collier was the largest supplier of nitrogen fertilizer on the West Coast, a
market using over 1.5 million tons per year and, in good years for agriculture, still
growing. By 1972, Collier's operating profit set a new record. When U.S. price
controls for products other than oil and natural gas were lifted in November

1973, domestic chemical prices rose. With worldwide supplies of fertilizer short, export prices more than tripled by 1974.

While the company faced mounting economic and political difficulties at home, development of its newly discovered Attaka field in Indonesia proceeded at a record pace. The logistical hurdles and physical hardships of drilling and construction in a remote tropical area proved daunting, but the need for rapid development of the discovery was all the greater given the slowdown in exploration and development activity in America.

The Attaka discovery well was completed in August 1970. Of the next four wells drilled to determine the extent of the field, three were good oil producers. Development began in March 1971.

"We gave ourselves a very short fuse — thirty months to develop this field," said Dick Stegemeier, then manager of operations for the project. Development was completed in 27½ months at some $6 million under the $115 million budget.

"Everybody worked long, long hours to get this thing done," he noted, "fourteen days on, seven off." With only primitive living quarters at the site in the beginning, many workers commuted the 1,000 miles from Singapore — and all supplies were routed through Union's facilities there as well.

When development was completed in 1973, oil from 52 wells on six platforms flowed to a central production platform, and from there 15 miles through an 18-inch pipeline to onshore processing and storage at the new Santan terminal. Production began in late 1972 and increased steadily to 101,000 barrels per day by the end of 1973.

SEA-FLOOR TEMPLATE

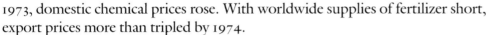

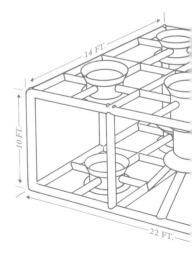

Meanwhile, Union picked up acreage on a concession south of Attaka. "We probably doubled our holdings," noted Chuck Schwartz, then general manager for the company in Southeast Asia. "As a result, we found a number of other fields."

Union's offshore acreage totaled 3.1 million acres. Commercial discoveries after Attaka included the Melahin and Kerindingan fields in 1972, and the Sepinggan field in 1973. (Further north, Union explorers made the first discovery of hydrocarbons in the Gulf of Thailand in January 1973. This led to a major natural gas development there later in the decade.)

In order to speed up the process of getting oil from its Indonesian discoveries to market, Union applied an idea that had been developed by the U.S. industry as a method to save exploratory wells for possible production: drilling

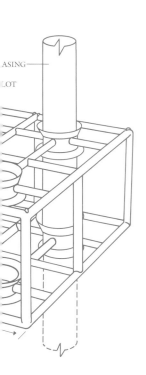

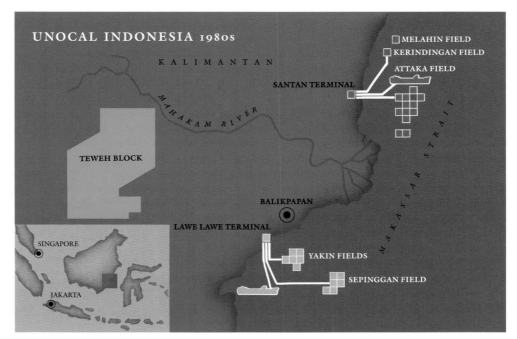

through sea-floor templates. In this way, the wells were drilled while the platforms were under construction. Once the platforms were lowered into place over guides, the drill slots lined up with the template configuration and the wells were rapidly completed.

"It's like putting a peg in a board," explained Stegemeier. "Within six weeks or so after you've set the platform, you've got production—instead of a year later. We have used the technique all over the world to save exploration wells and sometimes to do predevelopment work while waiting for the platform. It saves all kinds of money."

The Indonesian platforms were built to conform to standards set by the United States Geological Survey to prevent pollution of America's Outer Continental Shelf, per orders from Ray Burke. But Burke, then Union's senior vice president for energy resources, may have underestimated the "environmental" problem that would accompany his selection of the site for the project's housing facilities.

Burke spotted the site—a ridge overlooking the coastal town of Balikpapan—during a visit to Pertamina facilities. A community was designed that included air-conditioned housing, a water system, a generating plant, school, recreational facilities, and fire and police departments. Pasir Ridge (*pasir* is Indonesian for "sand") had been a Japanese antiaircraft installation during World War II, so the construction crews knew they might run into some ammunition. But they found more than they had anticipated.

"On the first day we had a bulldozer up there, it rolled over a five hundred-pound bomb that hadn't exploded," Stegemeier said. Over the next several days, construction workers found more unexploded bombs and shells—all of which they sandbagged and exploded on the site. The ammunition had been sitting on the ridge for 30 years and couldn't be defused. "There was so much live ammo that we almost abandoned the site," Stegemeier said. But they swept it clean and built the settlement. Every house had a panoramic view of the Makassar Strait.

Ray Burke, for whom the community recreation center on Pasir Ridge was named, said: "I felt that we should build a facility that would be attractive, serve its purpose, and be entirely compatible to the climate and neighborhood in which it was built." Instead of asking one of the oil service companies to handle the project, Burke found an architectural firm that could satisfy his requirements. The buildings incorporated local materials and were designed to become a permanent part of the Balikpapan community.

Opposite, top left: Korea's Kyung In Energy Company, in which Union held a 50 percent interest, completed a new 325-megawatt electric power generating plant — with a sophisticated control room — at Inchon in 1972. Opposite, top right: Korea's President Park Chung Hee (center) cut the ribbon at the dedication ceremony for the power plant, with the assistance of Fred Hartley (left) and Kim Chong Hee, president of Korea Explosives Company, another partner in the joint venture. Opposite, bottom: The Geysers geothermal project in California became the world's largest in 1973 when its generating plants had the combined capacity to produce 400,000 kilowatts of electric power.

Attaka crude was high-gravity oil with a very low sulfur content, making it environmentally desirable both in the United States and Japan, which was also becoming more concerned about environmental pollution. During the years of U.S. oil import restrictions, Union had developed substantial overseas markets. Unoco Limited, a subsidiary based in Hong Kong, had been set up in 1962 to market crude oil and petroleum products in the Far East.

By the 1970s, Japan was second only to the United States in refining capacity, and Union sold about 130,000 barrels of crude oil a day — both its own and other production — to Maruzen Oil Company, a refining and marketing company with headquarters in Osaka. Union held a 33 percent interest in Maruzen. Union also sold semirefined and refined products for distribution in Japan.

Union's other major Pacific Rim market was Korea. The company held a 50 percent interest in the Kyung In Energy Company, whose 325-megawatt electric power generating plant was completed at Inchon in 1972. The project included a crude oil topping plant to supply fuel oil for the power plant. Later, the topping plant was converted into a 60,000-barrel-a-day refinery producing a full product line. Gasoline and other refined products were marketed under the Sign of the 76 throughout Korea. Unoco supplied the crude oil. (Union sold its interest in Kyung In in 1983.)

Union also had an interest in another form of power in the Pacific Rim: geothermal resources that could be tapped to run steam turbines for electricity generation. The Philippine government had begun investigating the potential of its geothermal resources in the early 1960s. In 1971, Union formed a subsidiary, Philippine Geothermal, Inc., which contracted with the Philippine National Power Corporation to develop the Tiwi field for steam to power its generating plants. The first well, drilled in 1972, was successful and development began in 1973.

The U.S. Agency for International Development had referred the government of the Philippines to Union Oil because of the company's success in developing The Geysers field north of San Francisco. Since 1967, when Union had become field operator, company engineers had adapted oil-field technology to geothermal production. Drilling tools and techniques were modified to compensate for the harder rock and higher temperatures in geothermal formations. Natural gas reservoir technology greatly improved reserve estimation, and an exploratory drilling program in 1969 and 1970 established the existence of an extensive resource at The Geysers.

The results proved so good, in fact, that the Pacific Gas & Electric Company (PG&E) included geothermal energy in its long-range planning for the first time, and a sales contract was signed in May 1970. It was a welcome resource for PG&E, since construction of other types of power plants had been slowed by new state and federal environmental legislation.

In the late 1960s, few could see the potential for geothermal energy, but Union did. "It appealed to Mr. Hartley's instincts as a builder and an engineer," said Dr. Carel Otte, president of the Geothermal Division. "It was right in the spirit of our company's engineering-oriented corporate culture. And Ray Burke was incredibly supportive as a boss and as a good spokesman for geothermal."

The National Society of Professional Engineers honored Union Oil Company and three other firms for pioneering the development of commercial geothermal energy, selecting The Geysers project as one of the ten most outstanding American engineering achievements of 1972. By the end of 1973, The Geysers was capable of producing about 400,000 kilowatts of electrical power, making it the largest project of its kind in the world.

Environmental regulations had slowed development, but the geothermal industry was new enough to adapt more rapidly than others to changing requirements. When the first oil price shocks of the decade were instigated by Middle Eastern oil exporters in late 1973, The Geysers provided a working example of America's potential for developing domestic energy alternatives to supplement conventional oil and gas resources.

Union had also long been interested in another alternative source of energy: oil shale. As the country's oil and gas supplies declined, Union stepped up its research program to produce crude oil from vast oil shale holdings in Colorado. In 1973, a shale oil pilot plant was in operation at Union's research laboratories in Brea, California.

By spring of 1973, the crunch had come. Increasing energy usage coupled with reduced domestic production resulted in shortages. Union and other major oil companies instituted allocation programs to dole out supplies of gasoline to their dealers and distributors. At Union, deliveries were based on a percentage of 1972 purchases. President Nixon reacted by substituting import fees for quotas, and imports continued to rise.

While the price controls that had been set by Nixon to restrain inflation were dropped that summer, new price controls, related to May 1973 levels, were set for the oil industry. This gave birth to a two-level pricing system for domestic crude oil (which developed into a three-level system before controls were eliminated in 1981). Prices for "old oil" (in production before 1973) would be based on May levels. But market prices would prevail for "new oil" in an effort to stimulate domestic production.

Controls on dealers' margins allowed them to pass on most — but not all — of the cost increases to consumers. "This is an unbelievable government position," Hartley said, "since it calls for the dealers to absorb the increased cost of gasoline resulting from the increased crude oil costs for foreign and domestic crude as authorized by the same agency of government — the Cost of Living Council."

The effect of these regulations had barely been felt when turmoil in the Middle East created an opportunity for OPEC to demonstrate its influence over world oil supplies. On October 6, Egyptian troops attacked Israeli positions across the Suez Canal, igniting the Yom Kippur War. Eleven days later, ministers from OPEC's six Persian Gulf states agreed to raise their crude oil prices by 70 percent — from $3 per barrel to over $5. Several hours later, Arab oil-producing countries

LAND, LOTS OF LAND
During its early years, Union Oil preferred to purchase land rather than lease mineral rights for oil and gas exploration. Over time, the company's property portfolio grew as sites were also acquired for service stations and other facilities. In 1973, Charles Parker, senior vice president for finance, set up a separate Real Estate Division in order to better manage Union's considerable holdings. "One of the major functions of the group is to take jurisdiction over company-owned property that no longer has an operating need," said Parker. A subsidiary of the division, the Moreland Development Company, was formed to develop properties with good commercial, residential, or industrial potential. Moreland, which became the Unocal Land & Development Company, had grown out of an investment partnership formed in 1964. In one major project, the company's real estate specialists produced a development plan for the 250 largely vacant acres surrounding eastern region headquarters in Schaumburg, Illinois. In 1979, ground was broken for a Hyatt Regency Hotel adjacent to the company's office building. In the next few years, two office buildings, a restaurant, and a parkway named in honor of William S. McConnor, former Unocal Refining & Marketing Division president, were added. In 1989, the division completed a new master plan for 190 acres of the Schaumburg property, providing for office space, a regional shopping mall, and a convention center. In the late 1980s, Unocal's real estate specialists handled an increasing number of property sales as the company moved to streamline operations. These included the company's headquarters, Unocal Center, sold in 1988 for $205 million.

Above: King Faisal of Saudi Arabia and other Arab leaders, angered at Israel's supporters in the Yom Kippur War, agreed in late 1973 to embargo oil shipments to the United States. Opposite: The combined effects of the embargo and domestic shortages soon had American motorists waiting in line for gasoline.

agreed to institute an embargo against "unfriendly" (meaning pro-Israeli) countries, namely the United States and the Netherlands, and to cut the volume of their oil exports. Before the year was out, all OPEC producers agreed to price increases that at least doubled the cost of their oil. Arabian light crude, for example, went from $5 per barrel to $11.65.

In the United States, effects of the embargo, combined with domestic energy shortages, were greater than those caused by earlier supply disruptions following the Suez Canal closure in 1956 and the outbreak of the Six-day War (between Israel and Egypt) in 1967. By the end of 1973, most of America's 300 or so refineries were without an assured supply of crude. In late November, Congress passed the Emergency Petroleum Allocation Act to be administered by the newly created Federal Energy Office. The FEO took over all pricing matters of the petroleum industry from the Cost of Living Council and also established allocation priority systems.

Few had listened to the oil industry's warnings of impending domestic shortages and the dangers of growing U.S. dependence on Middle East producers. But once the shortage hit, fingers were quick to point at the industry — suggesting that the crisis had been manufactured to raise prices.

Claude Brinegar, who left Union to serve in the Nixon-Ford cabinets as secretary of transportation from 1973 to 1975, recalled an exchange with a U.S. senator who did not believe there was a real shortage. "I don't know how to prove it to you," Brinegar explained, "except perhaps to invite you to go down to the dock with me and watch the tankers no longer come in."

Americans had learned to take plentiful, low-cost energy for granted. Waiting in long lines to fill up their gas tanks made people angry. The public was largely unaware that the United States was importing a third of its crude oil in order to provide the abundance of energy that ran America's big cars, air-conditioned its homes and offices, and fueled its industry.

The Arab states lifted their embargo in March 1974. Prices rose, and so did the level of imports. Government policy kept U.S. domestic oil prices artificially low, continuing to discourage new development and production. Tightening environmental regulations also curtailed industry efforts. Between 1973 and 1977, average annual U.S. oil production slipped 1 million barrels per day. By the end of the decade, the country once more reeled under a supply disruption — this time triggered by revolution in Iran.

10   Shifting Balance in World Energy

Hartley and other oil company leaders faced a perplexing situation during the 1970s: American consumption of oil was rising, but government price controls on petroleum and its products discouraged domestic exploration and production. Opposite: Union discovered the Heather field offshore Scotland's Shetland Islands in 1973 and set the platform in 1977. Higher world oil prices spurred exploration and development in the difficult North Sea environment.

"The year 1973 was our country's introduction to an energy crisis whose duration and severity we are unable yet to determine," said Fred Hartley. "Certainly we Americans have come to the end of an era of cheap energy and to the beginning of a changed lifestyle."

Americans, however, were not ready to give up cheap energy. It had fueled the country's phenomenal development since World War II and was perceived as fundamental to continued growth. The U.S. government acted to keep domestic crude oil and product prices below escalating world market levels. In so doing, it discouraged domestic production, encouraged consumption, and virtually subsidized oil imports.

Domestic oil producers were soon trying to cope with an ever-deepening quagmire of federal price and allocation regulations — and imports continued to rise. By 1978, five years after OPEC began raising prices, Americans were consuming gasoline and other refined petroleum products at record levels — 19 million barrels a day. More than 46 percent of the country's crude oil supply was imported, compared with 33 percent in 1973.

The oil industry was targeted as the villain, accused of hoarding supplies, exhorted to find and produce more oil, and castigated for rising earnings. "I admit the expression 'dying industry' is an interesting one," said Hartley in response to a radio commentator's question about depletion of world oil supplies in January 1974. "A lot of people are trying to bury us."

Shortly after the Arab embargo was announced, Clay R. Warnock, then division sales manager in Seattle, was invited to speak to a group of legislators. When Warnock arrived at the appointed place — a school gym in Olympia, the state capital — he found the bleachers jammed with angry citizens. Warnock was directed to a single chair facing a row of more than a dozen state lawmakers, and the interrogation began.

"The crowd was hostile," Warnock recalled. "They were sure that we were putting gasoline underground and were contributing to this shortage. The price had gone up, and they just didn't understand the reasons for it. Some of the state senators were way off base. I was able to put some logic into the discussion. Before I left, I had the satisfaction of knowing that I made my message clear to at least some in my audience — but it was a very intimidating experience."

Oil company explanations continued to fall on deaf ears, particularly in regard to rising earnings. Union's earnings in 1973 were $180 million, up about 50 percent over 1972. "We are making a good recovery from the depressed earnings levels of the past three years," Fred Hartley said, "and our return on share-owners' equity has reached 10.9 percent, which was the average for all manufacturing companies during this period." In April 1974, Hartley was elected chairman of the board of Union Oil Company, in addition to his posts of president and chief executive officer.

Union announced a 22 percent increase in capital expenditures for 1974, with more than 70 percent earmarked for energy resource exploration and production. Later in the year, the capital budget of $490 million was revised to $700 million, topping the company's previous record of $533 million in 1968.

In 1974, Union's earnings rose 60 percent, totaling $288 million. The company projected capital expenditures of $750 million for 1975, more than two-and-a-half times earnings. "This is typical of the relationship between earnings and capital expenditures over the last ten years," explained Hartley.

Nevertheless, oil company profits were labeled "obscene" in Congress and by the media. In a nationwide poll taken in 1975, respondents guessed that oil companies earned 61 cents on every sales dollar, and that this was about double what other manufacturers earned. The truth was that oil companies earned 7.2 cents on each dollar in 1974. The average for all manufacturers was 5 cents.

The industry put its improving cash flows to good use. During the first half of 1974, the number of drilling rigs active in the United States averaged 1,389 — the highest level since 1965, and 42 percent more than the low of 976 rigs in 1971. But optimism in the domestic oil patch was short-lived as it became apparent that the government intended to tighten industry regulations.

In 1973, in response to the petroleum industry's changing economics, Charles Parker, Union's senior vice president of finance, had consolidated planning and development activities, including the one-year profit plan, the ten-year strategic plan, and a new three-year tactical plan. As government regulations mushroomed, the task of coordinating the company's response fell to the new department. "It became a very big, very time-consuming job," recalled Tom Sleeman, the department's first vice president.

"Early in the game," Sleeman explained, "there were certain regulations

VIEW FROM D.C.
In 1973, Union's Claude S. Brinegar, senior vice president, was asked by President Richard M. Nixon to serve in his cabinet as the nation's third secretary of transportation. "My sense of serving the country is that you take your turn; if asked, a person ought to step up and say yes," Brinegar said. His oil company background made him a key member of the President's advisory group during the oil embargo in 1973–74. In one of many tense situations, he found himself explaining to a group of angry airline pilots that the diesel fuel allocated to the trucking industry wouldn't fly airplanes and couldn't be converted to jet fuel. Brinegar's 20 years with Union Oil, particularly his direction of the integration of The Pure Oil Company into Union, had honed his management and analytic skills. In Washington, those skills helped him oversee the restructuring of the bankrupt Penn Central Railroad into Conrail, initiate movement toward deregulation of transportation, and prepare the first comprehensive outline of a national transportation policy. "It was a wonderful experience. You get challenged daily — your intelligence, integrity, and energy," he said. In 1975, Brinegar (serving under Nixon's successor, Gerald Ford) resigned his cabinet post, preferring the private sector, and accepted an offer to return to Union Oil.

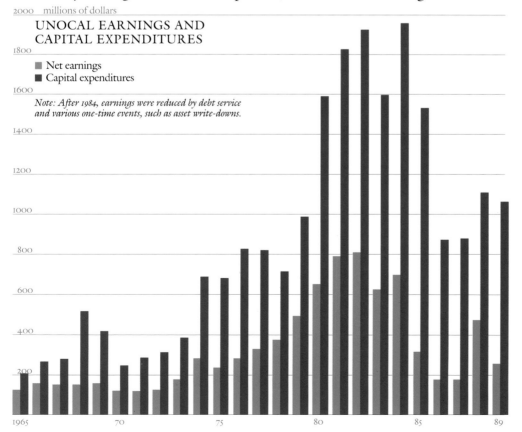

2000   millions of dollars

UNOCAL EARNINGS AND
CAPITAL EXPENDITURES

1800

■ Net earnings
■ Capital expenditures

1600

Note: After 1984, earnings were reduced by debt service and various one-time events, such as asset write-downs.

1400

1200

1000

800

600

400

200

1965   70   75   80   85   89

Charles Parker (top) consolidated Union's planning activities in 1973, creating a new Corporate Planning and Development Department headed by Tom Sleeman (above), who had joined Pure Oil in 1954 as an accounting management trainee. Opposite, bottom: As Union's earnings rose during the 1970s along with oil prices, the company was able to reinvest more and more in the widening search for new resources and in improved technology for cleaner, more efficient operations.

with regard to crude oil pricing that put us in a relatively favorable position and caused oil company profits to be quite high in 1974. That led to the federal government's crude oil entitlements program, which was so complex it was mind-boggling — and caused our profits to be quite low the next year."

The entitlements program, introduced in late 1974, was an attempt to even out the price of all crude oil flowing through U.S. refineries. The premise was that companies with access to less expensive price-controlled domestic oil were not "entitled" to refine it unless they paid refiners who were more dependent on expensive "new" domestic oil or imports. In this way, the benefits of price-controlled oil would be evenly distributed among refiners, and refined product prices would be more uniform.

"It is really a burden on us, because in the past our executives elected to build a higher share of domestic self-sufficiency in crude than the rest of the industry," noted Bill McConnor, president of the Union 76 Division. "The problem we're facing is that they have taken only one of the segments that make up the cost of getting gasoline to market and equalized that. They equalized the one in which we're the most proficient and competitive."

Starting in January 1975, the Federal Energy Administration (FEA) collected crude oil cost data from the nation's refiners, established a national average price, and published monthly entitlements notices specifying who would pay and who would receive. During the first three months of the program, Union paid out $22 million, of which $4 million went to a major oil company three times Union's size, and $1 million to a New York utility. Because of the FEA's two-month lag in publishing the notices, the companies that paid entitlements were delayed in recouping the cost in the marketplace.

Although aimed at protecting small, independent refiners, the program invited abuse and, in effect, subsidized imports. Within a few years, there were some 60 new or refurbished small refineries — called "teakettles" or "bias babies" — that had been built or restarted just to cash in on entitlements. Major integrated companies that processed a lot of foreign crude and municipal users of high-cost alternative fuels received disproportionate shares of payments.

The program was soon riddled with exemptions. While entitlements were supposed to equalize crude oil costs among refiners, in some cases they provided subsidies for nonrefiners, such as importers of residual fuel and petrochemicals. Some refiners were granted relief because of financial hardship, increasing the burden on others.

Joe Byrne, vice president of national marketing for the Union 76 Division, dubbed the entitlements program "Hydra," after a serpent in Greek mythology: Every time one of the monster's heads was cut off, two grew in its place. McConnor noted at the time, "You could spend every waking hour of your day and still not read all the FEA bulletins that come out."

Entitlements and price controls were not the only plagues on the oil companies after OPEC's price increases. The Tax Reduction Act of 1975 eliminated the depletion allowance for oil and gas. Other extractive industries, mining dozens of materials — sulfur, iron, zinc, gravel, peat, sand, coal, and uranium, to name a few — were not affected.

When the law was passed in March, Union immediately announced a reduction in its planned expenditures for domestic exploration and production by $45 million, and by twice that amount in 1976 when the natural gas provisions of the law took effect — "a result that is hardly consistent with the nation's long-term objective of energy self-sufficiency," Hartley stated in a wire to the joint conference committee that wrote the final bill.

Union's 1975 earnings were $232.8 million, representing a 19 percent dip from

Above: The Whitecap pumping station offshore Louisiana was completed in 1969 by a Union subsidiary, The Pure Transportation Company. The station feeds Gulf production into the Capline, which carries crude to midwestern refineries. Opposite, top: In the seventies, Union built self-serve stations—like this one in San Diego —for cost-conscious consumers. Opposite, bottom: By 1975, there were more than 300 Union 76 auto/truckstops—like this one in Winnemucca, Nevada —on major highways across the country. Below: By the late 1970s, Union owned or held interests in more than 3,000 miles of crude and product pipelines, part of a vast network that transports massive amounts of hydrocarbons.

1974. The decline was due to the loss of the depletion allowance, lower oil production, and government mandated delays in passing through entitlements costs to consumers.

When the embargo hit, the refineries were the first to notice the change in distribution patterns. Union's Beaumont refinery was on the Neches River, which empties into the Gulf of Mexico. "We were in a position to receive a lot of foreign crude," noted Roger C. Beach, then general superintendent at Beaumont. "Almost overnight, we went from processing a very routine slate of domestic crudes to processing about 50 percent foreign. We started receiving tankers from Nigeria and Algeria and other countries with exotic names."

In 1970, only 6 percent of the crude oil that ran through Union's refineries was imported. The percentage leaped to 25 percent by 1974 and to 44 percent by 1977, a reflection of declining domestic production and increasing consumer demand.

In early 1974, Union chartered four oil tankers, doubling the capacity of its fleet so it could meet its increasing need for imports. Capline, the major crude oil pipeline linking Gulf of Mexico ports with the central United States, increased its capacity by 50 percent in 1974 to handle the load, as did Chicap, the northern link between Capline and Union's Chicago refinery.

Another immediate effect of the embargo and price hikes was to halt the aggressive program of service station building that Union had been pursuing since its merger with Pure Oil in 1965. In fact, in the early 1970s, most companies were intent on expanding their retail networks. But higher priced oil and allocation of gasoline changed the approach. Union sold off its less profitable locations, modernizing and enlarging the remaining stations to serve more customers and handle bigger volumes. More self-serve islands and outlets were added, and the auto/truckstop network was expanded.

Company advertising during the 1970s was low-key. "We are trying to keep our name in front of the public, and we are advocating efficient utilization of fuel," said Bill McConnor at the time. "We provide good service and a good product, but we are not in any way promoting the sale of gasoline."

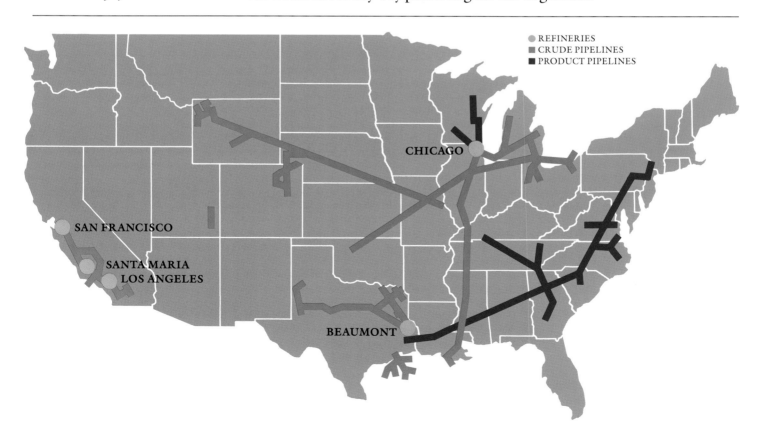

President Nixon, shown with his wife, Pat, resigned in 1974 and was succeeded by Gerald Ford.

In fact, Union promoted gasoline conservation. In late 1974, the company released the results of its Union 76 Fuel Economy Tests, giving new car buyers comparative information about gasoline mileage. Union conducted the tests in cooperation with the National Association of Stock Car Auto Racing, using procedures developed by the Society of Automotive Engineers. More than 80 foreign and domestic models were tested under actual driving conditions at the Daytona International Speedway in Florida. By contrast, the Environmental Protection Agency calculated its fuel-efficiency ratings based on laboratory emissions tests.

Fuel economy, however, was not a popular subject with Americans. Retail gasoline prices had gone up from 35 to 40 cents per gallon in 1973 to more than 60 cents in 1976, reflecting the regulated increase in the cost of crude oil; but that was not enough to encourage conservation. Hartley, in a 1975 interview, told of a customer's sending in a 1916 sales slip showing a price of 19 cents a gallon—equivalent to 95 cents a gallon in 1975, allowing for inflation. "That, adding thirteen cents for taxes, would make gas sell today for more than a dollar per gallon," Hartley said.

President Gerald Ford, who had taken office in August 1974 after the Watergate scandal forced President Nixon's resignation, wanted to let price and allocation controls on crude oil and products lapse on schedule in early 1975. Government studies suggested that decontrolling prices and letting them rise to world market levels would help reduce the nation's dependence on imports. But Congress didn't back Ford. Instead, the legislators passed extensions and developed a new set of price controls that actually lowered the cost of gasoline to consumers. Ford reluctantly signed the Energy Policy and Conservation Act in December 1975.

The EPCA was supposed to be the comprehensive national energy policy that would control utilization and promote supply, according to McConnor. "That was promised us after the embargo," he said in 1976. "But nothing very earthshaking has come out. The only crude we have now that we didn't have at the time of the crisis is, or shortly will be, North Slope oil. The rest of it has all been politics. Nothing has happened in shale or coal. The brakes have been put on nuclear energy. Very little has been done in solar energy. If you try to measure what we as a country have accomplished, I think the Alaskan pipeline is the only thing we can point to."

The EPCA provided for the establishment of the Strategic Petroleum Reserve (SPR), where 750 million barrels of oil could be stored as a precaution against another abrupt disruption in supplies. That amount of oil would, of course, provide only a short-term answer to future supply disruptions in a country that imported more than 7 million barrels per day. (The questions of how much oil should be set aside in the SPR, and how quickly, became controversial as the years passed. By 1990, the SPR held 580 million barrels of crude oil.)

Above: Bill McConnor, who was hired by Pure Oil in 1941 after graduation from Lehigh University, became president of the Union 76 Division when Claude Brinegar accepted a cabinet post. Below: The first phase of development of the Strategic Petroleum Reserve included excavation of huge 10-million-barrel capacity storage caverns in salt domes located along the Gulf Coast.

The EPCA also extended price controls for 40 months and created a third tier of oil prices that included most of the domestic production that had been exempt from controls under the prior rules. As months passed, the regulations got more tangled. They changed almost daily. From Union Oil's perspective, government administrators didn't seem to understand their own regulations.

"It's a very complicated set of rules that determines the price of different types of crude oil, requiring special record keeping to track our properties monthly to calculate production rates," said Donald A. Lindros, who administered Union's compliance with these regulations during the 1970s. "Another group of regulations controls the prices of refined products."

The EPCA mandated automotive fuel-efficiency standards, but Detroit's fuel-economy models turned out to be poor sellers. While sales of small cars rose from 43 percent of all car sales in 1973 to 53 percent in 1975, Americans soon resumed their penchant for gas guzzlers. In 1976, Detroit's big cars broke sales records. The small-car market was left to foreign manufacturers. Without the incentive of higher gasoline prices, American drivers did not take fuel economy seriously.

"I don't blame them," noted Claude Brinegar, who returned to Union as senior vice president of corporate affairs in 1975 after resigning his cabinet position as secretary of transportation. "We had the embargo and all the talk about shortages. But the shortage—in the sense of gasoline lines—went away. Prices went up, but then under the energy act that Congress forced on the President last December, prices went down....Politics notwithstanding, the best incentive for conservation is a high price. That's the one thing that causes a person to be prudent in his own resource trade-offs."

Indeed, American car buyers did become more prudent in their automobile choices and driving habits after the second energy crisis hit in 1979. By the early 1980s, sales of imported small cars quickly eroded Detroit's market share.

"However it is administered," Hartley said, "the new energy bill passed by

the Congress late in 1975 will result in a reduction in [available] capital needed to maintain our domestic oil production capacity. This then will increase our dependence on foreign oil....Congress has legislated in favor of the citizens of the OPEC nations and against ourselves."

From 1975 through 1978, dozens of "divestiture" bills, which Hartley characterized as serious threats to the very existence of the petroleum industry, were introduced in Congress. Vertical divestiture would have forced integrated oil companies to sell off operations, so that no single company would perform more than one function: production, transportation, refining, or marketing. Horizontal divestiture would have prevented oil and gas companies from producing other forms of energy, such as geothermal steam or shale oil.

"Either approach is bad economics," Hartley said. "Both would make capital harder to obtain to develop new energy sources, cause the consumer to pay more for energy, worsen the nation's long-term problem of inflation and unemployment, and increase our dependence on insecure foreign sources of energy."

The stage for such legislation had been set during the fuel shortages in the spring of 1973. California was the first of several states to sue various oil companies for antitrust violations. "The states seemed to think that there had been a conspiracy to create the shortage," said George Bond, who became Union's chief counsel in October 1973. "They went on that theory. They got nowhere with it, but it was a very expensive thing to defend." Eventually, a staff of more than 50 was assigned to gather data to defend against the lawsuit, and litigation lasted well into the 1980s.

Even though the oil industry was viewed as a monopoly, the fact was that in 1975 no company controlled more than 9 percent of the nation's total oil and natural gas production. More than 10,000 companies were competing in the search for oil and gas.

During the mid-1970s, Union and other oil companies had to fight off legislative attempts to break them up into smaller, less efficient organizations. Union ran this ad in national publications in 1975 in response to claims that oil companies acted as a monopoly.

In late 1974, U.S. Secretary of Transportation Claude Brinegar (left) conferred with President Ford at one of several conferences held around the country to solicit ideas about how to battle rising inflation. Brinegar resigned his cabinet post in 1975. He returned to Union Oil, where one of his first priorities was to consolidate government relations activities in a single department.

"What people didn't realize was that the oil industry is extremely complex," recalled Philip Blamey, Union controller during the mid-1970s. "There has always been a tremendous amount of competition and essentially distrust between oil companies. But collusion is presumed by outsiders because we have so many joint-venture operations for exploration and production, which simply serve to spread the risk; and we have so many agreements for exchange of products, which serve to reduce transportation costs."

The divestiture bills were not passed, thanks in large part to the oil industry spokespersons who worked hard to make their views known in Washington. Union's staff in the nation's capital spent long days presenting to legislators and government agencies the company's position and the facts that supported it.

"When I came to work for Union Oil in 1968, there were only three of us in the Washington office," recalled E. William Cole, vice president. "Now [in 1980] there are eleven people. That alone reflects the increased participation of government in our lives."

Union's representatives in Washington were frequently joined by Fred Hartley, Claude Brinegar, and many other Union executives in efforts to educate legislators and administrators about the complexities of the oil business. The need for such education was particularly evident to Brinegar, in light of his service in the capital.

"At the start [of the oil embargo] I was the only person in the cabinet who knew how many gallons of oil were in a barrel," he said. Brinegar initiated the development of an inventory of Union Oil's various and widely scattered government relations activities. These were consolidated in a new department.

"The seventies became a very contentious period," Brinegar recalled. "We had historically been something of a provincial West Coast company that tended to pull its head in. I certainly wanted to reverse that and influence actions in Washington as much as we could."

While Union Oil faced extraordinary regulatory burdens in the United States, the situation for the company's Canadian affiliate may have been worse. Higher oil prices after the 1973 embargo set off a ten-year tug-of-war between Canada's federal government in Ottawa and the provincial governments, particularly Alberta, the country's major oil-producing province.

Most of Canada's major oil discoveries were made during the 1960s and came on stream in the early 1970s. The Canadian government was beginning to enjoy tax revenues from steadily increasing production when, after the embargo, the provinces decided they wanted to share in the oil companies' so-called windfalls. Consequently, they doubled provincial royalties on oil-producing properties.

Union Oil of Canada, along with many other companies, was caught in a double taxation squeeze, according to Clement W. Dumett, Jr., president of Union of Canada since 1975. Capital for exploration and expansion of production was sharply curtailed. Drilling rig activity in Canada declined by 18 percent in 1974, while the United States enjoyed a 23 percent increase. In 1976, Union of Canada sold its refining and marketing assets to Husky Oil for $38.2 million, primarily because the investment that would be required to maintain and expand refining operations was needed for oil and gas exploration. In a capital reorganization, Union of Canada paid $73 million to its shareholders.

One aspect of the politics of energy in the United States was the promised development of alternatives to oil and gas. It was a popular theme, but hopes and expectations far exceeded technical realities. In reaction to the embargo in 1973, President Nixon had proposed Project Independence. The plan's objective was to eliminate oil imports and make the United States energy self-sufficient by 1980. Project Independence proved to be wildly optimistic and unworkable.

Some speculate that Nixon was hoping to divert attention from the growing Watergate scandal.

The fact was that development of energy alternatives was a long-term proposition. Technologies to replace growing U.S. dependence on oil imports were not sufficiently developed in the mid-1970s to produce the required amounts of energy within so short a time. Nor would domestic oil prices, which fell in real terms in 1974 and 1975, support development and production of such expensive alternatives as shale oil.

Union purchased oil shale properties in Colorado in the 1920s and had been developing technology for extracting oil from the ore since the early 1940s. In 1973, a three-ton-per-day pilot plant was built at the company's research center in Brea, California, as a prelude to designing an environmentally sound commercial plant. In 1976, Union's Synthetic Fuel Division completed engineering designs for a retort to produce 7,300 barrels of crude a day from 10,000 tons of oil shale. Union also completed environmental impact studies at the Parachute Creek site in Colorado. Progress toward commercial shale production seemed to be smooth and rapid.

But the politics and economics of energy continued to prohibit the commercial development of oil shale. The petroleum industry was choking on regulation and threatened with divestiture. The capital investment required to produce shale oil on a commercial scale could not be justified in the late 1970s.

The case for another valuable alternative fuel, geothermal energy, was already well established by the early 1970s. Union had aggressively developed geothermal resources and technology at The Geysers field in Northern California since 1965. By 1973, the field provided enough steam to Pacific Gas & Electric's power plants to generate 400,000 kilowatts of power, making Union the world leader in geothermal energy.

Union, criticized during the late 1960s for pursuing geothermal at a time when crude oil was cheap, was now applauded. The Geysers even drew presidential attention when Gerald Ford paid a visit in April 1975, along with Federal Energy Administration head Frank Zarb. Hosted by Fred Hartley, Dr. Carel Otte (Geothermal Division president), and PG&E chairman Shermer Sibley, President Ford and his party were given a full rundown on the operation, from drilling wells to generating electricity. Continued development of The Geysers

Opposite, top and bottom: In the late 1970s and early 1980s, Union's drilling at The Geysers increased the company's steam production to supply 1.1 million kilowatts of installed generating capacity. Opposite, center left: In 1975, as the politics of oil made alternative energies very attractive, President Ford (right) and FEA chief Frank Zarb (center) toured The Geysers with hosts Fred Hartley (left) and Dr. Carel Otte (in yellow jacket). Opposite, center right: A field operator opens a valve to test a well's flow rate. Below: Union introduced its driving simulators at an energy fair in Los Angeles in late 1976. The simulators, designed to teach energy-conserving driving techniques, proved popular and were used for several years at many expositions. Union's Lowell Morrill (center) assists a "driver."

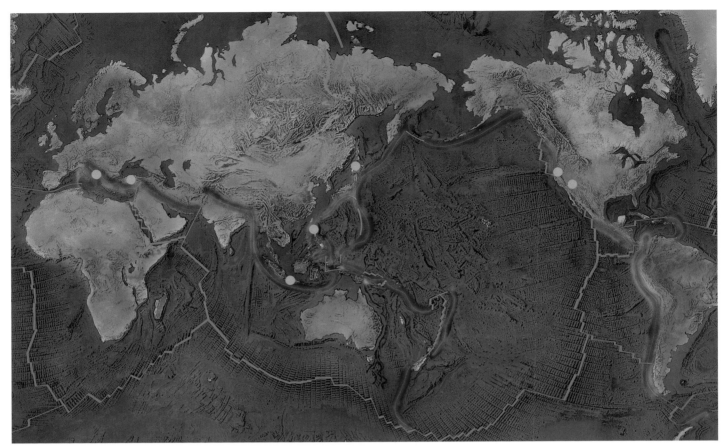

resource almost doubled the project's capacity by the end of the decade, making it a significant energy resource in Northern California.

Geothermal also played an important role in the Philippines' energy picture during the 1970s. Union had just initiated geothermal activities there in 1973 when the oil-poor country was stung by the combined effects of the embargo and higher prices. Dependent on imports for more than 90 percent of its energy requirements, the Philippines had been targeted by the Arab embargo because of a secessionist revolt by a minority Muslim population in the south. Oil account-ed for some 13 percent of the country's import bill in 1973, up to 32 percent by 1980. The Philippine government ordered rapid development of the geothermal resources at the Tiwi field in 1973. In 1975, Union's subsidiary, Philippine Geothermal, Inc., verified the potential of a second field at Makiling-Banahao, near Manila.

Increasing geothermal activity in both the United States and abroad helped offset a general decline in Union's total energy reserves and production during the 1970s, and so did international oil and gas activities. In 1974, Union's for-eign production (excluding Canada) set a record for year-to-year increases — up 13 percent over 1973. This was due largely to Union's share of the 100,000 barrels per day of crude oil being produced in the Attaka field offshore East Kalimantan. (The continuing success in Indonesia more than made up for the 4,000 barrels a day of oil lost in 1975 when Venezuela nationalized its petroleum industry, includ-ing Union's Lake Maracaibo property.)

The same techniques that had brought the Attaka field on stream so rapidly after its discovery in 1970 were applied to nearby discoveries in the Melahin, Kerindingan, and Sepinggan fields. When a fifth field, Yakin, was brought on stream in 1977, total production reached 147,000 barrels per day, with Union's share being a little more than half.

"The point of the rush to get on production was the growing dependence on imports in the United States," noted Dick Stegemeier, who directed the

Opposite: The red "ring of fire" symbolizes volcanic activity. This ring and the blue lines indicate deep cracks in the earth's crust where molten rock (magma) comes close to the surface and heats underground geothermal reservoirs. Dots indicate Union's geothermal operations in the 1970s and 1980s, including projects in California, the Philippines, and Indonesia. The company also explored prospects in California, Japan, Turkey, and Italy. *Below:* Union began development of geothermal resources in the Philippines at Tiwi in 1973 and at Makiling-Banahao in 1975. *Right:* The Sepinggan oil field offshore East Kalimantan, Indonesia, was brought on production in 1975, along with the Melahin and Kerindingan fields.

development of Union's offshore oil and gas operations and construction of support facilities in Balikpapan. "The company was looking for a controlled supply of crude oil."

The Indonesian project, Union's most ambitious to that time, presented enormous logistical problems. Everything, from steel pipe to food to toothpaste, had to be imported. Supply lines stretched thousands of miles to Singapore, Japan, the United States, and Australia. The crew was truly international. "We must have had people from a dozen countries speaking almost that many languages — Japanese, Korean, Indonesian, French, English," Stegemeier said. "And all these nationalities, speaking a polyglot of languages, had to work together as a team."

On one occasion, a few of them had to work together as a chorus. Graydon H. Laughbaum, Jr., then exploration manager, recalled a visit to a village in the Teweh area, which Union was preparing to explore, in the rugged jungle interior of Kalimantan. In accordance with local custom, Laughbaum and his Australian, British, and American coworkers were expected to sing to their hosts. They wanted to make a good impression; Union field crews would be spending a lot of time in the area. "We decided that we all knew the words and could possibly carry the tune of 'Jingle Bells' — an unlikely song in the surroundings, but it proved to be very popular," Laughbaum said.

Expatriate employees were carefully interviewed and warned about the problems of isolation and potential stress on their families in an Indonesian assignment. Stegemeier had expected that turnover might be high. "But we had very little," he recalled. "The people who came to Balikpapan loved it."

He was often called on to serve as counselor and confidant to members of the Union team. "I might have been a little better prepared if I had spent my graduate years in a seminary," he said.

The isolation of the project, linked only by unreliable shortwave communication to the telephones in Singapore, made it a unique experience. "In many

ways, it was like running my own company," Stegemeier said. "An exchange of letters could take two weeks. I couldn't always ask for a second opinion when a decision beyond my dollar authority needed to be made. We got great support from the home office staff, and Fred Hartley and Ray Burke were tremendous in giving me the opportunity to do the job. They simply said, 'You're on the firing line. You do what you think is best.'"

In 1975, Stegemeier, a vice president, was promoted to resident manager in Southeast Asia and moved his headquarters from Balikpapan to Singapore. He continued to supervise exploration and development activities in Indonesia and also oversaw exploratory efforts in many other countries, from Australia to India. In Bangladesh, Union hoped that the Bay of Bengal might become a second Gulf of Mexico, but exploratory drilling proved disappointing.

In 1973, Union's discovery of the Erawan gas field in the Gulf of Thailand presented the same kind of problem that had been posed by the company's initial natural gas discoveries in Alaska: Where was the market? Union contracted with a French company to do a marketing study on potential gas use in Thailand, and with a Houston-based company to study the feasibility of what would be, if built, the world's longest underwater pipeline. The pipeline would carry the gas 265 miles from the field to landfall at Rayong, 100 miles southeast of Bangkok.

"We determined that Thailand used a lot of electrical power," said Robert R. Roethke, then vice president of natural gas for the International Division. "While some of that electricity was generated from hydropower, most of it came from thermal power plants fueled by imported oil."

With the cost of imported fuel oil rising, the Electricity Generating Authority of Thailand became very interested in converting its power plants to burn domestic natural gas, according to Dr. Harold Lian, who was named president of Union's International Division in 1974 when John Sloat retired.

Union looked for ways to help the Thai government finance construction of the pipeline. Roethke approached World Bank officials, and Fred Hartley later followed up in conversation with the bank's president, Robert McNamara. The financing was approved. In 1978, the Petroleum Authority of Thailand was formed to buy and distribute the gas that Union produced, and negotiations began for the first gas sales contract.

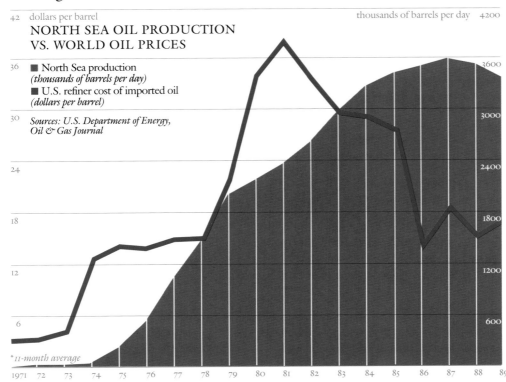

42   dollars per barrel   thousands of barrels per day   4200

NORTH SEA OIL PRODUCTION
VS. WORLD OIL PRICES

36   ■ North Sea production
     (thousands of barrels per day)
     ■ U.S. refiner cost of imported oil
     (dollars per barrel)

30   *Sources: U.S. Department of Energy,*
     Oil & Gas Journal

24

18

12

6

*11-month average

1971   72   73   74   75   76   77   78   79   80   81   82   83   84   85   86   87   88   89*

HEATH

UNITED
KINGDOM   N G

NORWAY

DENMARK

Halfway around the world, Union battled environmental extremes in Europe's North Sea. On even the best days, the ocean was rough and frigid. In winter, enormous storm waves generated up to twice the force whipped up by hurricanes in the Gulf of Mexico. The cost of one 12,000-foot exploratory well could exceed $5 million. Union had been active there since the late 1960s.

Huge discoveries were required to justify development costs in the North Sea, but the rising price of oil after 1973 expanded the options for oil and gas development. During the next decade, North Sea production became a major factor in the erosion of OPEC's markets.

Union and three partners were awarded four blocks in the United Kingdom sector of the North Sea in 1973. As operator, Union leased a gigantic $35 million drilling vessel, the *West Venture*, from a Norwegian company. The vessel's legs were 30 feet in diameter; its drilling derrick stood 160 feet high, 40 feet higher than rigs commonly used in the Gulf of Mexico. The first well, drilled 75 miles east of the Shetland Islands in almost 500 feet of water, struck oil. Platform Heather was set in 1977, after being towed 300 miles from Ardersier, Scotland. Its massive jacket (supporting structure) weighed 17,000 tons. Production started in 1978 and reached 20,000 barrels a day in 1980.

"When I went over there, you had to find a billion-barrel oil field to be in business," said John F. Imle, Jr., who moved to London as a senior drilling engineer for Union Oil in early 1973. "The oil field we found [Heather] turned out to contain reserves of one hundred million barrels. When we tested the first well, around Christmas of seventy-three, there was no way it could be considered commercial. But prices kept improving while we were doing appraisal drilling and development studies and ended up high enough to make development economically feasible. That was happening all over the North Sea, and it caused a tremendous surge in activity there."

Even the huge oil deposits discovered on Alaska's North Slope in the late 1960s were barely commercial at pre-embargo oil prices. But under the new price and supply regime, domestic producers and the U.S. government were eager to get those domestic supplies on stream. When Congress finally acted to expedite construction of the Trans-Alaska Pipeline System in 1974, Union made plans to drill on some of its North Slope acreage — and developed some unique technology

Left: A Union team built up an "ice island" as a drilling platform by freezing successive layers of seawater in shallow Harrison Bay above the Arctic Circle. Below: Giant legs on a drilling and production platform under construction in the Gulf of Mexico were designed to withstand hurricane forces.

in the process. For example, the company built its first "ice island" in the Beaufort Sea in the winter of 1976–1977.

Union's James R. Callender, Fred C. Duthweiler, and Michael E. Utt devised a scheme to take advantage of the Arctic Circle's most plentiful resource — ice. When winter froze the shallow waters of Harrison Bay, their team pumped seawater into a circular area on the ice sheet, forming a new three-inch layer each day. The ice sank, slowly building up a sturdy platform for drilling. The island was formed between November and January, the well drilled between February and April, and the rig removed just before the spring thaw. Union bore 25 percent of the cost, sharing expenses with other companies that wanted to participate in the new technology.

The major focus of Union's domestic exploration in the 1970s was in the warmer waters of the Gulf of Mexico. In 1974, the company spent $184 million for interests in more than 280,000 acres offshore. By year end, Union held interests in 11 platforms in various stages of completion in the Gulf.

Part of Union's strategy in bidding on Gulf properties in the early 1970s was to choose partners carefully in order to learn more about the then newly developed "bright spot" analysis technique that was helping geophysicists identify natural gas deposits on seismic records. "In 1972, we went to a Gulf Coast sale and did not buy one plot," explained Harry E. Keegan, who became president of the Oil & Gas Division in 1973. "But some companies were seeing more possibilities, and it was obvious then that two of them had something that the rest of the industry didn't have."

In the June 1973 sale, Union managed to get one of the two, Mobil, as a partner. By then, bright spot analysis was becoming an important factor in exploration, and Mobil had the expertise. Union compiled a remarkable 80 percent success rate in Gulf of Mexico drilling in 1975 with discoveries, many of them natural gas, in 23 of 29 wells.

During the 1970s, it became apparent that there were promising areas to explore farther and farther out in Gulf waters, so Ray Burke formed a deep-water technology team. The core members were Richard W. Yarbrough and Clifton A. Tannahill, both of domestic oil and gas operations; William K. Lewright, representing the International Division; and James A. Klotz, supervisor of reservoir, ocean, and arctic engineering for the research department. This team participated

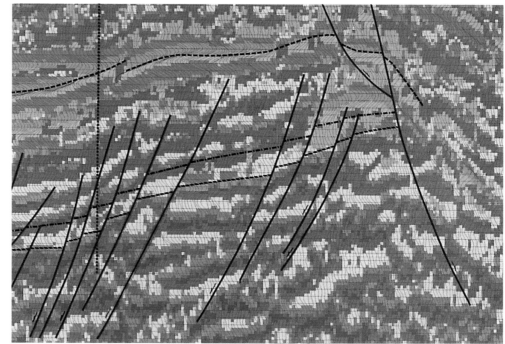

Since the 1970s, reservoir engineers have relied on computer simulations of oil and gas reservoirs to help maximize production. As technology evolved, the simulations grew more sophisticated. <u>Right:</u> By the late 1980s, Unocal researchers were able to cluster seismic data from many sources on one plot, creating a more detailed view of an oil reservoir, such as this one in the North Sea's Heather field. Based on geophysical analysis tools developed by company scientists, deep pink corresponds to likely high-porosity areas with good oil potential. Deep-blue areas are more likely to be compacted, indicating less oil flow. <u>Below:</u> This plot reveals — at least, to the practiced eye — the upper surface of a reservoir, located at a depth of 6,000 feet. Predominant areas of gas, oil, and water show up as yellow, green, and blue, respectively. The simulation is based on 1960s data from the Coalinga Nose field in California's San Joaquin Valley.

in some important early experiments in deep-water drilling from a prototype semisubmersible "tension leg" platform off Southern California; in laying pipeline in very deep water in the Gulf; and in subsea well completions (for wells not accessible to an offshore platform). In 1976, Union's International Division drilled some exploratory wells in the deepest waters yet for the company — 1,700 feet in the Andaman Sea off the west coast of the Malay Peninsula in Southeast Asia.

Even as the company looked to frontier environments for oil and gas discoveries, it also focused attention on producing more of the oil that had already been found. That was the reservoir engineer's province. The job has been compared with that of a physician trying to diagnose a patient from a mile away. The engineer cannot see into the reservoir. From tests and extrapolations, however, he can attempt to build a model of how a reservoir works and how it can be made to work better. Computer simulations became an invaluable tool in giving the engineer the capacity to analyze more data and consider more options.

"Reservoir engineers are determining the future — for another ten years at least — of the production of this oil company," said Union's Allyn T. Sayre, Jr., speaking of his own profession in 1976. "The reservoir engineer is the one who is trying to come up with the

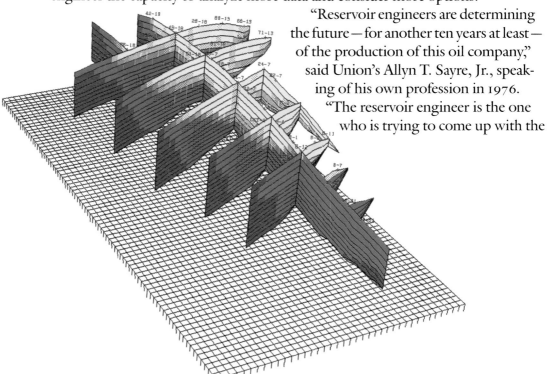

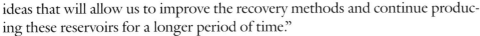

ideas that will allow us to improve the recovery methods and continue producing these reservoirs for a longer period of time."

Some two-thirds of the oil in any reservoir can be left behind by conventional production techniques. When a field is first developed, primary production relies on natural pressures. Natural gas or water in the reservoir pushes the oil through porous reservoir rocks and into the well bore. As these pressures decline, secondary techniques can be applied — pumping gas or water into the reservoir to keep the pressures up and the oil flowing. To assure maximum economic recovery over the long term, the reservoir engineer recommends which techniques should be applied, and when.

As the oil crisis grew in 1973, Union assigned its reservoir engineers the task of reviewing properties with marginal production. Production from 255 such wells was resumed or enhanced during 1974, with a projected increase in annual production of about 400,000 barrels. Additional drilling in existing fields (called "infill" drilling) also helped boost production. And with rising oil prices, Union renewed its efforts in tertiary or enhanced oil recovery, using advanced techniques to get more oil out of a reservoir. By 1977, the company was using or testing enhanced oil recovery processes in 17 fields in four states.

Union's Coalinga Nose field, producing since 1938 in California's San Joaquin Valley, was one of several chosen for experiments with the company's patented Uniflood process. The field was a "textbook reservoir," one without hidden underground faults to frustrate research efforts.

Uniflood had been in development since 1961. It used a combination of chemicals to "scrub" oil from reservoir rocks and then push it toward the well bore for production. L. Wally Holm, a senior research associate in the 1970s and the primary developer of the process, had started out in solvent-refining research. "It was natural for me to look at the reservoir and apply what I had been working with — solvents and detergents," he said.

Tests at Coalinga in 1977 proved successful, but Uniflood was still too expensive to be economic. The first license of Uniflood technology was not sold until 1980, after oil prices had doubled.

In 1986, Holm's lifetime work in enhanced oil recovery earned him membership in the prestigious National Academy of Engineering. In addition to the

development of Uniflood, Holm had gained the recognition of his peers for pioneering efforts in the use of carbon dioxide as a tertiary recovery method.

Union's most successful enhanced oil recovery projects in the 1970s were its thermal programs in central and coastal California. Since the 1960s, Union had been pumping steam into heavy oil reservoirs to help reduce the viscosity of the crude and make it flow more easily. The effort was given renewed emphasis in 1976, when the executive committee approved a five-year, 800-well program designed to develop 130 million barrels of potential reserves using the continuous steam drive technique. In just one year, production from five fields was increased by 8,500 barrels per day.

In Alabama, follow-up drilling to the company's late-1973 discovery 20 miles north of Mobile helped delineate the Chunchula natural gas and condensate field, which went on production in mid-1976. By the end of 1980, the Chunchula field produced a daily average of 35 million cubic feet of natural gas, 20,000 barrels of condensate, 2,800 barrels of propane, 1,700 barrels of butane, and 18 long tons of sulfur from 34 wells.

Chunchula was the sixth largest hydrocarbon discovery in the United States during the 1970s. But more than its size, the depth of the discovery—below 18,000 feet—gave it significance, according to Ray Burke. "It represents a new frontier," he noted in 1976. Deep drilling became a key strategy as Union worked to maintain the level of its domestic reserves.

In December 1976, the explosion of the tanker *Sansinena* in Los Angeles Harbor heightened public suspicion of the industry. The oil tanker, on long-term charter to Union, was 810 feet long and could carry 470,000 barrels of crude oil. Empty of cargo, it was taking on ballast water and fuel at Berth 46 when it exploded. The top deck blew off and landed ashore. Fire raged for several hours. Eight people died, including seven members of the ship's crew and a security guard. "It was a horrible disaster," said Neal E. Schmale, then a Union Oil attorney and one of the first company representatives on the scene.

Investigating agencies attributed the explosion to a build-up of vapors set off by a spark. At the first hearing of the Board of Harbor Commissioners, held within days of the explosion, Union 76 Division president Bill McConnor announced that the company was taking immediate steps to equip its carriers with inert gas blankets to prevent a similar tragedy.

Union quickly settled damage claims made by residents and businesses in the harbor area. The ship was a total loss. Temporary dock facilities were quickly arranged so the Los Angeles refinery could continue to receive crude shipments while the wreckage was removed and the berth rebuilt. The next tanker was due in port about a week after the disaster.

The *Sansinena* tragedy was the first of several tanker accidents in the industry that winter, most of which occurred on the East Coast. These accidents prompted new Coast Guard regulations to improve tanker safety.

By the end of 1976, public interest in energy issues subsided. Jimmy Carter was the President-elect, having defeated Gerald Ford in the November election. Carter's campaign proposal to create a cabinet-level energy department had failed to attract much attention, but energy—particularly oil—would not stay out of the spotlight for long.

The complex regulations that governed the price and distribution of petroleum in the United States after 1973 had upset the balance of supply and demand. Oil imports mounted, and the country's vulnerability to world supply disruptions increased. Although few saw it coming, in just two years the simmering political and religious conflict in Iran would boil over into bloody revolution, triggering the decade's second world oil supply crisis.

11

Moving Toward Decontrol

When Jimmy Carter took office as president in January 1977, the United States was ripe for the second energy crisis of the decade. Opposite: By 1979, revolution in Iran had triggered oil supply disruptions, long lines at gas stations, and the beginning of the end of U.S. domestic oil price controls.

While Jimmy Carter was being sworn in as the nation's thirty-ninth president in January 1977, Americans in the Northeast and Midwest were hard-pressed to stay warm. The winter was severe; fuel shortages, particularly of natural gas, made the suffering acute.

In one of his first acts in office, President Carter sent Congress emergency legislation providing him temporary authority over distribution and pricing of interstate gas supplies to allay the shortages. He then traveled to Pittsburgh, which had been particularly hard hit, to announce that the country probably faced a serious, permanent energy shortage.

In retrospect, it is ironic that the presidential campaign in 1976, bracketed as it was by two major oil price shocks, focused so little attention on energy issues. The United States had responded to the Arab embargo in 1973 and subsequent OPEC price increases by controlling domestic oil prices. As a consequence, Americans continued to view cheap and abundant energy as almost a birthright. Domestic oil production slumped while consumption soared.

By 1977, the United States was importing nearly half its oil and was ripe for another energy crisis. It came in 1979, when the Iranian revolution triggered the decade's second series of sudden oil price increases. The natural gas shortages of late 1976 and early 1977 were but a prelude, serving notice that energy was an issue that would not go away.

Consumers of interstate natural gas had been experiencing sporadic gas shortages since the beginning of the decade. This was the result of more than 20 years of federal government regulation, predating the price controls of the 1970s and making natural gas — like crude oil — both underpriced and oversold. Since federal regulations affected only those gas purchases made across state lines, consumers of intrastate gas were free to bid a little higher for their supplies. Significantly, intrastate consumers faced no natural gas shortages.

In 1976, the Federal Power Commission authorized an increase in the ceiling price to $1.44 per thousand cubic feet for "new" natural gas production brought on stream after 1974. But "old" gas, representing the largest part of Union's production, was selling below 30¢ per thousand cubic feet, the equivalent of selling crude oil at less than $1.90 a barrel, one-fourth the average domestic price.

Natural gas was undervalued in comparison to other fuels. Clean, efficient, and environmentally desirable as a fuel, it was also in demand as an important ingredient in the manufacture of fertilizer, plastics, and other essential materials.

Above: In 1979, a partial melt-down of the reactor core of a nuclear power plant at Three Mile Island, Pennsylvania, spelled the end of nuclear energy development for many years in the United States. *Left:* A grinding mill at Union's uranium mine and processing complex near Sweetwater, Wyoming, pulverized ore to the consistency of beach sand. The uranium project, planned when nuclear energy seemed the power source of the future, shut down after operating about 2½ years.

"There is a shortage because natural gas has taken over the market," explained Francis J. Barker, Union's vice president of natural gas and gas liquids, in 1977. "Other fuels, like coal, should have been used to help generate power. Natural gas, its price held down, rapidly rose in demand, out of proportion to its value."

Union's domestic natural gas production had doubled during the 1960s, peaking at 1.6 billion cubic feet per day in 1972 and exceeding the company's U.S. crude oil production on an energy equivalent basis. But rising exploration costs and low prices combined to slow petroleum exploration and production, and the company's natural gas production and reserves began to show the decline in 1973.

During the presidential campaign, Carter had promised to work for deregulation of producers' prices of new natural gas as a spur both to exploration and conservation of this valuable resource. But in the National Energy Plan he sent to Congress in April 1977, his proposals fell sadly short of what the industry had expected. Instead of calling for deregulation, the President's plan proposed continued price ceilings tied to domestic oil prices on new natural gas. This was supposed to put natural gas supply and demand back into balance as a first step toward deregulation.

The National Energy Plan was designed to reduce American dependence on imported oil. It recognized that both oil and natural gas prices would have to rise closer to world market prices in order to close the gap between what Americans paid for domestic resources and the replacement cost of those resources in imports. Carter insisted that oil companies should not benefit from such a "windfall" and that the increased revenues be shared with consumers through tax provisions.

The plan went to Congress, where it remained until the end of 1978. Meanwhile, Carter and Congress established the Department of Energy, which consolidated all the government's energy agencies in a cabinet-level department.

There was a popular belief in the late 1970s that the world was running out of petroleum resources at a fairly rapid rate. "Reserves were declining. The perception was that we were going to run out of oil and gas, and we had better find something more to do," said Tom Sleeman. "The economic forces that might have kept oil and gas production vigorous were not allowed to operate in the United States because of all the regulations during the 1970s."

U.S. oil companies began to diversify, some into very different kinds of businesses, such as computer software and retail sales. Union also pursued alternatives. The company had already proved the commercial viability of geothermal energy. Union's research was well under way into the mining and retorting of oil

HISTORY OF MOLYCORP

After the Civil War, prospectors moving west discovered an ore that looked like graphite in Sulfur Gulch, near Questa, New Mexico. According to local lore, the "graphite" mixed with animal fat made an efficient wagon-wheel lubricant and a not-so-efficient shoe polish. In truth, the ore contained molybdenum, whose usefulness as a toughening agent in steel was not recognized until the late nineteenth century. After 1914, the metal was in great demand as Europe and America armed for World War I. In 1918, the Western Molybdenum Mining Company acquired claims to the Sulfur Gulch deposit. Two years later, the Electric Furnace Reduction Company of Washington, Pennsylvania, a metal processing company, acquired the holdings of Western Molybdenum and incorporated as the Molybdenum Company of America (MCA). Men and mules did the backbreaking labor of digging for ore and hauling it out of twisting underground tunnels. By 1926, the Sulfur Gulch mine was the second largest moly producer in the world; and MCA was a major supplier of molybdenum, tungsten, and other specialty alloys to the steel industry. A search for new moly reserves, initiated in the late fifties, led to the start-up of an open-pit mine near Questa in 1965. By then, MCA also mined lanthanides near Mountain Pass, California, where a huge ore deposit had been discovered in 1949. The company also helped develop a niobium deposit in Brazil, in which MCA had acquired an interest in 1957. This venture led to the formation of CBMM, which became the world's largest niobium producer. MCA changed its name to Molycorp, Inc., in 1974, just three years before Union Oil acquired it.

Clockwise, from top: Molycorp's lanthanide mine and processing facilities near Mountain Pass, California; open-pit molybdenum mining near Questa, New Mexico; ferroniobium (iron-niobium alloy) smelting at the CBMM mine near Araxa in the Brazilian state of Minas Gerais.

shale, and the refining of shale oil into gasoline and other fuels. Union's Canadian subsidiary considered development of a thermal coal deposit and conducted research into thermal recovery of heavy oil deposits with vast potential.

In the spring of 1976, Union's Minerals Exploration Division undertook a feasibility study for a uranium mine and mill in southwest Wyoming. In 1979, the new Energy Mining Division, with John M. Hopkins as president, took responsibility for both the uranium and oil shale projects.

The uranium project proved short-lived. It went on stream in 1980, only to be derailed in 1983 when its primary customer canceled a purchase contract. The utility's planned nuclear power plant—and Union's uranium project—fell victim to the partial meltdown of a reactor core and the release of radiation at Three Mile Island in Pennsylvania in 1979. The accident brought intense public reaction. No new nuclear plants have been ordered in the United States since, and the one that Union was to supply was never completed. Union recovered most of its investment in the project in a $115 million cash settlement with the utility in 1987.

In 1977, Union acquired Molycorp, Inc., which had reported sales of $80 million and net earnings of $18 million in 1976. Molycorp produced molybdenum from its mine in Questa, New Mexico; lanthanides from its mine in

Mountain Pass, California; and niobium, through its interest in Companhia Brasileira de Metalurgia e Mineracao (CBMM), a mining operation in Brazil. The Mountain Pass mine contains the world's largest lanthanide ore body, and CBMM operates the world's largest niobium mine. Molybdenum and niobium are metals used in the production of high-grade steel. Lanthanides are essential elements in a growing variety of high-tech applications.

Molycorp and Union Oil were compatible businesses for two reasons: Lanthanide manufacture is basically a chemical rather than a mining business, and lanthanides are primary ingredients in many of the petroleum catalysts used in Union's refineries. Lanthanides have a strong affinity for combining with other elements, allowing the creation of new compounds with very specialized uses. Lanthanide phosphors, for example, make x-rays safer, reducing patient exposure time by intensifying x-ray images. Lanthanide-based magnetic alloys are used in miniaturized electronic motors.

"We bought Molycorp primarily for the lanthanides. By and large, they have met our expectations," said Tom Sleeman, president of Molycorp from 1979 through 1985. "With processing advances making a wider variety of lanthanide mixtures and purities available, there's just no telling what's down the road," he added. "The future for lanthanides keeps looking better and better."

Shortly after the acquisition, Union began studies that would lead to the expansion of Molycorp's molybdenum mining operation at Questa, New Mexico. And Molycorp upped its equity in the CBMM niobium mine, located near Araxa, Brazil, from 33 to 45 percent.

Union continued to expand its geothermal exploration in the late 1970s. Development of a demonstration project in the Jemez Mountains of New Mexico

LEGENDARY BUILDER
Clif Tannahill supervised the construction of more than 100 Unocal offshore platforms during his 30 years with the company. He joined Union Oil in 1956 as a civil engineer in the land department in the Gulf Region. In late 1964, he jumped at the chance to get into construction when he was tapped to supervise repairs to Union's Gulf platforms damaged by that year's devastating Hurricane Hilda. His use of ultrasonic inspection methods to check the platforms for cracks or other metal damage below the surface soon became accepted industry practice. When Tannahill suggested some basic improvements in platform design, he was offered the job of supervising platform construction in the Gulf. He initiated a review of all Gulf platforms. "We did a lot of modification and strengthening," he said. In the mid-1970s, Tannahill became a Houston-to-London commuter for three years during construction of the Heather platform, Union's first in the North Sea. His biggest challenge in terms of sheer size came in the Gulf of Mexico, where Platform Cerveza stood more than 1,020 feet high. Smaller but equally fascinating was the South Pass platform, set in 1980 in an area where the bottom was covered by a 50-foot layer of silt washed out from the Mississippi River delta. It was one of the first platforms successfully set on such a shifting sea bed, and it was installed in record time. Working from some research he had seen, Tannahill developed an idea to support the platform on an eight-foot diameter caisson that was firmly driven into the sea floor through the silt. Then, piles were driven in diagonal opposition so the platform would be level and secure. "No two platforms are alike," said Tannahill, thinking over his career. "There is always something different."

Above: Tiwi, one of two geothermal fields Union developed in the Philippines in the 1970s, came on stream in 1978. Steam is transported from wellhead to power plant via heavily insulated pipes. Loops in the pipes allow expansion and contraction as the temperature of the steam fluctuates. Opposite: Platform Cerveza was more than three years in planning and construction at the Bayou Boeuf yard near Morgan City, Louisiana.

began in 1978 but was abandoned in 1980 when rising costs made the project uneconomic. However, more than a decade's research into the vast but highly saline geothermal resources in California's Imperial Valley made good progress by 1980 with the completion of the 10,000-kilowatt Brawley demonstration project.

In the Philippines, the National Power Corporation completed its first 55,000-kilowatt power plant at Tiwi in December 1978. A month later, at the Malacanang Palace in Manila, President Ferdinand E. Marcos pushed a button for the formal start-up of the Tiwi plant, for which Union supplied the geothermal steam. By the end of 1980, geothermal energy was supplying 440,000 kilowatts of electricity to the Manila power grid.

In Thailand, Union and the government signed their first gas sales contract in 1978. Union had discovered the Erawan gas field five years earlier. At first, the Thai officials had been disappointed that the strike was gas and not oil. "But later they agreed that the gas was better," said William A. Greenwalt, Union's resident manager during the 1970s and early 1980s.

The gas sales contract virtually created Thailand's first hydrocarbon industry and would prove vital in helping to sustain the country's phenomenal economic growth, which had averaged 7 percent a year in the 1970s. The natural gas industry would greatly reduce the country's dependence on oil imports. Eventually, it might provide the raw material for a fertilizer industry needed to boost food production in Asia's largest rice-exporting country.

Before Union proceeded with development, the company drilled more wells to assess the Erawan field's potential. A Dallas firm, DeGolyer and McNaughton, took Union's drilling results and prepared an estimate of 1.5 trillion cubic feet of proven gas reserves. Later discoveries of numerous other fields added to the reserves.

That original Erawan estimate later proved to be too high. When the geologic complexity of the reservoirs was better understood, the reserves estimate was lowered — triggering a crisis in Union's relationship with the Thai government in 1983. But in 1979, the reserves estimate appeared more than sufficient to justify development. The first two platforms were set in 1980, and by then negotiations were under way for sales of gas from the newly confirmed Satun, Kaphong, and Platong fields.

In the United States, Union focused its attention on the Gulf of Mexico. Union made its first discovery of oil and gas in deep water — about 1,000 feet — in 1975. Development of East Breaks Block 160, located 100 miles offshore Galveston, Texas, occasioned a landmark in offshore construction: Platform Cerveza. Union worked with Ray J. McDermott, Inc., to design and construct the world's tallest single-piece platform jacket. The record, which stood until 1988, was impressive but incidental. "The real challenge was to try to come up with the most efficient design," said Clifton A. Tannahill, manager of offshore construction in the Gulf at the time.

Union had a small interest in another deep-water Gulf platform, Cognac, which was set in 1,025 feet of water in 1977. Cognac's jacket had been built and assembled in three pieces. Union's jacket, set in 935 feet of water in 1981, came in at one-third the cost of Cognac. Even so, the $95 million price tag was "a good example of the huge investments required to find and produce the additional domestic energy resources our nation must have," noted Fred Hartley.

In the spirit of competition that rules in the oil patch, Union took a cue from the French word *cognac* — a fine, expensive brandy — in naming its platform. *Cerveza* is Spanish for beer — a humbler, less costly libation than brandy.

Environmental considerations put some of the country's most promising areas for exploration off-limits. In 1976, Union spent $16.4 million for federal leases offshore New Jersey, only to have them canceled by a federal district court in February 1977. One year later, just before a second Atlantic lease sale, the state of Massachusetts and several environmental groups successfully sued to have the sale postponed. Union and some 50 other companies had registered to submit bids.

On the country's western coastline, memories of the Santa Barbara spill lingered even while the oil companies continued to operate their offshore platforms without further incident. In 1977, eight years after the spill, Union was finally allowed to install the Dos Cuadras field's third production platform in the Santa Barbara Channel. The field had produced more than 95 million barrels of oil since its discovery in 1968. By the end of 1977, it was producing 22,000 barrels a day, including 5,000 from the new Platform C.

In August 1977, President Carter signed into law a new series of amendments to the Clean Air Act, setting stricter rules for attainment of clean air standards. "We didn't realize the impact right away," noted Bill Cole of Union's Washington, D.C., office. But ten years later, after extensive good-faith efforts, dozens of U.S. cities were still unable to attain the rigorous federal standards and faced construction bans and loss of federal grants unless the law could be mitigated.

One immediate effect of the law on Union was to delay progress on some of the company's long-range thermal recovery programs in California. Union had planned to construct generators to inject steam into certain Kern County reservoirs that were nearing the end of their useful production. The oil was heavy; steam injection was needed to reduce its viscosity and prolong field production.

Under the new amendments, however, permit applications became more complex. The company's analysis of the project had to take into account not only any additional emissions into the atmosphere, but potential emissions should more facilities be built in the future. The company also had to consider how the effects of potential emissions might be offset by reduced emissions from other Union facilities in the area.

These reporting requirements delayed further development of the heavy oil fields, putting the government at odds with itself. Overly complex regulations served to stifle increased domestic oil production.

Between 1970 and 1977, Union's expenditures to comply with environmental regulations exceeded $300 million. More than half of the total had been spent at refineries and chemical plants, primarily to improve air and water quality. The figure doubled by the end of the decade.

Union's fertilizer sales steadily improved during the 1970s, bolstered by increasing demand and low feedstock (natural gas) prices. In 1977, Union broke into a vast new market. The company was invited to the People's Republic of China to make a presentation on the sale of bulk urea. When a sales contract was signed, Union became the single largest seller of urea to China.

In early 1978, the Union Chemicals Division was formed with T. Craig Henderson as president. It brought together the AMSCO and Collier operations, and was organized into three groups: nitrogen, petrochemical, and carbon. Sales rose by 56 percent in the next three years.

Union's specialty graphite company, Poco Graphite, Inc., was included in the new division in 1978. Poco, whose unique products have many high-technology applications, had just received a citation from the U.S. Energy Research and Development Administration for "substantial and invaluable contributions" to the nation's space exploration program. Poco graphite had been used as a shielding material for a nuclear power converter left on the moon by U.S. astronauts and proved useful on many other outer-space missions.

In 1979, the Molycorp subsidiary also joined the Chemicals Division following the retirement of William R. Kuntz, the Molycorp president who had helped negotiate the merger with Union.

Some eight years after the oil spill from Union-operated Platform A, the company was allowed to install its third platform in the Santa Barbara Channel. Production from the Dos Cuadras field rose from 17,000 to 22,000 barrels a day.

SPACE-AGE GRAPHITE

Carbon, one of nature's most common elements, is the basic material of a very uncommon product—Poco graphite, produced by a Unocal subsidiary in Decatur, Texas. In the late 1950s, Robert Carlson was assigned to develop a shielding material for the nose cone and wings of the U.S. Air Force's *Dyna-Soar,* a glider that would shuttle astronauts between Earth and orbiting spaceships. The *Dyna-Soar* never took off, but Carlson's unique, high-density graphite soon outshone its competitors. In 1969, it went to the moon as the black box protecting a nuclear power converter left there by the *Apollo 11* crew. It was aboard the *Voyager* deep-space missions and is specified for certain components in U.S. space shuttles. On Earth, Poco graphite's properties of strength, conductivity, and heat resistance have made it ideal for a variety of applications in many fields, such as electrical discharge machining, optoelectronics, high-energy physics, biomedical implants, and aviation. Dr. Hillis Folkins, a Pure Oil researcher who worked with Carlson early on, received a life-saving return on his efforts years later. In 1973, a surgeon replaced Folkins' faulty heart valve with a model made of Poco graphite. The Pure Oil Company, for which "Poco" is an acronym, acquired Carlson's graphite division from another company in 1964. A year later, Pure merged with Union Oil.

Clockwise, from top left: Poco graphite is a major component in virtually all artificial heart valves. Poco packages its products under clean-room conditions to maintain high degrees of purity for delivery to the customer. Specially processed grades of Poco graphite have much higher compressive, flexural, and tensile strengths than conventional graphites.

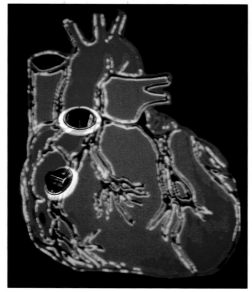

In 1978, an expansion of Union's nitrogen fertilizer manufacturing complex in Kenai, Alaska, was completed, doubling production capacity. New ammonia and urea plants contributed to a 21 percent gain in chemical sales revenues in their first year of operation.

Also in 1978, the *Cornucopia* was put into service. The ship, designed to transport liquefied ammonia from Union's plants at Kenai to West Coast terminals, replaced the barge *Kenai,* which broke loose from its tow and sank during a storm in late 1974. The loss of the *Kenai* was very serious. Under the Jones Act, only American-flagged vessels were allowed to ply between domestic ports, and there were none available capable of transporting liquefied ammonia. Union, with strong support from the West Coast farmers it supplied, was granted a waiver of the Jones Act by the U.S. Treasury Department so it could resume operations using foreign-flagged carriers until a suitable new ship could be built.

Union's Petrochemical Group acquired the polymer business of the A.E. Staley Company in late 1978 to expand its marketing, manufacturing, and research capabilities. Union research had made many strides in the development of emulsion polymer and adhesive products, and the Staley acquisition added more than 50 polymers to the product line.

Union's petrochemical markets had been in transition since the late 1960s when air quality regulations began to place tighter controls on the manufacture and use of hydrocarbon solvents, which are products of crude oil refining. Solvent-based paints and other products were being pushed off the market by water-based products made from emulsion polymers. The shift quickened after 1973 as the crude oil situation contributed to rising costs and shortages of solvents. Manufacturers, in turn, increased their use of emulsion polymers. In late 1978, Union announced plans to spend $34 million to double its output of aromatic naphthas (feedstocks for the manufacture of emulsion polymer building-block chemicals and other petrochemicals) at the company's refinery in Beaumont, Texas.

Carbon sales were also increasing, and Union increased its coke calcining capacity. Coke, the solid residue left over from a crude oil refining process, is calcined — heated at very high temperatures — to burn off impurities. The resulting carbon product is used in various metal-refining and chemical processes.

Union's coke expansion projects in the 1970s were designed as energy savers. At the Santa Maria (California) refinery, waste heat was converted to steam for use in the refinery — an energy savings equivalent to 140,000 barrels of fuel oil a year. A similar operation at the Chicago refinery saved the equivalent of 195,000 barrels of fuel oil a year.

American industry, unlike most of the consuming public, was acutely aware of the need for energy conservation in the 1970s. Given the huge amounts of energy that industries consumed and the rising price of oil, even small cutbacks in energy use could represent major cost savings. Many industries made significant strides in energy conservation during the 1970s.

Union formed a corporate energy conservation task force. A year after the oil embargo, the company boasted energy savings equivalent to the electrical needs of 65,000 homes. By 1978, the savings were nearly five times that. Union's refineries, already efficient energy users because of their 24-hour operation, reduced energy use by more than 20 percent from 1972 to 1979. (In 1977, Fred Hartley was the only energy company executive appointed to the board of directors of the new Alliance to Save Energy, a nonprofit research organization created to foster energy education and conservation.)

In 1978, Dick Stegemeier, having returned from his ten-year tour of duty in Southeast Asia, was named vice president of research on the retirement of Dr. Hal C. Huffman. A petroleum engineer by training and experience, Stegemeier had begun his Union career at the research labs some 27 years earlier. He was awarded seven patents for his work in enhanced oil recovery.

In January 1979, the research department became the Science & Technology

In 1979, Dick Stegemeier became president of the new Union Science & Technology Division. A petroleum engineer by experience and training, he had joined Union Oil in 1951 to work in research. Below left: In 1978, with the completion of expanded manufacturing facilities at Kenai, Alaska, Union Chemicals offered West Coast farmers a new product — high-quality granular urea (shown in storage before shipment).

In 1978, Craig Henderson was named president of the new Union Chemicals Division. An engineer, he joined Union Oil in 1949. Right: In the 1970s, Union engineers developed methods to recycle waste heat at company refineries, such as the one at Santa Maria, California. Recycling saved on fuel use in the production of steam, vital to many process operations.

Division with Stegemeier as president. In March, he announced plans to double the laboratory and office space. The change in status put the company's research activities on a par with other divisions. "It is recognition by top management," Stegemeier said, "that research has made very large contributions to the success of the company. As a division, we have a responsibility to take a greater leadership role in developing Union's vast energy resources."

As the company planned to expand its research in the areas of oil and gas exploration and production, as well as chemicals, it continued to reap the rewards of its work in refining technology. By 1978, Union's Technology Sales Group licensed the Unicracking process in 36 plants operating or under construction in eight countries around the world, making it the most widely used of all hydrocracking processes. Union had also developed related technology, Unicracking/ HDS, and installed the first plant at the Maruzen refinery near Tokyo in 1976. The process shared design elements with Unicracking but was designed to process heavy residual fuel oils, removing sulfur and metallic contaminants. (Union sold its one-third interest in Maruzen in 1978.)

In 1979, the company made the first sales of major petroleum refinery process technology to the People's Republic of China, agreements that called for licensing four Unicrackers and one Unionfiner.

"In the early seventies, when it became apparent that China was opening up, we had some of the technical papers relating to our successful processes translated into Chinese," explained William J. Baral, who became vice president of technology sales in 1979. "Then we arranged with friendly contractors to distribute these to the refiners and chemical plant users in China."

When Craig Henderson was invited to China in 1977 to make a presentation on urea, Baral went along and took the opportunity to talk informally about refining technology. He was invited back to make a formal presentation in 1978, which led to the refining technology sales in 1979.

Throughout 1978, Congress continued to debate and amend the National Energy Plan that President Carter had proposed in April 1977. Union was spending an estimated $3 million a year and the equivalent of 100 employees' time on compliance with pricing and allocation controls—which included a great deal of time on the front lines talking to legislators and other influential people in Washington, D.C.

"If we don't give the lawmakers the benefit of our knowledge," said corporate development manager Don Lindros, "and, because of that, they don't write a very good law, then it would be our own fault for not speaking. We have to make the attempt, even if we make our point only a percentage of the time."

About this time, Bill Cole had an inspiration. He proposed that Union employees would make very strong advocates for the company if they could interact with their own representatives in Washington. As voting constituents, they would have more personal and direct access to their legislators than professional industry representatives.

The task of designing and implementing a program based on Cole's idea was given to Karen A. Sikkema, then coordinator of government relations. By the spring of 1979, Union's new Key Contact program was born; 128 employees had received training in how to contact their representatives and present their views on issues affecting their jobs.

In November 1978, some 18 months after it had been submitted, about half of Carter's National Energy Plan was approved by Congress. The plan addressed such issues as fuel use and efficiency by utilities and industry, granted tax credits for the use of certain alternative energies, and — in the Natural Gas Policy Act (NGPA) — dealt with the highly politicized issue of how to control gas pricing and encourage production.

The NGPA provided for the partial, phased deregulation of some gas prices by 1985, the date when most gas found after April 1977 ("new" gas) would be allowed to demand market prices. "Deep" gas (from wells deeper than 15,000 feet) was immediately decontrolled, while "old" gas (discovered prior to 1977) remained under price controls.

The act created an administrative nightmare for gas producers. It made numerous distinctions in natural gas for pricing purposes, as in offshore versus onshore gas, resulting in 28 different categories with 28 sets of rules. Prices ranged from 30¢ to almost $6 per thousand cubic feet, all for the same commodity. Controls were extended to cover both intra- and interstate gas.

Natural gas pipeliners, fearful of more shortages in the face of rising demand, scrambled to buy up assured supplies of natural gas. They contracted for expensive, but plentiful, decontrolled gas and high-priced imports, and promised to pay whether or not they took the gas.

The situation changed in 1979, however, when OPEC announced a series of increases, doubling the price of OPEC oil from $17 to $34 per barrel. The increases had the effect of encouraging energy conservation, thus reducing demand for natural gas along with other fuels. Union had reversed its downward trend in natural gas production by the final quarter in 1978. Gas production held steady in 1979, then began to drop again with demand.

Pipeliners were forced to pay for expensive gas but delay acceptance of supplies they could not sell. Hence, the nation faced a period of excess deliverability, called the "gas bubble," for the next several years. NGPA regulations had the effect of creating higher consumer prices in a time of excess supply, which is contrary to the original intent of U.S. natural gas price controls.

OPEC's price increases followed the drastic cuts in Iranian oil production during that country's revolution. Few, if any, in the Western world had foreseen this event, believing the Shah to be firmly in command — although Ray Burke had spoken of Iran somewhat prophetically in 1976, when he commented on its sharp increases in tax rates on foreign oil producers.

"The Iranian government," Burke said, "wants to improve its take so it will be competitive with other countries in the Middle East. They are constantly threatening to renegotiate the deal. It hasn't carried overtones of kicking us out

Opposite: Claude Brinegar addressed one of the first groups of Union employees who agreed to serve as Key Contacts. Karen Sikkema (right) organized the program in 1979 as a method to improve the communication of oil industry issues to legislators. Below: Within a month of the Shah's overthrow in Iran in January 1979, Ayatollah Ruhollah Khomeini (in black turban) rode fundamentalist Islamic fervor to power.

so far, but who knows what's going to happen in the Middle East? The situation changes fast."

It was the policy of the National Iranian Oil Company (NIOC) to name its offshore fields after ancient and honored Persian dynasties. The field in which Union held a 12.5 percent interest was named for the Sassan dynasty, which had taken power in the third century and had been supplanted 400 years later when Arabs brought Islam to Persia.

Shah Mohammed Reza Pahlavi's dynasty, founded by his father in 1925, lasted little more than 50 years. The Shah's devotion to Westernization fomented fundamentalist Islamic opposition. Revolution forced him out in January 1979, and Ayatollah Ruhollah Khomeini took power within a month.

As the revolution heated up in late 1978, oil workers went on strike, disrupting production. Lavan Petroleum, the company that operated the Sassan field, ceased lifting oil. A negotiating team made up of representatives of Union and its joint-venture partners in Lavan made four trips to Tehran in 1979 to attempt to forge an agreement allowing them to resume operations.

W. Clyde Barton, then director of production operations for the International Oil & Gas Division, represented Union. By the time the last meeting was held, in October 1979, tension in Iran was extreme.

"The NIOC representatives finally agreed to receive our proposal for consideration, and I headed for the airport," Barton recalled. The airport was mobbed with people trying to leave, and the authorities were carefully searching luggage to confiscate gold and other valuables.

"It took about four hours just getting through the lines," Barton continued, "but I got on the plane. Nine days later, the revolutionaries took the American embassy. After that, of course, all negotiations with Iran were wiped out." In 1979, Union received none of its share, which had been 25,000 barrels per day.

Although the supply disruption in the United States was less severe than in 1973, President Carter took the opportunity to let domestic oil prices rise. He had long been convinced that this was necessary, but Congress had not acted on

the pertinent phase of his National Energy Plan. At the Bonn summit meeting in 1978, the President had promised other national leaders that U.S. oil prices would rise to world levels by 1980.

By 1979, other voices had joined the oil companies in calling for decontrol of oil prices. Environmentalists had begun to see that decontrol would encourage conservation and curtail energy growth. The *Wall Street Journal, Washington Post,* and *New York Times* took editorial stands in favor of it.

Carter exercised his option, as set forth in the Energy Policy and Conservation Act of 1975, to set pricing policy from June 1, 1979, until September 30, 1981, when price controls were to end. In April 1979, he announced that phased decontrol would begin June 1 and continue for 28 months. And he asked Congress to pass a tax to prevent the oil companies from benefiting from the "windfall" of higher prices arbitrarily imposed by OPEC.

The threat of an oil shortage panicked U.S. drivers. As in 1973, long lines of cars formed at service stations. The phenomenon started in California in April and spread east in May and June. Motorists waited as long as four or five hours to fill up their gas tanks. Scattered stabbings and shootings were reported as nerves wore thin and drivers fought for places in line.

One news report described the case of an unfortunate service station dealer: His customers filled up and drove off without paying when he went to the aid of his wife, who had been struck by a car pulling into the gas line. In some areas independent truckers, striking to protest rising diesel fuel prices, added to the disruption by parking their rigs to block gasoline deliveries to service stations.

In most cases, shortages were exacerbated by changes in driver behavior. People filled up their tanks and kept them full, which took them to the service station a lot more often and resulted in longer lines. A lot of gasoline was "in storage" in people's gas tanks. One study estimated that almost 150,000 barrels of gasoline per day were "idled" away by motorists waiting in line to buy more gas. The problem eased by summer.

Oil-importing countries also did some panic buying, putting Union in a precarious position. Before the price hikes, Union could rely on purchasing crude on short-term contracts at attractive rates on the spot market. But spot-market crude grew scarce, and demand pushed the price above $40 per barrel. By late 1979, Union was having trouble buying enough crude to keep its refineries going.

The company petitioned the government for an entitlements exception, an irony not lost on Union executives. Union was accustomed to being on the giving end — not the receiving end.

"We asked for a special allocation from some of the major oil companies, arguing that we were being discriminated against by their long-term relationships with their foreign suppliers," said Claude Brinegar. "Union, representing the midsized independent companies, was a vital part of the industry — and our future was being threatened."

Union won its point and was allowed to purchase some 6 million barrels of crude from the majors at their average acquisition cost, well below spot-market prices. "It was most welcome," said Brinegar. "Indeed, it saved us — at least until we could get a better idea about where to get the crude we needed."

"We had to totally reorganize our crude oil buying program," noted Bill McConnor. "We became a much larger factor in overseas oil." Union opened a London office to intensify its efforts to obtain more contracts directly with oil-producing nations.

In early 1980, Congress acted on President Carter's request for windfall-profit tax legislation. The tax was designed to extract at least $227 billion over a ten-year period from rising domestic oil prices. Congress also passed the Energy Security Act, creating the U.S. Synthetic Fuels Corporation. The greatest share of windfall-profit tax revenues was to be used — in the form of tax credits, grants, and low-interest loans — to subsidize synthetic fuel production.

At last, Union could proceed with its oil shale project. The company and the Department of Energy agreed in principle on a contract for the government to purchase shale oil. In the expectation that the company could negotiate the details satisfactorily with the incoming Reagan administration, Union began work on the nation's first major oil shale project. The first phase included a 13,500-ton-per-day room-and-pillar mine, a surface retort to produce oil from the shale ore, and an upgrading facility to process the raw shale oil. Capacity was 10,000 barrels per day.

In May 1980, ground was broken for the expansion of Union's research center, renamed the Fred L. Hartley Research Center. In December, Dick Stegemeier was elected senior vice president for corporate development, a director, and member of the executive committee. Cloyd Reeg replaced him as president of the Science

Left: Cloyd Reeg (left, center) and Dick Stegemeier (right, center) reviewed construction progress at the research center in 1980. At the end of the year, Reeg succeeded Stegemeier as president of Science & Technology when the latter was promoted to senior vice president, corporate development. Opposite: President Carter (right) was able to conclude negotiations for the release of the American hostages in Iran on the day his successor, Ronald Reagan (left), took the oath of office. Below: Oil drilling activity in the United States, which had declined during the 1970s, sharply increased once domestic oil price controls were lifted in the early 1980s. Activity dipped again with the dramatic world oil price drop in 1986.

& Technology Division. The research staff had been increased by about 170 people in two years to total more than 700. The largest part of the increase represented a doubling of the technical staff in exploration and production research, as Union prepared to expand its vigorous search for oil and gas.

In July 1980, the United States Justice Department and the Department of Energy issued the results of their studies on the oil industry's role in the energy crisis of 1979. The studies, which were ordered by President Carter to look into the possibility of oil company collusion in creating gasoline shortages, concluded that the shortages resulted from the combined effects of the sudden loss of Iranian crude, declining domestic production, and the federal government's own pricing and allocation rules.

"It is very gratifying," said Hartley, "to have two agencies of the federal government independently conclude what we know to be the truth."

In August 1980, Union and its partners in the Sassan field were notified that the National Iranian Oil Company had voided its agreement. Union protested, as did other companies that had invested in developing the Iranian oil fields, and wrote off some 80 million barrels of its reserves. A negotiated settlement was not reached until 1986.

The decade's second series of OPEC price increases, combined with oil price decontrol, was finally enough to slow down petroleum consumption in the United States. U.S. demand dropped 8 percent in 1980. Oil imports were down 19 percent.

Between 1974 and 1980, Union's crude oil reserves declined by some 350 million barrels, including the loss of Iranian reserves. Daily average oil production went down by 100,000 barrels per day over the six-year period, from 330,000 in 1974 to 230,000 in 1980. Foreign discoveries helped to slow these declines in reserves and production, as Union pursued an aggressive exploration program in more than two dozen countries.

A gas discovery made in 1979 in the Dutch sector of the North Sea led to development there, and the company also acquired interests in two blocks offshore Norway. Union also made important domestic discoveries in the Santa Barbara Channel offshore California and, in February 1980, announced plans to set two more platforms.

Union's 1980 earnings totaled a record $647 million, up 29 percent over 1979. Projected capital expenditures were almost $2 billion, more than three times earnings. The company split its shares of common stock two-for-one and increased quarterly dividends in 1980 for the second time in little more than a year.

U.S. ANNUAL AVERAGE ROTARY DRILLING ACTIVITY
(average daily count of rigs in operation)

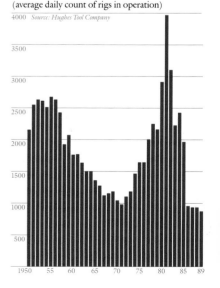

Source: Hughes Tool Company

Phased decontrol set in motion a veritable oil boom in the United States. The number of rigs drilling for oil and gas in 1980 averaged 2,915 per day, up 34 percent from 1979 and surpassing the previous record set in 1955 by 9 percent. Wildcat wells rose by 17 percent over 1979, with 30 percent of them finding oil or gas.

By the end of 1980, the federal entitlements program was doomed, collapsing under its own bureaucratic weight. Since 1974, more than $18.6 billion had changed hands among domestic refiners. Union Oil had paid out $700 million. Immediate decontrol of oil prices, announced by President Reagan shortly after he took office in January 1981, ended the program. However, since assessments lagged two months, the Department of Energy planned to publish final payment notices in January. The notices were never issued. Union, soon joined by other companies, challenged the action—but the matter was not settled for six years while debate raged in Congress and in the courts.

The Carter administration was on its way to defeat in 1980, as criticism intensified over the hostage situation in the American embassy in Tehran. Iranian student radicals took 90 hostages when they stormed the embassy in November 1979 and imprisoned 52 of them—all Americans—for more than a year. The radicals demanded the return of the Shah, who was terminally ill with cancer. In April 1980, eight American soldiers were killed and five wounded in an ill-fated attempt to rescue the hostages. In July, the Shah died in Egypt.

Ronald Reagan won a stunning victory in the November 1980 election. On the morning of Reagan's inauguration, January 20, 1981, President Carter concluded negotiations for the release of the hostages. After 444 days in captivity, the 52 Americans boarded a flight out of Tehran in exchange for the return to Iran of $8 billion in frozen assets. (Iran netted less than $3 billion; the balance was used to repay loans and cover other claims from creditors.)

In September 1980, Iran and Iraq went to war over claims to the Shatt al-Arab waterway that divides the two countries. Their attacks on each other's oil fields and facilities, including oil tankers in the Persian Gulf, curtailed Middle East exports—but without the global repercussions of previous supply disruptions.

World demand for Middle Eastern crude had declined, as OPEC's domination of the oil market eroded. High prices had inspired worldwide energy conservation, fuel switching, and increased development of petroleum resources not controlled by members of the cartel. Just as the American oil industry had been rocked by OPEC's price shocks in the 1970s, the decline of OPEC in the 1980s posed new challenges and heralded another period of turmoil and uncertainty.

FULL SERVICE: 1960–1990

In the early 1960s, Union Oil ads (opposite, top) touted the company's high standard of service by featuring graduates of its dealer training school and members of its Sparkle Corps (white-gloved cleanliness inspectors). After 1962, the large Union 76 signs over the canopies were replaced by distinctive rotating 76 spheres. Union's flexible station designs blended with local settings and architectural styles. In Thousand Oaks, California, a model 300-R station (opposite, bottom) featured a tile roof and shared its site with one of the area's namesake trees. In 1966, Lady Bird Johnson, who as First Lady headed a Keep America Beautiful campaign, called the 300-R design "an inspiration to travelers and residents alike." In 1967, the Union name was removed from the 76 sphere. Station designs in the next two decades continued to reflect concern for appearance and customer convenience. The Unocal 76 logo replaced Union 76 in 1985.

12 The New Oil Boom

After his first week in office, President Reagan announced the immediate decontrol of oil prices. Opposite: A living quarters platform in the Gulf of Thailand accommodates some 120 offshore workers. Union began producing natural gas in the Gulf in 1981. The development became a major success story, although it got off to a rough start when production levels proved lower than projections.

On January 28, 1981, after his first week in office, President Ronald Reagan announced immediate decontrol of oil prices — eight months early and almost ten years after controls had first been imposed during the Nixon administration.

"Our industry's business environment was substantially improved...by the decontrol of crude oil prices," noted Fred Hartley. "This change redirected our industry and the nation toward greater reliance on the market system rather than political considerations as determinants of economic decisions. The result has been new incentives, both for exploration and for energy conservation."

Full decontrol of oil prices gave a boost to the U.S. oil boom set off by partial decontrol in 1979. The total number of wells drilled each year in the United States had slowly increased after 1973 (the year OPEC doubled and then redoubled its oil prices), rising from fewer than 33,000 in 1974 to more than 51,000 in 1979, despite economic constraints. Over the next three years, the rate of increase tripled; the annual well count peaked at 88,000 in 1982.

The boom did not last. When OPEC doubled oil prices again in 1979, strong reactions in the world economy brought severe consequences. The economic slow-down that followed the first OPEC price shocks in 1973 was repeated, and this time Americans were no longer shielded from the full effects by price controls.

Those who had paid lip service to conservation in the mid-1970s found the economic incentive to take it seriously in the early 1980s. Americans drove less and demanded more fuel-efficient automobiles. Homeowners kept their houses warmer in summer and cooler in winter, and learned about insulation, solar water heaters, and other means to reduce energy costs.

Energy conservation and the use of cheaper fuels had reduced demand for oil worldwide by the 1980s. At the same time, oil production from non-OPEC sources — primarily Alaska, the North Sea, Mexico, and the Soviet Union — had been stimulated by higher prices. Much of this oil had been uneconomic to produce before 1973. OPEC countries continued to control their production in order to maintain prices, and non-OPEC production claimed growing shares in world oil markets. In 1976, for every non-OPEC barrel of crude oil produced, OPEC produced 1.7 barrels. By 1984, the ratio was reduced to 1 to 0.7.

As crude oil supplies began to outstrip demand, OPEC's grip on prices slackened. Market prices began to fall below the cartel's posted prices. In March 1983, OPEC finally responded to market forces and took the unprecedented action of announcing a price cut of $5 per barrel. Few in the oil industry, however, anticipated that the cartel would virtually lose control of the marketplace within three years and lower its prices drastically to regain market share.

In his report to shareholders in early 1983, Hartley said: "Depressed prices and lower demand for petroleum, chemicals, and metals products are showing no signs of recovery....Continuing our efforts to counter this situation, we are implementing further cost efficiencies and pursuing new tactics to expand the market for our products."

Hartley noted that in some areas lower oil prices dampened enthusiasm for petroleum exploration and development, as well as for the development of alternative energy resources. "But at Union, we have always prospered by striking our own course," he said. "Convinced that our long-term strategies are sound and should not be displaced by what we consider to be short-term conditions in the marketplace, we remain committed to expanding our resource base."

By the end of 1983, Union had halted the slow but steady decline in its domestic oil reserves that had begun in the late sixties. In fact, 1983 marked the beginning of a period in which the company annually replaced its worldwide crude oil and natural gas reserves.

Dick Stegemeier, senior vice president, corporate development, called research the "gateway to the future."

Union was committed to finding and developing new oil supplies, particularly in the United States; developing viable alternative fuels; and improving the energy resource technologies and products that would be vital to the human community in the future.

Symbolic of these efforts was the dedication in September 1982 of the Fred L. Hartley Research Center, the Science & Technology Division's newly expanded headquarters in Brea, California. Sleek additions, including a three-story administration building and three new laboratory buildings, almost doubled the office and lab space. The staff numbered some 800 scientists, researchers, and support personnel, representing a nearly 50 percent increase in four years.

"In terms of priorities, the major thrust of our work is to develop the technology for Union Oil Company to increase its production of energy resources," explained Cloyd Reeg, president of the division. "Fifty-six percent of our effort is directed toward research on the production of conventional oil and gas as well as alternative energy sources, such as geothermal and shale."

The Science & Technology Division reported to Dick Stegemeier, for whom a new position had been created in December 1980: senior vice president, corporate development. His mission was to develop new policy for moving Union into the 1980s. In addition to research and development, he was given responsibility for strategic planning and other company functions most involved in building future business. The Energy Mining Division (primarily oil shale) and the Corporate Engineering & Construction Department reported to him.

The early eighties would later be dubbed the "glory days." Benefiting from OPEC price hikes, the industry achieved the highest earnings in history and pursued ambitious goals for expansion.

Union Oil's earnings rose from $501 million in 1979 (the year OPEC doubled its prices) to $647 million in 1980, $791 million in 1981 (the year of full decontrol in the United States), and a peak of $804 million in 1982. (Included in the earnings were certain government incentives — energy and investment tax credits designed to revitalize the economy.)

During the difficult 1970s, U.S. oil companies had begun diversifying. Some purchased mining ventures, and others went far afield from natural resources businesses into such areas as retail department stores and computer software.

"History has shown that the industry diversified too much," Stegemeier said years later. "That's not a criticism of this company, it's a criticism of the industry. We misled ourselves into believing that oil prices were going to continue to rise.

At dedication ceremonies in September 1982, Fred Hartley (top left) noted: "This complex, with its visionary concepts, symbolizes Union's approach to the future." <u>Clockwise from top right:</u> The building's design reflected the high-tech activity inside; Cloyd Reeg welcomed guests; visitors included (from left) corporate secretary Bob Hedley, director Don Jacobs (partially hidden), Fred Hartley, Ray Burke, and Dick Stegemeier; research technician Lorene Ishii analyzed the surface of a catalyst using a photoelectron spectrometer; hundreds of employees, public officials, and others attended a series of open houses.

THE RUSH FOR SHALE
As petroleum consumption
increased during and after
World War I, oil companies
scrambled for new reserves.
Teams of geologists converged
on the oil shale lands in the
Uinta basin of Colorado, Utah,
and Wyoming. Union Oil dis-
patched geologist Roderick H.
Burnham and chemist Albert S.
Crossfield to Colorado in the
summer of 1920. Crossfield
devised a quart-size retort that
he attached to the running board
of the old Hudson Super-Six
Burnham acquired in Denver.
So equipped, the men criss-
crossed the rugged backcountry,
digging samples all day and
assessing the rock's oil content
at night, heating the portable
retort with a blowtorch. They
zeroed in on the best prospects
while competing field teams from
other companies waited for lab
results from far-off offices. In
the next four years, Burnham
directed the acquisition of more
than 20,000 acres of shale lands,
including the richest oil shale
deposit in a thousand square
miles — the Mahogany Ledge.
Most of the land was held under
160-acre placer-mining claims,
and Union crews had to work
each claim in order to hold it,
occasionally under fire from
competitors trying to scare them
off. Subsequent oil discoveries
relieved the 1920 oil shortage
scare, but Union continued
to hold its claims and advance
its research.

*Top left: The 108-foot upflow
retort is the heart of the shale
project on which Union began
construction in 1981 after receiving a government contract
assuring a guaranteed floor
price for the oil.*

Some people were so bold as to say that oil prices could go as high as fifty to seventy dollars a barrel; and that, of course, was the reason the government tried to come up with some alternatives."

Union had been anticipating the development of synthetic crude oil from its oil shale reserves in Colorado since 1920. Over the years, oil shortage scares had spurred research into the technology to extract oil from the rock—first in the twenties, then in the forties, fifties, and again in the seventies. By 1980, the economic and political circumstances finally seemed right.

"The Energy Security Act, passed by Congress in 1980 in fear of ever-rising prices of oil and more so-called shortages, really brought the oil shale project into focus," said John M. Hopkins, then president of Union's Energy Mining Division. "We had our project engineered and defined, so we were able to move quickly and establish a contract with the Department of Energy. It was fairly easy for us to deal with the DOE, because what we wanted was a price guarantee [requiring no immediate investment of government funds]," Hopkins added. "Many other companies were looking for loans, grants, or other direct financial assistance."

In the summer of 1981, Hartley announced: "I am very gratified that Union Oil is the first company to receive a Department of Energy award for the first commercial production of oil from shale in the United States."

Union estimated that its 20,000 acres on the western slope of the Rocky Mountains contained reserves of 1.6 billion barrels of recoverable oil. The

Above: The shale retorting complex was constructed near the mine entrance; a five-acre bench was carved out of the mountainside 1,000 feet above the valley floor. Above right: Inside the mountain, miners excavate large "rooms" but leave supporting pillars as they dig deeper into the earth. The miners use laser beams to guide their work.

Parachute Creek project was designed to produce 10,000 barrels of shale oil a day. Union would get the market price, but the contract assured that if the price fell below the contract floor of $42.50 per barrel, indexed for inflation, the government would make up the difference. The government had no liability or responsibility unless and until Union produced oil from shale.

"The oil price hit its peak about the time we signed the contract with the Department of Energy," said Stegemeier. "Then it began to slide."

By 1982, construction crews at the Parachute Creek site numbered 1,700 workers. John R. Pownall, who had been superintendent of the demonstration plant built at the site in the late 1950s, returned to supervise construction of the commercial facility. Arnold E. Kelley, who had also worked on the 1950s project and had supervised 1970s process research as vice president of engineering and development for Science & Technology, moved to Colorado in 1983 to assist with start-up.

"Every effort is being made to protect the environment and to mitigate the socioeconomic impact on this sparsely populated area of western Colorado," Stegemeier noted in April 1982. "To this end, we've already spent or committed more than sixty million dollars." Projects included two highway bypasses, a 15-mile paved county road, a $4.5 million middle school, 350 apartments and townhouses, housing for 750 construction employees, water and sewer systems, and facilities to provide public safety services. Another $85 million was earmarked for compliance with strict environmental requirements.

The $650 million oil shale complex — including the mine, retort, and upgrading plant — was completed in August 1983. Achieving sustained production was another matter. "We had the same experience that everyone else has had with a new technology based on solids — unexpected problems," said John Duir, vice president of engineering and development for the Science & Technology Division.

The most critical design feature, a rock pump 10 feet in diameter, worked reliably at start-up — pushing crushed shale up into an inverted cone some 34 feet high. As the shale flowed upward, hot gas flowed down through it. When the shale reached about 900 degrees F, kerogen (the organic material contained in the shale) decomposed into oil, gas, and carbon residue. The oil and gas were drawn off, and the retorted shale was cooled and conveyed down the hillside to a disposal and revegetation site. The retorted shale, however, proved hard to handle. The equipment was redesigned over the next three years.

Top left: In 1982, the Union Geothermal Division started up its Salton Sea plant in California's Imperial Valley. The demonstration plant tested techniques to use hot brines for electricity generation. Above: Development of Union's geothermal project in Indonesia, a joint venture with Pertamina, the national oil company, slowed in the early 1980s as the oil price dropped.

As the company attempted to achieve continuous operation of its shale facilities, Hartley and Union Oil were criticized in some quarters for pursuing an expensive alternative energy program as oil prices dropped. Other companies shut down experimental shale operations, but Hartley staunchly believed in the necessity of developing the nation's vast shale resources in light of future energy security. In late 1983, a financial analyst quoted in a *New York Times* story titled "Mr. Oil Shale" said: "Somebody has to take the long-term view in this industry. In the current time, Fred Hartley is one of the only ones willing to do that."

Even as Union pioneered oil shale technology, the company continued to be the acknowledged leader in geothermal energy. Union's geothermal projects at The Geysers in California and in the Philippines continued as major success stories in the early 1980s. The company's worldwide capacity for geothermal energy production rose from 10 million kilowatt-hours per day in 1980 to an average of 18.2 million kilowatt-hours per day in 1984.

Union boosted its ownership of The Geysers resource to 75 percent in 1984, purchasing a 25 percent share from Diamond Shamrock Corporation. Union produced steam for 984,000 kilowatts of generating capacity at The Geysers, and plans for expansion were under way. In the Philippines, Union brought two new 55,000-kilowatt generating plants on stream, boosting capacity to 660,000 kilowatts and providing 20 percent of that country's electricity.

Union's Geothermal Division, working closely with Science & Technology, faced one of its toughest technological problems in Southern California's Imperial Valley. Although the potential for energy production from underground steam and fluids was vast, the fluids proved highly saline and loaded with dissolved solids, causing corrosion and scaling (buildup of solids) in the production equipment.

Union built two demonstration plants in the Imperial Valley to learn more about handling the fluids. The plants, each with a 10,000-kilowatt electrical generating capacity, were located at Brawley and Niland, near the Salton Sea. Completed in 1980 and 1982, respectively, each tested different techniques to generate electricity from hot brines.

In 1983, a breakthrough was achieved in handling well-casing pipe corrosion. "It was something of a 'brute force' solution," said Dr. Carel Otte, president of the Geothermal Division. "We'd try one alloy, then try another that was a grade up, and then find out six months later that it didn't work. So we'd try a still more expensive alloy. We were losing time, and it was getting too expensive."

Ray Burke, senior vice president, energy resources, provided the inspiration

In the days when the West was still wild, Mike Murphy, gold prospector turned wildcatter, launched Wyoming's biggest industry. He drilled the state's first oil well in what would become Union's Dallas Dome field. The field celebrated its centennial year of oil production in 1984. In its first 100 years, Dallas Dome produced 10 million of Wyoming's 5 billion barrels of crude oil. By 1990, the field continued to produce about 350 barrels a day. Its longevity has been attributed to a natural waterflood that probably derives from snowmelt off the Wind River Mountains. Murphy drilled his well near a tar seep nine miles southeast of the town of Lander, just off the famous westward migration route, the Oregon Trail. He sold the oil to the railroad for lubricants and to ranchers for tarring their roofs and keeping the dust down in their yards. Later owners of the field cashed in on the huge markets that developed after the turn of the century. Oil was second only to agriculture in economic importance to Wyoming by the end of World War I. Union Oil acquired the Dallas Dome field in 1965 as part of its merger with The Pure Oil Company.

Wyoming's Dallas Dome field has been a steady oil producer for more than 100 years. Mike Murphy drilled the field's first well in 1884 near a tar seep that had long been used by Indians and trappers as a source of liniment and fire starter. Many nearby sites were excavated before Murphy started drilling.

for a single pipe made up of a series of alloys so several could be tested at once. The best results were achieved with beta C titanium, which stood up to the severest conditions. Union was granted a patent for the innovative application of titanium to geothermal production. The alloy was expensive, however, so the search for alternatives continued.

The Geothermal Division's exploration program for new resources focused on Japan and Indonesia in the early 1980s, meeting with greater success in Indonesia. In 1982, a joint-venture agreement was signed between Union and Pertamina, Indonesia's national oil company. But development slowed as the oil price dropped, because the agreement put a ceiling on the price for geothermal energy that was tied to oil prices.

"That ceiling started to depress us, driving us below the price where we had started," Dr. Otte explained. "What had been intended as a moderator against escalation became a price depressant, and we could not proceed. So the first power plant was not initiated until 1988, with a guarantee of a floor price."

Union's commitment to developing alternative energy resources was firm, but the company's emphasis continued to be on the expanding search for conventional oil and natural gas resources. A good portion of Union's high earnings in the early 1980s went to purchasing exploration rights. Through increasing sophistication in seismic techniques and geological and geophysical interpretation, the company would amass the finest position in exploration properties in its history before the end of the decade.

In the United States, much of the acreage Union acquired was in the Gulf of Mexico, particularly after the areawide leasing concept for the Outer Continental Shelf (OCS) was introduced in 1983. "Secretary [of the Interior James] Watt felt that the industry could best identify the tracts that it wanted to explore if the government declared them available for leasing," said Burke. "It was a welcome improvement over the prior system."

Before areawide leasing, the federal government took nominations from oil companies for OCS blocks and, based on the numbers of nominations various blocks received, offered a limited number at each sale. Beginning in 1983, much larger areas were offered at every sale. From 1981 through 1984, Union spent $675 million on federal leases acquiring the rights to explore in the Gulf of Mexico and offshore Alaska, California, and the Atlantic Coast.

Offshore oil drilling, however, had become a highly controversial environ-

mental issue in the 1970s. Opponents of offshore drilling managed, at least temporarily, to put millions of OCS acres off-limits to oil and gas exploration. This was accomplished through moratoria imposed by Congress beginning in 1982, which cut off the funding for certain lease sales, primarily those off the country's eastern and western coastlines.

Union set two platforms offshore Southern California in 1981: Gina and Gilda. By 1985, their combined daily production from the Santa Clara and Hueneme fields was 7,900 barrels of oil and 13 million cubic feet of gas, and additional discoveries had been made from both platforms.

In early 1983, about 100 miles up the coast, Union confirmed its discovery of the Point Pedernales field, an offshore extension of the highly productive Santa Maria basin. The company began the complicated permitting process to clear the way for development. Platform Irene was set in 1985.

The company's major domestic offshore activity, however, continued to be in the Gulf of Mexico. The highlight in 1981 was the setting of Platform Cerveza, which had the largest single-piece jacket built and launched to that time. As Cerveza's 952-foot-long jacket glided along narrow inland waterways on its way to the Gulf from the fabrication yard in Louisiana, its base towered 259 feet above the countryside. It took four days to tow the platform jacket 250 miles to its destination in the East Breaks field, 100 miles offshore Galveston, Texas.

A year later, the spectacle was repeated on a slightly smaller scale. The jacket for Cerveza Ligera (*ligera* is Spanish for "light") was only ten feet shorter but considerably lighter, shaving 5,000 tons off Cerveza's 26,000 tons. This was partly because the Ligera jacket did not have to bear the weight of production equipment, which was placed on the larger platform, and partly because of design refinements.

"In general terms, we improved our efficiency in a lot of little ways all along the line," noted W. Mike Isenhower, regional civil engineer in the Gulf Region, who worked closely with Clif Tannahill on both projects. The platforms came on stream in 1986 and 1987; initial combined production was 5,700 barrels of crude oil and 45 million cubic feet of gas per day.

From 1983 through 1985, Union doubled its offshore position in the Gulf of Mexico, from interests in 141 blocks to interests in 283. The net acreage the company acquired in areawide sales was 465,000. This included good acreage positions in the Gulf's two hottest geologic areas: the Flexure trend, a deep-water area off-

Opposite, left: When Platform Cerveza was set in 1981, it took four days to tow the jacket 250 miles through bayous and across open water to the East Breaks field offshore Texas. Opposite, right: Once the decks were added, Cerveza stood 1,023 feet above the sea floor. The jacket weighed 26,000 tons; decks and pilings added another 12,000. Below left: Thermal recovery techniques, such as the steam-injection program at the Guadalupe field, brought Union's production of heavy oil in California to about 14,000 barrels per day in 1982. Below center: Platform design has become increasingly more sophisticated as oil production has moved into deeper water and rougher climates. Platform Cerveza stands five feet higher than Los Angeles's tallest building, the First Interstate World Center.

Eva/1964
Offshore California
Height: 236 feet
Water depth: 58 feet

Heather/1977
North Sea
Height: 773 feet
Water depth: 469 fe

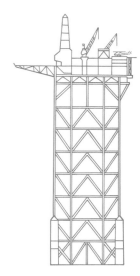

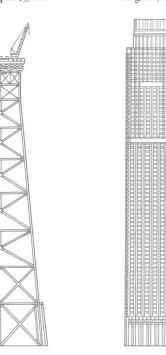

reza/1981
of Mexico
ght: 1,023 feet
r depth: 935 feet

First Interstate
Tower/1989
Los Angeles
Height: 1,018 feet

shore Texas and Louisiana, where reserve estimates ran as high as a billion barrels of oil equivalent; and the Norphlet trend offshore Alabama in Mobile Bay and federal waters, where the potential for natural gas below 20,000 feet was great.

Enhanced recovery, involving the injection of steam or chemicals into a reservoir in order to remove more oil from the field, continued to play an increasingly important role in building U.S. energy supplies in the early 1980s. Union operated 18 enhanced recovery projects in 1982 and estimated that such operations could yield an additional 600 million barrels of oil from the company's producing fields. In 1984, enhanced recovery projects using thermal and chemical techniques contributed 10 percent, or 15,000 barrels per day, of the company's total net domestic production.

Since world oil prices had taken their first giant steps upward in 1973, more challenging and more expensive oil frontiers had opened up to oil explorationists. At Union Oil, this translated into steadily increasing foreign crude oil production (through 1985) and exploratory efforts all over the world.

One major new non-OPEC source of oil was the North Sea, where oil production rose from less than 2 million barrels per day in 1979 to nearly 3.5 million in 1985. Union's Heather platform in the United Kingdom sector of the North Sea had come on stream in 1978. In 1979, after some 12 years of exploratory activity in the Dutch sector, Union found oil. A second discovery in 1980 confirmed the commercial potential. But the fields were small, so development costs had to be strictly controlled to make the project economically feasible.

The challenge fell to John Imle, who was promoted to general manager in the Netherlands in 1980. October 1982 was set as the target for starting production. Computer projections gave the project low odds of being completed on time, but those projections could not factor in Union's creative approach and the eager cooperation of the Dutch authorities.

For the Netherlands, Union's project would mean the country's first offshore oil development — and a doubling of the country's daily crude oil production. The memory of 1973, when the Netherlands had been targeted in the oil embargo by Arab oil exporters, was still fresh.

"We were very direct and open with the Dutch," said Imle. "We told them what we wanted to do and that we wanted to do it correctly. They said it would take years. We said that to make it feasible we needed to do it in months, not years — and we got them on our side."

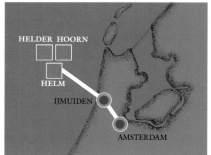

Union's long partnership in its Dutch oil venture with Nedlloyd, a Dutch transportation company, helped. Nedlloyd executives worked with the Union team to find the correct approach to negotiations, particularly on the local level when pipeline rights-of-way were required to get the offshore oil to the terminal in Amsterdam. The Dutch government streamlined its procedures to accommodate Union's timetable. The company was able to realize great savings in both time and costs by installing platforms of identical design in its three fields.

Ecological concerns were raised by an environmental group, the Werkgroep Noordzee. Visits were exchanged. Members of the Werkgroep traveled to the Heather platform for reassurance about Union's competence. John Imle and Tim McMahon, then Union's support services manager in the Netherlands, took a ten-mile bicycle tour of one of the delicate shore areas that the Werkgroep wished to protect. "The exchange of visits resulted in mutual respect and understanding of each organization's concerns and objectives," Imle said.

The first oil field Union developed was named Helm, which referred to a dune grass and, in honor of Nedlloyd, to a ship's helm. The Helder and Hoorn fields were named after Dutch towns. Production from both the Helm and Helder fields started a month ahead of schedule, in September 1982. Hoorn came on stream the following August. Production from the three offshore fields reached more than 30,000 barrels per day, 20 percent above earlier peak production estimates.

On the other side of the globe, Union was about to create a new hydrocarbon industry in Thailand. The company was developing a natural gas discovery made in the Gulf of Thailand in 1973. The Thai government was eager to begin converting the country's power plants to run on indigenous natural gas instead of expensive imported fuel oil. But the project ran into trouble.

Development of the Erawan field, which went on production in August 1981, was slowed as drillers encountered unexpectedly high temperatures. Several wells were shut in when down-hole equipment failed, but substitute materials were quickly found that could withstand the heat.

A second problem proved more difficult. The initial estimate of natural gas reserves in the Erawan field was too optimistic. Delineation drilling in the late 1970s had seemed to indicate vast reserves contained in several extensive underground reservoirs. As drilling proceeded and the production history of wells began to unfold, it became apparent that the reservoirs were smaller than expected — a

Top: Her Royal Highness, Queen Beatrix of the Netherlands, shown with Union host John Imle, participated in the dedication ceremonies for the Dutch fields in 1982. Above: A pipeline carries crude oil from Union's fields to a terminal in the port of Amsterdam. Above left: The Helder platform, along with its sister Helm platform, produced the first oil offshore the Netherlands in September 1982. Above center: Although Union's Dutch fields are located in relatively shallow water, averaging 75 feet, workboats still face the North Sea's rough waters and high winds.

result of erratic geologic deposition and complex faulting. The reservoirs, which proved to be thin beds of sand alternating with non-hydrocarbon-bearing sands, shales, and coal beds, were depleted relatively quickly.

Production in January 1982 was 120 million cubic feet of natural gas and 4,400 barrels of condensate per day. But it didn't improve much, averaging only about half of the projected rate of 250 million cubic feet per day.

For the Thai government, the situation was critical. The country was revamping its energy economy based on the natural gas resource. The Electricity Generating Authority of Thailand had built a new gas-fired power plant and was in the process of converting a second plant to use natural gas. The Petroleum Authority was nearing completion of a large and costly gas separation plant. Siam Cement Company had spent $41 million to lay a gas pipeline to its plant northeast of Bangkok.

The situation proved equally critical for Union. With the revised reserve estimate so far below original expectations, the economic viability of the project came into question, as did the company's future in Thailand.

Both Fred Hartley and Ray Burke were acutely aware that Union had made a commitment and could not let Thailand down. In Bangkok, headlines raged about low gas production and the revised reserve estimate. The government reduced the price it paid Union for gas. The company needed to take immediate action to demonstrate the strength of its resolve and its ability to deliver on its agreements.

Burke hit on the solution. Dr. Hal Lian, president of the International Division, had been involved in the Thai development almost from the beginning and was confident that the problems could be solved. He was sent to Bangkok as president of Union Oil Company of Thailand, sending a clear signal to the Thai government that the project had Union's top priority.

Lian was well known in Bangkok. When he arrived there in March 1983, production from Erawan was already turning around. Some officials remarked on how his arrival brought an immediate improvement. "I protested a little bit, but not too much," Dr. Lian admitted.

It was, of course, no miracle. Union had already stepped up drilling and explor-ation and made plans for additional Erawan platforms in order to maintain gas deliveries at a level between 120 million and 150 million cubic feet per day.

Union also accelerated the development of the Baanpot field, which was one of four included in the second gas sales contract, signed in 1982. Baanpot was

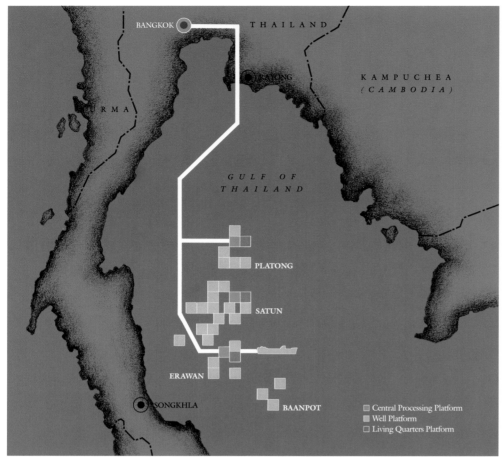

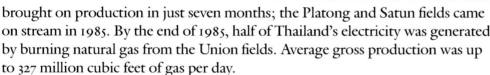

brought on production in just seven months; the Platong and Satun fields came
on stream in 1985. By the end of 1985, half of Thailand's electricity was generated
by burning natural gas from the Union fields. Average gross production was up
to 327 million cubic feet of gas per day.

As Union increased production by drilling more wells, reducing costs to
keep the project economically viable became imperative. Remarkable results were
achieved. The average time to drill a well dropped from 45 to 20 days between
1981 and 1986, and the average per-well cost went down from $4.5 million to $2
million. Average drill penetration of 200 feet per day improved to more than 900
feet per day thanks to the use of new technologies, including top-drive drilling
rigs, drill bits with diamond-cutters, and oil-based muds. Drilling crews also
improved, gaining speed as they gained experience.

Drilling accuracy was critical to keep down dry-hole costs, and Union had
two special weapons: three-dimensional seismic data collection, which had been
developed in the late 1970s, and a highly sophisticated prototype computer
program to help analyze and interpret the data. The program was designed by a
Dallas firm with funding from several companies, including Union.

Seismic data are records of energy waves reflected off underground geological
structures. Since the waves travel at different speeds through different kinds of
rock, they present a picture of the underground geology—at least to the practiced
eye. In a 3-D seismic survey, much more data are collected at the surface than in
an ordinary survey. After detailed computer processing, these data reveal a sharper
image of the subsurface.

The geology under the Gulf of Thailand is very complex. The gas-bearing
beds of sand were found to range from 5 to 40 feet in thickness, and each well that
Union drilled had to penetrate 6 or 7 beds—sometimes as many as 15—in order
to be economic. The 3-D seismic data helped Union's geophysicists plot optimum
well paths through a series of relatively small targets.

TECHNOLOGY TRANSFER

Since Thailand's labor force had no experience in the oil and gas industry, Union set up a training program to help staff its offshore development and production operations. The company's objectives were to transfer technological skills and knowledge to Thai nationals, as well as to reduce the costs of maintaining an expatriate workforce. A basic training center, located in Songkhla, the company's staging area in the south of Thailand, opened in 1979. By the end of 1989, 434 students had graduated. From the start competition for trainee positions has been intense, since only 60 of some 1,000 applicants for each class can be accommodated. Trainees are recruited from all areas of Thailand, with technical school graduates preferred. Basic training includes a year's study of several subjects, including "platform" English, petroleum technology, and safe work practices. Trainees then move offshore for on-the-job instruction as mechanics, electricians, operators, and technicians. Each trainee must complete a list of objectives and master certain tasks before achieving journeyman status, a process that takes about three years. A continuing education program offers employees opportunities to enhance their technical knowledge and learn supervisory skills. They may also be selected for work exchanges with company operations in other parts of the world.

In 1979, Union of Canada discovered the Slave field in Alberta's Peace River country. In 1982, a second oil pool was identified. Much of the ground is muskeg, a mixture of moss, leaves, earth, and water that becomes a quagmire after the spring thaw, restricting drilling activities to the colder months.

In 1982, Union and the Thai government began negotiations to settle their dispute over payment. Thailand's leaders contended that Union should have foreseen the delivery shortfalls. Union's executives held that the lower levels of natural gas reserves and production fell beyond the company's control. Discussions continued for a year and a half. During the final four weeks, Ray Burke met with senior Thai officials in Washington, D.C., New York City, and Bangkok. In the agreement reached in May 1984, Union received a cash reimbursement for underpayments amounting to $28.4 million and incentive prices for Erawan gas production above 150 million cubic feet per day.

Shortly after Hal Lian moved to Bangkok, John Imle in the Netherlands received a call from Ray Burke inviting him to dinner in Los Angeles. Imle soon found himself installed as the new president of the International Division, responsible for all foreign operations except Thailand and Canada.

Imle continued to expand Union's international activity, with the emphasis on discovery. "Our exploration vice president [William A. Sax] was spending a lot of time in China negotiating a contract," Imle said, "and I thought he should have been exploring. So we set up a separate negotiating group [New Ventures under Bob Roethke] and purposely kept it out of the exploration department so there would be no conflicting demands. I wanted the explorationists to focus one hundred percent of their attention on finding oil."

While exploration and production improved for Union in most parts of the world, the situation in Canada was very different. Earnings dropped 33 percent in 1981 — from $18 million to $12 million (Canadian dollars), largely due to the higher taxes that were part of Canada's National Energy Program initiated in the fall of 1980.

One of the program's objectives was to encourage greater Canadian ownership of the oil industry. Many foreign-owned companies, such as Union, were asked to consider selling out to Canadian companies. New tax rules and an incentive system for exploration of federal lands heavily favored Canadian-owned companies. Union of Canada, facing a drastic reduction in net earnings and cash flow, cut back its operations to the minimum.

The Calgary economy had been overheating in the late 1970s, according to Clement W. Dumett, Jr., president of Union of Canada. "A little cooling off would have been welcome," he said, "but we got the deep freeze."

By the spring of 1981, Union's board had decided to sell the conventional oil and gas operations of Union of Canada. The company stopped trading its stock on the Toronto Exchange and bought back the 2 million shares (about 14 percent of the stock) that it did not already own. "We were organized to sell by about October of '81," said Dumett, "but the second version of the National Energy Program hit and slapped more tax on us. By then, nobody wanted — or had any money — to buy anything."

In late 1982, Union of Canada took down the For Sale sign and began to rebuild. The company focused on the development of discoveries made in 1979 and 1982 in the Slave field near Peace River in northern Alberta. Estimated oil in place was 25 million barrels, of which about 30 percent was recoverable.

Union of Canada explorationists also began to reexamine old properties, looking for geologic anomalies that might have been passed over as uneconomic in the days of low oil prices. Exploration of the company's Beaufort Sea properties was put on hold, since Union of Canada, as a foreign-owned company, was at a distinct disadvantage when it came to federal incentives for drilling in the difficult arctic environment.

Union also had an interest in Canada's vast resource of unconventional reserves, an estimated 1 trillion barrels of oil contained in the Athabasca tar sands and the Grosmont heavy oil (bitumen) deposits located in northeastern Alberta. Research efforts begun in 1977 to use steam injection to produce the sticky bitumen yielded excellent results but were stopped when the world oil price dropped dramatically in 1986. The Alberta Oil Sands Technology Resource Authority, a government agency, funded half the research costs.

Late in 1982, Union of Canada began construction on the Obed thermal coal project in west central Alberta, near Hinton. It was designed to produce 3 million tons of coal per year. The first coal was shipped in August 1984.

The business environment improved in Canada in 1984 when a new government, headed by Prime Minister Brian Mulrooney, was elected. "We got back to a more reasonable accommodation between the provincial and federal governments," noted Dumett.

The slowdown in activity for foreign-owned oil companies in Canada was unique at the beginning of the eighties, a period when oil exploration and production were booming in other parts of the world. The steel industry shared in the boom, supplying millions of tons of steel for use in oil fields. And Union

Opposite, left: Molycorp's new underground mine and modernized mill outside Questa, New Mexico, were dedicated in late 1983. Opposite, right: These thickening tanks are just two of the numerous steps in the production of molybdenum concentrate from crushed ore. One ton of ore yields 6 pounds of concentrate, which is then shipped to Molycorp's plant in Washington, Pennsylvania, for processing into compounds required by industry. Below: Construction of the Obed thermal coal mine in Alberta included a huge "glory hole" with a 45,000-ton capacity for coal storage.

completed plans to provide two critical materials to the steel industry: molybdenum and needle coke.

Molybdenum adds strength and corrosion resistance to steel, making it an ideal alloy for such oil industry applications as drill pipe, high-pressure pipelines, and offshore platforms. Needle coke, a premium quality petroleum coke, is manufactured into electrodes for electric arc furnaces that melt down scrap steel.

In New Mexico, about 250 miles southeast of Union's Parachute Creek oil shale project, the company dedicated its new underground molybdenum mine near Questa in September 1983. Construction had begun in 1978, when open-pit mining operations were phased out.

The $250 million development of the mine and modernization of the mill were massive tasks, involving the excavation of more than ten miles of underground tunnels and installation of an underground railroad. The Questa mine, with a 60-year history in northern New Mexico, was the area's major employer. Molycorp kept its open-pit miners on the roster during the years of construction, training them to work underground. Mill workers became construction workers as well.

The new mine proved highly efficient, operating on the principle of "gravity block caving": Tunnels were cut under the ore deposits, which were blasted out with explosives. The ore tumbled down "by gravity" through a series of excavated chutes to rail cars; it was then transferred up to the surface by conveyor belt and fed into the mill for processing.

"This ultraefficient moly mine and mill will allow us to become one of the nation's lowest-cost primary molybdenum producers," said Tom Sleeman, president of Molycorp, at the mine dedication. Efficient production was key, since some of the company's competitors produced molybdenum at a very low cost as a by-product of other mining operations.

The Questa mine was designed to produce 18,000 tons of ore per day. By the end of 1984, production was up to 12,000 tons. The markets, however, had begun to shrink in 1983 with dropping oil prices. Demand for steel was down, not just in the oil patch but for all industrial applications. The American steel industry in particular was in a devastating slump, suffering from overcapacity and inefficient methods of production. Molycorp's mine was shut down in 1986 after the oil industry cut back operations following the collapse of oil prices. The mine did not reopen until markets improved in 1989.

As with the Questa molybdenum mine, Union's needle coke project had been

approved during a time of high oil prices and brisk steel sales. Union Chemicals had been investigating the market for needle coke for more than a decade, and the early 1980s looked to be the time to move forward. Electric arc furnaces, which required graphite electrodes made from this specialty coke, represented a growing segment of the worldwide steel industry.

Keith L. Openshaw, then senior vice president for Union Chemicals, asked Science & Technology to develop the technology in the mid-1970s. The strategy was to use low-cost feedstocks to produce the high-purity, crystalline coke.

In 1977, John Duir and Milan Skripek conceived the basic process. By 1981, the process — a unique scheme to desulfurize the feedstock without disturbing essential molecular characteristics — was ready for commercial development. "The trick was to find processing conditions that would pull out sulfur atoms while minimizing the addition of hydrogen," noted Duir. Electrode manufacturers specified strict tolerances for the quality of the coke, specifications that grew tighter as Union worked to develop the process.

Union began producing needle coke in 1985 at its new facilities, built as a joint project between the Chicago refinery and the adjacent Union Chemicals carbon plant. Electrode manufacturers praised the product's quality, giving it a competitive edge in a depressed market. "We are producing one of the best needle cokes in the world," noted Cloyd Reeg at the time.

However, Union had trouble maintaining consistent quality and getting production rates up to design capacity. The company shut down needle coking operations in October 1987 so that research and operating people could correct the problems. When the facilities were restarted in May 1988, the quality, quantity, and efficiency of production had been substantially improved.

Aside from molybdenum and needle coke, Union Chemicals sales were generally strong in the 1980s, as the division moved to enhance its traditional businesses with specialty product lines. Markets for lanthanides, for example, had virtually exploded in the 1960s and 1970s. Shortly after Union acquired Molycorp in 1977, the market for samarium-cobalt magnets took off. The magnets were used in a number of new miniature electronic applications, such as tiny earphone speakers for wallet-sized tape players.

"We saw a demand for samarium that looked like it would exceed existing production capacity," recalled R. Gene Dewey, then Molycorp's vice president for mining and exploration. "Union made the decision to build a plant to separate samarium and gadolinium, another lanthanide then just starting to be in demand for use in x-rays and laser beams. This was a brand-new development for Molycorp, and for the most part, brand new for the world."

The separation facilities, which employed a solvent extraction process developed by Union, opened at Molycorp's lanthanide mine in Mountain Pass, California, in 1982. After only two years of operating the new facilities, Molycorp reported a 38 percent increase in lanthanide sales.

In late 1980, the Petrochemical Group continued to expand its polymers operations, this time with the purchase of the emulsion business of the Celanese Plastics and Specialties Company. In addition to new talent and technology, Union acquired a stronger position in paint and textile markets, and an introduction to the paper-coating business. In 1982, the Petrochemical Group completed construction of a technical service center in Charlotte, North Carolina, to assist customers with product development, chemical formulation, and production process refinement.

The group also expanded its national network of warehouse distribution centers that marketed solvents and other chemicals in less-than-carload lots. By 1984, 24 centers served a growing number of chemicals customers who needed quantities ranging from 5 gallons to 7,500 gallons, as compared with a 30,000-gallon rail-car load. Less-than-carload lot sales had been initiated a half-century earlier by the American Mineral Spirits Company, one of the companies that originally formed the Union Chemicals Division. In 1931, AMSCO had begun selling naphthas, coal tar solvents, industrial alcohols, and other products in relatively small quantities to paint, varnish, and lacquer manufacturers.

"There is a lot of opportunity in responding to the marketplace—finding an edge, looking for solutions, and seeing how they are accepted," said Nicholas E. Lynam, senior vice president, Petrochemical Group. "You've got to do good

market research up front, find out what the needs are, and develop the technology to satisfy them."

Union's Nitrogen Group, the largest supplier of nitrogen fertilizers to the West Coast agriculture industry, also looked for a new marketing niche. The group found it in "plant protection" chemicals as environmental concerns in the early 1980s widened to include areas of health and safety.

"It was already becoming obvious in the mid-1970s that it was going to be very difficult to register a new pesticide or herbicide," said John W. Jost, Science & Technology's vice president for chemicals research. "Don Young [a senior consultant for research] saw that we would have a competitive advantage if we developed agricultural chemicals that were effective without having the environmental problems of the existing chemicals." Young's inspiration led to the creation of several new agricultural products.

The growing public concern about issues of health and safety had major effects throughout the company. As new technologies and new chemicals were developed, regulations mounted. For example, under the rules of the 1976 Toxic Substances Control Act, products refined from shale oil were defined as new chemicals. As such, they had to be thoroughly tested to define their characteristics and identify possible hazards before the products could be registered for sale.

In 1983, the federal Occupational Health and Safety Administration published a revised Hazard Communication Standard. This greatly increased the levels of documentation that companies were required to develop and disseminate to employees, customers, and others about the materials used in manufacturing as well as in products. Union rapidly built up its staff of medical and environmental specialists to help meet the growing regulatory demands.

The Union 76 Division, which encompassed refining and marketing activities, also had to adjust to a changed business environment in the eighties. After decontrol in 1981, the price of gasoline in the United States rose at first but began dropping by summer as competition among gasoline retailers increased. Total U.S. demand for petroleum products fell 5 percent in 1981, the third straight year of decline. Demand fell again slightly in 1982 and then leveled off until 1986 when the price of crude oil dropped dramatically.

Union 76 Division earnings were strong during the early 1980s, as the company's marketers carved out specialized niches where Union could successfully compete for sales of gasoline and lubricants. The key for refining operations was

Opposite: In 1983, Union expanded the capacity of its Chicago refinery to process heavy residual oils by 45 percent with the addition of two new coker drums, each weighing 147 tons. Below left: A PureGro truck sprays an orchard in California's central valley. PureGro, a Union subsidiary, is a major supplier of fertilizers and crop-protection products to western farmers. Opposite, below: A mechanic uses an "oscilloscope" to diagnose engine problems at dealer Jim Dawson's Protech-certified station in Burbank, California.

efficiency. Rebuilding the coker at the San Francisco refinery and expanding the coker at Chicago increased the refining system's capacity to process lower-cost, heavy crude oils into high-value fuels. Waste heat from operations was harnessed and recycled to conserve energy use, and other modifications were made to increase product yields.

Union's refineries ran at about 75 percent of capacity during the early 1980s, while the U.S. industry averaged about 70 percent. The company's fuel conversion units—the Unicrackers and fluid catalytic crackers—operated at near capacity to churn out gasoline "because that's where the margin is—in the lighter product," said Don Hanley, then vice president for western refining. In 1982, the Unicracker at the Los Angeles refinery set a new throughput record, processing more than 22,000 barrels of crude oil per day.

The level of service given customers at gasoline stations had declined throughout the industry during the 1970s when government controls on profit margins dampened dealer incentive. In the 1980s, some companies cut back on services to position themselves as "no frills" operations. Questioned about this during a presentation to Union's executive committee, Clay Warnock, vice president of western marketing, responded: "Whatever the competition is doing, we should do just the opposite." The Union tradition of offering good quality and friendly service remained a valid marketing position, given that others were abandoning the customers who still valued service.

Union emphasized full service through its dealers in the West and, at the same time, continued to expand the number of self-serve islands at its stations. The full-service concept included marketing leaded premium gasoline, even when other retailers dropped it as more and more cars on the road ran on unleaded.

In 1981, the Union 76 Division introduced Protech, an automotive service and repair program with a money-back guarantee that was rapidly expanded throughout the western marketing region. Union also began to build high-volume "superfacilities." Forty were in operation by 1984, each averaging sales of 150,000 gallons of gasoline per month. The high volume of sales helped offset increasing overhead costs of land and construction.

Union followed a different marketing strategy in the East. "We sell the major portion of our gasoline through marketers—independent petroleum firms that purchase our products and resell them through their own dealer and convenience store locations," noted Thomas W. Matthews, vice president of eastern marketing.

While it was practical in the West to work directly with dealers, who were concentrated in large metropolitan areas, distribution in the East was more efficiently handled through marketers, with each serving a group of dealers scattered throughout many smaller communities.

In the East, Union's marketing strategy included the combination of high-volume, self-serve fuel outlets with convenience stores offering grocery products and fast food items. By 1984, the company operated 124 of these convenience stores (C-stores), providing models for its eastern region marketers. The number of C-stores operated by Union 76 marketers grew from fewer than 500 in 1980 to more than 3,000 by 1987.

In 1988, 12,000 U.S. marketers surveyed by the Petroleum Marketers Association of America voted Unocal the best supplier of all the major oil companies and independent suppliers in 48 states.

"Both the quantity and quality of marketer growth have been outstanding in the East," noted Tom Matthews in 1990. "An average of eight hundred new marketer retail facilities have been added each year since 1982, while some four hundred fifty older, nonproductive marketer outlets have been removed from the system. This has improved both our retail image and sales volume."

Another key to marketing profitability in the early 1980s was the expansion of the company's national auto/truckstop system. These outlets, located on highways spanning the country, catered to the needs of truckers and other long-distance travelers, offering restaurants and convenience stores along with truck and auto services.

"We got in there first with something different," explained Matthews. "In the late 1950s, Pure Oil bought out a business in Ohio from a man named J.V. 'Jerry' Sanner. It included two facilities we called truckstops that were selling about a hundred thousand gallons of diesel fuel and gasoline monthly. That opened some eyes, since Pure's service stations were then averaging a swift six thousand gallons per month. Jerry came on the payroll and built a system."

The truckstops were constantly improved and numbered about 200 at the time of Union's merger with Pure in 1965. Union expanded the system, but competition built up during the 1970s.

"In the early 1980s, we found ourselves rapidly losing our number-one position," Matthews said, "so we turned it around."

New outlets and services were added, and the system set volume records for diesel sales in 1983. By 1984, the company operated 150 auto/truckstops on major U.S. interstate highways and 150 smaller truckstops on other routes—all open 24 hours a day, 365 days a year.

As Union's marketing operations adjusted to the new realities of decontrol, so did the company's crude oil supply operations. A new department was formed in 1981 under Roger Beach, who had been named vice president of crude supply in December 1980, just a month before full decontrol.

"It took us a while to understand the structural changes that were occurring in the marketplace," Beach said. "Regulations had bred a lot of uneconomic small refiners and a lot of traders—third-party people in our business who weren't normally there. After deregulation, a lot of them went broke in a hurry."

Beach consolidated Union's three crude oil supply organizations — domestic east and west, and foreign—into a coordinated unit. "We were much more efficient when we pulled the group together," he explained. "Then we could do a crude exchange from east to west, or vice versa, more easily. It opened up all kinds of possibilities.

"And there was an intangible benefit," he continued. "The intelligence of the marketplace is very important when you're buying and selling crude every day.

Roger Beach kept in touch via computer with world oil markets after his promotion to vice president of crude supply in 1981. He had worked for Pure Oil for four years when that company merged with Union Oil in 1965. Right center: In the 1980s, Union's eastern region marketers developed a network of self-serve marts, like the one in Elgin, Illinois. Bottom, left and right: The company also expanded its network of truckstops.

The fact that we all talked to each other every day improved our intelligence of the marketplace tremendously."

The people in charge of crude oil supply face a formidable challenge: They not only sell the company's crude oil production but also supply the necessary crude oil to keep the company's refineries going. Those functions must remain separate in order to assure the best sale and purchase prices for the company. So the crude oil supply department works with independent oil producers, foreign producers, other integrated companies, and crude oil traders, as well as with the company's own production and refining people.

The size and complexity of the international crude oil marketplace in the 1980s made computerization essential to track prices and trades around the world. By 1984, a new computer service offered instant information on crude oil prices, shipping, and transactions throughout the world, with continuous updates as conditions changed. Union's crude oil supply specialists could base their decisions on up-to-the-minute information. With offices in Hong Kong, Los Angeles, and London — each separated by about eight hours — Union had a constant watch on international developments.

"After peaking in 1981, crude oil prices started to fall because supply was outstripping demand," Roger Beach said. "OPEC started losing control of the pricing mechanism. That's when the crude oil futures market began to revolutionize the way we do business. It reduces our risk, if we use it properly." As in the futures market for any commodity, the buyer or seller locks in a price for a later delivery, thus hedging losses against fluctuating prices.

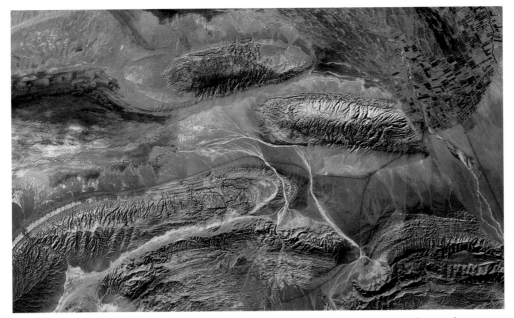

EYES IN THE SKY
The art of aerial reconnaissance — or remote sensing — has reached amazing heights with the coming of the space age. Sensors on board orbiting satellites are an important tool for those caught up in the search for energy and mineral resources. These sensors pick up and record visible and infrared light waves, and microwaves reflected or emitted from earth. Wavelengths vary, providing information about the composition of the surfaces from which they emanate. When the data are combined to form an image, they present a surprisingly detailed "picture" with important clues about topography and geology. Union established a remote sensing department at its Science & Technology labs in 1983. Dr. Alfredo E. Prelat, who headed the operation, was soon working with the National Aeronautics and Space Administration to evaluate remote sensing data for mineral exploration. Remote sensing technology, particularly when combined with other kinds of information-gathering techniques, helps scientists pinpoint potential hydrocarbon and mineral formations and geothermal resources. This technology is also used to site wells, roads, and production facilities. In Alaska, it helps chart ice movements and plan shipping lanes. In one case, remote sensing helped a field team navigate an uncharted river; the data revealed the channels where the water was deep enough to allow a boat's passage.

On July 23, 1984, a devastating event sent shock waves throughout the company. A high-pressure tower at the Chicago refinery ruptured, resulting in a series of explosions and a major fire. Fifteen employees and two contract security guards were killed; many others were injured. The effects reverberated in Lemont, Romeoville, and the other towns around the refinery, located about 25 miles southwest of Chicago.

"It's a small community," said A.J. Eliskalns, then refinery manager. "Almost everyone had a friend or relative who worked at the refinery." In the midst of grief, employees worried, too, about their own livelihoods. Would the refinery reopen?

"It was a very difficult time," said Bill McConnor, then president of the Union 76 Division. "The refinery employees were badly shaken. It happened to their people — people they knew well. The employees were anxious just to have us get back into business again. They were behind us one hundred percent."

Union worked closely with community leaders to provide grief counseling services and to hold a memorial service a week after the accident. "It will take a long, long time to get over this. Now we just need to help each other out and get through it all," said Richard J. Fuhrman, a refinery employee and committeeman for the Oil, Chemical, and Atomic Workers Union, Local No. 7517, when interviewed by one of the many television reporters covering the tragic event and aftermath.

The problem started as a small crack in a high-pressure vessel. Emergency crews responded promptly and worked to shut down the unit, but the crack expanded and the vessel exploded — "like a rocket," noted one eyewitness. Fire spread throughout the refinery, nearby buildings were destroyed, windows were shattered for miles around, and the ground shook as far as 30 miles away. Fire fighters from 30 neighboring communities joined Union's crews to quell the raging inferno.

Within days of the explosion, the company decided to rebuild. "We put people to work right away," said Eliskalns. "The labor union gave us a special dispensation to put aside work rules so people could come back to work to begin clearing away the debris."

With the abrupt shutdown of the Chicago refinery, Union's crude oil supply department quickly rerouted crude oil shipments. The marketing people purchased products to meet the immediate needs of Union 76 customers in the Midwest. Production was stepped up at Union's refinery in Beaumont, Texas.

Some nine months after the shutdown, Union restarted its operations to process crude oil at Chicago, running everything except the alkylation unit and

Top left: Company scientists use data relayed from orbiting satellites to create pictures of the earth's surface that can provide important clues about mineral deposits, geothermal activity, and other geologic features. In this false-color image, vegetation is bright red, salt formations are bright orange, and shale is dark gray.

the damaged fluid catalytic cracker. "We brought our throughput up to a reasonably high level," said McConnor, "and we made arrangements to get our gas-oil processed elsewhere until the cat cracker was back in operation." The cracker was restarted in May 1985; the alkylation unit, in October.

By that time, the company had survived a very different type of crisis. An investment group led by T. Boone Pickens, Jr., attempted a hostile takeover in the spring of 1985. Pickens, chairman and founder of Mesa Petroleum and self-styled champion of the small stockholder, had been involved in several attempts to take over oil companies since the late 1970s, as had several other so-called corporate raiders. Many target companies had been forced to take on new debt or merge with other firms.

In June 1984, Fred Hartley commented on such activities in a speech entitled "Capitalism in Chaos?": "I am deeply troubled by these events. I believe they reduce needed exploration investments, quash innovation, and destroy rather than build....I recognize that there is a place for takeovers and buyouts....But when a strong company making profitable, long-term investments is threatened by financial takeover artists and their bankers simply to make a short-term profit, I see red. It is the destruction of entrepreneurship for a fast buck."

In 1984, a Pickens investment group had forced Gulf, the fifth largest U.S. oil company, into the arms of Chevron, the fourth largest, in the biggest corporate merger to that time. Later that year, Pickens led an attempt to take over Phillips Petroleum. Combined after-tax profits for the Pickens group from both deals have been estimated at close to $300 million.

"We anticipated that we were going to be on the list for a takeover sometime," said Dick Stegemeier. "We had done most of the obvious things you can do, given some time and opportunity to prepare a defense. Certainly the Delaware laws were more favorable to fighting off such takeovers than California laws."

Union had adopted an internal plan of reorganization in 1983 in which Union Oil Company of California, a California corporation, became the operating subsidiary of Unocal Corporation, a new Delaware holding company. At the end of 1984, Union planned a campaign to advertise that it would begin doing business as Unocal in 1985; but events made such a campaign unnecessary. Unocal became a familiar name in headlines across the country as it struggled to survive as an independent company.

Below: U.S. domestic oil prices were controlled below world prices in the mid-1970s. Below right: When adjusted for inflation, U.S. oil prices have often hovered in the $12 to $18 per barrel range, where they returned after the world oil price crash in 1986.

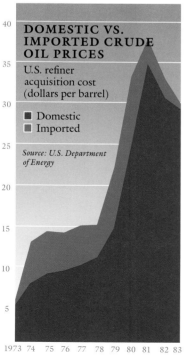

DOMESTIC VS. IMPORTED CRUDE OIL PRICES

U.S. refiner acquisition cost (dollars per barrel)

■ Domestic
■ Imported

Source: U.S. Department of Energy

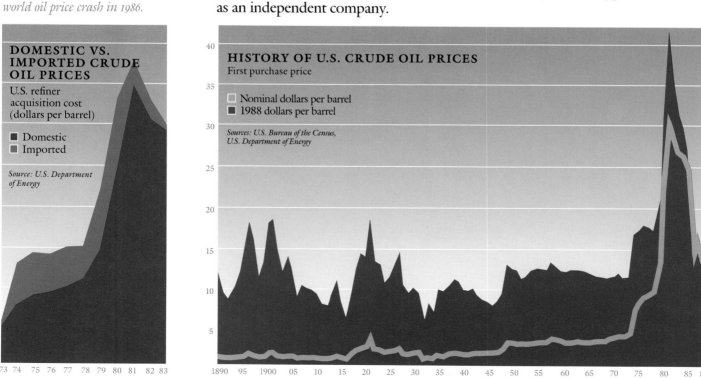

HISTORY OF U.S. CRUDE OIL PRICES
First purchase price

□ Nominal dollars per barrel
■ 1988 dollars per barrel

Sources: U.S. Bureau of the Census, U.S. Department of Energy

Late
Sports

Los Angeles Times

Morning
Final

Circulation: 1,064,392 Daily / 1,334,666 Sunday   **Tuesday, April 9, 1985**   MF/92 Pages Copyright 1985 Times Mirror Co. **Daily 25¢**

Battle for Union Oil Begins

Hartley Vows to Fend Off Pickens Takeover

By DEBRA WHITEFIELD, *Times Staff Writer*

After weeks of verbal sparring, the opening round of what is expected to be a bruising corporate fight finally began Monday, with Texas oilman T. Boone Pickens ____ing the first blow: an offer to ____ of the parent of Union

Inc. is now trying to raise on Pickens' behalf. Mesa Petroleum is much smaller than Unocal, with revenues of $413.5 million last year compared to Unocal's $11.5 billion.

His next step, Pickens sold __ interest needed to ta__ cost about $3.4__

13   Defeating
a Raider

T. Boone Pickens, depicted as the loser by artist Bill Schorr, may not have bargained on Union Oil's tenacity in fighting off a hostile takeover attempt in 1985. Opposite: The struggle for control of the company pitted Union and Fred Hartley (left) against a group of investors headed by Pickens. As an unexpected benefit, the publicity helped Union Oil in its transition to begin doing business as Unocal.

On Valentine's Day, February 14, 1985, T. Boone Pickens, Jr., and his investment group, Mesa Partners II, made a 13D filing — required of an investor within ten days of accumulating more than 5 percent of a company's stock — with the Securities and Exchange Commission (SEC). Pickens stated that his group had acquired 7.3 percent of Unocal's stock "for investment purposes only."

A federal judge subsequently declared that the "investment purposes" statement was false and that to believe it "defied common sense."

Fred Hartley certainly didn't believe it. In fact, he considered it a declaration of hostilities. Hartley thought the worst of those he referred to as the "pious piranhas" of Wall Street. Corporate raiders, he said, were "financial barbarians with self-righteous facades."

In the petroleum industry, several old, established companies — Conoco, Marathon, Superior, Cities Service, Getty, and Gulf — had already been dismantled or swallowed up by other companies, providing profits for corporate raiders and the Wall Street arbitrageurs who swarmed around them. Phillips Petroleum, having paid a heavy price to fend off a Mesa group takeover, labored under a debt that cost the company almost $2 billion in divested assets.

Unocal itself had been the subject of takeover rumors. In fact, a halt was called in trading the company's stock on July 13, 1984, triggered by an imbalance in buy and sell orders based on rumors that turned out to be false.

In early February 1985, only a few days before Pickens revealed his group's Unocal holdings, *Business Week* magazine reported: "Wall Street sources say that, privately, Hartley has made no secret that his company is for sale at the right price."

Hartley fired off a sharp response. "Let me quickly set the record straight: Unocal is not 'my company,' and it certainly is not for sale....One of your other statements — accurate this time — reflects the success of our long-term approach: 'Unocal is different. It has been among the most successful of any major [oil company] at finding oil and gas, and it has an efficient refining operation.'"

Unocal management, in preparation for what might come, had adopted a number of "shark repellent" measures: staggered terms for directors, the elimination of cumulative voting, and the requirement for a vote of 75 percent of the shareholders to approve certain key events, such as a change of control opposed by a majority of the board of directors.

In addition, a group was formed within the company to study corporate take-

EVOLUTION OF THE OIL INDUSTRY

1890	1900	1910	1920	1930	1940	1950	1960	1970	1980	1990

UNION OIL — **UNOCAL**

PURE OIL

ROYAL DUTCH (NETH.)
SHELL TRNS. (UK) — ROYAL DUTCH/SHELL GROUP — **SHELL OIL**

WOLVERINE PETROLEUM — SHELL UNION OIL (US)
AMERICAN PETROLEUM
NATIONAL OIL

SUN OIL — **SUN**
SUNRAY OIL — **ORYX ENERGY**
MIDCONTINENT PETROLEUM

THE TEXAS COMPANY — **TEXACO**

GETTY OIL

PHILLIPS PETROLEUM — **PHILLIPS PETROLEUM**

GENERAL AMERICAN

AMERADA HESS — **AMERADA HESS**
OCCIDENTAL PETROLEUM — **OCCIDENTAL PETROLEUM**

CITIES SERVICE

ANDERSON & KERR DRILLING — **KERR–MCGEE**
COASTAL STATES GAS — **COASTAL**
COLORADO INTERSTATE GAS

AMERICAN NATURAL RESOURCES

TEXAS OIL & GAS — Acquired by USX 1986 — **USX (TEXAS OIL & GAS)**
BURLINGTON RESOURCES

STANDARD OIL TRUST

OHIO OIL — Acquired by USX 1982 — **USX (MARATHON OIL)**
SOLAR REFINING
STANDARD OIL (OHIO) — Acquired by BP 1987 — **BP AMERICA**
CONTINENTAL OIL — Acquired by DuPont 1981 — **DUPONT (CONOCO)**
MARLAND
STANDARD OIL (NEW JERSEY) — **EXXON**
ANGLO AMERICAN
EUREKA PIPELINE
SOUTH PENN OIL — **PENNZOIL**
NATIONAL TRANSIT
SOUTHWEST PENNSYLVANIA PIPELINE
STANDARD OIL (NEBRASKA)
STANDARD OIL (INDIANA) — **AMOCO**
STANDARD OIL (KANSAS)
RICHFIELD
ATLANTIC REFINING — **ARCO**
PRAIRIE OIL & GAS
SINCLAIR
SOUTHERN PIPELINE
CUMBERLAND PIPELINE — **ASHLAND OIL**
ASHLAND
GALENA SIGNAL
SOCONY VACUUM OIL — **MOBIL OIL**
STANDARD OIL (NEW YORK)
SUPERIOR OIL
STANDARD OIL (KENTUCKY)
STANDARD OIL (CALIFORNIA) — **CHEVRON**
GULF OIL

over battles, particularly those involving oil companies. The group included staff attorneys, economists, and financial experts. They collected and studied legal briefs, SEC filings, court testimony, news articles, and information about litigation and state statutes.

The group searched for patterns in corporate takeovers and tried to identify the modus operandi of each corporate raider. Sam A. Snyder, assistant general counsel, spent many an evening at home, eating a sandwich at his computer terminal, studying the daily accumulation of material.

"It was quite obvious that Unocal might be a target," said Snyder. "Intelligence is the prime resource in any war. We began to marshal information. We had to know the players better than they knew us."

In turn, Unocal came under the close scrutiny of Wall Street analysts. What the experts saw was a financially stable but conservative company that, from their point of view, had not moved quickly enough to shed unproductive assets and split the proceeds with shareholders. The analysis fit many oil companies that had diversified their investments, often too widely, during the cash infusions that

Claude Brinegar chaired the command group of Unocal executives who concentrated their efforts on takeover defense. Opposite: The breakup of the Standard Oil Trust in 1911 resulted in a proliferation of oil companies. Since then, the industry has experienced several periods of consolidation, particularly in the 1960s and the 1980s.

accompanied the OPEC oil price run-ups in the late 1970s and early 1980s. Unocal, moreover, was a company with a lot of cash and an unfashionably low ratio of debt to equity of 18 percent.

On February 15, Hartley quickly put his defense team in place. Unocal's top managers had already decided that if it came to a takeover battle, they would not follow the pattern of other oil companies under siege. They would not turn decision-making over to outside legal and investment banking firms but would control the fight and play the lead role in developing strategies.

Hartley appointed a small command group to concentrate on the takeover defense. The chairman was Claude Brinegar, senior vice president, administration. Other members of the group were Phil Blamey, vice president and chief financial officer; Neal Schmale, director of budgets, planning, and economics; and Sam Snyder, who was preparing to succeed George C. Bond as Unocal's general counsel.

Bond, only two months away from retirement, was under physician's orders to avoid stress. "However, the adrenaline was flowing," he said. "There was no way I could or would avoid going all out to defeat any attempt to take over Unocal....Sam Snyder became the field commander of our many legal battles while I ran the general staff at headquarters."

Snyder, who had been ready to board a plane to Bangkok on an arbitration matter on February 15, canceled his plans and stayed in Los Angeles to take charge of the legal team.

Twelve of Unocal's 74 staff lawyers were involved almost exclusively in takeover defense strategies. Jasmina A. Theodore, assistant counsel, was put in charge of confidential files associated with the takeover attempt, for which Bond commandeered three rooms on Unocal Center's executive floor where security could be maintained. "Security throughout the center was increased," Theodore noted. The open and friendly atmosphere at the center became more subdued as guards appeared at every entrance, and employees began to wear their identity badges. There was a general feeling that it was time to circle the wagons to prepare for the attack.

"The first event before us," recalled Brinegar, "was the February twenty-fifth board meeting. It was our first chance to discuss possible antitakeover strategies with the outside directors. It was also our last chance to change the bylaws that would govern the annual meeting scheduled for April twenty-ninth."

The directors took the opportunity to adopt a bylaw, which had earlier been contemplated by company management, that required 30 days' notice for any matters to be transacted at the annual meeting. They also amended an existing bylaw to require 30 days' notice for nominations for the election of directors.

The board agreed that Pickens was not just an investor, as he maintained, but a serious takeover threat. Moreover, they shared Hartley's conviction that Pickens meant to dismember Unocal if he got his hands on the company. The board took the firm position that Unocal would best serve its shareholders by not allowing the company to be acquired at an inadequate price.

The company, nevertheless, did need outside financial and legal expertise. Blamey recommended Goldman Sachs & Company, a large firm with experience in takeover fights.

Hartley also wanted New York investment bankers Dillon Read & Company as advisers. Unocal's relationship with the firm went back to 1939, when Reese Taylor had called on James Forrestal for help in obtaining financing to turn a Depression-battered Union Oil Company around.

In 1985, Hartley called on Dillon Read's Nicholas Brady, who would later become U.S. Secretary of the Treasury, to help develop financial strategies in mounting the takeover defense. Brady might also prove an effective voice for

Unocal in Washington, D.C., as the company urged Congress and the regulators to take steps to curb takeover mania.

Unocal lined up law firms in New York; Washington, D.C.; Los Angeles; Houston; and Wilmington, Delaware. Already under retainer was the proxy-soliciting firm D.F. King, whose president, Artie Long, personally took on Unocal's campaign. To assist in the effort to gain public support for Unocal's position, the company engaged Hill & Knowlton, an international public relations firm head-quartered in New York. The firm not only brought solid expertise in takeover battles but provided an instant nationwide communications network through its branch offices in major cities.

Hartley and Unocal took the offensive, firing the first real salvo of the war. On March 12, Unocal sued Security Pacific National Bank, its principal bank, for breaches of contract and fiduciary duty and for deceit and misrepresentation in making loans to a partnership controlled by Pickens.

Sam Snyder, who became Unocal's general counsel in 1985, took command of the company's legal defenses during the takeover attempt. He celebrated 30 years with the company in 1985, having joined as a landman in Midland, Texas, in 1955. He moved to the Law Department in Los Angeles in 1961.

Earlier, Snyder's team, in combing through the 4-inch-thick file on the Mesa group's raid on Phillips Petroleum, discovered that Security Pacific had extended Mesa II a line of credit of up to $185 million dollars. The same line of credit appeared in the 13D filing concerning Unocal. Privately, officers of the bank denied to both Snyder and Blamey that the funds could be used for take-over activities, insisting that the loan had been for working capital only. Despite such disavowals, the Mesa investors were free to use the money as they chose and may well have used it to buy Unocal stock.

The issue was a critical one for Unocal. Security Pacific had been the company's bank for 40 years, managing Unocal pension funds, financing large Unocal projects, and serving as the primary depository for the payroll. As custodian for the company's employee stock ownership plan, Security Pacific held at least 10 percent of Unocal's stock.

The bank — with access to a lot of confidential information about Unocal — appeared to be lending money to the enemy. Beyond that, Security Pacific's loan to Mesa Partners II lent credibility to a takeover campaign that depended almost entirely on borrowed money.

For Snyder, the loan provided the legal opening he was looking for — a "nonfrivolous novelty," as he called it, that would catch the other side off balance. Once Unocal filed suit, Hartley took the issue public. "If you can't trust your banker, who can you trust?" he asked in a speech. He sent a letter to Paul Volcker, chairman of the Federal Reserve Board, with copies to every member of the United States Congress:

"The bank breached explicit promises made by its highest officers to this company and has abused its relationship of trust with this company," Hartley wrote. "After a relationship of some forty years, in which the bank continually received confidential financial, geological, and engineering information from this company, the bank turned around and loaned money to a group intent on taking Unocal over or putting it into play as an acquisition target."

The Volcker letter and copies had been mailed in unmarked envelopes, which, to Boone Pickens, at least, seemed a sneaky thing to do. He made a point of mentioning it later, whenever he retold the story.

The truth was that the company had not yet printed envelopes or stationery with its new Unocal logo. Rather than send the letters out under the old Union mark, Karen A. Sikkema, director of corporate communications, had simply decided on plain envelopes.

In fact, events had caught Unocal without an official logo. Public relations manager W. Barry Lane had to improvise a Unocal letterhead for his mushroom-ing output of press releases. Sikkema had received sample Unocal stationery pro-

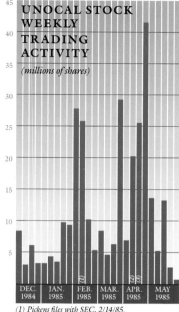

UNOCAL STOCK WEEKLY TRADING ACTIVITY
(millions of shares)

(1) Pickens files with SEC, 2/14/85.
(2) Pickens launches offer, 4/8/85.
(3) Unocal announces offer, 4/16/85.

The New York Stock Exchange recorded heavy trading in Unocal stock at key moments during the takeover struggle.

posed by a New York design firm, but company executives hadn't had time to make a final choice.

One night after Sikkema had gone home, Brinegar and Robert O. Hedley, corporate secretary, entered her office, took the samples from the file, and chose one on the spot. Hartley later said that Pickens saved the company several million dollars that had been earmarked for a national campaign to advertise the new name. Thanks to Pickens, Unocal was frequently in the headlines, and the ad campaign became unnecessary.

The Security Pacific suit struck home, drawing return fire from Pickens. On March 21, Mesa sued Unocal for interfering with its banking relationships. "Apparently we hit a sore nerve," George Bond recalled later.

By this time, Mesa II had used its bank loans to acquire much of the 16.8 million Unocal shares it now owned—increasing its stake to 9.7 percent. On March 27, Mesa II announced that it had upped its holdings by another 6.7 million shares, raising its total to 13.6 percent of Unocal's stock. Ultimately, however, Snyder's legal attack proved to be very damaging to Mesa II's lines of credit. Bankers, growing edgy in the public spotlight, began to withdraw their support from the takeover war.

Until now, Pickens had maintained that his group was acquiring shares solely for investment. In its new filing with the SEC, however, Mesa II revealed that it might seek to control or force a restructuring of Unocal. And, in an attempt to get around the 30-day requirements, Pickens declared that Mesa II would solicit proxies to delay the annual meeting scheduled for April 29.

On April 1, the Unocal board responded by stiffening the requirements for transacting business at the annual stockholder meeting. The directors adopted a new bylaw: One-third of the company's shares entitled to vote would be required for a quorum. On the same day, Unocal sued Mesa Partners II, alleging violations of federal securities laws in its purchase of the company's common stock.

On the following day, April 2, Hartley and Pickens argued their cases publicly as both testified before a congressional committee investigating corporate mergers. Hartley denounced the takeover activity in the oil industry, calling it a "speculative binge that must eventually collapse, leaving the wreckage of ruined companies, lost jobs, and reduced U.S. oil production."

The public animosity turned personal. Before their congressional testimony, Pickens and Hartley met in the hallway. Hartley refused to shake hands with Pickens, who later called Hartley "arrogant" before the committee.

"I decided he wasn't entitled to shake my hand," said Hartley.

"That's a strange way to treat your largest shareholder," Pickens retorted.

In criticizing Hartley's management, Pickens — during his testimony — asked why a Unocal corporate jet carried a piano for the personal use of the chairman. "Who paid for this?" Pickens asked — and quickly answered, "The shareholders."

Hartley explained that the piano, a small electronic model, had been a gift from the company pilots, who had bought it and installed it in the plane on their own time. It was meant to welcome Hartley back to work in 1976 after he recovered from open-heart surgery. Moreover, the piano had long since been removed. As Unocal's expanding interests had led to more overseas flights, the piano took up space needed for additional life-saving equipment.

"I had to decide which would be better," Hartley later said, "to have the life-saving equipment available after we hit the water or to play 'Nearer My God to Thee' on the way down."

Above: Security Pacific, with head-quarters in Los Angeles, had been Unocal's bank for 40 years. Unocal filed suit when company lawyers discovered that the bank had extended a line of credit to the Mesa group that appeared in the 13D filing concerning Unocal. Below: Unocal mounted a major effort on Capitol Hill to urge legislators to take action to make takeover attempts less attractive to raiders. Many measures became law—but too late to assist Unocal's defense in 1985.

Hartley was not the only Unocal presence in Washington, D.C. The company mounted a major political effort to get new regulations and legislation that would make hostile takeover attempts less attractive to raiders, but no actions were taken in time to address Unocal's immediate problem.

"The irony is that an awful lot of the measures we urged then — and didn't get — have since been put into effect," said John L. Rafuse, Unocal's manager of government relations, three years after the takeover attempt. "Tax law changes have been extensive, and the SEC now looks at a lot of takeover cases in a different way."

At Unocal's headquarters in downtown Los Angeles, antitakeover operations were centered in room 437, a windowless conference room that became known — not fondly — as the "dungeon." As the New York financial, legal, and proxy experts crowded in, the dungeon was the scene of constant briefings, meetings, strategy sessions, and conferences at all hours of the day and night, seven days a week.

As the tempo picked up, the pressure on the Corporate Communications Department grew intense. Not only was the department preparing for the upcoming annual meeting and trying to keep shareholders and employees informed, but the public relations staff also had to coordinate press conferences and field constant queries from a growing army of news media. Frequently, manager Barry Lane composed news releases before dawn in Los Angeles to hit the newswires by 6:30 A.M. — which corresponded with the opening of the New York Stock Exchange at 9:30 A.M.

Unocal's legal staff was also caught up in the frenzy to process and disseminate information as the takeover situation grew more complex. All documents prepared for the SEC — as well as all other company communications, including press releases, advertisements, shareholder letters, and proxy solicitations — had to be carefully reviewed to be sure they adhered strictly to SEC rules. Dennis P. Codon, assistant counsel assigned as liaison with the investment bankers, took on

Unocal Targets Mesa and Pickens In Antitrust Suit

By a WALL STREET JOURNAL Staff Reporter
LOS ANGELES

Unocal Board Rejects Mesa Takeover Bid

Pickens Group Says
It Ha
Up

By NAN
and DEE
Times St

Unocal
board of di
jected as
tender offe
Boone Pic
group.
    The decis
cial board n
cal said in a
statement.
offer, for 64
each, from M
Mesa Easter

Unocal Sues Pickens, Alleges Antitrust Violation

By Jim Bates, *Investor's Daily*
    Unocal Corp. yeste

nominate its own directors to fill the three seats on the board up for consideration this year.

Pickens tangles with target

First they squabbled about a piano. Then they squabbled about a handshake. Then they got down to business.

chairman wouldn't shake hands with me" before the hearing began.
    Hartley said the plane was 13 years old and worth less

money they bo
stock in target
    Hartley calle
other raider
nhas." The
nance them
of liquidator

Unocal's Fred Hartley to Boone Pickens: No greenmail, no leveraged buyouts, no stock buybacks. Get lost, buddy.

Pickens Opens Fight to Gain Control of Unocal

Group Offers $54 Each for 64 Million Shares of Stock; Hartley Vows to Keep Firm Independent

By DEBRA WHITEFIELD, *Times Staff Writer*

After weeks of verbal sparring, the opening round of what is expected to be a bruising corporate fight finally began Monday, with Texas oilman T. Boone Pickens delivering the first blow: an offer to buy control of the parent of Union Oil Co. of Californ
    Pickens a
    are

interest. The additional shares needed to take control will cost about $3.46 billion, an amount the New York investment banking firm of Drexel Burnham Lambert Inc. is now trying to raise on Pickens' behalf Mesa Petroleum is much sm   Unocal, with

Millions for defense, not one cent for tribute

Lawrence Minard

THE French statesman
d that Fred Hartley is up
t's T. Boone Pickens.
gone pretty nicely for
Time magazine cover.

visits. He is getting pretty good at the Robin Hood bit. Made him bold enough to move in on $11.5 billion (revenues) Unocal Corp., where his Mesa Partners II already has a 9 7 beachhead and nearly $500 left to the added responsibility of keeping the company in compliance with SEC rules.

On April 7, Easter Sunday, Lane received a call at home from a *New York Times* reporter. Looking for a quotable comment, the reporter told Lane that the next morning's paper would carry a Mesa "tombstone"—a wordy, legalistic advertisement announcing an offer to purchase shares of a company. Lane promptly notified the appropriate Unocal executives. On April 8, however, the early edition appeared without the ad. The Unocal team breathed more easily—but not for long.

Hartley heard the news on his car radio as he rode to work later that morning. The Pickens group had placed the tombstone in the newspaper's second edition, announcing a $3.46 billion bid to buy a controlling interest in Unocal. Mesa Partners II proposed a tender offer of $54 a share for 64 million shares, which would bring their total holdings to over 50 percent of the company. The balance of the stock would, as a result, be devalued, and shareholders would face the choice of holding it or exchanging it for paper backed by high-risk "junk" bonds.

Shortly thereafter, the Mesa group mailed out proxy materials asking Unocal shareholders to approve a 60-day delay of the annual meeting. Pickens wanted time to line up his own candidates for the three upcoming vacancies on the board of directors.

"Mesa was coming not to build, but to destroy," Hartley said. "They were out to loot and liquidate Unocal."

Even more shocking was the fact that, within a week, Pickens announced that the investment banking firm of Drexel Burnham Lambert had commitments for $3 billion from more than 130 investors to finance his campaign.

Now Unocal was engaged in two battles: a proxy fight and a hostile tender offer. Shaping a response to the tender offer took first priority because there was so little time.

In the dungeon, morning and afternoon conference calls helped keep all parties informed across the country. Brinegar and either Snyder or Codon were usually at the center of communications. Sometimes the phone conferences would last as long as an hour. Out of the brainstorming in the dungeon, the Unocal forces came up with a plan for counterattacking Mesa's tender offer: a self-tender to buy back Unocal stock.

Neal Schmale, director of budgets, planning, and economics from 1981 through 1985, helped develop Unocal's antitakeover strategy. In 1968, he joined the company as a drilling engineer. After completing a law degree in 1974, he moved to headquarters, working first in law, then in planning. He was promoted to vice president in 1986 and senior vice president, corporate development, in 1988. Below: The Mesa group's offer to Unocal shareholders included paper backed by high-risk junk bonds in a deal structured by Drexel Burnham Lambert. The firm's offices in Beverly Hills, California, were headquarters for the so-called junk bond king, Michael Milken. In 1990, Milken pleaded guilty to six felony counts involving securities fraud, and Drexel declared bankruptcy.

This chart details the return to an investor who purchased 100 shares of Unocal stock just before the takeover attempt and held them for five years. Adding up each year's revenue and then subtracting the purchase price yields a return of $3,211.

UNOCAL RETURN ON INVESTMENT
December 31, 1984 to December 31, 1989
Summary: Investment of $3,700 earned $3,211, a 25% compounded annual return over five years.

	STOCK PRICE $/SHARE	STOCK BUYBACK $/SHARE	DIVIDENDS $/SHARE	NUMBER OF SHARES	REVENUE TOTAL $
BUY 12/31/84	37.00			100	(3,700)
1985		29.25[1]	1.15[2]	61	2,995
1986			1.59	61	97
1987			1.00	61	61
1988			1.00	61	61
SELL 12/31/89	29.75		0.55	122[3]	3,697

(1) 39% of stock repurchased @ $75; equates to $29.25 per share, based on 100 shares
(2) Dividends paid on 61% of stock left after buyback   (3) 2:1 stock split in 1989

Said Schmale, "The thing I most vividly recall was sitting down in this fourth-floor conference room repeatedly going over scenarios with Goldman Sachs and Dillon Read — and who knows how many lawyers.

"It was constant strategizing," he continued. "What do we do? What do they do? How many shares do we buy back? What do we offer if we buy back so many shares? Then, how many shares do they have, and what is the stock likely to trade at, and what will their next move be? It wasn't chess, but it was some sort of game where we were always trying to look two moves ahead."

On April 14, Unocal's directors rejected Pickens' tender offer as "grossly inadequate." On April 16, the directors followed with the announcement of a conditional back-end tender offer designed to make certain that Unocal shareholders got full value for their stock if the Mesa group took control of the company.

The plan had several unique features. Unocal's repurchase of its stock would be conditional on Pickens' success in acquiring over 50 percent of Unocal shares. If Mesa II succeeded, Unocal would buy back the remaining shares at $72 per share, a figure recommended by Unocal's investment advisers. That was considerably higher than Pickens' tender offer of $54 — and would leave Unocal with so high a level of debt that the Mesa group, once in control, might have difficulty maintaining operations.

Unocal had intended the offer as a self-tender, but the company — under siege — was unable to borrow the necessary cash. So the self-tender became an exchange offer, with Unocal issuing its own secured notes — backed by the value of the company's assets — to shareholders in exchange for their stock.

The notes would be senior to debt that Pickens would incur. In other words, the Mesa partners, along with the financial backers who had lent them capital through junk bonds, would have to wait for their money until the senior debt had been satisfied.

Under the company's exchange offer, up to 87.2 million Unocal shares, or about 49 percent of the total, could be exchanged for a package of notes with a total face amount of $72 per share — if Mesa II were successful in its takeover attempt. Since then-current SEC rules specified that the time for self-tenders was shorter than for third-party tenders, the Unocal offer expired three days ahead of Pickens' offer — forcing stockholders to make an early decision.

Behind the scenes, however, Unocal's investment advisers argued forcefully that this offer was confusing and left Wall Street too much up in the air. "Within

Gary Sproule (right, on the trading floor of the New York Stock Exchange) was the company's executive representative in New York in 1985. As such, he developed close contacts with analysts and portfolio managers whose clients and firms held Unocal stock. When the time came, Sproule helped arrange meetings where Unocal executives could explain management's position on the takeover situation to major shareholders.

a week, our advisers made it clear that the arbitrageurs of Wall Street — who now owned a majority of our stock — weren't taking our conditional 'back-end tender' seriously," said Brinegar.

"We recognized that firm action was needed," he continued. "Consequently, after another long board meeting, we announced on April twenty-third that we would buy, on a pro rata basis, fifty million shares for seventy-two dollars a share, whether or not Pickens was successful." Unocal's offer amounted to a $3.6 billion swap of equity for debt, using senior secured notes.

Unocal reserved the right to exclude Mesa Partners II from its offer. The Mesa group promptly challenged the exclusion in a federal district court in Los Angeles and in a state chancery court in Delaware. Wall Street suddenly began to take Unocal's novel strategy seriously.

Putting together the exchange offer involved an enormous amount of legal paperwork, including detailed financial disclosures required by the SEC. It all had to be accomplished quickly and quietly to keep from revealing Unocal's strategy. Charles S. McDowell, assistant comptroller, was placed in charge of a team — with members from Unocal's law, accounting, finance, tax, and treasury groups — to put the offer together.

"We went underground," said McDowell. "We worked day and night at Pandick Press [a Los Angeles financial printer]. It was a very difficult time. We were doing everything we could to save the company." In one evening, McDowell counted close to 90 people working on Unocal's material within the confines of the printing plant. Some of them — including Brinegar, Schmale, Codon, and McDowell — stayed overnight.

"Confidentiality was absolutely paramount," said McDowell. "We knew that Pickens' people were trying to find out what we were doing. They were calling all the major printing plants in Los Angeles, trying to locate Unocal, and they called Pandick. But we had a security system and it worked very well. Most of the Pandick employees just didn't know who we were."

Meanwhile, the annual meeting scheduled for April 29 was shaping up as the most important in the company's history. During a rehearsal on April 26, however, word came that U.S. District Court Judge A. Wallace Tashima had ordered

TAKEOVER CHRONOLOGY

February 14	Mesa Partners II announces that it has purchased 7.3 percent of Unocal's common stock (13.8 million shares) "for investment purposes only."
February 22	The Mesa group makes additional purchases, increasing its stake in Unocal to 9.7 percent—more than 16.8 million shares.
February 25	Unocal directors adopt a bylaw requiring 30 days' notice of matters to be transacted at the annual meeting and amend an existing bylaw requiring 30 days' notice for nominations for the election of directors.
March 12	Unocal sues Security Pacific National Bank for breaches of contract and fiduciary duty in connection with Security's extension of a line of credit to the Mesa group.
March 21	The Mesa group sues Unocal for interference with its banking relationship with Security.
March 27	The Mesa group announces its purchase of another 6.7 million Unocal shares, increasing its stake to 13.6 percent of the company's stock.
March 28	Mesa says it may seek to control Unocal or force a restructuring of the company. First order of business: soliciting proxies to postpone the company's April 29 annual meeting for two months.
April 1	Unocal sues the Mesa group, alleging violations of federal securities laws in its purchase of Unocal common stock.
April 8	The Mesa group announces a $3.46 billion bid for a controlling interest in Unocal. If successful, the group's tender offer of $54 per share for 64 million shares would give it 50.1 percent of the company.
April 14	The Unocal board of directors unanimously rejects Mesa's offer as "grossly inadequate."
April 16	Unocal announces an exchange offer for up to 87.2 million shares of its common stock for a package of senior secured notes having an aggregate par value of $72 per share. The offer is conditioned upon completion of Mesa's 64-million-share offer.
April 19	Unocal announces that its executive committee will recommend the board approve formation of a master limited partnership to contain most of the assets of the company's Gulf Region oil and gas operations. The move is approved by the directors on April 30.
April 22	A Delaware state court rules that Unocal cannot block the Mesa group from making proposals at the annual meeting if it is adjourned for 60 days.
April 24	Unocal amends its exchange offer; the company will buy 50 million shares from non-Mesa shareholders whether or not the Mesa group's tender offer is successful.
April 26	A U.S. district court in Los Angeles orders Unocal to delay its annual meeting until May 13 so that both Unocal and the Mesa group can send corrected proxy materials to shareholders.
April 29	A Delaware chancery court judge grants a temporary restraining order prohibiting Unocal from excluding the Mesa group from the $72 exchange offer.
May 2	The Delaware Supreme Court delays an appeal of the Unocal case and returns it to chancery court, but notes that companies incorporated in Delaware "may deal selectively with their shareholders" under certain circumstances.
May 13	After Unocal's annual meeting, Pickens concedes that the Mesa group has probably lost its proxy fight to block election of three directors (including Hartley) and adjourn the meeting. In Delaware, the chancery court upholds its earlier ruling.
May 15	Two days of settlement talks between Unocal and Mesa representatives break off without result.
May 17	The Delaware Supreme Court reverses the chancery court ruling; Unocal may exclude the Mesa group from its $72 exchange offer.
May 18–20	Unocal and Mesa resume discussions and reach a settlement.
May 29	The proxy vote count is completed with Unocal management receiving overwhelming support from non-Mesa shareowners.
June 6	The count of common shares properly tendered for exchange is more than 151 million (86 percent of all shares outstanding). Unocal accepts about 59 million (39 percent of the shares tendered) for exchange.

the meeting postponed until May 13. The delay was intended to allow both sides time to correct "false and misleading" information in their printed proxy materials. In addition, the judge took Pickens to task for his stated intentions for Unocal and misrepresentations in Mesa's description of its financing.

For weeks Unocal had prepared for overflow crowds at the April 29 meeting. With the company auditorium clearly too small to hold the hundreds of share-holders expected to attend—let alone representatives of the electronic and print media—video monitors were set up in the cafeteria and in a covered parking area where overflow seating for shareholders had been erected. Facilities were also set up to broadcast the meeting to nine other company locations in California, Georgia, Illinois, and Texas.

To accommodate the press, a meeting room was equipped with a direct feed from a video camera in the auditorium. Television stations would be able to tape the proceedings or transmit them live.

With the meeting delayed, all the electronic equipment had to remain in place for two weeks. Employees and visitors to Unocal headquarters dodged the rivers of cable snaking from the auditorium to the cafeteria and the parking garage.

Judge Tashima's decision seemed, on the face of it, a minor victory for Pickens, and spirits sank at Unocal. "That was a heartbreaker of a day," Snyder recalled, "but in retrospect, it was probably good."

Said Brinegar: "As it turned out, those two extra weeks were a blessing, because they enabled us to focus a major effort on getting votes."

Ken Cory (top), California state controller, and Jesse Unruh (above), state treasurer, trustees of California state pension funds, supported the position of Unocal management during the take-over attempt. Unruh, who was influential with other industrial investors, pledged a million proxy votes to Unocal and carried the company's message to other fund managers.

The mood of Unocal's employees rose or fell with each tactical victory or perceived defeat. Employees, who by themselves constituted the second largest block of the company's shareholders, tended to feel uneasy about the takeover attempt. Most were as convinced as Hartley that if Pickens managed to seize control of the company, their jobs would be threatened by a selling off of assets. They pored over newspapers and the growing volume of Hartley's com-muniques. Many wrote postcards and letters to their congressmen asking that Pickens be stopped.

The proxy fight was in full swing. Shareholders, whose mailboxes were stuffed with proxy solicitations from both sides, could choose Pickens' slate of directors or Unocal's three incumbents, including Hartley.

Corporate secretary Bob Hedley took command of Unocal's proxy solicita-tion with the help of Artie Long and Dennis Codon. They set up phone banks in a seventh-floor conference room dubbed the "boiler room." More than 700 employees, all volunteers, called individual shareholders and urged them to vote against the Mesa proposals. Department managers were assigned to phone stock-holders who held 200 or more shares.

Senior managers—including Claude Brinegar, Phil Blamey, Ray Burke, Bill McConnor, and Dick Stegemeier—presented Unocal's case to its large institu-tional investors, such as mutual funds, pension plans, and insurance companies. As a group, these investors held 42 percent of Unocal's stock. Foreign investors were contacted by International Division management.

"Our message was simple," Brinegar said. "Unocal alive can do more for you than Pickens can with his vague, two-tier, front-end loaded, junk-bond, bust-up takeover plan."

Slowly, the votes started coming in, and the momentum appeared to go Unocal's way. On the last day of proxy solicitation, Hartley announced that he had brought a stockholder into the Unocal camp with 600,000 shares.

Perhaps the most significant proxy victory occurred when California state treasurer Jesse Unruh and state controller Ken Cory were invited to lunch at Unocal headquarters a few days before the annual meeting. Unruh controlled the

UNOCAL 76

DOING BUSINESS AS UNOCAL
By 1984, Union Oil Company of California was well established as an international company, but it was still doing business under a regional name. Company executives made plans to update the corporate image and adopt a new logo: Unocal 76. The new name received lots of exposure in the media in the first half of 1985, since it was hot news during the attempted takeover of Unocal. Unocal 76 signs first appeared on service stations in Los Angeles in the spring of 1985, in time to introduce the new look to shareholders attending the annual meeting at corporate headquarters in May. From Los Angeles, new signage spread rapidly in all directions across the country. Tank trucks — which serve as moving billboards for the company — were spiffed up with new Unocal 76 decals. New labels appeared on products from batteries to motor oil. The famous 76 symbol assured an easy transition from the consumer's point of view, reinforcing the message that the name change would not alter the high quality of 76 products and services. Robert R. Tompkins, then manager of graphic art production for marketing, noted: "The name Unocal may take a while to catch on, but the important thing is still that little circle with the 76. That's the real magic, that 76."

Top right: After an annual meeting rehearsal in the company auditorium, where he learned that the meeting would be postponed from April 29 until May 13, Hartley strode back to his office. His entourage included corporate communications director Karen Sikkema (right), in charge of producing the meeting, and government relations manager Jack Rafuse (behind Hartley).

California state pension fund, which held a substantial number of Unocal shares; he also wielded considerable clout as the head of the Council of Institutional Investors, which included the managers of other large funds around the nation. After talking to Hartley and Brinegar, Unruh not only pledged a million proxy votes to Unocal, he made calls to other managers to urge them to follow his lead.

On the legal front, the stacks of depositions grew with Hartley and Pickens each having to sit still for several. Snyder's legal attack was unrelenting and highly creative. By this time, there were lawyers, lawyers everywhere.

"At one time," said Snyder, "I was running fifteen law firms and two hundred lawyers." The largest group was from the Los Angeles firm of Gibson, Dunn and Crutcher, which at various times assigned more than a hundred attorneys to the Unocal cause. Later, when the dispute moved to a Delaware chancery court, George Bond, on hand to watch the action, was startled to see a lawyer in almost every seat in the courtroom, all representing Wall Street arbitrageurs.

Among the numerous actions Unocal took was an antitrust suit filed in Louisiana. It accused Mesa of participating in an unlawful conspiracy to restrain competition in domestic oil and gas exploration in the Gulf of Mexico. The suit claimed that Pickens' activity as a raider had resulted in heavy debt for several oil companies, thereby diverting funds that would have otherwise been risked in competitive offshore bids.

The suit was dropped after the eventual settlement, somewhat to the lingering disappointment of Unocal attorneys. A pro-Unocal decision could have resulted in heavy financial damage to Mesa.

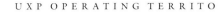

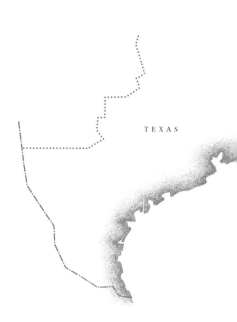

TEXAS

Another unusual suit, also eventually dropped, was brought by Mesa share-holders. It charged that Mesa, which had acquired so many shares of publicly traded companies for "investment purposes," really was an investment company but had failed to register as such under the Investment Company Act of 1940.

Unocal's executive committee announced on April 19 that it would recommend to the board the formation of a master limited partnership. The partnership would contain virtually all of the assets of Unocal Oil & Gas Division's Gulf Region. Units in the partnership would be offered to the public and distributed to shareholders. On April 30, the board approved the plan.

In May, as the takeover battle continued to rage, a massive effort was launched to produce a prospectus describing the new partnership — Union Exploration Partners, Limited (UXP). The financial, planning, and legal groups in Los Angeles and Houston coordinated their efforts. Oil & Gas Division comptroller Richard Goddard, Chuck McDowell, and others from Unocal headquarters took up temporary residence in Texas. More lawyers were summoned. Tom Stoy, Gulf Region vice president, reported in awe that at one time there were 19 lawyers crowded into his office.

Part of the task included a detailed inventory of Gulf Region assets. All the information had to be current for the prospectus and, subsequently, for the transfer of virtually everything — down to every lease, boat, and platform — to UXP. Several editions of the prospectus were issued, and Unocal finally received SEC approval in July. UXP came into existence August 1.

Meanwhile, in Los Angeles, the rescheduled annual meeting was finally convened at 10:00 A.M. on May 13. More than 1,700 people attended, including Boone

Pickens himself. At one point, he made a 15-minute statement, then answered questions from shareholders.

Brinegar noted that he appeared to be mortal after all: "He turned out to be an ordinary guy of ordinary size, not the financial superman portrayed on television talk shows or in the recent *Time* magazine cover story. He was capable of making ordinary statements — even dumb ones as, in fact, he did in answer to some of the questions from employees in the audience. He also looked to me like he could be beaten or, indeed, knew that he was likely to be beaten."

Although it would still be several days before all the proxy votes could be counted, Pickens conceded to the press after the meeting that the Mesa group had probably lost the vote to block the reelection of the three incumbent Unocal directors, along with the vote to delay the meeting for 60 days. It was the latest in a series of setbacks for Pickens. A week earlier, news reports had indicated that Mellon Bank had pulled out of the 12-bank consortium that helped finance Mesa II's attempted takeover of Unocal. Several other banks had pulled out earlier in the year.

During the annual meeting, disquieting news for Unocal arrived from the Delaware courtroom where Vice Chancellor Carolyn Berger ruled that the company could not exclude Mesa Partners II from its back-end exchange offer. Earlier, on April 29, Berger had also decided against Unocal, but hopes were revived three days later when the Delaware Supreme Court delayed an appeal of the lower court ruling and sent the case back to the chancery court for a rehearing.

Unocal's fate seemed to hang precariously on this single legal dispute, as the case once again returned to the Delaware Supreme Court on appeal. If Pickens could share in Unocal's exchange offer, he could profit by as much as $175 million just by selling back his Unocal stock.

Observers noted that both Hartley and Pickens appeared unusually subdued in their remarks about each other at the annual meeting. Unknown to the public, a mutual acquaintance from Texas had arranged a meeting between the two. On both sides, the pressure to settle was intense. Unocal faced an uncertain outcome in the Delaware court, and Mesa was spending $7.5 million every 45 days to hang on to its $3 billion financing.

The meeting was set for the morning after the annual meeting, but things

Left and above: Following the annual meeting on May 13, Fred Hartley (at podium) presided over a press conference. It drew some 50 reporters, photographers, and cameramen — but the big story still awaited a decision from the Delaware Supreme Court.

seemed to go wrong from the beginning. "We had sought a secret place and settled on a suite at the New Otani Hotel in downtown Los Angeles," Brinegar recalled. "The Unocal team sneaked in, one at a time, only to see Pickens and three of his associates arrive in a white stretch limousine, accompanied by two bodyguards!" Later, when the two parties departed, they took the precaution of riding down in separate elevators, which ended up arriving in the lobby simultaneously anyhow.

With the Delaware Supreme Court decision still pending, neither side was ready to make any serious concessions. A second meeting was held but ended when Pickens stood up, made a show of resetting his gold Rolex to Amarillo time, and announced he was going home. "I don't remember either side saying goodbye," said Brinegar.

On May 16, A. Gilchrist Sparks III, Unocal's Delaware lawyer, argued his appeal of the chancery court decision before Delaware Supreme Court Judge Andrew Moore II in Wilmington. The next morning, May 17, about 100 people returned to the courtroom to hear the decision. The courtroom doors were locked until Moore finished reading, which took 14 minutes.

Five minutes later, Sparks was back in his office. Shortly after 6:00 A.M. Pacific time, he called Snyder with the good news: Judge Moore had ruled that Unocal exercised valid business judgment when it defended itself against a "grossly inadequate and coercive two-tier, front-end loaded tender offer" by excluding Pickens and Mesa from its own $72-a-share offer.

"I found out yesterday that I am being promoted to general counsel," Snyder told Sparks, "and now you've just told me there will be a company for me to be a general counsel of."

Brinegar received a phone call about the same time as Snyder, this one from a New York banker. "Just coming over the ticker reflecting a nine A.M. Delaware court decision," Brinegar recalled, "were these wonderful words: 'Delaware Supreme Court rules in Unocal's favor.' It was clearly the start of a great day!"

Unocal had won. By the time Brinegar reached his office at 7:30 A.M., Goldman Sachs in New York had received a call from Pickens' lawyers asking to resume discussions. Pickens would have to settle for the best deal he could get. Unocal's executives, firmly in the driver's seat although aware of Pickens' power as a major company stockholder, were ready to talk.

"We met at one of our outside lawyers' offices in Los Angeles late on Saturday,

Below: The corporate seal carries the date of March 18, 1983, when Unocal Corporation was formed as a Delaware holding company. Union Oil Company of California, which became the corporation's operating subsidiary, began doing business as Unocal in 1985 — and gained rapid name acceptance thanks to headlines generated by the takeover fight.
Bottom: After the May settlement, Unocal's corporate secretary Bob Hedley (standing, left) and assistant secretary Jim Courtney (right) visited the proxy countinghouse. Excluding the Mesa shares, the ratio of shareowner support for the company's management was nearly three to one.

May eighteenth, and again on Sunday," Brinegar said. "By six A.M. on May twentieth, we had the final agreement ready for signing.

"Its terms were simple," he explained. "Mesa would be permitted to tender thirty percent of its stock at seventy-two dollars per share — rather than thirty-nine percent, as the other shareholders would. It would dispose of its remaining stock through a slow process, subject to our approval. All lawsuits [by and between Mesa and Unocal] would be dropped, and Mesa and Pickens would leave us alone until 2010!"

Snyder and Brinegar reviewed the terms with Hartley by phone. It was approved by the board of directors at a meeting that afternoon, signed by Hartley and, about an hour later, signed by Pickens via telecopier from Amarillo, Texas.

"We estimated that Pickens' pretax cash loss from this war was about $200 million — his first big defeat," Brinegar said. (Some time later, after the Mesa group sold its Unocal shares, Unocal's manager of economics Jack J. Laak estimated that Mesa realized an after-tax gain of $30 million, having used Unocal losses to offset gains from raids on Gulf and Phillips.)

Under the agreement, Unocal agreed to use its best efforts to maintain the level of dividends to stockholders and to distribute UXP units. Early in August, the first UXP units were issued to shareholders. Unocal was UXP's managing general partner and owned almost 97 percent of the units.

In addition, the settlement placed severe restrictions on what Mesa could do with its Unocal shares. Mesa and its chief financial backer, Drexel Burnham Lambert Inc., were effectively prevented from working together to gain control of Unocal for the next 25 years.

When the proxy votes were finally tallied, 87 percent of the total shares had been voted. Ninety million shares were voted against Pickens, and Unocal's management had been endorsed overwhelmingly.

It was a satisfying victory, but Unocal was suddenly in a much different financial position. The company had spent upward of $10 million in legal fees defending itself against Pickens, but that was scarcely a drop compared with its new obligations.

What the takeover attempt had done, as Hartley pointed out, was force Unocal to convert shareholder's equity into debt. The company now moved

THE SETTLEMENT
May 20, 1985

■ Unocal agreed to allow Mesa Partners II to participate in its $72 exchange offer. Ultimately, Unocal purchased some 32 percent of the 23.7 million shares held by the Mesa group as compared to 39 percent of the 127.3 million shares tendered by non-Mesa stockholders.

■ The Mesa group agreed to honor a "standstill" agreement concerning the Unocal shares it continued to hold.

■ The Mesa group agreed that it would not purchase any new Unocal shares for 25 years, and that it would cease all efforts to acquire control of Unocal or to influence its policies.

■ Drexel Burnham Lambert, the Mesa group's investment banker, agreed not to buy or finance the purchase of any Unocal shares for three years, except in the ordinary course of its brokerage activities.

■ Unocal agreed to use its best efforts in the judgment of the board to maintain the level of cash dividends to shareholders and to distribute units of Union Exploration Partners Limited as dividends to shareowners.

Top left: Dick Stegemeier was made Unocal's president and chief operating officer in December 1985, just before the collapse of world oil prices.

quickly to borrow $4.8 billion to refinance its senior notes, which carried high interest rates ranging up to 14 percent, and retire other debt obligations.

"With hindsight, our timing was ideal," said Unocal treasurer Edwin H. Powell. "It took us most of the summer to put the financing together. It closed in late October — before the big oil price drop in 1986."

"Had we tried to refinance six months later," said Neal Schmale in 1988, "we might still be saddled with high-interest debt."

The refinancing, one of the largest such programs in corporate history, involved several elements. Unocal borrowed $3.3 billion from a group of banks and $1.5 billion through a private placement primarily with institutional investors. On a single day, the company borrowed more than $4 billion.

"The result," noted Phil Blamey, "was a one-hundred-million-dollar-a-year reduction in the company's interest costs and an increase of about sixty million dollars in the overall debt."

Once the takeover fight had ended, many looked back on that short, intense period as the most exciting time of their professional careers. The teamwork and camaraderie involved in meeting Pickens' challenge had, if anything, left the company, its management, and employees closer knit in spirit and more determined to succeed.

Sometimes it seemed as if the takeover fight was the only thing happening; but, in fact, the company had steadily continued to produce and market petroleum products, chemicals, and metals. While Hartley and the takeover combat team had been at center stage for three months, the other senior executives had been overseeing Unocal's day-to-day operations.

"We were charged with running the company," said Dick Stegemeier. "You can't stop everything just because you're fighting a takeover. Ray Burke continued to run the oil, gas, and geothermal operations; Bill McConnor continued to run refining and marketing; Craig Henderson, the chemicals side. I continued to work on research, oil shale, strategic planning, and the budgeting process — because that had to keep going. Otherwise, the whole cash flow would have disappeared during this battle."

In the anticlimactic months following the foiled takeover, Hartley returned to more pleasant duties. In June, fresh from victory, he traveled to Thailand to participate in the dedication of three natural gas and condensate fields, Baanpot,

Above and right: A Buddhist monk, making a mark for prosperity, participated in the religious ceremony that helped mark the formal dedication of Unocal's Baanpot, Satun, and Platong natural gas fields in the Gulf of Thailand in June 1985. *Below right:* In October 1985, Unocal and Pacific Gas & Electric celebrated 25 years of power production at The Geysers. Unocal attendees included (from left): Joel Robinson, Santa Rosa district operations manager; Ray Burke, executive vice president; and Dr. Carel Otte, president of the Geothermal Division.

Satun, and Platong. Development of these fields more than doubled Unocal's productive capacity in Thailand.

Prime Minister Prem Tinsulanonda, who presided over the dedication ceremonies, noted: "The event we are celebrating today is an important milestone on Thailand's road to energy independence. In the years to come, natural gas will occupy center stage in supplying our nation's growing energy needs."

In October, Hartley participated in another energy milestone — the twenty-fifth anniversary of The Geysers geothermal project in Northern California. Pacific Gas & Electric Company had completed its first power plant at The Geysers in 1960.

After Unocal became involved as a steam producer in 1965, the company introduced drilling and production technology that quickened the project's development. In his remarks at the ceremony, Governor George Deukmejian called The Geysers "a very critical component of California's energy supply."

In December, the Unocal board of directors began the transition of corporate leadership to Richard J. Stegemeier, who was appointed president and chief

Late Sports

Los Angeles Times

Morning Final

Circulation: 1,076,466 Daily 1,346,343 Sunday   Tuesday, May 21, 1985   MF/110 Pages Copyright 1985 Times Mirror Co.   Daily 25¢

Unocal Defeats Takeover Bid

Private Firms

On Patrol:

Pickens May Lose Money on Attempt

By DEBRA WHITEFIELD
and NANCY RIVERA,
Times Staff Writers

operating officer. Hartley remained chairman and chief executive officer. Ray Burke and Claude Brinegar were each elevated to executive vice president. Phil Blamey retired, and in January, Brinegar took on the additional responsibility of chief financial officer.

Having survived one major threat to the company, however, Unocal management now faced another. One event soon overshadowed all others: the precipitous drop in the price of crude oil in early 1986.

As OPEC, and particularly Saudi Arabia, boosted production, a worldwide crude oil glut developed. From $27 a barrel in late 1985, the average price of crude plummeted to a low of $11 by July 1986 before it began to rise again. Some domestic crudes sold for less than $10 per barrel in July and August.

The number of drilling rigs in the field declined along with oil production as domestic costs exceeded prices and cheap foreign crude flooded the market. For oil service businesses it was a catastrophe; many went out of business. Oil-based local and regional economies, such as Houston's, were severely depressed.

For Unocal, the pinch was particularly severe. Although the company was intact at the end of 1985, it was quite different from what it had been a year earlier. Caught between payments on the company's enormous debt and falling oil revenues, Stegemeier and Hartley faced some difficult choices in a highly uncertain future.

Top: When the takeover fight hit the headlines in April, it was dubbed the "battle for Union Oil" (page 246). In just six weeks, the company was recognized as "Unocal"—removing the need for an advertising campaign. Left: Fred Hartley (with tie) led a group at the Los Angeles refinery in a round of "thumbs up" shortly after the victory. The other Unocal employees were (from left): Don Pierce, Dick Miller (then refinery manager), Jerry Johnson, Ambrose Russo, Bobby Deal, and Stanley Sutton.

Part 4

1986–1990

Challenge and Response

Bold Steps

Richard J. Stegemeier:

A NEW LEADER

When Richard Joseph Stegemeier was a college student in the late 1940s, he wanted a career that promised excitement. His first choice, metallurgy, soon paled by comparison to the oil business, and he changed his major to petroleum engineering.

"Exploration and production," he recalled, "seemed to be on the frontier of adventure — promising the unknown quantity of other countries."

Perhaps young Stegemeier had picked up a yearning for distant lands watching the boats on the Mississippi. He was born April 1, 1928, in Alton, Illinois, an industrial center on the river, and grew up in nearby Wood River, which, while small (only about 5,000 people), had two oil refineries.

The eldest of three sons, Dick spent his childhood in the shadow of the Depression. His machinist father managed to keep his job in a munitions factory, but at reduced wages.

"They were tough times, hard times," Stegemeier recalled, "but we were always a very close family."

Stegemeier's grandparents lived on their farm outside Wood River while Dick was growing up. When the United States entered World War II in 1941, all the young field hands enlisted. Dick, then 13, rode his bicycle 15 miles out to the farm every weekend to help out.

Dick's parents were determined their sons would be well educated. The boys were good students, and Dick earned straight A's in high school. He was also captain of the baseball team, class president, and valedictorian.

In 1946, he enrolled at the Missouri School of Mines (later part of the University of Missouri at Rolla). Dick threw himself into his studies, carrying a full schedule of classes.

His first petroleum job was for The Texas Company (Texaco), working as a roustabout in the fields near Okemah, Oklahoma, in the summer of 1949. In a letter to his Uncle Ed, he described the work:

"Foremost among the [jobs I enjoy] is being derrick man....I climb up to the top of these 87-foot derricks when we are replacing a pump. Besides being a pretty responsible job, it is equally dangerous....You have to hang on with one hand and foot and reach out into the center of the derrick."

In Okemah, Dick met Marjorie Spess. Her sister, married to one of Dick's coworkers, suggested that Marge might want to come down from Tulsa to meet Dick. In the fall, when he returned to finish his degree at Rolla, they kept up a correspondence.

After Rolla, Stegemeier earned his master's degree at Texas A&M on a fellowship from the Tennessee Gas Transmission Company. His thesis, a study of high-pressure natural gas flow in reservoirs, required that he build his own lab equipment — and it was often difficult and dirty work. The project took longer than he expected, which explains how Union Oil's legendary recruiter, J.P. Rockfellow, found him in school that summer of 1951.

But for Rockfellow's persistence, Stegemeier might have spent his career at another oil company. He had already accepted a job. When Rockfellow arrived looking for students to interview, Dick made it clear that he would interrupt his lab work only as a favor to his faculty adviser, Dr. Harvey Kennedy — and that he wouldn't change out of his lab clothes.

"So I went in, dirty and disheveled," Stegemeier recounted. "Mr. Rockfellow had an outstanding ability to relate to

Clockwise from top left: Dick Stegemeier (center, front) as captain of a league-leading basketball team at the research center in 1954; reviewing expansion plans at the research labs in 1980; in the headlines as CEO in 1990; with a guest at 100th annual meeting; with wife, Mar decorating a sweepstakes-winning Rose Parade float in 1988; as campaign chai* for United Way's Los Angeles region, k* off a fund-raising street fair at Unocal *ter in 1989; with a student at the John* Clinic for the hearing impaired.

people. He couldn't care less that my shirt was torn. He made me feel like he had only one job to do all year long and that was to hire me."

Rockfellow showed Stegemeier pictures of Union's new research center, surrounded by orange groves in California, and Dick—though still feeling obligated to the other company—began to weaken. Rockfellow assured him that a young man in his situation could change his mind.

The next day, Stegemeier decided to join Union as a research engineer. He went on payroll November 1, 1951. The following February, he and Marge were married and settled in Fullerton, not far from the Brea labs.

Stegemeier divided his time between the laboratory and the field for the Natural Gas Department, to which he was assigned full-time in 1961. In 1964, he was sent to Japan to represent Union in a proposed project to liquefy natural gas. He gained valuable international experience, although the company later decided against the project. He and Marge also got their first taste of living abroad, moving to Tokyo with their two sons and two daughters, who ranged in age from three months to ten years.

In 1966, the family returned to California, but only 18 months later they began an overseas odyssey that lasted 10 years. They first moved to Australia, where Dick became part of the team that negotiated Union's first production-sharing contracts with Indonesia. The Stegemeiers lived in Sydney until 1970, when Dick was promoted to vice president and transferred to Singapore.

Dick traveled frequently to Indonesia. While spending some weeks in the steamy jungles of Sumatra, he gave up shaving. Soon, the company's chairman, Fred Hartley—who didn't appreciate beards—paid a visit.

"I had to think of something clever very quickly," Stegemeier explained. "So I said I'd decided to grow a beard for good luck until we made a discov-

ery in Indonesia. Fred said, 'Don't shave it off until you do!'"

When the Attaka field was discovered in 1970, Stegemeier had more than one reason to celebrate. Not only was the oil high-quality crude, but Hartley wired him: "Congratulations. You may now shave off your beard."

To develop Attaka, Union built its own settlement in Balikpapan. Stegemeier was in charge as general manager and moved his wife and daughters there (the boys were in college in the States) in July 1973. With every move, Marge recalled, there was concern about new languages and customs. "But," she said, "you just tell yourself 'I'll handle that—and then I'll have some fun!'"

In remote Balikpapan, the Stegemeier home frequently doubled as an inn. Half the time, the family had house guests—Union people, suppliers, and traveling dignitaries.

"We didn't have television," Stegemeier recalled, "so we spent our time in conversation, playing cards, or listening to music. I wouldn't trade that time for anything."

The family moved back to Singapore in 1975. Dick, as resident manager, traveled widely in Southeast Asia. "That was the kind of adventure," he said, referring to all his years overseas, "people pay a fortune for. And here I was, being paid to experience it."

In 1977, the Stegemeiers returned to the United States, where Dick soon headed up Union's research. In 1980, he was elected senior vice president, corporate development.

Placing a high priority on community service, Stegemeier gave generously of his time to many organizations, including Junior Achievement, the YMCA, and United Way. He also became active on the boards of numerous business and educational institutions.

When Dick was named Unocal's CEO in 1988 and chairman in 1989, the Stegemeiers were once again travelers, visiting Unocal installations around the world. For them, it was part of a continuing grand adventure.

14 Challenge and Response

In early 1986, new Unocal president and chief operating officer Dick Stegemeier faced a challenging business environment as world oil prices collapsed. Opposite: Platform Irene, whose installation offshore California's Point Pedernales was completed in late 1985, came on stream in 1986 and reached production of 20,000 barrels per day in 1987.

I t felt like a life or death situation," said Dick Stegemeier, Unocal's president for scarcely a month when the bottom fell out of oil prices in early 1986. "The company was over six billion dollars in debt, and the oil price was about to be cut by half. We tightened up the screws on everything we did. We had to survive—by reducing our capital expenditures, cutting our operating costs, and trying to maximize revenues at a time when prices—of both natural gas and crude oil—were falling."

Unocal's earnings for 1985 were $325 million, less than half the 1984 earnings of $700 million. Antitakeover expenses and the cost of servicing the debt took a toll, as did a partial write-down (reduction in recorded value) of the shale project amounting to $250 million ($125 million after taxes). A cut in capital expenditures from $2.1 billion in 1984 to $1.85 billion in 1985, combined with cash on hand, allowed the company to reduce its debt some $200 million by January 1986.

As it became apparent that oil prices were dropping rapidly and that no one could predict the bottom, Unocal took steps to revise its spending plan for 1986. The capital budget had been set at $1.5 billion, based on an oil price of $24.50 per barrel. By February, oil prices had dropped well below $20 per barrel, and Unocal's executive committee cut the capital budget to $1.2 billion. "Our revenue stream was falling," Stegemeier explained, "and we had this enormous debt that had to be serviced."

Claude Brinegar, executive vice president, recalled: "Both 1985 and 1986 were extraordinarily tumultuous years. I know of no other major corporation that suffered two such body blows [the takeover attempt and the oil price drop] in succession."

Brinegar worked closely with Unocal's treasurer, Ed Powell, to manage the debt. The $3.3 billion in bank loans, which had helped retire the company's senior notes in late 1985 prior to the oil price drop, was short-term, floating-rate money. The loans carried what Brinegar characterized as an "enormous, heart-stopping balloon payment" due in 1992. And, of course, floating interest rates made the company subject to rate increases.

Unocal's money managers focused on refinancing to stretch out the maturity of the company's loans and to lock in advantageous fixed rates of interest. "Year by year, month by month, we've leveled off that huge spike of debt we had maturing in 1992," Powell noted.

"Ours was a pretty quiet existence when we didn't have very much debt," he stated in late 1988. "We did maybe one financing every two or three years. Since

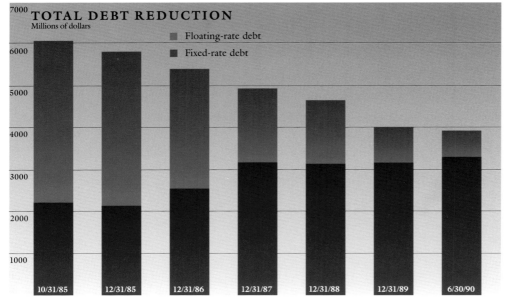

TOTAL DEBT REDUCTION
Millions of dollars

■ Floating-rate debt

■ Fixed-rate debt

7000 · 6000 · 5000 · 4000 · 3000 · 2000 · 1000

10/31/85   12/31/85   12/31/86   12/31/87   12/31/88   12/31/89   6/30/90

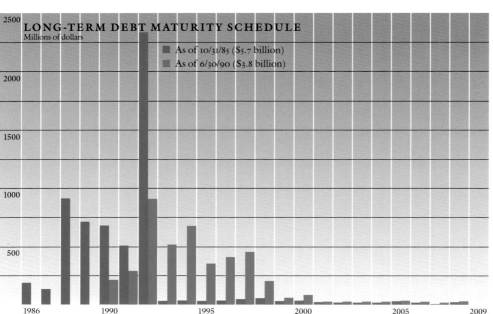

LONG-TERM DEBT MATURITY SCHEDULE
Millions of dollars

■ As of 10/31/85 ($5.7 billion)

■ As of 6/30/90 ($3.8 billion)

2500 · 2000 · 1500 · 1000 · 500

1986   1990   1995   2000   2005   2009

1985, we've been doing several a year. We're utilizing every tool we can find to
reduce the overall costs of the debt."

In April 1986, Fred Hartley reported to shareholders that the company had
paid down an additional $150 million on the debt just since January. He also
noted the company's success in converting $660 million of the floating-rate bank
debt to long-term, fixed-rate obligations. "Today, we have achieved a balance of
approximately fifty percent floating-rate and fifty percent fixed-rate," he said.

By the end of 1987, Unocal had reduced its total debt from the October 1985
peak of $6.1 billion to just under $5 billion. Debt repayment in 1987 totaled $452
million, slightly more than the 1986 reduction of $436 million. The proportion of
floating-rate to fixed-rate debt was further reduced, from 48 percent to 33 percent
of total long-term debt.

Gary W. Sproule, appointed assistant treasurer in April 1986, observed: "Our
luck has been pretty good. We've been able to call the cycles right and lock in
interest rates at the low point." Indeed, in a speech in early 1988, Brinegar suggested that Unocal's Treasury Department—particularly Powell and Sproule—
should get a "Nobel Prize for timing."

Because Unocal's debt-to-equity ratio soared from 18 percent to 78 percent
as a result of the takeover settlement, the company's credit rating dropped sharply.

Fortunately, the drop stopped just above junk-bond level, barely avoiding the extreme limitations on financial flexibility that such a rating would entail, not to mention the uncomfortable irony for a company whose chief spokesman so decried junk bonds.

In June 1985, in testimony before the securities subcommittee of the Senate Banking Committee, Fred Hartley said: "The issue here isn't mergers, it is raids. In particular, I oppose hostile takeovers in which corporate raiders use junk financing to convert a large part of a company's equity into debt, milk its assets to repay the debt, and ultimately destroy or nearly destroy the company for their personal gains."

Earlier, Hartley had denounced the creation of "a destructive new weapon ...added to the corporate raiders' arsenal — junk-bond financing. These high-risk, low-rated bonds have supported a number of stock raids and takeover attempts. Now corporate raiders can borrow virtually one hundred percent of the cost of an acquisition—with little or no security—on the promise they will bust up the target company to repay the loan. This is...short-term thinking gone wild."

The skill with which Ed Powell and his financial team managed the debt became a key factor in rebuilding Unocal's credit rating. Powell, in turn, relied heavily on the support of Neal Schmale, who became vice president, budgets, planning, and economics in early 1986, and Chuck McDowell, promoted to company comptroller as of July 1986.

"My role was to monitor the budgets," recalled Schmale. His group moved quickly to set up a communications network to closely track the flow of funds in and out of the company. It was vital that deviations from budget plans be reported in a matter of days rather than weeks, so that budget controls could be maintained and the company's cash flow could be put to optimal use—both in operations and in managing the debt.

The information network also proved critical to meet the reporting requirements of certain debt covenants. Unocal's lenders, and in some cases the Securities and Exchange Commission, had to be informed of developments affecting the company's financial health.

"I was responsible for making sure that everything we were doing made financial sense," said McDowell, "and that we could implement all of our planning strategies." One of the comptroller's key functions was to work with Unocal's Tax Department to ensure that no tax losses were overlooked and that returns were filed early. Tax refunds in 1986 and 1987 totaled about half a billion dollars, money sorely needed to help pay down the debt.

By late 1987, Unocal had lowered its debt-to-equity ratio from 78 percent to 72 percent. Four credit-rating agencies upgraded Unocal, basing their decisions on such factors as the company's improving balance sheet and financial flexibility, debt reduction without the sale of core assets, and the operating strength of up-stream and downstream businesses. The agencies also noted that Unocal's capital-spending program was funded at high enough levels to preserve the company's resource base. "We made extraordinary progress," said Brinegar, "helped along by the total company adjustment to the situation."

The adjustment included acknowledgment of some very harsh realities. Early in 1986, the company considered an enhanced retirement program. Since dropping oil prices curtailed operations, it made sense to reduce the workforce. Joe Byrne, vice president, human resources, had been quietly studying such plans since the threat of takeover the year before; so he was able to put a plan together quickly — within ten days of Dick Stegemeier's request.

Unocal's Voluntary Retirement Incentive Program — announced on March 31 and available to employees who turned 55 years of age as of June 30 — added three years to eligible employees' ages and three years to their company service records for purposes of calculating the retirement benefit. (Certain groups, including senior management and employees represented by collective bargaining agents, were excluded or offered limited participation.) During the two-month election period, from April 15 through June 16, more than 1,000 Unocal employees decided to retire, representing a 5 percent cut in the workforce. While the company lost years of invaluable experience, it also benefited.

Below: In 1986, more than 1,000 employees enrolled in the company's voluntary early retirement program. As a group, they represented 32,000 years of service to the company. All around the country, their coworkers honored them. At Unocal Center, five after-work parties hosted by senior management were held the week of June 23, with white carnations and orchids denoting the retirees.

EXPO 86

Expo 86 in Vancouver, British Columbia, turned out to be one of the largest world trade and technology fairs ever held in North America. With 54 nations represented—along with some 30 major corporations—the fair, held May through October 1986, showcased international achievements in transportation and communications technology—including the actual 5-ton command module of the *Apollo 14* space mission. Unocal's Fred L. Hartley represented the United States as ambassador to Expo 86 and commissioner general to the U.S. Pavilion. At dedication ceremonies, he noted that it was a homecoming for him. "After all," he said, "I was born only about a mile from here." Behind the scenes, Hartley proved instrumental in helping to assure the success of the $3.5 million California Pavilion. Through his efforts, more than 100 businesses contributed to the $1 million fund required to qualify the project for matching state money. "We had to convince people that Expo 86 was going to be first class," Hartley said, "and that there was a real need for California to participate, since the state is one of Canada's biggest trading partners." Unocal cosponsored an exhibit with Pacific Gas & Electric Company. The multimedia presentation told the story of The Geysers geothermal project in California, tracking steam energy from its underground origins through development and production. The city of San Francisco, which uses electricity produced at The Geysers, was represented in the exhibit by a scale-model street scene with working streetlamps and cable cars.

"The retirement program created some excitement in the company in terms of younger people moving into jobs with greater responsibility," said John Imle, then president of the International Division. "Many of them began succeeding in their new assignments faster than anyone could have expected. The bottom line has been that a leaner workforce has done an outstanding job of keeping us profitable and competitive. I can't say enough about the high degree of dedication our employees at all levels have demonstrated."

Also in 1986, the company instituted freezes on salaries and hiring. Through attrition, and the shutdown of the molybdenum mine in New Mexico early in the year, the company reduced the workforce by another 5 percent by year end.

"These were very, very painful things to do," Stegemeier emphasized, "but it was a question of survival. We could not run the risk of going into default on some of our debt. We let the employees know what was happening, and they backed us one hundred percent."

During those difficult years, Unocal maintained its reserve position and levels of production on everything from crude oil to chemicals. "By the end of 1986, we were healthier than we were at the start of the year," Stegemeier noted. "Fortunately, in 1986, even though oil and gas prices were down, refining profitability was up—so that helped carry the day for us. And at the same time, our operations in Thailand strengthened quite a bit."

In 1986, refiners paid an average of $14.50 per barrel of crude oil, compared with $27 during 1985. The price rose somewhat in 1987, averaging $18. "Our earnings were about the same in 1986 and 1987," said Stegemeier, "about one hundred eighty million dollars each year. But the roles were reversed. We didn't make much profit on the refining side in 1987, but we made more on the oil and gas side."

During this critical period for the U.S. oil industry, Fred Hartley focused much of his attention on national energy policy. One possible response to OPEC's price cuts was for the United States government to impose a tax on imported oil, thus shoring up domestic prices. Hartley proposed a flexible fee that would rise and fall as necessary to keep domestic prices on a level of about $25 per barrel. In speeches, articles, and testimony before Congress, he hammered home the point that America's strategic position in the world petroleum market was being badly damaged by cheap oil.

In a *New York Times* editorial, Hartley stated: "Some consumers and policymakers oppose an oil import fee, believing it would interfere with the free market and unfairly penalize certain sectors of the economy. But oil is a strategic commodity necessary to national security. Without it, we cannot defend ourselves."

He warned that low oil prices would boost demand even as it slashed domestic production. "At thirteen dollars and fifty cents," he noted early in 1986, "most domestic enhanced oil recovery [EOR] production stops, as do all such future projects. This is a major loss."

EOR production then averaged 650,000 barrels per day. Before the price drop, it was projected that EOR would account for 25 percent of the production from reserve replacement during the last 15 years of the century.

Ultimately, the oil import fee proposal received little sympathy within many sectors of the industry; executives, recalling the heavy-handed role government had played in oil pricing during the 1970s, were reluctant to invite anything that resembled government participation. While some support for an import fee existed in the Reagan administration and Congress, political considerations proved overwhelming. Consumers welcomed low prices, discounting the possible long-term consequences.

The drop in oil prices triggered Unocal's partial write-down of its oil shale project for 1985, as it became obvious that the high oil prices of the early 1980s

HIGHEST HONORS
In the spring of 1988, Dr. Carel
Otte became the third Unocal
engineer to receive one of the
profession's highest honors:
membership in the National
Academy of Engineering (NAE).
He joined an elite organization
of about 1,400 engineers that was
established in 1964. Unocal's
Fred L. Hartley had become
a member in 1980; and L. Wally
Holm, in 1986. Potential academy members are voted in by
their peers on the basis of their
contributions to engineering
theory and practice, or their
accomplishments in new fields
of technology. Hartley, as chairman and president of Unocal,
was honored for the development of oil shale and geothermal
steam and fluids as alternative
energy resources; Dr. Otte, for
his pioneering work in the development of geothermal energy.
Unocal was the first to successfully harness geothermal energy
for large-scale, commercial use.
Holm, cited for his lifetime
work on enhanced oil recovery
techniques to recover otherwise
unproducible oil, pioneered the
use of carbon dioxide injection
to prolong oil-field production.
He also developed Uniflood, a
unique surfactant process that
"scrubs" additional oil from reservoirs. NAE membership is
not just an honorary position;
academy engineers are often
called upon to provide technical
advice to U.S. policymakers.
NAE studies and assessments
of technological events and
issues offer both the executive
and legislative branches of the
U.S. government vital background information.

that had justified shale oil production at more than $40 per barrel would not soon
return. Although the technology for processing oil from shale continued to hold
promise, the project could move ahead only with the help of government price
supports administered through the U.S. Synthetic Fuels Corporation (SFC).

The SFC, controversial almost from the beginning, held its first directors'
meeting in October 1980. Ronald Reagan, who defeated Jimmy Carter in the
presidential race in November 1980, stood opposed on principle to providing
government subsidies to support private sector enterprises. His transition team
recommended the SFC's dissolution in January 1981.

As world oil supplies increased in the early 1980s, alternative fuels lost their
appeal in the United States. Legislative actions reduced the SFC's funding several
times. In October 1985, Unocal received a second SFC award, which proved to be
the agency's final award for alternative energy development. It totaled $500 mil-
lion in price and loan guarantees for Unocal's installation of new technology to
improve the efficiency of its shale-processing facility.

Although the SFC was dissolved in December 1985, the 1980 award of $400
million—which Unocal had negotiated with the Department of Energy before
SFC's formation and which was earmarked for price supports—remained available. Senator Howard Metzenbaum of Ohio, however, challenged the 1985 award
in a lawsuit that never went to trial. In mid-1987, Unocal announced that it would
not use the funds, since the capital costs of the proposed installation were higher
than anticipated. By that time, Unocal's plant produced 5,000 barrels of shale
oil per day, about half its design capacity.

*Top left: The retort at Unocal's
oil shale project in Colorado
operated at half capacity—about
5,000 barrels per day—by 1986.
Start-up took 34 months, an
average time for a solids processing plant, according to one study.*

Above: Tom Sleeman was appointed president of the Unocal Chemicals Division in April 1986. *Below:* An Idaho potato field is sprayed with Enquik, a desiccant that dries out the potato vines and makes harvesting easier. Enquik, which also acts as a weed killer, decomposes into naturally occurring soil nutrients. The product was first marketed in 1988. In the 1970s, Unocal had begun development of a variety of useful agricultural chemicals that would not leave harmful residues in the environment.

"It was a difficult period for the shale project," said Cloyd Reeg, then president of the Science & Technology Division, who had assumed additional responsibility as president of Energy Mining when John Hopkins retired in January 1986. "But," Reeg continued, "we achieved sufficient production of shale oil by July of 1986 to ship our first synthetic crude oil [in December] to the Chicago refinery. By then, we were the only company still working on a commercial-scale facility to develop new technology."

The long start-up time was not unusual. "Solids processing is just not at the same level of development as fluids processing," noted Allen C. Randle, vice president of the Energy Mining Division. A study by the RAND Corporation, comparing data from about 50 solids processing plants, reported an average start-up time of 33 months, compared with the Parachute Creek facility's 34 months.

During the first quarter of 1988, the company wrote down its remaining investment in the shale facility—$350 million pretax. Fred Hartley, an unflagging champion of the Parachute Creek project, explained: "I would like to stress that the write-down...does not mean we have given up on oil shale. Rather, the likely level of crude oil prices makes it increasingly improbable that we will generate enough cash flow to recover the original plant investment."

Hartley's commitment to the development of oil shale remained consistent with the view of energy development he had long espoused for Unocal. In November 1987, in a letter to employees, he wrote: "In my view, America has become a shortsighted society, committed to making the quick buck at the expense of innovative, long-term projects. At Unocal, we have resisted this kind of thinking, despite the hostile takeover attempt in 1985 and the oil price collapse of 1986. Unocal has been in business for nearly a century. Year after year, we reinvest a significant share of our earnings in an ongoing research and development program that has led to a series of innovative products and processes."

Indeed, even in 1985, behind all the sound and fury of the takeover struggle, Unocal inventors filed a record 105 patent applications. Of the 69 granted (the most for Unocal since 1972), 15 dealt with refining catalysts and processes; 10 were for shale-retorting processes or shale-oil refining technology; others involved fertilizers and herbicides, geothermal resources, oil production, lubricant and gasoline additives, needle coke production, carbon products, solar technology, and animal feed supplements. In 1989, a new record was set when 75 of 108 patent applications were approved. From 1985 through 1989, Unocal achieved record high royalties for the use of its technology in hundreds of facilities around the

world. The Unicracking process, for example, accounted for more than 60 percent of the world's licensed hydrocracking technology.

Research has played a key role in Unocal's expansion of its specialty chemical products. "Our historic businesses are nitrogen fertilizers and related products, petroleum coke, and solvents," said Tom Sleeman, who became president of the Chemicals Division in April 1986 after Craig Henderson's retirement. "We've been in these businesses for a long time. They're commodity-type businesses — big but not growing very fast.

"So, for long-term growth prospects," Sleeman continued, "we're emphasizing specialty products such as lanthanides, polymers, Poco graphite products, plant-protection chemicals, and Unipure. All of these are very research-oriented."

In 1985, the Petrochemical Group of the Chemicals Division began full-scale marketing of its new Unipure technology, a patented procedure for removing heavy metals from industrial wastewater. Sales of the technology doubled each year in the first three years after its introduction.

The development of Unipure provided a good example of the entrepreneurial spirit that can arise within a corporation where research and development expertise is available to the operating groups. Early in the 1980s, sales of ammonia to industrial customers in California began to drop because the ammonia (used to neutralize acidic wastewater) interfered with the removal of toxic heavy metals from plant effluents. Unocal Chemicals' Nitrogen Group brought the problem to the attention of the Science & Technology Division. Dr. Douglas Walker developed a wastewater treatment system that proved more versatile and cost efficient than conventional methods. Since the system relied on chemistry, manufacturers would not have to make expensive investments in new equipment.

The process proved effective in its first demonstration at a small plant in Los Angeles, and that's when Nick Lynam, senior vice president, Petrochemical Group, became aware of it. "I spent two days with Doug at the metal-plating plant," Lynam said, "and another half-day in the laboratories....I convinced myself there was a business opportunity."

Below left: By May 1988, the cogeneration plant at the Los Angeles refinery was in full operation, able to produce 44 megawatts of electricity and 300,000 pounds of steam per hour. The refinery produces more electricity than it can use, exporting the surplus to the Los Angeles Department of Water and Power. Unocal receives credit that can be redeemed by other company facilities in the area. Below: Roger Beach was appointed president of the Refining & Marketing Division in 1986.

OUT IN FRONT

For nearly 80 years, Unocal products or their predecessors have demonstrated superiority on the auto industry's most rugged and demanding proving grounds — the nation's automotive race tracks. In 1965, through its merger with The Pure Oil Company, Union Oil became involved with the National Association for Stock Car Auto Racing. Pure's tradition in stock car racing dated back to 1951, when the company supplied gasoline for a Pure dealer, Marshall Teague, who drove a Hudson Hornet in a 500-mile Labor Day race at Darlington, South Carolina. In 1958, Pure was given the option to be the official fuel supplier at any NASCAR race. In 1959, NASCAR inaugurated annual performance trials, which provided the first public comparison of new car makes and models. In 1968, Union received NASCAR's Industrial Award of Excellence for its sponsorship of the trials. The award recognized the company's outstanding contribution to motor sports and the motoring public. All NASCAR Winston Cup competitors must use Unocal 76 gasoline. Many also rely on 76 motor oils, gear lubes, and greases. In 1988, a new Unocal unleaded racing fuel was used for the first time in a NASCAR race. Conceived in 1947 at a small meeting of race promoters in Daytona Beach, Florida, NASCAR has become the premier organization in automobile racing, sanctioning more races on U.S. tracks than any similar group.

Top right: A superfacility in San Marino, California, offers full-serve and self-serve options, and Protech maintenance and repair.

In turn, Lynam and Craig Henderson convinced Unocal's executive committee to let them form a new business group. "It's a relatively small business experiencing some very nice growth rates," Lynam said, "but it's the foundation for what I think is going to be a significant business for Unocal."

Unipure was developed as a response to concerns about finding economic and effective methods to reduce industrial pollution. By the end of the decade, Science & Technology had produced or was working on several other products and processes to address a growing body of environmental and health concerns and regulations.

One long-standing health concern was the effect of lead in the atmosphere. In 1970, Unocal had been one of the first companies to sell low-lead gasoline as its regular grade to help reduce the lead content in automobile emissions. Given the advent of catalytic converters (requiring unleaded fuel) on automobile exhausts in the mid-1970s, the market for leaded fuel had declined. Even so, in March 1985, the United States Environmental Protection Agency (EPA) moved to hasten the reduction of lead in the atmosphere by establishing a lead phasedown schedule for refiners that required a 90 percent reduction by January 1986.

At the time, Unocal still sold leaded premium gasoline in the West to serve those customers whose cars required it — but to a shrinking market. In 1986, Unocal became the first oil company to sell only unleaded gasoline in the West, six years before proposed legislation would ban lead. The company introduced a new Super 76 Unleaded Premium with a 91-octane rating (92 in California). At the same time, to accommodate its leaded-fuel customers, the company introduced Valve Saver, a new product designed as a lead-substitute additive. Valve Saver, developed to lubricate the less durable valve seats in engines designed to run on leaded fuel, helped prevent valve-seat wear under severe driving conditions.

Gearing up to meet the increased demand for high-octane unleaded fuel, Unocal's refining system began construction of two 7,400-barrel-per-day isomerization units, one at San Francisco and one at Chicago. They came on stream in 1987 and 1988, respectively.

Unocal's Refining & Marketing Division underwent a major restructuring in 1986, led by Roger Beach, who became division president following Bill McConnor's retirement in April. Since the merger with The Pure Oil Company in 1965, refining and marketing activities had been divided into eastern and western regional operations. After 20 years, distance was less of an issue since communication systems had become highly sophisticated.

VAN: A SUPERGIANT
In March 1986, Unocal's Van field in East Texas produced its 500-millionth barrel of crude oil, putting the field in the ranks of "supergiants" in the United States. The field, discovered in 1929 by The Pure Oil Company, became part of Union Oil in 1965. Pure leased 17,000 acres of land in East Texas in 1927 and struck oil in W.T. Jarman's pasture at a depth of 2,710 feet on October 14, 1929. The widowed Mrs. Jarman decided to use part of her share in the profits to buy a new set of teeth. Van, meanwhile, became a boomtown almost overnight; the population soared from 200 to 2,000. The chaotic overdrilling that often followed such a discovery was avoided at Van. Pure owned some 80 percent of the acreage and reached a development agreement — known as the Van Joint Account — with the other companies concerned. Signed in November 1929, it was the first unitization agreement for development of a large, privately owned oil field. As such, the agreement provided the industry model for orderly and efficient oil production. Before unitized development, oil finders often pumped oil out of the ground so fast that natural reservoir pressures depleted quickly and production played out, leaving as much as 90 percent of the oil still in the ground. The Van field's production peaked at more than 46,000 barrels of oil per day in 1972. That rate diminished over time to less than 5,000 barrels per day, but drilling in the mid-1980s doubled the field's daily production to more than 9,000 barrels per day. In 1986, the Jarman No. 1 discovery well — still a producing well — was dedicated as a state historic site.

"I wanted to reduce the redundancy inherent in having two separate organizations," Beach said. "And more important, I wanted everyone to work as a team. So we reorganized by function instead of by geography."

The restructuring resulted in a single organization with overall national responsibilities for refining, auto/truckstops, crude supply and transportation, and administration. Marketing, however, remained divided to better serve the unique characteristics of the company's operations in the East and West.

With the oil price drop in 1986, consumption rose. Unocal's refineries operated at 85 percent of capacity in 1986 and 87 percent in 1987, compared with an average of 75 percent during the early 1980s. Efficiency continued to improve, too. In 1987, a new 49-megawatt cogeneration plant at the San Francisco refinery began to produce power and steam, which led to a substantial reduction in utility costs. In 1988, a similar plant started up at the Los Angeles refinery.

During 1986 and 1987, U.S. consumption of petroleum products rose by about 800,000 barrels per day. At the same time, the nation's production fell by nearly one million barrels per day. All key indicators of industry activity dropped dramatically in 1986. Oil company expenditures for exploration, development, and land acquisition fell by about 40 percent. The average number of drilling rigs searching for new oil and gas fell by 50 percent. In fact, during one week in the summer of 1986 the rig count dropped to 663, the lowest level in 46 years. As a result, U.S. proved reserves of crude oil dropped by 5.4 percent in 1986, and natural gas reserves by nearly 1 percent.

With consumption increasing and domestic production falling, U.S. oil imports rose from 32 percent of consumption in 1985 to 39 percent in 1987 and to 43 percent by spring of 1988, higher than at the time of the first OPEC-led oil price increase in 1973. Hartley and Stegemeier repeatedly warned of the potential consequences of the situation, pointing to OPEC's possible return to control of world oil prices and supplies.

Even as the domestic oil situation worsened, Congress and the Department of the Interior agreed on a compromise in July 1986 that effectively delayed leasing activities for three years in California's highly prospective Outer Continental Shelf area. The debate continued and was soon joined by controversy over proposals to grant oil exploration leases in the Arctic National Wildlife Refuge. The area adjacent to the huge North Slope oil fields was believed to have tremendous poten-

Opposite, left: The orange pipes carry carbon dioxide for injection into the reservoirs at the Dollarhide field in West Texas. The injection program, combined with infill drilling, boosted field production 150 percent in three years — from 1,000 barrels per day in 1985 to 2,500 in 1988. Below: Production engineers Connie Cheyney and Tom Collier use a computer to design a rod string for a well in one of Unocal's West Texas fields, where precise well completions helped boost production in the 1980s.

tial to boost U.S. oil reserves and production, but development was staunchly opposed on environmental grounds.

Unocal, meanwhile, did what it could to maintain both its production and reserves. Unocal's crude oil and condensate reserves held steady at about 750 million barrels in 1985 and 1986, rising to 771 million barrels in 1987. Natural gas reserves dropped less than 2 percent to total 6,093 billion cubic feet in 1987. Unocal maintained its reserves despite a cutback in capital spending for exploration of almost 50 percent—from $1.1 billion in 1985 to $590 million in both 1986 and 1987.

The success of the company's exploration program was in part due to the excellent domestic land position that had been developed, particularly since the areawide leasing program was instituted in 1983 for federal lands in the Gulf of Mexico. By the end of 1987, the company's prospective properties in the United States totaled 2.9 million acres.

"When oil prices began to collapse in 1986," Dick Stegemeier observed, "there were abundant opportunities to acquire prime lands at bargain-basement prices. Many other companies backed off almost entirely, but we continued to acquire lands even though we had a lot of cash difficulties. We believed in the future. It was a bit of a gamble, but now we have the best land position that the company's ever had."

The strategy was consistent with that of the company's founder, Lyman Stewart, who always bought up lands even when his business partners objected. "The point is," said Stegemeier, "if you don't have the properties, you can't make the discoveries."

"By March of 1986, the oil price was in full retreat," recalled Harry Keegan, then president of the Oil & Gas Division. "We had to curtail projects that ten- or twelve-dollar oil just wouldn't support. We constantly reevaluated the projects we were working on and shut down those that no longer had economic viability. The budget cuts were large. We even shut in some production, mainly the heavy oils on the West Coast. We shut in as much as two thousand barrels a day from wells that could no longer pay their direct lifting costs."

Even with the shut-ins, which numbered 550 wells in the United States, production in both 1986 and 1987 remained steady at 1985 levels—about 154,000 barrels per day. This was achieved by accelerating an ongoing program of infill and extension drilling to boost production in the company's older fields, particularly in Alaska, California, Texas, and Louisiana. In UXP's Van field in East Texas,

Left: Unocal launched Platform Irene, the first offshore structure in California's Santa Maria basin, in August 1985. Once gusty winds and turbulent waters had calmed, the 260-foot-tall jacket slid into the ocean. The launch was the culmination of two years of intense effort, with at least half the time devoted to getting the necessary permits from more than 60 local, state, and federal government agencies. Opposite, portraits: On March 18, 1987, Ray Burke (top) and Dr. Hal Lian received a very high honor: the Royal Decoration of Commander of the Most Noble Order of the Crown of Thailand. The awards, granted by King Bhumibol Adulyadej, are given to those who perform noble deeds for the country. Opposite, right: Natural gas drilling and production platforms dotted Unocal's fields in the Gulf of Thailand as development continued. Thailand's dependence on imported oil dropped from 95 percent of its energy supplies in 1981 to 60 percent by 1988.

for example, a drilling program had doubled that field's production to 9,000 barrels per day between 1984 and 1986. Some of the increase came from wells completed in a previously undeveloped reservoir. The Van field, which had started producing in 1929, joined the ranks of 45 other "supergiants" in the United States in March 1986 by producing its five hundred-millionth barrel of oil.

By 1987, more than 25 percent of Unocal's total oil production in its Central Region—including West Texas, Oklahoma, Wyoming, Illinois, and Montana—came from some 300 infill wells drilled since 1981. In 1987 alone, the infill and extension drilling program in the region added 9 million barrels to the company's crude oil reserves.

In the Western Region, Unocal participated—with a 10.5 percent interest—in the first production from the area offshore Alaska's North Slope. The Endicott field in the Beaufort Sea started producing more than 100,000 barrels of oil per day in late 1987. Farther south, Platform Irene, set in late 1985 offshore California, achieved production of about 20,000 barrels per day in 1987. Because of the improved oil prices that year, Unocal resumed production from some of its California thermal recovery projects shut in the year before.

In 1988, the Western Region also gained significant reserves through a property exchange with Chevron. Net increases included 10 million barrels of oil, primarily in the Swanson River field in Alaska and from Platform Edith, offshore Southern California. Unocal's natural gas reserves in Alaska also increased by some 80 billion cubic feet.

Over the years, technical data processing services had become a vital tool in oil exploration and production. As seismic data interpretation and computerized reservoir simulation gained in sophistication, the company enhanced its computer power in these areas. In 1986, the Science & Technology Division in Brea, California, consolidated these technical services for improved efficiency.

As oil prices climbed in 1987, Unocal again picked up the pace of its foreign operations, where it had a strong land position. "We did extensive geological studies in these areas before taking them," noted John Imle. "It's taken several years for us to build up our present portfolio. There's a good representation of areas that have a reasonable potential of making a large impact on the company."

Unocal's natural gas project in Thailand continued as a star performer, with natural gas production in 1987 up by 43 percent over 1986. Condensate production also increased, reaching some 15,000 barrels per day.

In late 1987, Unocal celebrated the twenty-fifth anniversary of its operations in Thailand. The company's development of Thailand's natural gas resources had boosted the kingdom's economy. Almost completely dependent on imports for energy supplies in 1981, when gas production started from the Erawan field, Thailand relied on natural gas from Unocal's fields for more than one-quarter of its total commercial energy by the time Hal Lian retired as president of Unocal Thailand in March 1988.

Since the first natural gas delivery in 1981, Thailand had reaped an estimated $1.5 billion through royalties, taxes, and reduced energy costs. The country had also initiated its Eastern Seaboard Development Project. Based on the use of natural gas to develop petrochemical and other industries, the project would create thousands of new jobs. The first gas separation plant started up in 1985.

The natural gas development in Thailand represented Unocal's largest single investment in any project, totaling more than $1.4 billion by the end of 1987. "We expect to invest at least that much more in the future," said John Imle at the time of the anniversary. "There is still a lot of natural gas to be found and produced in the Gulf of Thailand."

In the Netherlands, Unocal took another direction — literally — to boost production. The company conducted the North Sea's first horizontal drilling program, begun in late 1986 in the Helder field to reduce the amount of water being produced with the oil — and the results proved better than predicted. By mid-1988, the Helder field produced 7,700 barrels of oil per day, 70 percent more than projections for conventional vertical development of the field. Water production dropped by 60 percent, from 100,000 to 40,000 barrels per day.

The Helder field also became the site of the world's first unmanned tripod tower oil platform, Helder B. Installed in late 1986, the platform provided an economical method for recovering marginal reserves.

In another innovative North Sea project, Unocal served from 1986 through 1989 as technical adviser to Statoil, the Norwegian national oil company, for the

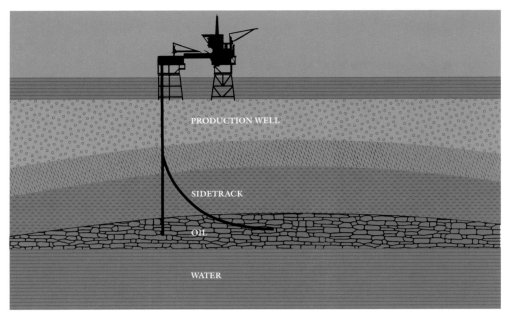

PRODUCTION WELL

SIDETRACK

OIL

WATER

Left: In late 1986, Unocal began the North Sea's first horizontal drilling program and achieved a dramatic boost in oil production from the Helder field offshore the Netherlands. The first well was sidetracked from an existing vertical well to cut costs. Results were so positive that another nine sidetrack wells were drilled by mid-1988. *Opposite:* As a result of continued development of its fields offshore Borneo, Unocal produced its five hundred-millionth barrel of Indonesian oil in July 1988. *Below:* Seven huge storage tanks at the Lawe Lawe terminal, which serves Unocal's Yakin and Sepinggan fields and Pertamina's Balikpapan refinery, have a combined capacity of 4.6 million barrels of crude oil.

development of the Veslefrikk field. The project involved the conversion of a semi-submersible drilling rig into a floating production unit. In 1989, Unocal put its 18 percent interest in the field up for sale.

In 1986, Unocal finally received some compensation for investments in the Persian Gulf that had been expropriated by Iran in 1980. Unocal filed for compensation in late 1981 before the Iran–U.S. Claims Tribunal in The Hague, Netherlands, according to Timothy R. Thomas, the Unocal attorney assigned to the case. By then, the American hostages held for more than a year by Iranian militants had been freed. As a condition of the hostage settlement, the United States released certain frozen Iranian holdings, and Iran set aside funds to settle claims on foreign assets it had nationalized.

Claims litigation proceeded slowly. According to Bob Roethke, who represented Unocal along with Clyde Barton and Tim Thomas, no action occurred in direct negotiations with Iran until that country became more concerned about its position vis-a-vis the Western democracies.

"In 1986," said Roethke, "we received an indication that the Iranians would be interested in settling out of the tribunal, so we set up a meeting with them in London. We were a long way apart between what they thought we should get and what we thought we should get."

"The big issue," noted Thomas, "was whether the company should be paid

CAPACITY : 800 000 BBLS
PRODUCT   : CRUDE OIL

something for the lost opportunity on the oil that we had discovered and had put the capital in to develop — but were never allowed to produce."

"It was a tough negotiation," recalled Barton, "but both sides wanted a resolution. In the end, we settled for thirty-six and a half million dollars."

In January 1988, Unocal marked the twentieth anniversary of its production-sharing contract with Pertamina, the Indonesian national oil company. In July, Unocal produced its five hundred-millionth barrel of Indonesian oil. Natural gas production from Unocal fields reached a cumulative total of 775 billion cubic feet. Just the year before, Unocal had signed a 20-year agreement with Pertamina for the delivery of a net total of more than 400 billion cubic feet of natural gas from the Attaka field to government-owned liquefied natural gas and fertilizer plants. In 1988, this represented a 120 percent increase in daily natural gas production.

By the time the anniversary was celebrated at a reception in Jakarta in October, Richard Stegemeier — who had been the company's first general manager in Indonesia — had become the chief executive officer of Unocal. In the late 1960s and early 1970s, Stegemeier had honed his leadership abilities on the remote jungle coastline of Kalimantan. He had molded a team that worked together under the pressures of physical hardship, harsh climate, long supply lines, and relative isolation to initiate one of the company's most successful ventures. In 1972, when Stegemeier turned the valve on the Attaka field's first producing well, he could not have guessed that he was destined to lead the entire company before the end of the following decade.

By early 1988, a plan was in place for Stegemeier to take over leadership of the company from Fred Hartley before the end of the year. In June, the directors announced that Hartley had recommended Stegemeier be elected chief executive officer of Unocal as of August 1. The announcement stated further that while Hartley would remain as chairman of the board, he would retire as an employee of the company no later than November 30, 1988. The transition, however, proved far more sudden.

In July, the directors disclosed that Hartley had elected to retire as of June 30. At the time, few people knew of Hartley's cardiac arrest and coronary bypass surgery. Obvious health concerns had led him to accelerate his retirement plans.

"He has been a distinguished leader who maintained the highest moral standards," said Stegemeier. "During Fred Hartley's tenure, Unocal grew from a small regional oil company to its present position as a worldwide natural resources company. He leaves Unocal with a solid foundation for future growth."

15

Bold
Steps

Above: *In July 1989, President George Bush signed legislation ending more than three decades of federal price controls on natural gas, allowing for increased production of this undervalued fuel.*
Opposite: In 1990, Unocal CEO Dick Stegemeier posed with some of the more than 8,000 heavily polluting, pre-1971 vehicles destroyed under SCRAP, a company project designed to help clean up the air in Los Angeles.

A change in chief executives always means some changes in management philosophy," said Dick Stegemeier, after taking office as Unocal's new CEO in July 1988. "However, I'd like to stress that there will be no radical shift in our basic operating philosophy."

He rededicated Unocal to improved productivity and profitability. He emphasized the need for innovative thinking at all levels and asked all employees for their participation in strengthening the company. He stressed safe operations and reaffirmed the company's commitment to environmental protection.

Stegemeier quickly emerged as an open and diplomatic communicator with the financial community and Unocal's other publics. He understood the importance of effective communication with shareholders, employees, government, customers, and the media.

In August 1988, the new CEO was interviewed by the *Los Angeles Times, New York Times,* and *Wall Street Journal.* In September, he traveled to several eastern cities to meet with investment managers, securities analysts, and major shareholders. He outlined the steps Unocal was taking, both long- and short-term, to increase productivity and profitability. He received praise for being accessible to the press and for providing more details, such as business segment earnings, in Unocal's financial reports.

Stegemeier revived the CEO's monthly employee newsletter — first issued by Reese Taylor — using it to clearly articulate the company's goals, activities, and progress. He set forth four key operating goals: (1) expansion of the energy resource base; (2) development of a satisfactory rate of return on all assets and the sale of underperforming assets; (3) improved profitability through control and reduction of costs, increased revenues, and increased production; and, to help accomplish these goals, (4) the encouragement of innovation and creativity.

Stegemeier's will to act quickly became apparent, as he accelerated the corporate restructuring begun under Hartley after the attempted takeover and the 1986 collapse of oil prices. In one of his first actions as CEO, Stegemeier announced that Unocal sought a buyer for all or part of the 13 acres of prime real estate in downtown Los Angeles where the corporate headquarters building stood.

Many speculated that Hartley would have resisted such asset sales; yet some were announced before Hartley's June retirement. Given Unocal's debt combined with low oil prices, the question of selling underperforming assets became largely a matter of timing: When could the best price be had for certain properties? According to Neal Schmale, promoted to senior vice president for corporate

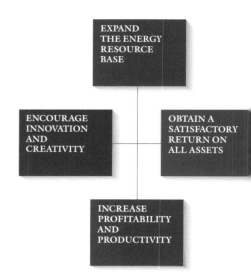

development in July 1988, "All of these things were in the mill for a long time. There's a time to hold your cards and a time to cash in — and Fred was patient."

In May 1988, the company announced the phasedown and eventual closure of its chemicals manufacturing plant in Brea, California. Unocal opted to expand operations at its West Sacramento facility in Northern California rather than continue to operate in an area whose character had changed over a period of 30 years from rural to densely populated.

In late June 1988, Unocal announced the shutdown of petroleum fuels manufacture at its Beaumont (Texas) refinery. Built in 1924 by Pure Oil, the refinery had been designed to process crude oil with low sulfur content.

"The relatively higher cost of these crudes," Stegemeier noted, "combined with the low profit margins on petroleum product sales in the Gulf Coast area, has made it uneconomic to continue to produce petroleum fuels at this facility." While the Beaumont refinery continued to manufacture lubrication oils and solvents, the company wrote down $31 million of its investment in the facility in the third quarter of 1988.

In the first quarter of 1988, the company took a $525 million write-down of other assets. The total included the remaining investment — $350 million — in the Parachute Creek (Colorado) oil shale project; half the investment — $105 million — in the molybdenum mine and processing facilities in New Mexico and Pennsylvania; and 40 percent of the investment — $70 million — in needle coke facilities at the Chicago refinery.

"Based upon recent analysis, we have concluded that these assets have little chance of generating sufficient cash flows to enable the company to recover its full investment in them," Hartley said at the time.

The Unocal Center property sold in December 1988, some 30 years after its opening. In 1958, the headquarters building had dominated the Los Angeles skyline; its design captured the spirit of a company riding the crest of economic expansion that followed World War II. By 1988, the company had weathered some of the most difficult challenges in its history, and its headquarters building stood dwarfed by the proliferation of highrises in Los Angeles. Downtown property values had soared; Unocal could use the money.

"By selling the property," Stegemeier noted, "we can make a substantial amount of cash available to repay debt and to search for energy resources."

The sales price was $205 million. The purchaser, UC Land Associates, an affiliate of Hillman Properties of Newport Beach, California, stated its intention

Opposite, left: The Los Angeles of early 1990 presented a very different profile than in the late 1950s, and Unocal Center (foreground) no longer dominated the skyline. Unocal sold its downtown Los Angeles property, including the center, in late 1988. Opposite, right: As CEO, Stegemeier established four key operating goals for Unocal. Right: In late 1989, the Chicago refinery and certain other midwestern assets were sold to UNO-VEN, a joint venture between Unocal and the national oil company of Venezuela. Below: On October 31, 1989, Dick Stegemeier (left) and Juan T. Chacin, president of Petroleos de Venezuela, signed the joint-venture agreement in Caracas.

to develop the property as a commercial office center. Unocal leased back the headquarters building for three years and made plans to move its headquarters.

Also in December 1988, Stegemeier announced that a "heads of agreement" had been signed with Petroleos de Venezuela, S.A. (PDVSA). The intention was to form a joint venture that would own Unocal's Chicago refinery and certain related marketing and other assets. After almost a year's worth of discussion, the details were settled.

Definitive agreements to create a petroleum refining and marketing general partnership — The UNO-VEN Company — were signed October 31, 1989, in Caracas, Venezuela, and the deal closed on December 1. Each partner, Unocal's Union Oil Company of California subsidiary and PDVSA's Venezuela Petroleum Holdings, Inc. (VPHI) subsidiary, held 50 percent. Unocal generated a $500 million pre-tax cash flow from the transactions involved, money that was quickly reinvested in other areas where the company anticipated significant growth. The new company agreed to accept 135,000 barrels per day of Venezuelan crude oil as feedstock for the refinery.

Venezuela was not the first OPEC country to invest in downstream operations in importing nations like the United States. "I think it's a positive trend," said Roger Beach, president of the Unocal Refining & Marketing Division. "It helps the security of supply for the oil-importing nations, and it modifies the political position of the exporting countries. When they move into the downstream side, they are no longer solely producers. They are directly linked to the consuming nations, and that makes for more stability in the world oil marketplace."

Assets transferred to UNO-VEN included the refinery, 13 product terminals and other plants, and more than 100 Unocal 76 retail service stations. The new company also assumed existing contracts with a network of approximately 190 marketers serving more than 3,300 service stations in a 12-state area of the Midwest. The transaction did not include Unocal's marketing operations in the southeastern United States.

Midwest 76, Inc., and VPHI Midwest, Inc., were formed as UNO-VEN's managing general partners. A second general partnership, The Needle Coker Company, was set up to handle the operation of needle coking facilities, located at and adjacent to the Chicago refinery.

Some 1,100 Unocal employees were transferred to UNO-VEN. Edward T. DiCorcia, formerly of Exxon, was appointed chief executive officer February 1, 1990. He reported to an operating committee made up of three members each

UNO-VEN MARKETING AREA
UNOCAL MARKETING AREA
REFINERIES

HAWAII

Left: Under the UNO-VEN agreement, the joint venture took over a 12-state marketing area, with products and services offered under the Unocal 76 logo. Below: The UNO-VEN Company became the operator for more than 100 Unocal 76 service stations in the Midwest and assumed contracts with marketers operating another 3,300 stations. Opposite, below: This station in Issaquah, Washington, is in the more populous western part of the state where Unocal began to concentrate its marketing activities in late 1989.

from the managing general partners. Midwest 76's members—from Unocal's Refining & Marketing Division—were Al Eliskalns, manager of planning and economics and former manager of the Chicago refinery; Tom Matthews, vice president, eastern marketing and auto/truckstops; and Ed Scott, vice president, crude supply and transportation.

As Unocal finalized its agreement with Venezuela, it launched another major initiative that yielded $322 million. The Norwegian assets, including an 18 percent interest in the Veslefrikk field and varying interests in three other license areas, went up for sale. "Our future in Norway beyond Veslefrikk production [which began in early 1990] is very uncertain," stated John Imle. "By selling now, we can redeploy the value of that asset into longer-term opportunities with more strategic value for us." In May 1990, Total Marine Norsk A/S, a subsidiary of Total Compagnie Francaise des Petroles, purchased Unocal Norge A/S.

In 1989, the company sold its interest in the THUMS joint venture in Long Beach, California, amounting to 5,500 barrels of crude oil per day. Reserve losses resulting from the sales of producing properties were recovered through a carefully planned program of acquisitions. Unocal also sold its Obed Mountain thermal coal mine near Hinton, Alberta, yielding an after-tax cash flow of $70 million ($80 million Canadian). The sale of several surplus properties, including the 45-acre Torrance (California) tank farm, netted $64 million.

Unocal's Real Estate Division created an Environmental Site Assessment

and Remediation Group to prepare company properties — like the tank farm — for sale and development. The new group, which was transferred to Engineering & Construction, used bioremediation techniques to clean up soil and groundwater at several contaminated domestic sites.

In 1990, Unocal entered an agreement with Kennecott Corporation for its Green Mountain Properties joint-venture to take over Unocal's mothballed uranium mine and processing facilities in Sweetwater, Wyoming.

In marketing, Unocal announced plans in late 1989 to restructure its operations in the Pacific Northwest. The company began to withdraw sales of motor fuels from marginally profitable locations to concentrate its efforts in the more heavily populated western areas of Washington and Oregon.

In late 1989, Unocal suspended all manufacturing operations at its Beaumont refinery. Phasing out petroleum fuels manufacture had cut the refinery's losses; but petrochemical, lube oil, and solvent operations could not sustain profitability. "The facility has continued to lose money every month since the downsizing last year," noted Stegemeier.

"It was an extremely difficult decision," said Roger Beach, "and a painful one. Beaumont…had a lot of excellent employees trying their best to make a go of it." The plant employed about 450 people. Unocal continued to operate the facility as a storage terminal.

Unocal also took a harder look at its oil shale project in Parachute Creek. Given the climate of corporate restructuring, the project needed to achieve a level of cash flow at which revenues covered the costs of operation — or it would be shut down. Both in 1988 and 1989, the project produced close to a million barrels of raw shale oil (yielding more than a million barrels of syncrude because of volume gains during processing). In 1989, that amounted to break-even operation for about half the year.

For the first five months of 1990, production was up, totaling 670,000 barrels of raw shale oil. During a two-month turnaround, adjustments were made to increase the yield and improve efficiency still further.

"The plant has run consistently this year at about 6,000 barrels per day," said Stephen C. Lipman, newly appointed president of both the Science & Technology and Energy Mining divisions in July 1990. "This is very encouraging; 1990 should be the best year we've ever had. With continuing government price supports, we can achieve our goal of covering our costs."

"Down the road," Lipman added, "price supports will run out. So we've

begun to investigate ways to produce more valuable products at our raw shale oil upgrading plant. It's a small but efficient refinery with the potential to help us realize improved profits." (By the end of 1989, Unocal had received a total of $76 million under the terms of its federal price-support agreement, leaving a balance of $324 million still available.)

Unocal kept the shale project open to recover part of its investment and to demonstrate the basic technology for the future. "Whether we want to accept it today or not," said Stegemeier, "shale oil is a potential transportation fuel in the United States over which we have some control."

While company operations were under close scrutiny, Unocal's management also was restructured. In addition to Neal Schmale's appointment as senior vice president, several other new corporate officers were named in 1988, helping to create a vigorous attitude in the company as the new decade approached. Karen A. Sikkema became Unocal's first woman officer when named vice president, corporate communications, in April. At the same time, Thomas F. Hairston became vice president for the Washington, D.C., office, succeeding Bill Cole. In July, Gary W. Sproule was named vice president, budgets, planning, and economics; Wellman E. Branstrom, vice president, human resources (succeeding Joseph Byrne, who retired); and Darrell D. Chessum, assistant treasurer (who succeeded Ed Powell when he retired as treasurer in 1990). In September 1988, Donald L. Hanley was named to a newly created position as vice president, health, environment, and safety.

In November 1988, Ray Burke retired as executive vice president, energy resources, after a 37-year career with Unocal. Coworkers presented him with a plaque acknowledging that under his leadership company explorationists had found 2.4 billion barrels of oil.

Burke's retirement, and Harry Keegan's a month earlier as president of the Oil & Gas Division, triggered many other changes in the energy resources group. John Imle was promoted to senior vice president for energy resources and a director; H D Maxwell moved up to replace Keegan; and Harry C. Lee moved up to replace Imle as president of the International Oil & Gas Division.

Dr. Carel Otte, president of the Geothermal Division, also announced his intention to retire. In February 1989, Steve Lipman was appointed the division's new president, and Dr. Otte stayed on as a consultant until September. In April 1990, Darcel

L. Hulse, formerly vice president in charge of engineering and construction, became president of the Geothermal Division. Lipman was tapped to replace Cloyd Reeg, who retired as president of the Science & Technology and Energy Mining divisions. John R. Dietzman was named director of the Corporate Engineering & Construction Department, replacing Hulse.

At the highest level, the composition of Unocal's executive committee changed significantly in the three years between late 1985, after the defeated takeover attempt, and late 1988, after Stegemeier was elevated to chief executive officer. In 1985, the six-member executive committee included Fred Hartley, Dick Stegemeier, Claude Brinegar, Ray Burke, Bill McConnor, and Craig Henderson. McConnor and Henderson, heads of the Refining & Marketing and Chemicals divisions, respectively, had retired in 1986 and were replaced by Roger Beach and Tom Sleeman. Beach and Sleeman were promoted to corporate senior vice presidents in 1987 and elected directors in 1988. After Hartley and Burke retired in 1988, Stegemeier and Brinegar became the senior members on the executive committee, having been joined that year by Beach, Imle, and Sleeman.

In April 1989, Fred Hartley stepped down as Unocal's chairman, and Stegemeier was elected in his place. A few months later, Brinegar, executive vice president and chief financial officer, was elected vice chairman of the board.

Hartley's fellow directors accorded him unique status as chairman emeritus, honoring him for 50 years of service to Unocal, including 24 years as CEO. He had led Unocal through some very difficult years and presided over many of the company's most notable achievements. In his farewell remarks, Hartley said: 'I have been truly blessed to spend my career working with and for such fine people.' With obvious emotion, he waved goodbye to shareholders and employees attending the annual meeting on April 24, 1989.

From 1988 through 1990, Unocal's board elected five new outside directors, including the company's first woman director: Ann McLaughlin, visiting fellow and trustee, The Urban Institute, Washington, D.C., and former U.S. Secretary of Labor. Other new outside directors were MacDonald G. Becket, chairman, The Becket Group; Malcolm R. Currie, chairman and chief executive officer, Hughes Aircraft Company; Frank C. Herringer, president, Transamerica Corporation; and Charles R. Weaver, chairman and chief executive officer, The Clorox Company. Three outside directors, with accumulated service on the board totaling more than 60 years, retired in 1990: William H. Doheny, William F. Ballhaus, and Lewis B. Harder.

Throughout the company, changes were made or planned to push authority deeper into the organization, increasing accountability at the operating level and encouraging quicker, more flexible responses to fluctuations in the business environment. In the International Oil & Gas Division, management restructuring began after the early retirement program in 1986.

"That program," recalled John Imle, "was an opportunity for us to shrink ranks at the higher levels. The post-eighty-six situation has meant fewer managers, more people with their hands on the work, and more decisions being made in the field than were before. All that has been very positive."

Above: Unocal, a leader in the auto/truckstop industry, operated 270 facilities nationwide in 1990, including the one shown in Jackson, Georgia. *Left:* In 1987, Unocal initiated Trucker Appreciation Month at its participating truckstops, offering prizes, food, free blood pressure and cholesterol checkups, and dietary information to these very important users of Unocal's products and services. *Far left:* Unocal's own truckers, such as Nancy Malm, work around the clock to keep stations and truckstops supplied with gasoline. *Below:* A 65-foot truck-and-trailer rig has an 8,600-gallon capacity.

In 1989, Unocal streamlined its marketing operations on the West Coast. Offices in Seattle and San Diego were closed and operations consolidated in San Ramon (east of San Francisco) and Los Angeles. "Our strategy," said Clay Warnock, vice president of western marketing, "is to move decision-making on pricing and capital expenditures down to the sales division level in an effort to be more responsive to dealers, distributors, and commercial accounts."

The company also reorganized its domestic Oil & Gas Division, creating six separate business units—each operating as a profit center—from three larger, regional groups (Western, Central, and Gulf). In October 1989, when Unocal's Canadian subsidiary became the seventh business unit, the new organization was renamed the North American Oil & Gas Division.

Expansion of the resource base was the first of the four key operating goals Stegemeier had set forth when he became CEO, and progress on that front was impressive. As oil prices began sliding in the early 1980s and then plunged in 1986, Unocal—with a record as a low-cost producer—maintained the levels of its crude oil and natural gas reserves. At the same time, the energy resources group worked to expand and improve its enviable land portfolio. John Imle described Unocal's position in late 1988:

"Capital is less available to the petroleum industry because of low oil prices—and less available to our company because of our debt. So we have to be a lot more selective in the acreage we pick up. We have many more explorationists than we did in the past assigned to do regional studies of various parts of the world before we even think about applying for exploration license areas. We've done our homework. Both domestically and internationally, we have an outstanding portfolio."

Unocal's exploration efforts during 1989 met with a high degree of success: More than 30 percent of the exploratory wells Unocal drilled found commercial quantities of oil or gas. Extensions to existing fields also yielded important new reserves. The company replaced 123 percent of its worldwide crude oil and natural gas production on a crude-equivalent basis. Total hydrocarbon reserves worldwide were up 2 percent. Earnings from 1989's petroleum activities totaled $450 million, a 38 percent increase over 1988 earnings of $325 million. (Results included a $53 million after-tax gain from natural gas contract settlements.)

The natural gas market "bubble" seemed finally to be deflating in 1989, at least in the winter's peak demand periods. As oil prices rose, electric utilities switched to cheaper natural gas as a fuel. Gas burns cleaner than oil, giving it an environmental advantage. And Congress acted to end 35 years of federal regulation of natural gas prices with full decontrol slated for 1993. President George Bush signed the legislation on July 27, 1989.

Unocal held an enviable position in the United States of having a ratio of natural gas reserves to production of 15:1, compared with an industry average of 10:1. Union Exploration Partners, Ltd. (UXP), Unocal's operating unit in its Louisiana and Texas/Southeastern regions, sold record volumes of natural gas throughout 1989. For the year, gas sales averaged 416.3 million cubic feet per day, up nearly 12 percent from 1988.

In May 1990, UXP entered an agreement to purchase the stock of Prairie Holding Company, a crude oil and natural gas subsidiary of Placer Dome Inc. The acquisition, completed July 3 and valued at $336 million, added more than 20,000 net acres of promising exploratory lands to UXP's holdings in East Texas and Louisiana. Net daily production from Prairie's wells included 36 million cubic feet of natural gas and 4,100 barrels of hydrocarbon liquids.

In June, UXP announced that it would change from a Texas limited partner-

UNOCAL PLATFORMS

1	EVA	4	GINA	7	B
2	ESTHER	5	GILDA	8	C
3	EDITH	6	A	9	IRENE

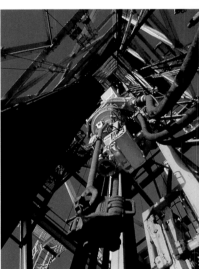

Top left: By 1988, Unocal operated nine platforms offshore Southern California. In the two decades since the oil spill from Platform A in 1969, no further such incidents had occurred. Top: A worker inspects a walkway beneath Platform Irene. Above: The view of the derrick from Irene's drilling floor can be dizzying. Unocal drilled the West's longest horizontal well from Irene in the summer of 1989.

ship to a Delaware corporation, the Unocal Exploration Corporation (UXC). Tax revisions and other considerations had made the partnership less attractive.

Unocal, which first employed horizontal (extended-reach) drilling to improve oil production from its fields in the Dutch sector of the North Sea, set a record with the technology offshore California in August 1989. The well, drilled to a total depth of 14,387 feet from Platform Irene, extended 12,739 feet horizontally. The longest reach well in the western United States, it bottomed out at only 4,057 feet vertically below the ocean floor.

In mid-1990, Unocal extended its holdings in southern Alaska through the acquisition of Amoco's 62.5 percent interest in the Chakachatna Group, owner of four platforms in the Cook Inlet. Combined production averaged about 5,100 barrels of oil per day. Unocal also boosted its Canadian production by some 2,000 barrels of oil per day through the acquisition from Saskatchewan Oil of interests in 25 oil and gas units and other properties.

Overseas, long-established projects continued to yield new oil and gas resources. Unocal Indonesia had maintained crude oil production of more than 65,000 barrels per day since 1982 (more than 70,000 barrels per day in 1990), thanks to good geologic and engineering work that identified new reserves in producing fields. Unocal also produced 80 million cubic feet (net) of natural gas per day. Most went into the manufacture of fertilizer or was liquefied and exported to Japan, South Korea, and Taiwan. As demand for natural gas grew in Southeast Asia, Indonesia itself consumed increasing amounts for power generation.

Unocal's natural gas development in the Gulf of Thailand continued to be vigorous. A fifth field, Kaphong, was brought on stream in 1989. A few months later, on October 17 — the ninety-ninth anniversary of Unocal's founding — the company signed an agreement for a third gas sales area with the Petroleum Authority of Thailand (PTT). The agreement, called Unocal III, allowed for the development of six additional fields: Funan, Jakrawan, Surat, Trat, Gomin, and Pakarang.

The plan was to bring on new production incrementally, increasing daily average production from 530 million to 700 million cubic feet per day; but the underwater pipeline carrying the gas to shore had only a capacity of 540 million cubic feet per day. In 1990, compression facilities installed by Unocal and PTT increased the capacity to 800 million cubic feet per day.

"Unocal III is a major reinvestment, underscoring our confidence in Thailand's economy," said Graydon H. Laughbaum, Jr., president of Unocal Thailand.

"It also raises the level of our partnership with Thailand. We have PTT Exploration and Production as a five-percent partner in Unocal III and have built the thirty-million-dollar compression platform together with PTT."

On February 13, 1990, Unocal delivered its one trillionth cubic foot of natural gas to PTT. Thailand's demand for energy boomed, and Unocal was the primary natural gas producer in the country.

Success, however, was marred by disaster in late 1989. The drillship *Seacrest* capsized during a sudden and severe typhoon in the Gulf of Thailand. Owned by a Unocal subsidiary and operated by a drilling-services company out of Singapore, the ship carried 97 people.

"We have mobilized every available resource to aid in our search for the ship," said Stegemeier after the first reports came in, "and we pray that we will find the *Seacrest* and the people on board in good shape."

The typhoon, the worst to hit Thailand in 35 years and the only one known to have formed in the Gulf, struck in the early morning hours of November 3 with little warning. Before it was over, Typhoon Gay killed hundreds of people, destroyed 29,000 homes, and sank some 600 boats, including 4 heavy freighters. Unocal workboats, joining the massive rescue effort, picked up nine survivors.

Storm winds of 100 miles per hour whipped up 50-foot waves. Despite the best efforts of the *Seacrest*'s crew, the ship could not withstand the sudden, violent reversals in wind and wave conditions when the eye of the storm passed over it. Only six crew members survived. Unocal moved quickly to offer financial support to the families of those lost at sea. To help avert similar disasters, the company cooperated with the Royal Thailand Meteorological Service to install a state-of-the-art typhoon warning system, which enhanced the advance storm-warning capability for all of Southeast Asia.

In the late 1980s, a key element in Unocal's international strategy was a focus on underexplored regions. Many countries previously closed to foreign petroleum activities began to welcome outside expertise in resource development. In November 1989, Unocal signed a production-sharing contract with the Union of Myanmar (formerly Burma) — "an example," noted John Imle, "of how 'enlightened aggressiveness' has paid off for us in obtaining an early land position."

By mid-1990, Unocal actively explored in a dozen countries outside North America. "The best basic exploration asset," Imle observed, "continues to be a good, solid geologist or geophysicist with an active imagination, access to the best technology, and a burning desire to work hard to find oil and gas."

Imle also noted that the company's oil and gas reserves were higher in 1990 than they had been at the end of 1982. This increase was achieved during a particularly tough time for the company. In 1985, the debt had soared from $1.2 billion to $6.1 billion, following a hostile takeover attempt.

"In the five years since then," Imle said, "despite precipitous price drops, we have paid off two billion dollars of that debt while at the same time paying out two billion dollars of extra interest payments on the new debt. It is sometimes forgotten that during the same period of time, Unocal replaced its worldwide oil and gas reserves on an equivalent barrel basis.

"This is a tribute to our exploration and development organization worldwide," Imle continued, "whose staff of geologists, geophysicists, and engineers numbered the same in 1982 — a peak year for the industry — as in 1990. Not many of our competitors can say that, and it puts us in a very advantageous position."

Unocal increased its capital spending budget for 1990 by 20 percent over 1989, up from $1.1 billion to $1.3 billion. For the first time in company history, the amount budgeted for foreign exploration for energy resources exceeded that for domestic exploration: $111 million to $106 million. This reflected both the

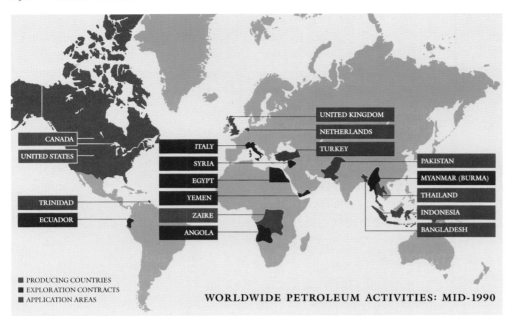

CANADA
UNITED STATES
ITALY
SYRIA
EGYPT
YEMEN
ZAIRE
ANGOLA
TRINIDAD
ECUADOR
UNITED KINGDOM
NETHERLANDS
TURKEY
PAKISTAN
MYANMAR (BURMA)
THAILAND
INDONESIA
BANGLADESH

■ PRODUCING COUNTRIES
■ EXPLORATION CONTRACTS
■ APPLICATION AREAS

WORLDWIDE PETROLEUM ACTIVITIES: MID-1990

Above: John Imle, elected senior vice president for energy resources in 1988, fostered a policy of "enlightened aggressiveness" to obtain early exploration acreage positions in promising areas of the globe. Left: In 1990, for the first time in the company's history, Unocal budgeted more money for foreign than domestic exploration.

maturation of the United States as an oil province and constraints against exploration in high-potential domestic areas, such as the Outer Continental Shelf and Alaska. While Unocal participated in the first exploration drilling in Alaska's highly prospective Chukchi Sea during 1989, many other promising areas in the United States continued to be closed.

Year-end figures for 1989 reported a record decline in U.S. oil production, which dropped by a half-million barrels per day. Imports averaged 44 percent of petroleum demand in 1989 and reached a record high of 48 percent in the first half of 1990.

On June 26, 1990, President Bush announced a ten-year ban against new oil drilling in many prospective areas offshore the continental United States. Affected areas included the eastern seaboard north of Rhode Island; most of the Pacific coastline, including prime areas offshore California; and 14 million acres surrounding the Florida Keys.

"Ironically," said Dick Stegemeier, "this policy entails a greater risk to the very marine environment we are trying to protect. That's because almost all of our imported oil comes to this country in tankers....When you check the record, you find that tankers are a much greater source of spillage than offshore platforms and pipelines.

"Nor does the public seem to realize," he added, "that a moratorium on offshore production effectively restricts the search for new sources of natural gas — the cleanest of all fossil fuels."

Unocal's geothermal projects expanded as the 1990s approached. In January 1989, the company announced that it was ready to proceed with its Indonesian geothermal project in the Gunung Salak area 40 miles south of Jakarta. In its joint operations contract with Pertamina, Unocal agreed to provide steam for 165,000 kilowatts of generating capacity to power plants owned and operated by PLN, Indonesia's electricity authority. The first plant, a 110,000-kilowatt facility, was scheduled for completion in early 1993.

In Southern California's Imperial Valley, Unocal Geothermal achieved a major milestone in February 1989. With the opening of its Salton Sea Unit 3 power-generating plant, Unocal became an electricity supplier in addition to a geothermal resource producer. The plant, owned and operated by the company's Desert Power subsidiary, could generate 49,900 kilowatts of energy, enough to fill the electricity demands of 50,000 residential customers and equivalent to a savings of 500,000 barrels of crude oil per year.

In 1987, Earth Energy, another Unocal subsidiary, had taken the first step toward commercial-scale electricity production with the purchase of a 10,000-kilowatt generating plant in the Salton Sea area. Until then, Unocal had functioned only as a resource producer selling steam to utilities. This experimental venture showed promise, so Unocal proceeded with Salton Sea Unit 3. In 1990, the company's third electricity-generating plant, also built and operated by Earth Energy, was brought on-line with a capacity of 20,000 kilowatts.

Sales of electricity from Unit 3 proved to be the primary factor in increased geothermal earnings in 1989. Power was transmitted by the Imperial Irrigation District to Southern California Edison's substation in the Coachella Valley.

Unit 3 marked the culmination of years of Unocal research in the handling of the salty, corrosive brines typical of the Imperial Valley geothermal resource. A great deal of progress had been made over a decade, not only in corrosion resistance, but in the reduction of scaling inside well casings. Scaling, the buildup of solids dissolved in the brine, plugged and corroded the casings of wells used to reinject brine into the reservoir after it was cycled through the power plant. Unocal developed technology that not only reduced such buildup, but also recovered a compound from the geothermal fluids that contained some valuable metals.

Production from Unocal's largest geothermal project, The Geysers north of San Francisco, declined as the field matured. Unocal began operating the field in 1967, supplying steam to Pacific Gas & Electric Company (PG&E) for producing electricity. Net production, which peaked at 5 million megawatt-hours in 1987, had dropped to 4.2 million megawatt-hours by 1989.

"Faced with declining production," said Darcel Hulse in July 1990, shortly after becoming president of the Geothermal Division, "our main objective is to maximize the benefits of the remaining energy."

Unocal identified immediate steps that would help lengthen the life of the field. These involved finalizing a new agreement with PG&E concerning steam sales, one that would modify the pressure requirement for steam supplied to

In February 1989, Unocal opened its Salton Sea Unit 3 generating plant and so became an electricity supplier as well as a geothermal resource producer. Unit 3 was proof of the success of the company's extensive research efforts in handling the corrosive brines typical of the Imperial Valley resource.

turbines and encourage improved efficiency in the generating plants. The new agreement would also permit PG&E to load cycle. That is, during peak usage hours (such as hot afternoons when people turn on air conditioners), the utility's generators could draw steam at the field's maximum production rate. In off-peak hours, however, less power would be needed and production could be reduced to conserve the resource.

"For the longer term," Hulse explained, "we are studying the effects of water injection to help replenish the geothermal reservoir. Initial results are encouraging, but success requires a sufficient water source. We may also be able to increase production if we can find ways to control the corrosivity of steam that is now unusable. The benefits of all of these programs will allow us to prolong the life of The Geysers field and be more effective stewards of this important natural resource."

In the Unocal Chemicals Division, specialty products represented a different approach to the corporate goal of "expanding the resource base." Poco Graphite, Inc., producer of graphite materials with a wide variety of high-tech uses, posted record sales and earnings in 1988 and 1989. Sales of new agricultural products increased. Sales of wastewater treatment products and services, offered by the company's Unipure Group, grew 50 percent in 1989.

The company continued to expand its production of emulsion polymers for a variety of uses, although it suffered a serious temporary setback in July 1988. An early-morning explosion and fire destroyed the company's emulsion polymer plant in Bridgeview, Illinois, as workers prepared to start up equipment after the weekend shutdown. Four employees were injured; one eventually died. Unocal, tracing the cause to human error, acted quickly to prevent similar events at other locations. The Bridgeview plant was not rebuilt. To make up for its lost capacity, a new plant was built in Kankakee, Illinois, and two others were expanded.

Unocal continued to improve its lanthanide production capabilities. In 1989, Molycorp, the company's metals subsidiary, began to produce dysprosium oxide and increased its output of neodymium, products required by the growing neodymium-iron-boron permanent magnet industry. The company anticipated increased demand for cerium, which reduces the transmission of ultraviolet radiation through automobile and architectural glass.

By 1990, lanthanide processing facilities at Molycorp's Mountain Pass mine in California had been greatly expanded to produce the unique concentrates that

Below left: Molycorp's Mountain Pass lanthanide mine is located in the high desert country of California near the Nevada border. Below: A worker removes a tray of gadolinium oxide (used to intensify x-ray images) from a furnace at Mountain Pass. During the late 1980s, Molycorp greatly expanded its lanthanide separation facilities at the mine.

PureGro Centennial
The PureGro Company, a Unocal subsidiary, had its beginnings as a guano supplier. It was founded May 23, 1890, in the kingdom of Hawaii by George Norton Wilcox, a grower who saw the need for a commercial fertilizer industry to supply a burgeoning sugar cane business. With George D. Freeth, Wilcox started the North Pacific Phosphate and Fertilizer Company to exploit guano deposits on Laysan Island in the northwestern part of the Hawaiian chain. In 1894, the company opened a fertilizer plant in Honolulu and became The Pacific Guano and Fertilizer Company. A dozen years later, it constructed a fertilizer and bone-char plant on tidelands in West Berkeley, California. The company grew rapidly and in 1920 merged with the Hawaiian Fertilizer Company. In 1935, Pacific Guano Company was formed to take over the mainland assets. In 1961, Union Oil bought Pacific Guano and subsequently expanded the subsidiary through acquisitions in the Rocky Mountains region and the Midwest. After the merger of Pure Oil with Union, Pacific took over the agriculture operations of the Pure Gas and Chemical Company. In 1967, Pacific changed its name to PureGro. An award-winning advertisement at the time noted: "If your name was Guano, you'd change it, too." During its 100-year history, PureGro has played a major role in the growth of California as one of the world's great agricultural producers. Throughout the West, PureGro offers technological assistance and a wide variety of products to meet the needs of agriculture.

accounted for 40 percent of lanthanide revenues. "It's a very high-tech industry," said Gene Dewey, who became president of Molycorp in 1985. "The products that have significant value must be produced in highly pure forms. I'm talking about at least three nines—99.9 percent pure. For some products, specific identified impurities cannot exceed one part per million."

Molycorp also took steps to boost its production of yttrium, which, while not a lanthanide, was often demanded by customers who used lanthanides as phosphors. In 1985, Molycorp had become involved in yttrium production in a Canadian venture and, in the same year, discovered a deposit of yttrium and zirconium on Indian lands in southeastern New Mexico. In May 1989, Molycorp and the Mescalero Apaches announced a joint leasing-operating agreement to evaluate the deposit, estimated to contain 10 million pounds of yttrium.

"This could become the first commercial deposit of yttrium in the United States," said Dewey. "It contains sufficient quantities to supply this country's requirements for many decades."

Market conditions allowed Molycorp to reopen its molybdenum mine and mill in Questa, New Mexico, in 1989. Initial production ran about half the annual capacity of 20 million pounds.

In January 1990, Molycorp announced a joint venture with Sumitomo Metal Industries, Ltd., to develop and market lanthanides and yttrium products in Japan. Molycorp held a 33 percent interest.

The eastern edge of the Pacific Rim also drew the attention of Unocal's Refining & Marketing Division in 1990, as it sought to expand its markets. In 1906, Union Oil Company's general manager, the young Will Stewart, had first been authorized by the board of directors to negotiate contracts to sell fuel oil and refined products in China and Japan. Over the decades, Unocal's interests in Asia had ebbed and flowed with changes in the markets and in the political climate.

"The potential for expanding our downstream activities into that part of the world has always been attractive," explained Roger Beach in 1990. "For the past year or so, we've been developing several entrepreneurial business ventures."

These included a distribution business to sell lubricants under the Unocal 76 brand in Indonesia, Thailand, Hong Kong, Singapore, Malaysia, the Philippines, and the People's Republic of China. The company also entered into a crude oil processing agreement with Sinopec, China's national oil company. In return for crude oil supplied to Sinopec, Unocal would receive gasoline and diesel for marketing in the Far East.

The development of new business opportunities, streamlining of operations, and sales of underperforming assets improved Unocal's profitability and productivity. A renewed emphasis on safe operations was also key. In 1986, when Stegemeier had just been elected president, he spotlighted safety. Ultimately, safety depends on well-designed equipment, proper procedures, and thoughtful employees who know their jobs and act with care. But Stegemeier gave operating groups the added support of a new corporate-level safety department.

"There is no excuse for running an unsafe operation," Stegemeier said at the time. "In my years with this company, I have never seen management at any level turn down a project that would improve the safety of an operation."

Stegemeier wrote to all supervisors telling them that henceforth all lost-time accidents must be reported to the president—not as a punitive measure, but to underscore the importance of thinking and acting with safety in mind.

In September 1988, Stegemeier announced the creation of another new corporate department, consolidating several groups under Don Hanley as vice president, health, environment, and safety. Departments reporting to Hanley included: Environmental Sciences, Health Services, Medicine, and Safety & Risk Management. The new organization was designed for the realities of the 1990s, with health and safety issues closely tied to environmental concerns.

The caliber of company operations was an important factor in reducing risk not only to the health of employees and customers, but also in reducing risk to the environment. The direct link between safe operations and environmental protection was dramatically illustrated in the 260,000-barrel oil spill from the Exxon tanker *Valdez* in the Gulf of Alaska in March 1989.

"The *Valdez* spill was a tragic accident in several respects," said Stegemeier. "Tragic, because of the damage it caused to the marine ecology of Prince William Sound. Tragic, because it was, by all reports, eminently preventable, the result of gross human error. Tragic, also, because of the suspicion—even downright hostility—it has generated toward the entire U.S. oil industry."

In the wake of the *Valdez* spill, the petroleum industry developed several initiatives. Unocal, for example, began a rigorous and comprehensive review of its entire spill prevention and response system. Unocal also joined other companies in forming the Petroleum Industry Response Organization, organized to create five regional response centers around the continental United States.

"Those of us in the business of extracting earth resources bear a special responsibility," said Stegemeier. "Our activities are essential to America's economic vitality and national security, but our activities—by their very nature—disturb the environment."

Instead of the oil industry continuing to be perceived as the bad guy in all environmental discussions, however, Stegemeier advocated a search for common ground. "Resource development and environmental protection," he said, "do not represent mutually exclusive policy goals....We can have both."

The *Valdez* spill evoked a strong public reaction reminiscent of the response after Unocal's Santa Barbara Channel spill 20 years earlier. While the two accidents were very different—one from an offshore platform and the second, much

Left: The fire school at Unocal's Los Angeles refinery trains employees to handle emergencies. The company has conducted fire schools since the 1920s. Opposite: Training programs, such as this one in Southern California's Ventura harbor, keep employees current in the latest methods of oil-spill containment.

Right: Bill Lovell, safety manager for oil and gas operations in the Louisiana Region, climbs aboard a rescue capsule with coworkers during a marine rescue training exercise in the Gulf of Mexico.

larger spill from a tanker — both became rallying points for environmental activists.

After the Santa Barbara spill, offshore drilling practices were improved, and regulations governing offshore activities were strengthened. On the twentieth anniversary of that spill in January 1989, Stegemeier noted that in the two decades since the spill more than 900 wells had been drilled offshore California without further incident.

Stegemeier worked to make his and Unocal's position on improving environmental quality unmistakable. In April 1990, he restated the company's position in his monthly newsletter: "Please let me stress that Unocal intends to become an industry leader in safety and environmental protection. We're fully committed to taking all action necessary to protect our employees, the communities in which we operate, and the environment. This commitment goes beyond mere compliance with the law. We're determined to prevent environmental damage, and we're prepared to respond to any environmental emergency."

As the 1990s began, issues such as global warming, destruction of the ozone layer, toxic waste disposal, and acid rain focused intense interest on environmental protection. The social and political movement that exploded into prominence in the 1970s had gained momentum and complexity during the 1980s.

Energy companies had made tremendous strides in cleaning up the industry since the 1950s, when smog became all too obvious a problem. Unocal had led the way in at least one area. By 1990, 221 petroleum facilities in 22 countries used Unocal-developed technology to remove from the atmosphere every year 5.5 million tons of sulfur dioxide — the principal contributor to acid rain. But formidable challenges remained.

"We're in for a revolution on the refining side," Roger Beach said, "not only for Unocal but industrywide." Enormous investments of time and money would be required to develop technologies to comply with tougher restrictions on refinery emissions and to develop cleaner-burning transportation fuels.

In Los Angeles, the 1990s were heralded by the South Coast Air Quality Management District's three-stage plan to clean up the air in the basin by 2008. "Quite frankly," said Dick Stegemeier, shortly after the plan was approved in May 1989, "some of the regulations as currently written appear to be totally impractical, and we're doing our best to have them reconsidered.

"If we mandate the use of today's knowledge and technology 20 years down the line," he continued, "we'll impose on ourselves a technological straitjacket rather than encourage the innovation that could ultimately solve the problem."

Stegemeier called for a reasoned approach to solving environmental prob-

lems, balancing political and social goals against scientific realities. "Wherever possible," he said, "we should replace complex rules and regulations with basic environmental goals and standards, then give industry the freedom and flexibility to meet them. In other words, we need more collaboration, less confrontation. We need more innovation, less litigation. We need more results, and fewer rules. As one law professor recently said: 'Our environmental law has become so complex that the tax code is child's play by comparison.'"

In 1986, Unocal had been a founding member of the Petroleum Environmental Research Forum, a consortium of petroleum companies that was formed to coordinate environmental research and problem solving. In another effort inaugurated in 1989, Unocal joined with 13 other oil companies and the three major U.S. auto manufacturers. They planned to coordinate the development of new engines and new fuels to achieve lower automobile emissions.

Unocal, however, took immediate steps to help clean up the air in the Los Angeles basin before new technology and fuels could be developed. In April 1990, Unocal announced three innovative programs targeted to reduce the vehicle emissions that cause at least 60 percent of the area's smog. Taken together, Stegemeier called the measures small steps — "but indicative of what can be done if everyone participates."

Under the South Coast Recycled Auto Program (SCRAP), Unocal pledged to remove 7,000 old cars (1970 models and earlier) from the streets. Such cars spew 30 to 60 times more pollutants into the air than newer models. The 7,000 vehicles Unocal planned to scrap were estimated to emit 6 million pounds of carbon monoxide, reactive organic gases, and nitrogen oxides annually. Vehicle emissions tests of a representative sample of the scrapped cars were made with the assistance of the California Air Resources Board.

Unocal agreed to pay $700 each to the owners of qualifying vehicles, with total costs to Unocal for SCRAP amounting to more than $5 million. The company expanded the program after receiving a donation from Cypress Semiconductor of San Jose. Cypress's chief executive officer T.J. Rodgers sent a check for $700 and a note on behalf of his employees asking Stegemeier to "buy and bury

Above: Unocal's Los Angeles refinery operates around the clock. Refining operations faced tough new environmental legislation in the 1990s. Unocal's Dick Stegemeier advocated a reasoned approach that would allow industry room for innovation in exploring alternatives to achieve the desired results. Opposite, bottom: On June 14, 1990, Stegemeier held a press conference to launch the 76 Protech Patrol, a fleet of vehicles offering free emergency assistance to motorists during rush hours to keep stalled cars from clogging traffic.

one for us, too." Unocal undertook to match all such donations in an effort to scrap an additional 200 vehicles.

In July, Ford Motor Company agreed to purchase another 1,000 vehicles to be scrapped through Unocal's program—and offered the owners a $700 credit on certain new low-emission Fords. Ford and Lincoln-Mercury dealers in the greater Los Angeles area contributed an additional $63,000 (covering the purchase of 90 old cars). In August, the South Coast Air Quality Management District donated $100,000 to the SCRAP project. The district's board chairman Norton Younglove noted that the program was achieving immediate reductions in air pollution. "We are grateful to Unocal for taking the lead in getting rid of a number of the oldest and dirtiest cars on our roads," he said.

Unocal offered program participants a free one-month pass to ride Los Angeles Rapid Transit District buses. First Interstate Bank stepped forward with special auto loans with lower payments on certain 1982 or newer used cars.

The overwhelming public response to SCRAP—more than 12,000 car owners applied—left the company with a long waiting list. The first cars were scrapped in Los Angeles on June 1 at Hugo Neu-Proler Company's Downtown Metal Center. Neu-Proler operated the world's largest scrap metal recycling and exporting operation at its Terminal Island facility in the Los Angeles Harbor area.

Unocal also introduced two other initiatives for drivers in the greater Los Angeles area: Smog-Fighter and the 76 Protech Patrol. Smog-Fighter offered owners of pre-1975 vehicles free smog checks and free low-emission tune-ups at participating Unocal Protech stations during the "off-year" of state-required biennial smog checks. The program was designed to keep cars running cleaner.

The 76 Protech Patrol provided free services to assist motorists stranded on freeways during rush hours, keeping traffic flowing and getting motorists who needed help to the nearest service station. "Getting stranded cars back on the road helps eliminate stalls in the traffic flow and cuts the level of harmful emissions," said Stegemeier. The patrol was inspired by a similar program in Sacramento, partially sponsored by Unocal dealers in late 1988. By mid-1990, Protech vehicles cruised the freeways in several California communities.

In 1990, Unocal faced a difficult decade in which the environmental challenge would be one of many. But restructuring in the late 1980s had put the company in a greatly improved position. During 1988, Unocal reduced its total

76 IN HOLLYWOOD
The first Union Oil television commercial was aired in 1949 after then president Reese Taylor acted on advice from Hollywood movie director Hal Roach: namely, get on board the hottest new advertising medium—TV. Union started out with a bombshell: In the only television commercial she ever made, Marilyn Monroe, in her trademark breathy voice, asked a Union station attendant to put a quart of Royal Triton Motor Oil in her pink convertible's "tummy." Union launched various television campaigns over the years. In the early 1970s, fashion model and aspiring actress Farrah Fawcett appeared in one of a string of Union Oil commercials known as the "George and Marge" series. In 1973, Union found the man who would come to personify the Spirit of 76 for millions of television viewers. Richard X. Slattery, a one-time New York cop turned actor, became "Murph," the prototypical 76 dealer (above)—solid, unflappable, dependable. Slattery was chosen over more than 70 other actors in 1973 auditions for the role. In the first commercials, station attendant "Billy" was played by Larry Wilcox, who later gained fame as California Highway Patrol Officer Jonathan Baker in the TV series CHiPs. In 1985, the familiar and friendly figure of Murph was on hand to assist customers through the transition from Union 76 to Unocal 76. Murph remained as 76 spokesman in 1990, with the commercials filmed—as usual—at the Unocal 76 station at Dodger Stadium before the start of the baseball season.

debt by $389 million, and by another $550 million in 1989. In September 1989, after third-quarter results were in, the directors voted a 40 percent increase in the dividend, from 25¢ to 35¢ per common share, and a two-for-one stock split.

"Today's dividend increase reflects our strengthened financial position and our confidence in Unocal's future," said Stegemeier. "The stock split reflects the substantial increase in the price of Unocal shares and is intended to expand the marketability of the stock to a broader range of investors."

By the beginning of 1990 — Unocal's centennial year — total debt stood at $4.1 billion, some $2 billion less than its peak four and a half years earlier. The debt ratio had been driven down from 79 percent to 64 percent over the same period. "Unocal can begin to move away from liability management and toward investment management," noted Neal Schmale.

During his first two years as Unocal's CEO, Dick Stegemeier proved himself the strong and sure leader that the company needed. "After the takeover battle in 1985 and the crude oil price collapse in 1986, we had to change our game plan," he said. "Unocal had to adjust to new realities. We went from being cash rich to cash poor. But I like to think that we became 'opportunity rich.'

"We couldn't do everything," Stegemeier continued, "but we could do those things that were possible with limited cash. We had to think beyond the obvious, beyond the operating problems — and look out into the future. That's the CEO's role, as I see it."

The 1990s presented enormous technological and social challenges. Environmental problems with global implications demanded attention. The Eastern European Communist bloc had disintegrated, and the Soviet Union struggled to achieve economic and social reform. Moves toward greater democracy swept the globe, and the dream of world peace seemed almost at hand.

Yet, the situation in the Middle East remained as volatile as its history. On August 2, 1990, Iraqi troops invaded Kuwait. The price of oil, already on the rise in international markets from about $15 to $20 per barrel, quickly shot up another $8 on the spot market.

Opposition to the Iraqi action formed rapidly, creating some unlikely alliances among Arab and Western nations. The United Nations Security Council imposed mandatory sanctions, forbidding its member nations to conduct business with Iraq in the hope that an economic embargo could force Iraq out of Kuwait.

Above: At a press conference at Unocal Center on April 26, 1990, Dick Stegemeier announced Unocal's new environmental programs for Southern California: SCRAP, Smog-Fighter, and the 76 Protech Patrol. Below: Protech mechanics performed a free smog test and low-emission tune-up on a pre-1975 car under the Smog-Fighter program. Opposite, top: Emission checks of cars accepted for Unocal's SCRAP program helped assess the program's effectiveness. Opposite, bottom: Cars were scrapped at the Hugo Neu-Proler yard near downtown Los Angeles. Here, a vehicle — drained of fluids and stripped of engine, transmission, and wheels — enters the jaws of a crushing machine.

The United States and several other nations, at the request of Saudi Arabia, massed troops and armament in that country. When the Arab League denounced the Iraqi invasion of Kuwait, several Arab countries also sent troops to defend Saudi Arabia. The United States, Japan, and the European Economic Community froze Kuwaiti assets. Iraq refused to release U.S. citizens and other foreign nationals whose countries participated in the embargo.

As a standoff developed and war threatened, American consumers responded angrily to increases in the cost of gasoline. Although prices for both crude oil and gasoline on the spot market had risen by about 20¢ per gallon shortly after the invasion, Unocal at first increased its wholesale price to most of its dealers by only 4¢ to 6¢ per gallon.

At a White House press briefing on the Middle East situation, President Bush asked the U.S. oil industry to restrain price increases, and many companies responded. On August 8, Unocal announced a short-term freeze on the price of gasoline charged to its retail dealers.

Nevertheless, the economic embargo against Iraq and occupied Kuwait reduced available oil supplies by some 4 million barrels per day. World oil prices climbed and so did the cost of gasoline and other petroleum fuels. (The outcome of the Iraq situation—the third Middle East oil crisis in less than 20 years—remained uncertain as of this writing.)

Events in the Middle East in the 1970s had shown that neither the oil industry nor the U.S. government could shield the American public indefinitely from the effects of increasing world oil prices. History seemed to be repeating itself. Oil-importing nations were once again reminded of their vulnerability.

As the new decade opened, the world stood on the brink of unpredictable and monumental change. Businesses would require creative and aggressive management in order to thrive.

Lyman Stewart had faced a similar prospect when he boarded a train for California in 1883. He was looking for oil, a resource whose potential had only begun to be suspected then. It was used as a lubricant and a paving material. Its primary product was kerosene, an effective substitute for whale oil in lamps. Stewart could not have guessed that oil would literally reshape the world as the source of gasoline, which fueled the internal combustion engine. Nor could he have known that twentieth-century science would create a fantastic array of hydrocarbon prod-

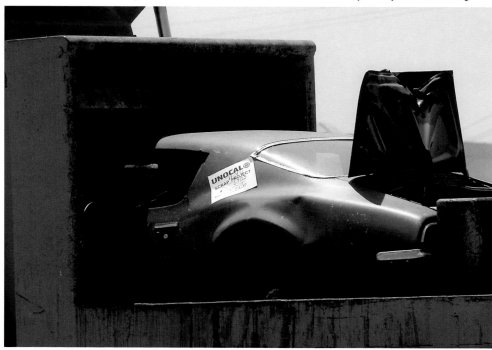

1. Union Oil's original headquarters in Santa Paula, California, where the company was founded in 1890, was rededicated as the new Unocal Oil Museum on March 24, 1990. 2. Unocal chairman and CEO Richard Stegemeier was one of the first to sign the museum's guest register. 3. Stegemeier talked with Art Stewart, grandson of company cofounder Lyman Stewart. 4. Guests waited outside the museum, located at the corner of Main and Tenth streets, for the ribbon-cutting ceremony. 5. Dick Robb, who retired from the Union 76 Division in 1981 after nearly 33 years with the company, was one of 500 guests at the opening. 6. Santa Paula Mayor Les Maland viewed an exhibit with another guest. 7. Mayor Maland and Dick Stegemeier prepared to cut the ribbon. The Unocal contingent included, from right: Barry Lane, manager, public relations; Karen Sikkema, vice president, corporate communications; Darcel Hulse, vice president, corporate engineering and construction; Joseph B. Jenkins, project manager; and Robert R. Oberg, manager, project engineering.

THE UNOCAL OIL MUSEUM
In March 1890, an elegant two-story office building opened in the small California town of Santa Paula. Built by local oil-men Lyman Stewart and Wallace Hardison, the structure combined the simplicity and grace of the Queen Anne style of architecture with an italianate use of columns and arches. The red brick in the building's facade was manufactured in Santa Paula, and the distinctively purplish Sespe brownstone was quarried nearby. In October 1890, Stewart, Hardison, and Thomas Bard formed Union Oil Company of California, headquartered in the new building. Union moved the center of its business to Los Angeles in 1901 but continued to house district offices in the Santa Paula building until restoration began almost a century later. The Pioneer Petroleum Society of California established an oil museum on the building's first floor in 1950. Refurbishment to return the building to its original splendor began in 1988. The new Unocal Oil Museum, dedicated in March 1990, used multimedia exhibits to tell lively stories about the company and the petroleum industry's past and present. A massive, century-old cable tool rig, once used to pound through the rocky California soil, was housed in a museum annex and rigged to move as if it were still drilling for oil. Several of the upstairs offices were returned to 1890s style. Two rooms were recreated as a 1930s bedroom and kitchen, such as those used by company superintendents housed in the building during the Depression. The building itself, one of the finest examples of late-nineteenth-century architecture in Ventura County, became a county landmark in 1977 and was listed on the National Register of Historic Places in 1986.

ucts that would prove essential to an improved standard of living. But he believed that oil offered opportunity, and that was enough for him.

One hundred years later, Stegemeier elaborated on that theme: "From the beginning, our leaders have been people who wanted to build. They weren't satisfied with the status quo, and they met every challenge head on.

"With each problem our company has faced over the last century, we've risen to the occasion and become stronger. I can't say exactly where Unocal will be in the twenty-first century, but we know who we are. Our management is responsive. We have a strong corporate culture characterized by an innovative spirit. If we stay attuned to what's going on around us, we can identify the best opportunities for our company."

Even as Unocal moved to face the challenging 1990s, the company honored its past. Tributes to 100 years of doing business filled the centennial year. The celebrations began in Santa Paula, the small California agricultural town where Unocal was founded on October 17, 1890. In March 1990, the newly refurbished Unocal Oil Museum was dedicated in the company's original headquarters building. As fall approached, plans for the October board meeting, to be held in Santa Barbara (about 50 miles from Santa Paula), included a museum tour with a visit to the second-floor conference room where the original incorporation papers had been signed a century earlier. In August and September, centennial picnics were held in various company locations, providing barbecues and entertainment for employees and their families.

The grandest celebration was held April 30, when Unocal's annual meeting was transformed into a centennial gala. The meeting, held at the Pasadena Civic Auditorium some ten miles east of company headquarters in downtown Los Angeles, drew almost 2,000 shareholders and guests. Two very special guests were featured speakers that day: Arthur C. Stewart, grandson of the company's cofounder Lyman Stewart; and Lester Todd, a retiree who, like Unocal, also celebrated his one hundredth birthday in 1990.

Stewart shared his memories of a stern, aging grandfather (Lyman was 65 when Art was born in 1905) and provided glimpses into Union Oil Company as it weathered the Great Depression of the 1930s, geared up to help supply the armed forces during World War II, and expanded operations in the booming postwar economy. "Our company has a remarkable history," he noted, "and I'm sure it will have an equally remarkable future."

Lester Todd, then just three and a half months short of his personal centennial, attended the meeting and shared his memories with the audience via videotape. Todd had worked in Union Oil's Southern California oil fields from 1922 through 1955. He recalled how he had first become a Unocal shareholder. He was working in the Montebello field when the company decided to terminate its Provident Fund and pay employees in cash and stock for their interests.

"Some of the boys were complaining about having to take stock," Todd recalled. "They wanted all cash." So he volunteered to buy their stock, and he held on to it for the next 50 years. "They pay what I'd call a pretty good little dividend," he said.

Although Lester Todd worked for Union Oil for 33 years, he never received a gold watch. In the 1950s, employees were given a gold watch after 35 years of service, a practice that was later changed to honor 30 years of service.

"With our respective centennial birthdays approaching," Stegemeier announced, "we'd now like to present you with a very special centennial watch."

The presentation closed the meeting, and the guests adjourned to lunch where Dick Stegemeier led off with a toast: "To Unocal's second century—may it build on our legacy of spirit and success."

1

5

2

7

3

6

8

4

9

11

12

A CENTENNIAL CELEBRATION

The annual shareholders meeting, held at the Pasadena Civic Auditorium a few miles from company headquarters on April 30, 1990, drew close to 2,000 people. Before the business meeting, guests viewed historical and educational exhibits — some borrowed from the Unocal Oil Museum in Santa Paula. The meeting featured a videotaped history of the company and speakers who could bring alive bits of the company's past. A luncheon was held, during which Unocal was honored with proclamations from the cities of Los Angeles and Pasadena and the state of California. The finale was the presentation of a multitiered anniversary cake led through the hall by a drum major to the tune of "76 Trombones." During the meeting, Arthur C. Stewart, grandson of cofounder Lyman Stewart, recalled the day in 1915 when John D. Rockefeller telephoned Lyman to wish him a happy seventy-fifth birthday. And he described some of what life on an oil tanker was like in the 1920s. Another Union Oil retiree, Lester Todd, shared memories of Southern California's oil fields in the 1920s and 1930s. His recounting included a story about how he and his coworkers alternated shifts — one week on, one week off — during the worst days of the Great Depression so no one had to miss a paycheck. "If you're working for Union Oil," he concluded, "you're lucky. I don't think there's anybody that can beat them."

1. Art Stewart. 2, 3, & 6. Exhibits from the Unocal Oil Museum in Santa Paula. 4 & 5. Close to 2,000 guests enjoyed coffee, conversation, and sweet rolls. 7. Los Angeles Mayor Tom Bradley took the podium at the centennial luncheon, flanked by host Dick Stegemeier (left) and Jess Marlow, noted television news anchor who emceed the centennial luncheon. State controller Gray Davis (second from right) also spoke. 8 & 13. The grand finale — a towering one hundredth anniversary cake. 9. Executive vice president Claude Brinegar (left) presented centenarian Lester Todd with a gold watch in honor of more than 30 years of company service. 10 & 12. Dick Stegemeier presided at the meeting and, at the luncheon (11), toasted Unocal's future.

BIBLIOGRAPHY

Bartlett, Anderson G. III, Robert John Barton, Joe Calvin Bartlett, George Anderson Fowler, Jr., and Charles Francis Hays. *Pertamina: Indonesian National Oil.* Jakarta: Amerasian Ltd., 1972.

Beaton, Kendall. *Enterprise in Oil: A History of Shell in the United States.* New York: Appleton-Century-Crofts, Inc., 1957.

Boesch, Donald F., Carl H. Hershner, and Jerome H. Milgram. *Oil Spills and the Marine Environment.* Cambridge, Massachusetts: Ballinger Publishing Company, 1974.

Cowan, Edward. *Oil and Water: The Torrey Canyon Disaster.* Philadelphia and New York: J. P. Lippincott Company, 1968.

Davis, L. J. "The Biggest Knockover." *Harper's* (January 1985) 53–70.

Ghosh, Arabinda. *OPEC, the Petroleum Industry and United States Energy Policy.* Westport, Connecticut: Quorum Books, 1983.

Glasner, David. *Politics, Prices and Petroleum: The Political Economy of Energy.* Cambridge, Massachusetts: Ballinger Publishing Company, 1985.

Goodwin, Craufurd D., ed. *Energy Policy In Perspective: Today's Problems, Yesterday's Solutions.* Washington, D.C.: The Brookings Institution, 1981.

Greenberger, Martin, with Garry D. Brewer, William W. Hogan, and Milton Russell. *Caught Unawares: The Energy Decade in Retrospect.* Cambridge, Massachusetts: Ballinger Publishing Company, 1983.

Harris, Michael T., and Roger Skrentny. "Unocal's Fred Hartley." *California Business* (August 1985) 48–64.

Henry, James O. "Black Oil and Souls to Win." *The King's Business* (February 1958) 11–41.

Hoyer, A.S. *Service Beyond the Sale: A History of the Petrochemical Group of the Chemicals Division of Union Oil Company of California.* Schaumburg, Illinois: Union Oil Company of California, Chemicals Division, 1983.

Hutchinson, W. H. *Oil, Land and Politics: The California Career of Thomas Robert Bard* (2 volumes). Norman: University of Oklahoma Press, 1965.

Itchon, Gabriel Y., Perla A. Segovia, and Arturo P. Alcaraz. *A Short Story of the National Power Corporation, 1936–1986.* Quezon City, Philippines: National Power Corporation, 1986.

Johnston, Moira. *Takeover: The New Wall Street Warriors, The Men, The Money, The Impact.* New York: Arbor House, 1986.

Kalt, Joseph P. *The Economics and Politics of Oil Price Regulation: Federal Policy in the Post-Embargo Era.* Cambridge, Massachusetts: The MIT Press, 1981.

Kruger, Paul, and Carel Otte, eds. *Geothermal Energy: Resources, Production, Stimulation.* Stanford University Press, 1973.

Levy, Walter J. *Oil Strategy and Politics, 1941–1981.* Boulder, Colorado: Westview Press, 1982.

Nash, Gerald D. *United States Oil Policy, 1890–1964.* University of Pittsburgh Press, 1968.

O'Hanlon, Thomas. "Fred Hartley and His Well-Oiled Multiplying Machine." *Fortune* (April 1967) 156–161+.

Petrow, Richard. *In the Wake of the Torrey Canyon.* New York: David McKay Company, Inc. 1968. ©1968 by Richard Petrow as *The Black Tide.*

Prast, William G., and Howard L. Lax. *Oil-Futures Markets.* Lexington, Massachusetts: D. C. Heath and Company, 1983.

Roscow, James P. *800 Miles to Valdez: The Building of the Alaska Pipeline.* Englewood Cliffs, New Jersey: Prentice-Hall, Inc., 1977.

Soberg, Carl. *Oil Power.* New York: Mason/Charter, 1976.

Steinhart, Carol E., and John S. Steinhart. *Blowout: A Case Study of the Santa Barbara Oil Spill.* Belmont, California: Duxbury Press, 1972.

Tucker, William. "The Energy Crisis is Over!" *Harper's* (November 1981) 25–36.

———*Progress and Privilege, America in the Age of Environmentalism.* Garden City, New York: Anchor Press/Doubleday, 1982.

———"The Wreck of the Auto Industry." *Harper's* (November 1980) 45–60.

Whitaker, John C. *Striking a Balance: Environment and Natural Resources Policy in the Nixon-Ford Years.* Washington, D.C.: American Enterprise Institute for Public Policy Research, 1976.

White, Gerald T. *Formative Years in the Far West: A History of Standard Oil Company of California and Predecessors Through 1919.* New York: Appleton-Century-Crofts, Inc., 1962.

Williamson, Harold F., and Arnold R. Daum. *The American Petroleum Industry: Volume I, The Age of Illumination, 1859–1899.* Evanston, Illinois: Northwestern University Press, 1959.

Wise, T. A. "The Curious Pursuit of Pure Oil." *Fortune* (July 1965) 112–115+.

PHOTO AND
ILLUSTRATION
CREDITS

TIMELINE
Page xii: Fireworks, *Westlight*. T. Boone
Pickens cartoon, *Bill Schorr, Tribune Media
Services*.

CHAPTER 1
Page 4: Los Angeles in 1883, *Security Pacific
Historical Photograph Collection/Los Angeles
Public Library*.
Page 8: Edwin Drake, *The Bettmann Archive*.
Drake's first well and the Lady Stewart well,
*Drake Well Museum/Pennsylvania Historical
and Museum Collection*.

CHAPTER 2
Page 22: First auto built in Los Angeles,
*Security Pacific Historical Photograph
Collection/Los Angeles Public Library*.
Page 24: Rockefeller cartoon, *Horace Taylor,
Department of Special Collections/University
Research Library, UCLA*.
Page 32: Spindletop gusher, *UPI/Bettmann
Newsphotos*. Train on Maui, *AP/Wide World
Photos*.
Page 35: Skeleton of sloth, *George C. Page
Museum/The Natural History Museum of Los
Angeles County*.
Page 38: Ship traffic in San Pedro harbor,
California Historical Society. Olds Runabout,
*National Automotive History Collection,
Detroit Public Library*.
Page 39: 1906 San Francisco earthquake,
UPI/Bettmann Newsphotos.

CHAPTER 3
Page 42: Ford assembly line, *UPI/Bettmann
Newsphotos*.
Page 46: Milton Stewart and Hunan Bible
Institute, *Chartered For His Glory/Biola
University*.
Page 47: Lyman Stewart at Bible Institute
dedication, *Chartered For His Glory/Biola
University*.
Page 53: Signal Hill oil field, *UPI/Bettmann
Newsphotos*.
Page 54: Taxis drafted for war service, *AP/
Wide World Photos*. Kaiser Wilhelm cartoon,
W. A. Rogers, UPI/Bettmann Newsphotos.
Page 55: Los Angeles, Eighth and Broadway,
California Historical Society.
Page 57: Ruth Elder, *P&A Photo*.

CHAPTER 4
Page 58: Los Angeles in 1920s, *California
Historical Society*.
Page 68: San Luis Obispo tank farm fire,
San Luis Obispo County Historical Society.
Page 71: Depression apple seller, *UPI/
Bettmann Newsphotos*.
Page 74: "Spirit of 76" painting by A. M.
Willard, *UPI/Bettmann Newsphotos*.

CHAPTER 5
Page 82: Soldier guarding oil pumper, *UPI/
Bettmann Newsphotos*.
Page 85: Wilshire Boulevard's Miracle Mile
in 1947, *Security Pacific Historical Photograph
Collection/Los Angeles Public Library*.
Page 92: Scrap rubber truck and New York
school kids, *UPI/Bettmann Newsphotos*.
Page 95: Oil drums on Iwo Jima, *UPI/
Bettmann Newsphotos*.

CHAPTER 6
Page 102: Cahuenga Freeway in 1950s, *UPI/
Bettmann Newsphotos*.

CHAPTER 7
Page 124: 1964 Alaska earthquake, *UPI/
Bettmann Newsphotos*.
Page 130: Daniel Ludwig, *UPI/Bettmann
Newsphotos*.

CHAPTER 9
Page 164: Los Angeles in 1973, *Los Angeles
Times Photo*. Crowded Los Angeles freeway,
UPI/Bettmann Newsphotos.
Page 165: President Richard Nixon, *AP/
Wide World Photos*.
Page 166: Earth Walk in Philadelphia and
Earth Day parade in St. Louis, *UPI/
Bettmann Newsphotos*.
Page 167: Earth Day in New York, *UPI/
Bettmann Newsphotos*.
Page 176: TAPS construction, *UPI/Bettmann
Newsphotos*.
Page 178–179: Sea-floor template
illustration, *Bob Massey*.
Page 182: Gas line at Union 76 station, *AP/
Wide World Photos*.
Page 183: King Faisal of Saudi Arabia, *AP/
Wide World Photos*.

CHAPTER 10
Page 186: U.S. Capitol, *UPI/Bettmann
Newsphotos*.
Page 190: Richard and Pat Nixon, *UPI/
Bettmann Newsphotos*.
Page 191: Salt cavern at Strategic Petroleum
Reserve, *U.S. Department of Energy*.

CHAPTER 11
Page 204: Last car in line, *Westlight/
Larry Lee*.
Page 205: President Jimmy Carter, *AP/Wide
World Photos*.
Page 206: Three Mile Island reactor, *AP/
Wide World Photos*.
Page 215: Ayatollah Khomeini and followers,
AP/Wide World Photos.
Page 216: Gasoline line, *Westlight*.
Page 219: President Ronald Reagan taking
oath of office, *AP/Wide World Photos*.

CHAPTER 12
Page 223: President Reagan, *UPI/Bettmann
Newsphotos*.
Pages 230–231: Offshore rigs illustration,
Linda Yaussi.

CHAPTER 13
Page 246: Fred L. Hartley, *Los Angeles Times
Photo/Ken Lubas*. T. Boone Pickens, *AP/
Wide World Photos*.
Page 247: Pickens cartoon, *Bill Schorr,
Tribune Media Services*.
Page 251: New York Stock Exchange, *AP/
Wide World Photos*.
Page 248: Oil industry chart, *based on chart
in Fundamentals of the Petroleum Industry by
Robert O. Anderson, University of Oklahoma
Press*.
Page 258: Jesse Unruh, *AP/Wide World
Photos*.
Page 259: Fred Hartley at Unocal Center,
AP/Wide World Photos.
Page 266: Hartley and L.A. refinery
employees, *Bruce W. Talamon*.

CHAPTER 15
Page 286: Dick Stegemeier, *Steven Burr
Williams*.
Page 288: Aerial view of Los Angeles,
The Los Angeles Center.
Page 295: President George Bush,
Susan Biddle/The White House.

Credit also belongs to the many staff and
free-lance photographers whose work has
chronicled the company's activities over the
years. Among those represented in this book
are: *John T. Barr, Bart Bartholomew, Ray
Engle, Lon Harding, Ed Holcomb, Larry Lee,
Sergio Ortiz, Robert Pacheco, Larry Paulsen,
Ernie Rodriquez, George Rose, Chuck
Schoenfeld, Tim Smight, Marc Solomon, Chris
Springmann, Mark Stephenson, Bob
Thomason, Dick Tolbert, Steven Burr
Williams, and Bob Witkowski*.

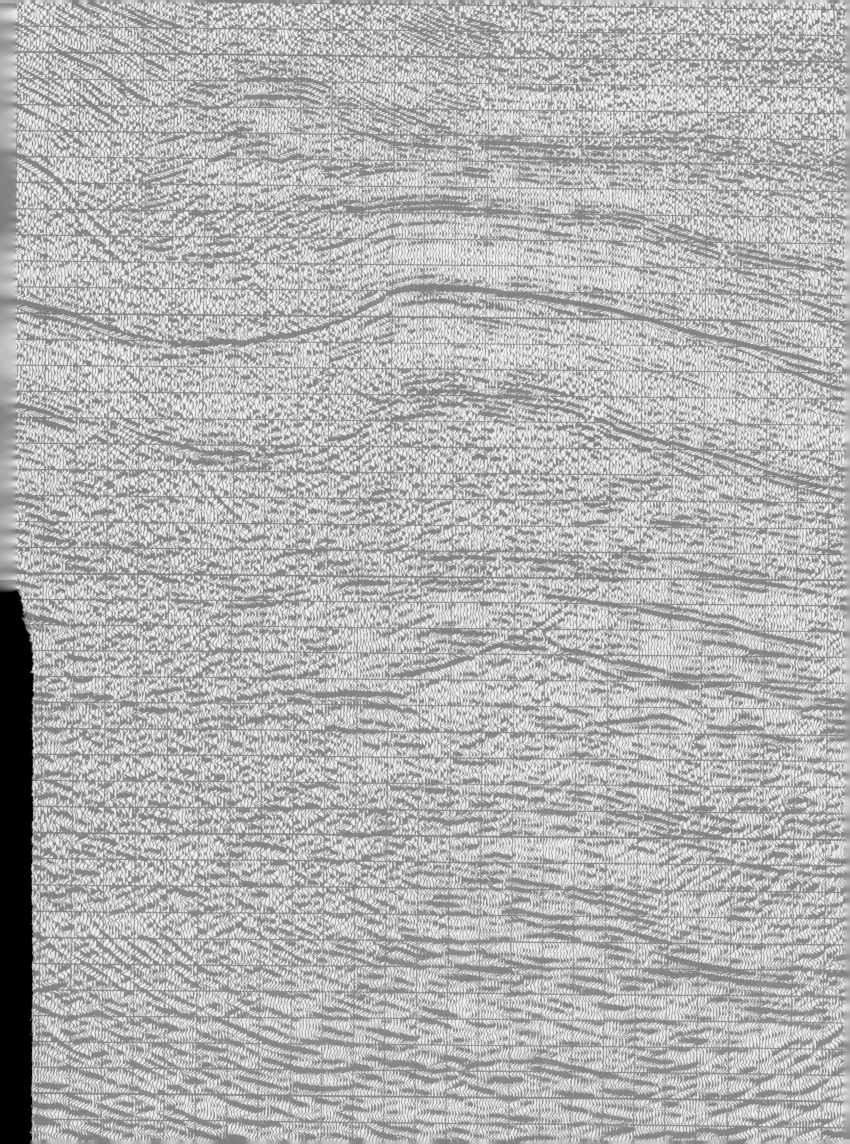